T0329395

CAMBRIDGE LIBRARY COLLECTION

Books of enduring scholarly value

Technology

The focus of this series is engineering, broadly construed. It covers technological innovation from a range of periods and cultures, but centres on the technological achievements of the industrial era in the West, particularly in the nineteenth century, as understood by their contemporaries. Infrastructure is one major focus, covering the building of railways and canals, bridges and tunnels, land drainage, the laying of submarine cables, and the construction of docks and lighthouses. Other key topics include developments in industrial and manufacturing fields such as mining technology, the production of iron and steel, the use of steam power, and chemical processes such as photography and textile dyes.

The Industrial Resources of Ireland

Sir Robert Kane (1809–90) was a noted Irish chemist, becoming a professor at the age of twenty-two. His work on compounds of ammonia were considered internationally important. His 1,200-page textbook, *Elements of Chemistry* (1841–3) was considered 'the best extant in the English language' and was widely used in England and America. *The Industrial Resources of Ireland*, published in 1844 and reissued in 1845, had originated in a series of lectures to the Royal Dublin Society, and contains a mass of factual detail on the energy, mineral, agricultural, capital and labour resources of the country. Kane believed that Ireland did not lack natural resources so much as the knowledge of how to exploit them, and technical education was necessary. The book outlines an ambitious plan to harness the raw materials which Ireland possessed, or was believed to possess. However, the outbreak of the Famine overtook his schemes.

Cambridge University Press has long been a pioneer in the reissuing of out-of-print titles from its own backlist, producing digital reprints of books that are still sought after by scholars and students but could not be reprinted economically using traditional technology. The Cambridge Library Collection extends this activity to a wider range of books which are still of importance to researchers and professionals, either for the source material they contain, or as landmarks in the history of their academic discipline.

Drawing from the world-renowned collections in the Cambridge University Library, and guided by the advice of experts in each subject area, Cambridge University Press is using state-of-the-art scanning machines in its own Printing House to capture the content of each book selected for inclusion. The files are processed to give a consistently clear, crisp image, and the books finished to the high quality standard for which the Press is recognised around the world. The latest print-on-demand technology ensures that the books will remain available indefinitely, and that orders for single or multiple copies can quickly be supplied.

The Cambridge Library Collection will bring back to life books of enduring scholarly value (including out-of-copyright works originally issued by other publishers) across a wide range of disciplines in the humanities and social sciences and in science and technology.

The Industrial
Resources of Ireland

Robert Kane

CAMBRIDGE
UNIVERSITY PRESS

CAMBRIDGE UNIVERSITY PRESS

Cambridge, New York, Melbourne, Madrid, Cape Town, Singapore,
São Paolo, Delhi, Dubai, Tokyo, Mexico City

Published in the United States of America by Cambridge University Press, New York

www.cambridge.org
Information on this title: www.cambridge.org/9781108026857

© in this compilation Cambridge University Press 2010

This edition first published 1845
This digitally printed version 2010

ISBN 978-1-108-02685-7 Paperback

THE

INDUSTRIAL RESOURCES

OF

IRELAND.

BY

ROBERT KANE, M.D.,

HONORARY MEMBER OF THE ROYAL DUBLIN SOCIETY, AND OF THE FLAX
IMPROVEMENT SOCIETY OF IRELAND;
SECRETARY TO THE COUNCIL OF THE ROYAL IRISH ACADEMY;
PROFESSOR OF NATURAL PHILOSOPHY TO THE ROYAL DUBLIN SOCIETY, AND
OF CHEMISTRY TO THE APOTHECARIES HALL OF IRELAND.

𝔖econd 𝔈dition.

DUBLIN:

HODGES AND SMITH, GRAFTON-STREET.

LONGMAN AND CO., AND SIMPKIN AND CO., LONDON.

MACLACHLAN AND STEWART, EDINBURGH.

MDCCCXLV.

PREFACE

TO THE FIRST EDITION.

———◆———

SOME time since, being engaged with the delivery
of a course of Lectures on the physical principles
and mechanical construction of the prime movers
of machinery, I entered into some details regarding the circumstances under which the sources of
mechanical power exist in Ireland, and took occasion to correct the exaggerated ideas usually entertained of the disadvantages under which this country labours, in regard to mechanical industry.

The discussions, into which I then entered, although but collateral, attracted some attention, and
I was requested by the Council of the Royal Dublin
Society to proceed further with those inquiries.
Passing beyond the question of mere mechanical
industry, I had occasion to examine the relations of
the country to the prime materials of the chemical
and metallic manufactures, and finally to discuss
some important statistical and moral problems, affecting the industrial progress of Ireland.

These inquiries inovlved, besides the examination and comparison of the works of various independent authors, a great number of series of new mechanical and chemical investigations. For these the materials had to be gradually collected, and I take this opportunity of returning my thanks to the numerous individuals, who kindly, indeed enthusiastically, in their separate departments, placed specimens and documents at my disposal, without the assistance of which it would have been impossible for me to proceed.

The facts I had thus collected, and the general conclusions to which I had arrived, were embodied in a course of public Lectures on the Sources of Industry which exist in Ireland, delivered by me at the Royal Dublin Society in the commencement of the present year. On the conclusion of the course, the Council of the Royal Dublin Society expressed their sanction of the general facts and principles therein contained, and requested that I should prepare those Lectures for publication.

Such is the origin of the present work, in which, however, I have not retained the form of the Lectures described above. The discussion of each subject has been rendered more precise, and carried more into numerical detail, than a lecture to a mixed auditory would allow, and many topics which, owing to the limited time of public lectures, were not then noticed, are now treated of in their proper place.

In arrangement and extent the work has thus

assumed another form, but in no case have I found occasion to correct a statement, or modify any conclusion, which I had expressed at lecture.

It must be understood, that in sanctioning the general principles which I embodied in my course, so far as to call upon me to prepare those Lectures for publication, the Royal Dublin Society only wished to draw public attention to the eminently important subject of the industrial resources of Ireland, and not to thereby specially adopt all or any of the conclusions to which I have arrived. The various materials for this work have been collected by me as an individual; all the experimental investigations which were carried on for its illustration, were conducted in my laboratory; and, therefore, the responsibility of all facts, where no author is quoted, and for all opinions expressed, or conclusions drawn, where not otherwise described, rests with myself.

In a work thus undertaken and carried out, it is inevitable that many imperfections shall be discovered, which more extensive means and greater facilities for investigation should have enabled me to obviate. The subject is, in itself, of such a nature, that the progress of experiment and of inquiry must tend continually to modify our existing views, to extend our actual knowledge, and to substitute for the limited observations of our present field, the wider and more exact investigations, which may naturally result from the discussion of the great question of our industry. In all such cases, the first step, though the most difficult and the least accredited, is still the most essential.

In other countries it has been the most anxious care of Government, and of those intrusted with the superintendence of education, to ascertain the nature and amount of their means of promoting industry, and extending the employment of the people. It is thus that every year sees the Continental nations making such giant strides in manufacturing activity. It is thus that the physical disadvantages, which had so long kept them back, are gradually being lessened in importance.

If similar zeal and intelligence were manifested in developing the resources of this country, there would be no fear of the result. As circumstances, however, do not admit of this being done, the publication of even the short and imperfect sketch, which alone could be drawn up by an unaided individual, may be useful in awakening the attention of those practically engaged upon such subjects, and may lead to more extensive observation, and more detailed inquiry.

R. K.

June 1, 1844.

PREFACE

TO THE SECOND EDITION.

In presenting to the Public a Second Edition of " The Industrial Resources of Ireland," I feel it my duty, and certainly it is one peculiarly agreeable to an author, to express my grateful recognition of the kindness with which the work has been received, and the very favourable judgments which have been pronounced upon it by various competent authorities.

I had, indeed, for many years devoted all the time and energy, which an individual could well command, to obtain materials for the discussion of the problem that presented itself to me upon every side, and under various aspects; the problem of,—what field for *work* does Ireland really present? I had always found that real progress was effected only by genuine labour. I knew that all that is sound and permanent in England's industrial power grew, not out of oratorical elegancies, but from hard-handed, stern, and persevering work. By such work alone,

work of mind and of body, can a people hope to
advance, and the consideration of what departments
of industry presented most prospect of success, and
by what modes of action that success could be rendered most facile and least remote, presented itself
to my mind, naturally, as of vast importance.   The
expression of public opinion regarding the present
work has certainly proved that I was not wrong in
my general conceptions.   The imperfections, and
even, perhaps, inaccuracies, almost inevitable in a
work embracing so wide a range of subject, have
been kindly overlooked by my indulgent critics,
who, agreeing with me in the importance of the
object, gave it their approval.

I did not, however, presume upon this forbearance,
but availed myself of every opportunity of adding to
the number of the facts, and to the accuracy of the
statements which the work contains.   The interval
which has elapsed since its first publication has
been too short to allow of any very material alteration, but in a variety of places, which it would be
tedious to enumerate, I have inserted additional
information, and rendered more definite and precise
that already given. In order also to represent to the
reader the more important physical features of the
country, I have caused to be prepared, to accompany this edition, four maps illustrating,

1. The geological structure of Ireland.
2. The elevation of its surface.
3. The distribution of bog and drainage.
4. The means of internal intercourse.

Although not of large size, I believe these maps will be found to supply a good deal of useful general information. Detailed references to their contents will be found in those chapters of the work where the subjects to which they refer are specially discussed.

In putting forward the Second Edition of the "Industrial Resources of Ireland," I have done so without pretension of any very material alteration from the former, but still revised and corrected to the present limits of our knowledge. The subject of promoting the development of industry and of industrial knowledge in our country is one that I have taken up, as the steady and well-considered object of my life; yet whilst following out, in the laboratory or the workshop, the inquiries subservient to that object, I have felt myself assisted and encouraged in no ordinary degree by the approbation which my countrymen of all classes and parties have awarded to a work, which I consider but a preliminary effort.

R. K.

Royal Dublin Society,
February 1st, 1845.

ERRATUM.

Page 359, line 28, *for* " Ballina." *read* " Ballinamore."

CONTENTS.

———◆———

CHAPTER I.

PAGE.

IMPORTANCE of Fuel in the industrial Arts. Circumstances of Ireland
as to Fuel. Absence of Wood. Its former Abundance in Ireland.
Geographical Position of the Coal Districts. Coal Fields of Leinster,
of Tipperary, and of Munster. Their Geological Structure and Extent of Beds. Cost of the Coal produced. Anthracite of the South.
Bituminous Coal of the North of Ireland. Coal Fields of Tyrone,
of Antrim, Monaghan, and of Connaught. Their geological and
economic Conditions. Position of the Lough Allen Coal Field. Its
Productiveness not well ascertained. Composition of the Irish Coals,
their Cost and practical Value. Numerical Results of their economic and ultimate Analyses. Peculiarities in the Use of Anthracite as Fuel. Its conversion into a flaming Coal by Steam. Its Use
with locomotive Engine Boilers. Wood Coal of Lough Neagh. Its
Situation and Extent. Results of its chemical Analysis, and of its
economic Examination. Extent and Mode of Formation of Bog in
Ireland. Different Kinds of Bog. Composition of Turf, its Cost
and practical Value. Modes of preparing it. Influence of the Water
contained in Turf on its heating Power. Compressed Peat. Its Cost
and economic Value. Products of the Distillation of Turf. Preparation and Value of Charcoal from Turf, ... 1

CHAPTER II.

Necessity for determining the Influence which the Cost of Fuel exercises
on the Cost of Power, and the Means of economizing it. General
Principle of Steam Power. Evaporative Powers of different Kinds
of Fuels. Comparison of Anthracite with bituminous Coal. Unit
of Steam Power. Consumption of Coal with ordinary Steam Boilers.
Economy of Fuel obtained with Cornish Boilers. Mode of employing Steam in Cornwall. Principle of Expansion. Money Value of
Coal in Ireland. Cost of Steam Power, with native and imported
Coals. Employment of Turf as Fuel. Its absolute and relative

PAGE.

Cost. Results of practical Trials. Practical Results of the Employment of Turf in the Steamers on the Shannon and under fixed Engines. Cost of the Horse Power of Steam with Coal and Turf in different Districts in Ireland and in England. Influence of the Cost of Fuel on the final Cost of the Products of Manufacture. Statistical Analysis of the different Elements of Expenditure besides Steam Power in the Cotton Trade, in the Woollen Trade, in the Flax Trade. Final Conclusion as to how far the Cost of Fuel necessarily affects Industry in Ireland. Elements of Calculation for evaporative Steam Power, ... 45

CHAPTER III.

Of the Water Power of Ireland. Mode in which it originates. Amount of Rain and Evaporation in different Parts of Ireland. Average assumed. Influence of the Nature of the Surface on Evaporation. Elevation above the Sea of the Surface of Ireland. Limestone Plain of the Centre. Mountainous Districts of the North and South. Average Elevation assumed as the average Height of Fall of Water from the Land to the Sea. Total Amount of mechanical Force thus generated; its Distribution. Arrangement of the principal Rivers by which the Surface of Ireland is drained. Drainage of the central Districts by the Shannon and its Adjuncts. Wicklow and Wexford. Drainage Basins of the Blackwater and the Lee. Basins of Lough Neagh, of Lough Erne, and the Foyle. Relation of the Extent of Surface drained to the mechanical Force. Water Power of the Shannon: of the Lee at Cork; of the Upper Bann; of the Connaught Lakes. Description of the most important Water Engines. Different Forms of Water Wheels. Of the Water Pressure Engine. Reaction Mill. Of the Turbine. Principle of its Action; its Economy; Constancy of its Power. Disadvantages of Water Power. Necessity for economizing the Waters of Floods. Examples of the Power of Floods. Formation of Reservoirs to secure Uniformity of Water Power. Results of those erected on the Upper Bann and on the Shaw's Water at Greenock. The Dodder. Lough Ennel and the Brosna. Estimates of the Cost of Water Power. Relative Values of Water and Steam Power as Movers of Machinery. Extent to which Water Power is economized in England and in Ireland. Combination of Steam with Water Power. Application of the Force of the Tide to mechanical Purposes. Peculiar Advantages of the Turbine as a Tide Mill. Advantageous Situation of many Points on the Coast for employing the Tide as a Source of mechanical Power, . . 71

CHAPTER IV.

Importance of Iron in the Arts. Ancient Manufacture of Iron in Ireland. Ores of Iron. Magnetic Ironstone. Hematites. Bog Iron Ores.

PAGE.

Clay Ironstone of the Coal Districts. Distribution, Properties, and Composition of the Ironstones of the Leinster Coal Field. Connaught Coal District. Iron Ores of Arigna and Slieve-a-Nieran; their Abundance; their Composition, compared with the British and Scottish Ores. Sketch of the Process of Iron smelting, and Analyses of the Elements of its Cost in Staffordshire and in Wales. Probable Cost of making Iron at Lough Allen. Effects of the Hot Blast on the Iron Manufacture in Scotland. Its possible Influence in Ireland. Of the smelting of Iron by Anthracite in Wales and Pennsylvania. Its Feasibility in the Leinster Coal Field. Conversion of Pig into Bar Iron. Analysis of the comparative Cost in England and at Lough Allen. Employment of Turf in the Manufacture of Iron in Germany and France. Analysis of the Cost of Production of Iron by Turf. Refining of Iron with Turf; its superior Quality. Influence of the Cost of Fuel on the Iron Manufacture. Recent Processes for economizing the waste Heat of Iron Furnaces. Utilization of Fuels of inferior Quality, ... 118

CHAPTER V.

Geological Structure of Ireland. Granitic Rocks; their Distribution and Composition. Mica Slate; its Extent. Clay Slate, upper and lower; its Mineral Contents and Area. Veins and Protrusions of Quartz Rock. Sandstone Formations; old Red and Yellow Sandstones; Conglomerates; their Distribution. Carboniferous Slate. Relations of the Limestone and Coal Measures to the underlying and superincumbent Rocks. New Red Sandstone. Chalk of Antrim. Basalt and Trap Rocks of the North of Ireland.

Mining Districts of Ireland. Copper Mines. Ores of Copper. Mines of the Wicklow District; their Distribution; Mode of working and Produce. Mines of the Waterford District; their Structure and Produce. Copper Mines of the South-Western District; their geological Relations and Produce. Copper District of Tipperary. Mines in the Clay-slate north of Dublin. Metallurgic Treatment of Copper Ores. Economy of Fuel in smelting.

Of the Lead Mines of Ireland. Ores of Lead. Lead Mines of Wicklow and Wexford; their Structure and Produce. Lead Mines of the Northern and South-Western Slate Districts. Deposits of Lead Ore in the Limestone of Ireland. Mines near Dublin. Mines of Clare. Preparation and smelting of Lead Ores. Extraction of the Silver from Lead. Richness of the Irish Ores in Silver. Economy of Fuel in the Treatment of Lead Ores, ... 168

CHAPTER VI.

Gold Mines of Wicklow; their Situation and Produce. Native Silver. Mines of Manganese, Antimony, Cobalt. Minerals of Zinc, Nickel, and

PAGE.

Tin. Sulphur Trade of Wicklow. Iron Pyrites. Deposits at Silvermines.
Decomposable Pyrites of the Coal Fields. Means of manufacturing
Copperas and Alum. Native Alums of Clare and Kerry. Varieties
of Clay found in Ireland. Porcelain Clay of Baltinglass and Tullow.
Pipe-Clay of Cahir and Roscommon. Clays of Coal Island, Kil-
kenny, Arigna, and Howth. Flints and Quartzoze Sand. Manufac-
ture of Glass and Earthen Ware. Building Stones of Ireland; their
Varieties and Qualities. Roofing Slates of Killaloe, Valentia, and
Wicklow. Minerals of Barytes and of Magnesia. List of Varieties
and Localities of Marbles, ... 219

Chapter VII.

Of the Agricultural Industry of Ireland. Its Importance as an Occupation. Relations of Agriculture to Manufactures. Natural Fertility
of the Soil of Ireland. Statistical Valuation of its Produce. Distribution of the Surface of the Country. Office of Plants. Correlative Functions of the Mineral, Vegetable, and Animal Kingdoms.
Composition of Plants. Origin of the Soil. Connexion between the
Fertility of the Soil and its Composition. Examples of fertile Districts. Nature of the Soils of various Parts of Ireland. Composition
of Subsoils, Organic Elements of the Soil. Mechanical and Physical Offices of the soil. Of Drainage: its Importance to Irish Agriculture.
Action of Plants on the Soil. Of Exhaustion. Composition of the most
important Crops. Of Manures. Composition and Properties of the
most important native Manures. Of Lime and Limestone; Marl;
Sea Sand. Coral Sand; its Nature. Value of those Sands dredged
upon the North and South Coasts. Of Gypsum; of Sea-weed; of
Bones; Farm Yard Manure; its Composition and relative Power.
Importance of its Preservation and suitable Economy to practical
Agriculture, ... 249

Chapter VIII.

Agricultural Industry continued. Of Rotations. Relation of Corn Crops
and Green Crops. Amount of Food produced by various Systems of
Culture. Influence of different Cultures in the Exhaustion or Amelioration of the Soil. Size of Farms in Ireland. Principle of Consolidation, not as applicable to agriculture as to Manufactures. Relation of the Size of Farms to the Population. Relative Profit and
Employment afforded by large and small Farms. Average available Farms for existing Population.
Secondary Uses of Food Crops. Manufacture of Potato Starch, Sugar,
and Spirits. Composition of different Kinds of Potatoes. Manufacture of Beet Root Sugar; its economic Circumstances. Of Fibre
Crops. Cultivation of Flax and Hemp. Composition of ligneous

PAGE.

Fibre. Mode of Culture and Preparation of Flax. Principles which
it gives off in steeping. Average Crop of Flax; its Value. Uses of
the Flax Products as Food and as Manure.

Flax Manufacture and Linen Trade. Total Value of Flax grown in Ire-
land. Exertions of the Royal Dublin Society and Flax Improvement
Society, and their Results. Employment given by the Flax and
Linen Trade. Tables of Mill Power and of Exportation of Flax and
Linen. Localization of this Industry. Favourable Situations for it.
Culture and Composition of Hemp. Conclusion. 295

CHAPTER IX.

Importance of Means of internal Communication to the Industry and Morality of a People. Influence of the Construction of Roads on the
social Condition of the Inhabitants. The Expense repaid manifold
by the Increase of Revenue. Utility of public Grants to assist in the
Execution of Works of local Improvement.

Of Inland Navigation. Favourable natural Condition of Ireland. Na-
vigation of the Shannon. Expenditure on its Works. Amount of
Employment given. Traffic on the several Parts of the Shannon by
Steam and otherwise. Other navigable Rivers of Ireland. The
Barrow Navigation. Extent and Direction of the Canals of Ireland.
Grand and Royal Canals. Amount of Traffic and Tolls. Their
Branches. Lagan Navigation. Newry and Ulster Canals. Tyrone
and Boyne Navigations. Proposed Canal to place in Connexion
Lough Neagh, Lough Erne, and the Shannon.

Of the Irish Lakes in Relation to the Means of Intercourse. Loughs Neagh
and Erne. Lough Gill. The Connaught Lakes. Importance of
developing their Navigation. Probable Benefits to the Inhabitants
of that Province, and to the Country at large.

Of Railways as regards Ireland. Existing Lines. Dublin and Kingstown. Ulster Railway. Drogheda Line. Report of Railway Commissioners. Lines recommended therein. Notice of the general
Conditions of the various Lines of Railway now proposed to be
formed. Cost of locomotive Power. Of the Atmospheric Railway.
Its peculiar Relations to this Country. Its mechanical and economical Advantages.

Importance of the Railway System as a Means of Intercourse to the People. Notice of the Question of Governmental Control in the Construction and Management of Railways, ... 344

CHAPTER X.

Circumstances of Ireland regarding certain staple Articles of Industry.
Cotton, Wool, Salt. Of the Cost of Labour in Ireland. Skilled and
unskilled Labour. Cheap Labour and low Wages not identical.
Labouring Force of Men estimated. Skilled Labour rare and dear

PAGE.

in Ireland. Freedom of Labour necessary to all industrial Progress. Combinations in Ireland more injurious than in Great Britain. How to be counteracted. Evidences of Improvement in the Habits of the Working Classes.

Supposed Want of Capital in Ireland. Real Extent of its Influence. English Capital not available for active Industry. Useful for the secondary Operations of passive Industry, and thus leaving native Capital free for the more active Pursuits.

Necessity for industrial Knowledge in Ireland. Possessed by England in an eminent Degree. Observations of M. Briavionne. False Ideas of Education. Union of Science and Practice necessary for Industry. Industrial Knowledge more extensive and more difficult to acquire than professional Knowledge. Manner of conducting it. Exertions of the Royal Dublin Society for promoting industrial Education. Special Education in Agriculture, by the Royal Dublin Society, the Royal Agricultural Society, and private Agricultural Schools. Of the System of National Education, in regard to Agriculture. Relations of Industry to Morality, Temperance, and Intelligence. Conclusion, ... 391

THE

INDUSTRIAL RESOURCES

OF

IRELAND.

———◆———

CHAPTER I.

IMPORTANCE OF FUEL IN THE INDUSTRIAL ARTS. CIRCUM-
STANCES OF IRELAND AS TO FUEL. ABSENCE OF WOOD. ITS
FORMER ABUNDANCE IN IRELAND. GEOGRAPHICAL POSITION
OF THE COAL DISTRICTS. COAL FIELDS OF LEINSTER, OF
TIPPERARY, AND OF MUNSTER. THEIR GEOLOGICAL STRUC-
TURE AND EXTENT OF BEDS. COST OF THE COAL PRODUCED.
ANTHRACITE OF THE SOUTH. BITUMINOUS COAL OF THE
NORTH OF IRELAND. COAL FIELDS OF TYRONE, OF ANTRIM,
MONAGHAN, AND OF CONNAUGHT. THEIR GEOLOGICAL AND
ECONOMIC CONDITIONS. POSITION OF THE LOUGH ALLEN
COAL FIELD. ITS PRODUCTIVENESS NOT WELL ASCERTAINED.
COMPOSITION OF THE IRISH COALS, THEIR COST AND PRAC-
TICAL VALUE. NUMERICAL RESULTS OF THEIR ECONOMIC
AND ULTIMATE ANALYSES. PECULIARITIES IN THE USE OF
ANTHRACITE AS FUEL. ITS CONVERSION INTO A FLAMING
COAL BY STEAM. ITS USE WITH LOCOMOTIVE ENGINE
BOILERS. WOOD COAL OF LOUGH NEAGH. ITS SITUATION
AND EXTENT. RESULTS OF ITS CHEMICAL ANALYSIS, AND
OF ITS ECOMONIC EXAMINATION. EXTENT AND MODE OF
FORMATION OF BOG IN IRELAND. DIFFERENT KINDS OF BOG.
COMPOSITION OF TURF, ITS COST AND PRACTICAL VALUE.
MODES OF PREPARING IT. INFLUENCE OF THE WATER CON-
TAINED IN TURF ON ITS HEATING POWER. COMPRESSED PEAT.
ITS COST AND ECONOMIC VALUE. PRODUCTS OF THE DIS-
TILLATION OF TURF. PREPARATION AND VALUE OF CHAR-
COAL FROM TURF.

THE question which presents itself almost on the threshold
of every industrial enterprise, is that of the amount and cost
of the fuel necessary to be consumed in executing the work:

B

for in the existing condition of the Arts, it may almost universally be considered, that, directly or indirectly, the changes which are to be produced, whether in composition or in form, in the raw materials of any manufacture, are effected by the operation of heat.   If we look to any of the various chemical or metallurgic arts, we find the agency of heat necessary to give liquidity to the substances employed, so that they may be run into moulds, or separated from infusible components; to effect their perfect mixture, or to bring into play those chemical affinities, by which their constitution may be altered, and new and more valuable products formed.   Hence it is impossible to carry on those branches of industry in localities destitute of fuel: and where this is scarce and high priced, the cost of production of the manufactured article may be so augmented, as to absorb all profit, and render the prosecution of that trade only a source of loss.   In a similar manner, although not in the same degree, the mechanical arts are influenced by the cost of fuel.   In localities where water power is not available, it is necessary to employ steam.   To produce any given motion, to spin a certain weight of cotton, or weave any quantity of linen, there is required steam; to produce the steam, fuel; and thus the price of fuel regulates effectively the cost of mechanical power.   Abundance and cheapness of fuel are hence main ingredients in industrial success.   It is for this reason that in England the active manufacturing districts mark, almost with geological accuracy, the limits of the coal fields.   Hence it is easily conceivable, that in attempting to describe the materials which exist for the prosecution of industry in Ireland, the first step must consist in such an account of the sources of fuel at our disposal, as may determine its practical value, its distribution, its nature, its probable cost, and, as far as possible, its abundance.

The materials which we employ as fuel for our domestic and industrial purposes, are all derived from the vegetable kingdom, being either wood of modern growth, or else turf or coal, which are themselves but masses of vegetable matter of ancient growth, compressed and decomposed until they present their well-known aspect.   In this country we may practically

exclude wood from our consideration as a fuel; there is no
feature of an Irish landscape more characteristic than the
desert baldness of our hills, which, robbed of those sylvan ho-
nours that elsewhere diversify a rural prospect, present to
every eye a type of the desolation which has overspread the
land. This barrenness of trees is but of recent origin. Numerous localities, in every part of Ireland, derive their names
from having been originally embowered in forests. In every
district where man's neglect, combined with nature's rank
luxuriance of vegetation, has given occasion to the formation
of those bogs, for which our country has become a bye-word,
it is found that immersed in the turf are quantities of large
timber, generally fir, birch, and oak; the former so impregnated with resinous material, that a splinter burns like a can-
dle, and may be employed as such. This resin is partly the
native turpentine of the tree, but, for the most part, consists
of peculiar bodies produced by the decomposition to which the
wood is subjected, and by which, if the action were continued
for a sufficient length of time, true bituminous coal might be
produced.

That the country was some centuries ago remarkable for its
extent of forests, as it is now by the reverse, appears from all
our histories. Many causes conspired for their destruction.
In some districts they were extirpated to increase the arable
surface. In others in order to destroy the shelter which bands
of outlaws found in their recesses. An extensive export trade
in oak was at one time carried on, and two centuries ago the
manufacture of iron was in great activity throughout this
country, and led to the cutting down, as Boate says, of innu-
merable trees in order to prepare charcoal. During all this
time, no one planted; all sought their immediate profit and
cared not for the future, and the final result has been, that at
present the timber grown in Ireland is not sufficient for those
uses to which it specially is adapted, and as a fuel we may consider it never to be employed.

There is no doubt but that the coal has had its origin in the
amassing together of great quantities of trees and plants, which
constituted the vegetation of our globe at a period far antece-

dent to the appearance of man upon its surface. There is
reason to suppose, that vegetable growth was then more active than it is now in the same localities. The plants whose
forms may still be recognized in the beds of coal, belong, in
great part, not to the vegetation of the temperate climes, but
to that which characterizes the scenery of the tropics. In the
convulsions to which the superficial crust of the earth has been
subjected, these forests have been destroyed; the growth of
an immense surface, probably carried together by currents,
has been engulphed and covered with mud and sand, and was
thus subjected, under the influence of enormous pressure, and
probably of an elevated temperature, to those decomposing
agencies, by which vegetable matter, when in contact with
moisture, is incessantly affected.

Under such circumstances, wood is converted into coal.
The change is not sudden nor direct. It would be difficult to
recognize in the masses of coal we usually burn, the forms of
the plants from which it had its origin. But there are many
varieties of coal. In the deposits of the true coal formation,
the chemical changes have been carried on through such a
lapse of ages, and under circumstances so favourable to their
action, that it is now completed. But in geological epochs
less remote, masses of vegetable remains have also been imbedded, in which we can study the intermediate states of
change. It is thus by connecting the fossil wood or brown
coal with recent wood upon the one hand, and with true coal
upon the other, that we obtain an accurate view of the course
of alteration which has produced this important fuel.

The alteration in the chemical composition of wood, when
it is converted into coal, is capable of being accurately traced,
and requires attentive study, as on it rest the comparative
values of different kinds of coal as fuels. The composition
of wood, and of some of the most important of British coals,
is given in the following table: in which, however, they are
supposed to be free from ashes.

	CARBON.	HYDROGEN.	OXYGEN.
Oakwood, . . .	52·5	5·7	41·8
Fossil wood, . .	73·0	5·0	22·0
Cannel coal, . .	85·5	5·8	8·7
Caking coal, . .	89·0	5·4	5·6
Anthracite,. . .	92·8	3·9	3·3

The alteration will hence be seen to consist in the removal of most of the oxygen and some of the hydrogen of the wood. These elements pass off combined with carbon, and are found haunting the recesses of the coal mine, under the forms of those *damps* or vapours so fatally known to miners, the oxygen and carbon forming the carbonic acid, termed choke damp, the hydrogen and carbon constituting the light carburetted hydrogen or fire damp. The quantity of carbon removed from the wood being comparatively small, this element preponderates the more in the residual coal as the decomposition has been more perfect, until finally in the anthracite or stone coal we find some specimens almost pure carbon.

When I bring before the reader the individual composition of the varieties of Irish coal, I shall again notice this table, and point out in what way the heating power of any kind of coal is connected with its composition. For the moment I shall lay it aside, in order to notice somewhat further the geological relations of the various fuels.

The formation of coal in great masses appears to have occured but in one geological period, though this may have extended over a great length of time, as we find the various portions of the coal formation to be separated from each other by strata of slaty rock or sandstone, of such thickness as must have required long years to form. Still the coal formation stands quite distinct from the formations that lie under and above it. In these there is no coal. In some localities of the most recent (tertiary) geological age, limited deposits of fossil wood are found, but they are unimportant, and we may consider coal as limited in its distribution to those rocks which lie

between the mountain limestone on the one hand and the new
red sandstone on the other.

It would not suit the objects of this work to attempt a consecutive description of the geological structure of Ireland, or
to enter upon the examination of its rocks and minerals in any
general point of view, as it is only in reference to their industrial uses that they interest us, and the individual rocks can
be best noticed in relation to the products which they furnish
to the arts.   On subsequent occasions, therefore, those rocky
strata which are inferior in position to the limestone shall be
noticed, as well as those more limited in their development in
this country, which lie above the coal formation; but at present the structure of the districts in which fuel is to be found
need alone occupy attention, briefly premising the description
of the rock, the limestone, upon which our coal formation
rests.

In this country the limestone formation is more developed
than any other portion of the geological series.   It is often
called the mountain limestone, because in England, where it
was first examined, it rises into hills of considerable elevation,
as in Derbyshire.   With us that title cannot be applied.   Its
extent may be inferred from the fact, that a direct line of 120
miles, drawn east and west, from Dublin to the Bay of Galway,
touches no other rock, and from north to south, although its
boundaries are irregular, its mean breadth may be considered
at 100 miles.   Over this immense area, the surface is almost
entirely flat; its average elevation over the sea not exceeding
250 feet, and, although undulating in its surface, the elevations which it forms seldom rise more than two or three hundred feet above the general level.   This peculiar feature of
our country brings with it many disadvantages and some advantages, to each of which I shall advert in the proper place.

The great scale of the limestone formation in this country
has allowed of its being recognized to be, not one homogeneous
rock, as it had been formerly described, but to consist of three
formations, essentially different in character, and even in
some degree as to the animal remains which they contain.   Of
these divisions the lowest is by far the most widely extended.

It prevails most in the midland and southern counties, and furnishes us with some of the marbles of Galway and Kilkenny, Carlow, Mayo, and other places, which shall be again noticed.

The neighbourhood of Dublin is occupied by the middle limestone, to which the name of calp was given by our celebrated countryman, Richard Kirwan. It extends rather towards the northern counties of Leinster, as Westmeath and Longford. It occurs also in Galway. It is much less pure than either of the other divisions of the limestone strata, containing often layers of soft shales, of impure coaly matter, of earthy ironstone, and of flinty slate. The uses to which it is most applicable shall be hereafter stated and its chemical composition shewn.

The upper limestone occupies a small area, and is at once distinguished from the others by the physical character of the country which it forms. This is steep and rugged, presenting crags and precipices, with numerous caverns. To the localities of this rock belong the peculiar interest, that on it the coal formation rests. We hence find it encompassing those districts in which coal is found, or in which it may be expected to be discovered. To specially describe its distribution is, therefore, needless, as in examining the limits of our local deposits, I shall in fact, point out the localities where it is found. It is only useful to remark, that its greatest development is on the southern and eastern coasts of Galway Bay, where, rising from under the great coal formation of the Munster district, it constitutes the rugged mountains of Burren, and forms much of the country between Galway and Sligo, the hilly character of which distinguishes it so remarkably from the greater flatness of surface of the calp, and of the lower limestone counties of the centre and south.

Interposed between the limestone and the true carboniferous beds, there exists a great sandstone deposit, which, from one of the most important uses of its materials, is known as the *millstone* grit. The relations of this rock are so identified with the coal measures, that the notices of localities are the same for both, and need not be separated.

In the geological map which accompanies the chapter specially devoted to the mineral resources of Ireland, those sub-
divisions of the limestone are not individually marked, but may
easily be traced by the reader according to the localities described; the object of the map being only to indicate such
important geological features as influence practical industry.
The different shadings represent the different systems of rocks,
and for distinction sake, the space occupied by the limestone,
which is more than one-third of the entire area of the island,
has been left unshaded.

The coal formations, as marked on the map, include all strata
between the limestone and the new red sandstone (Permian).
Thus the area occupied by the millstone grit is contained in
that of the coal field of Lough Allen. Were these minor features of the rocky structure represented, the map should become so crowded, and its parts so minute, as to be unsuited for
general reference, and unintelligible, except to those already
conversant with the subject.

The coal formation of Ireland consists of a series of sandstone and slaty rocks, which rest upon the upper limestone,
and give an aspect of considerable elevation to the districts.
They are seven in number; of these one is in Leinster, two
are in Munster, three in Ulster, and one in Connaught. These
districts differ materially in their produce, according as they
are situate to the north or to the south of Dublin. Those to
the north yield bituminous or flaming coal: those to the south
yield only stone coal or anthracite, which burns without flame.
There is no doubt but that this difference results from the geological circumstances of those portions of the island, but it
would not suit our purpose to enter into that question.

We will commence the history of our coal districts with that
of Leinster.

This deposit occupies the greater portion of the county of
Kilkenny, of the Queen's County, and part of Carlow. It is
bounded on the east, west, and south, by two great rivers, the
Barrow and the Nore, which run immediately at the base of
the Colliery Hills. Its general appearance, when viewed from
a distance, is that of a very steep ridge of high land running

in a direct line for many miles, rising from 800 to 1000 feet above its base, and apparently flat on the summit. It presents this character on every side, but, when viewed from the eminence itself, it resembles a barren table land rising precipitously above a flat and highly cultivated country.

This district constitutes a great mineral basin; its strata consequently incline from the edge towards the centre, the undermost appear on the outer edge, and the uppermost in the interior of the district. The strata consist of beds of slate clay, containing abundant thin veins and nodules of ironstone, compact sandstone, and sandstone slate; with these are interposed beds of fire clay, and the coal beds, of which there are altogether eight workable, arranged in regular succession. These strata require to be more specially described.

Slate clay is usually the most abundant rock of the coal formation. It is a dull earthy mineral, which easily divides into thin flakes. It decomposes rapidly when exposed to air; its colour varies from black to grey; it is sometimes very hard or even flinty, which especially occurs where it comes into contact with the subjacent limestone. The quantity of ironstone associated with this rock is very large, its composition and uses will be hereafter noticed.

The sandstone of the coal formation consists of silicious sand cemented by a paste of lime or clay. It contains numerous vegetable impressions. This sandstone frequently becomes micaceous and slaty, so as to split easily into layers, producing the well-known Carlow flags.

The roof of the coal bed is sometimes sandstone, and sometimes slate clay. The floor of the bed is generally a clay, locally termed *coal seat*. This substance is soft and earthy; I shall hereafter describe its composition, at present I need only mention that it is equal to the best Stourbridge clay, for all the purposes for which that substance is employed.

The beds of coal in the Leinster district are, as already stated, eight in number, distinguished by the following names, arranged in the order of their position from below upwards:

1. The Rossmore foot coal.
2. The first bed of slate coal.

3. The second bed of slate coal.
4. The four foot coal.
5. The second foot coal or Drummagh coal.
6. The first three foot coal.
7. The double seam.
8. The second three foot coal.

The seventh and eighth beds, being those lying next the surface and easiest worked, have been exhausted; the sixth bed,
or first three foot coal, which for the last century has principally supplied the wants of the surrounding country, is now
considered by Mr. Griffith as nearly worked out. The inferior
beds have been but little, some not at all touched, and must be
the theatre of future mining operations. Of these the most
important is the four foot coal, and its description will serve
as an example of the rest.

The upper part of this bed is composed of five feet five inches
of slaty coal (locally termed *kelves*), under which there are three
feet of hard coal, containing some sulphur pyrites, then a bed of
black slate clay of six inches thick, and lastly one foot of coal,
containing a thin bed of kelve near the bottom, making altogether a height of coal, kelve, and slate of ten feet, of which
but four feet are solid coal. Mr. Griffith estimates the area
occupied by this coal at 5000 acres (Irish), and as its specific
gravity is 1·591, the total quantity of pure solid coal may be
calculated at rather more than sixty-three millions of tons. On
the average this bed appears to lie about eighty yards below
the first three foot bed of coal, and at a depth of from 100 to
140 yards from the surface.

Formerly the extraction of the coal was very badly managed.
The imperfect methods of drainage obliged many shafts to be
abandoned when they arrived at a certain depth, a large quantity of coal was left behind, and the amount of labour was excessive. Hence coal was high-priced; 20s. a ton for coal, and
from five to eight shillings for small coal or culm. But since
Mr. Griffith's report, and especially by the exertions of the late
Mr. Aher, much progress has been made in introducing a better
system. The use of the steam engine for draining has enabled
shafts to be re-worked that had been totally abandoned. The

quantity of coal raised is estimated at 120,000 tons per annum, and it is sold at a price of about 11s. 6d. per ton for coal, and 4s. per ton for culm.

The chemical and economic qualities of this coal will be described, when I have noted the geographical circumstances of the remaining anthracite basins.

The Tipperary coal field is indeed a portion of that already noticed, being separated from the Kilkenny coal field by a narrow intervening neck of limestone. It extends about twenty miles in length from Freshford to near Cashel. It is about six miles broad in its widest part; the towns of Killenaule and of New Birmingham mark its centre. It forms a range of hills from 300 to 600 feet in height, abrupt on the north-western, but sloping on the south-eastern side into the limestone plain. The general nature and arrangement of the strata is the same as has been above described, but they dip at a steeper angle and undulate. Hence the coal lies in deep troughs, from which arises a peculiar mode of working, the shaft being sunk in the centre of the trough, and the coal wrought by working upwards on both sides of it.

This district appears to contain but three beds of coal. The lowest is but nine inches, the others are each two feet thick. The quantity of coal at present raised has been estimated at 50,000 tons per annum. The price at which it is at present sold may be estimated at 12s. per ton for good coal, and 4s. per ton for culm.

Proceeding further to the south and west we arrive finally at what is peculiarly termed the Munster coal field. This tract, the most extensive development of the coal strata in the British Empire, occupies considerable portions of the counties of Clare, Limerick, Cork, and Kerry. In all four counties coal has been discovered, and coal mines worked. The physical features of the country are similar to those described in the Tipperary district. The coal consequently lies in a series of troughs, the hills usually striking from east to west, and the strata dipping on either side, north and south, at considerable angles, often perpendicular. From this peculiarity of structure, the estimate of the precise condition of the coal becomes difficult. The same beds frequently re-appear in different parts of the country, thrown up by contortions of the strata to the surface, and might then, on superficial observation, be counted as distinct deposits. From Mr. Griffith's investigations it appears, however, that there are six distinct layers of coal. Of these, three of the most valuable, locally known as the bulk-vein, the rock-vein, and the sweet-vein, have been recognized on the opposite sides of three of the undulations. The detailed examination of this district has not, however, been as yet carried on to a sufficient extent to enable us to trace the entire arrangement of the strata.

The most extensive collieries at present worked in this district are situate in the barony of Duhallow in the county of Cork. The beds of culm present themselves in numerous places over the west coast of Clare, and along the estuary of the Shannon. The beds, although thus of enormous superficial extent, are unfortunately not thick; the coal is softer and more slaty than in the Tipperary and Kilkenny districts. This applies, however, only to the thinner beds; the veins mentioned above in Duhallow, and which are from two to three feet in thickness, produce an excellent anthracite, of which some analyses shall be hereafter given.

Such are the beds of non-flaming coal or anthracite which occur in Ireland. We shall now pass to the description of the coal of the northern portions of the country, which is bituminous coal.

A small but highly-interesting coal field occurs in Tyrone. The country round it resembles a great geological museum, containing rocks of every epoch, from the granite rising from beneath all, to those tertiary clays which constitute the latest term of the geological series, and of which, in relation to the stores of fuel they contain, I shall soon have occasion to speak. The limestone of Dungannon may be considered as forming the base of the Tyrone coal district. It is covered by strata of sandstone, limestone, and slate clay, with clay-ironstone, fire-clay, and coal. The external character of the country is similar to that of the southern coal field: it is an assemblage of low hills, with steep acclivities and flattened summits. Here, however, when the hills exceed a couple of hundred feet in height, they are capped with new red sandstone or trap, or even with both. This district is geographically subdivided into the Coal-island and the Anahone basins, the former of which is by much the larger and the more important.

The Tyrone coal burns rapidly with flame, and evolves great heat: its composition and economic power will be hereafter noticed. The sandstone and slate are generally analogous to those rocks in other coal fields, and need not be further noticed. The ironstone and fire-clay will be specially described further on.

The linear dimensions of the Coal-island field are six miles by two; its area about 7000 acres. The Anahone district contains only 320 acres, yet recognized, but it may extend under the new red sandstone through a much larger area.

Notwithstanding the smallness of this basin, its strata are so much contorted and disturbed, as to cause great irregularity in the workings by changes of level, and the occasional disappearance of the bed of coal from amongst the broken strata. Slips and shifts of the layers of rocks also occur, and rather more frequently than in other coal fields. But notwithstanding these drawbacks, this basin merits special attention. The coal is excellent : it is not difficult to raise, and its quantity is such as to be capable of diffusing the blessings of industrial prosperity over an extensive area.

From Mr. Griffith's report, it appears that there are in this basin six workable beds of coal. The names of these beds, and their usual thickness, are as follows:

BEDS OF COAL.	THICKNESS.			
	Ft.	In.	Ft.	In.
1. Annagher coal, ...	8	0 to	10	0
2. Yard coal, ...	2	0 ,,	3	0
3. Braghaveel coal, ...	4	9 ,,	5	0
4. Balteboy coal, . · . . .	0	9 ,,	3	0
5. Derry coal, ...	4	6 ,,	5	0
6. Gortnaskea coal, ...	2	0 ,,	6	0
	22	0 ,,	32	0

From 22 to 32 feet of solid workable coal is thus found within a depth of 120 fathoms, and it is remarked by Mr. Griffith that amongst the numberless pits of the English coal fields, there is no example of the same thickness of coal within the same distance from the surface. The collieries in this district are worked, some by the Hibernian Mining Company, and some by private companies of persons belonging to the neighbourhood. The industry of the latter has been and is profitable. The works of the former have hitherto been carried on at a loss. Whence comes this difference? The materials for answering this question may present themselves in a subsequent portion of this work.

The Anahone coal strata occupy a mineral trough about a mile in length, and half a mile in breadth. It is bounded on the north by the carboniferous limestone, but on the other sides it is met by the new red sandstone which lies over the coal measures. The deepest pit sunk in it was to fifty-seven yards, and there were found three beds of coal, one of three feet, one of nine feet, and the lowest of two feet in thickness. In some parts of the field certain other beds have been noticed : the only one actually worked was that of nine feet, and this appears to have been nearly exhausted. It is an excellent coal, and bears carriage without breaking. The working of this basin has been carried only to the limits of the coal strata on the surface, but there is no doubt but that the beds penetrate under the new red sandstone, and probably to a considerable extent. Investigations, under that point of view, still remain to be made, and deserve attention.

At the northern extremity of Antrim is found a coal district, unimportant as to magnitude, but remarkable from its association with the great basaltic mass from which the characteristic scenery of Fairhead and the Causeway is derived. This coal field differs from all the others in this country in wanting the underlying limestone, and resting directly on mica slate. In this, certainly very rare peculiarity, it is not, however, without parallel: the coal district of St. Etienne in France being similarly circumstanced. The face of the precipices to the sea, where sufficiently free from the debris of the basaltic rock, presents sections of this coal formation which fully illustrate its structure. At top the entire is covered by from 50 to 100 feet of the columnar greenstone, which spreads over the entire district. Under this are beds of reddish sandstone, slate, and coal. At Murlough Bay, the beds of coal are six in number, of which four are bituminous and two anthracitous. The latter are found, one immediately above, and the other close below a range of columnar basalt of seventy feet in thickness, which lies in amongst the coal strata. It might hence appear that these beds also had been originally bituminous, and that the basalt injected at an intense heat had distilled off their volatile portions, converting the residue into anthracite. There are, however, other and strong reasons against such an idea. Thus the beds of coal which lie close under the upper range of basalt are fully bituminous, and the effects of heat shewn where trap dykes traverse the bituminous beds, and convert them into true coke, is quite different from anything visible in the lower beds, which consist of a real anthracite.

The quantity of coal which remains in this district is so small, that further detail concerning it is unnecessary. It appears to have been the oldest worked colliery in Ireland, perhaps in the empire, as during the year 1770 the miners broke into an old gallery, the walls of which were lined with stalactites, evidently of great age, and antique mining tools were found therein. The residents in the district had never heard of a tradition of the mine having been anciently worked, and the excavation must have been made at a very remote period indeed.

The bituminous beds of coal are each about two feet six inches thick. The upper bed of anthracite is also of the same thickness: this latter appears, however, to be impure and sulphurous.

In Monaghan a small coal basin rests on a patch of the carboniferous limestone which is insulated within the slate district. The strata dip at so large an angle as to render the working very difficult; and as no beds exceeding twelve to fourteen inches in thickness have been found, this coal district need not be considered as of any value.

We arrive now at the last of the coal fields of this country, the Connaught district. It is one worthy of attention from its peculiar geographical position, and from the circumstances connected with the attempts made to establish the manufacture of iron within its bounds. Those attempts, part of the history of the too notorious Arigna Company, shall be treated of hereafter. The localities of the coal only need occupy us now.

The Shannon, the largest river in the British islands, rises in the centre of the Connaught coal field, and falls into the Atlantic Ocean: dividing the counties of Clare and Kerry, and cutting through the centre of the Munster coal formation. Expanding in its inland course into a chain of extensive lakes, it intersects, through a line of 247 miles, some of the richest lands in Ireland, washing the banks of ten of the thirty-two counties of which our island is made up. It has its origin in the recesses of the Leitrim hills, where it springs almost with its full power from a vast gulf, the depth of which has not been yet ascertained, and almost immediately expanding forms Lough Allen, of which the area is 8900 acres. The picture of this district, as I saw it some two years since, has never left my mind. The dark brown hills, heather clad, rose abruptly from the water, excepting towards the south, where they were separated from the lake by level spaces of marshy bog. The patches of cultivation, small and rare, far from relieving the aspect of the scene, served but to render its dreariness more oppressive. The lake, smooth as a mirror, reflected the brilliant sky of midsummer. No wave disturbed it: the noise and bustle of active industry were far away. The melancholy solitude of my walk was only broken by the approach of some wretched men, who had heard of the phenomenon of a stranger's presence in their wilds, and pressed around, asking whether I was about to do anything for the country, to give employment. Alas! it was not in my power. As I walked on, there lay around my path masses of iron ore, equally rich with the best employed in England. I knew that in those hills, whose desolate aspect weighed upon my mind, there were concealed all the materials for successful industry. A population starving, and eager to be employed at any price; a district capable of setting them at work, if its resources were directed by honesty and common sense; but all sacrificed to the stock-jobbing speculations of a few men acting on the gross ignorance and credulity of some others. If the industrial circumstances of this country were really known, such events as the jobbing of the Arigna Company could not have occurred. Let us hope that by the progress which science and education have since made, and are now making, the occurrence of aught similar may be for the future prevented.

The hills which surround Lough Allen form the Connaught coal field; they occupy large parts of the counties of Roscommon, Sligo, Leitrim, and a portion of Cavan in Ulster. The greatest length of the district is sixteen miles, which is also its greatest breadth. The total area is about one hundred and fourteen thousand Irish acres. Seen from the south, they present a steep and straight ridge of from 1000 to 1200 feet in height; the summits flat, and usually covered with bog. The centre of this district is occupied by Lough Allen. The circuit of the lake may be conveniently divided into four parts, with respect to its content in coal. The rocks are similar to those of the other coal fields: they consist of sandstone, sandstone slate, slate clay, clay ironstone, and fine fire clay. The strata are very regularly arranged, conformably to the limestone on which they rest, and contrary to the declivity of the hill. Slips occur, as in all coal fields: they do not present anything peculiar here.

West of Lough Allen the River Arigna divides the field into the southern and western portions. The former consists of one great mountain ridge named Brahlieve: at its base are the Arigna Iron Works. The western division extends between the Arigna and Dorobally rivers. These two portions have almost the same internal structure. Upon the limestone rests slate clay, in thickness from 300 to 600 feet. This rock is remarkable for the rich beds of ironstone which it contains. These are exposed in the channel of the River Arigna in incredible numbers. Higher up occur numerous beds of sandstone, and next, the fire clay, which, as in the Leinster district, forms the seat of the coal.

The beds of coal found in this district are three in number, and were first described with detail in Mr. Griffith's Report on the Connaught coal formation. As the extent and character of these beds of coal will be found of high importance, and that opinions differ regarding them, I shall transcribe, in full, the most important of Mr. Griffith's observations.

" *Of the first Bed of Coal.*—The fire clay is succeeded by a bed of coal, which varies in thickness from one to three feet: it is known in the country by the name of the *crow* coal. It contains numerous thin laminæ of black slate clay, which render it of little value, except for burning lime. When first brought to the surface it is moderately solid, but on exposure to the air it soon divides into thin flakes.

" This bed has never been wrought. If it were, I have little doubt its average thickness would be found to amount to three feet, but it has never been seen excepting at the outgoing. In the vale of the Arigna, near the iron works, where the fire clay was wrought, this coal was three feet thick. This coal runs parallel to the three foot coal which lies above it, and its outgoing may be traced along the face of the hills through the greater part of the southern and western division of the district.

" *Of the three Foot Coal.*—The future prosperity of the Connaught coal district may be said to depend entirely on the produce of this bed, which, though of moderate thickness, is fortunately of great extent. Its quality as fuel for domestic purposes is excellent, and if used for smelting iron, it is among the best in the empire. According to the analysis of Kirwan, 100 grains are composed of

71·42, carbon.

23·37, mixture of asphalt and maltha.

5·21, grey ashes.

" Specific gravity, 1·351.

" The thickness of this coal is rarely less than three feet, or more than three feet four inches.

" In its outgoing, commencing at the iron works, it may be

traced without difficulty along the northern face of Brahlieve mountain, without any material interruption, for four miles and a half, by Aughabehy colliery, nearly to Geeva point in the county of Sligo, and from thence back again on the opposite side of the hill to Tullylions colliery, and afterwards round the eastern end of the mountain to the point above the Arigna works.

" In the western division of the district the extent of coal is not so great as in the southern. This division may contain about 1200 acres of the three foot coal, which, added to 2800 acres contained in the southern division, make a general total of about 4000 acres.

"From this calculation we should deduct one-fifth part to allow for impurities in the coal and the loss occasioned by slips and undulations. This, at the rate of 7840 tons per acre, will leave upwards of thirty millions of tons of coal as the probable quantity which may be raised out of the southern and western divisions of the district.

" *The third bed of Coal* varies from eight to nine inches in thickness. It is the uppermost bed of coal in the district, and has not been met with except in the southern division."

On the three foot coal several collieries are worked. Of these the Rover and the Aughabehy are the principal : the former are situated very near the iron works, the latter farther distant. Coal from the Celtnaveena and from the Meenashama pits will also be found amongst those of which the composition will be given farther on.

These coal beds being at a higher level than the general surface of the country, admit of being worked under the most favourable circumstances. The expense of raising the coal is very small; Mr. Griffith calculated that the cost of it at the pit's mouth was four shillings per ton, and when the iron works were in operation, it was contracted for at five shillings per ton.

At the time that Mr. Griffith visited the locality and reported on it, the collieries were in such a wretched condition, flooded with water, their machinery out of repair, and the persons engaged about them so ignorant, that complete accuracy in the information he obtained could not be expected, and it would appear that the results above given require some alteration. I shall, therefore, in order to indicate as fully as possible the special circumstances of the district, detail, though briefly, the results of examinations of certain portions of it, made by mining engineers, none of whom, however, it must be remarked, inquired into the general structure of the locality, as Mr. Griffith did, nor were any of them in that position which would justify equal authority being attributed to their individual reports.

After the first exposure of its extraordinary proceedings, when it became indispensable to pay some attention to its proper business, the Arigna Iron Company commissioned Mr. Twigg of Chesterfield, a person practically conversant with collieries and iron works, to examine their holdings in this district, and he made several reports on the subject, of which a very excellent digest has appeared in the Survey of Roscommon, published by Mr. Weld.

From Mr. Twigg's reports it would appear that the bed of coal, as it sinks into the mountain, rather diminishes in thickness. He found it in the chisel pit at Aughabehy two feet seven inches thick. Mr. Weld found it in a pit which he examined to be less than two feet. Mr. Twigg estimated the working coal ground at Aughabehy at 160 English acres, and that at an average of 2550 tons per acre it should yield 408,000 tons of coal. The working area of the Rover colliery he valued at from 80 to 100 English acres. Mr. Twigg made no survey of the general area of coal in the district, such as that made by Mr. Griffith (4000 Irish acres).

In 1825 the Mining Company of Ireland instituted some inquiries as to the conditions of a portion of this coal field, and had reports prepared by mining engineers of reputation, for access to which documents I am indebted to the kindness of Mr. Purdy. The coal beds on Mounterkenny Hill were found by Mr. Kenneth to consist of two distinct patches, that to the north containing 204½, and that more southerly 106 Irish acres of coal. No workings were carried on in the larger, but Tullynaha colliery is situated in the smaller portion. In this pit, which was twenty-two yards deep, and very badly worked, he found the coal but 20 inches thick, consisting of twelve inches of head coal, 2¾ inches of slaty coal, and 5¼ inches of crow coal. The coal was then laid on the bank for 4s. 6d. per ton, but he considered that, by proper workings, it could be done for 3s. or 3s. 6d.

Mr. Kenneth calculates the total qnantity of coal in the Mounterkenny part of the field as follows : the north portion, containing 204½ acres, averaging two feet thick, gives

House coal, . . 667,897 tons.

Slaty coal, . . 400,820 ,,

The south portion, 106 acres, same thickness,

House coal, . . 345,869 tons.

Slaty coal, . . 207,564 ,,

making a total of 1,622,150 tons, of which, however, a third must be subtracted, to allow for loss in actual working for sale.

Mr. Geddes, examining the Tullynaha pit almost at the same period, reported that it shewed two beds of coal, the upper, or crow coal, three feet thick, the second, eight yards lower, two feet thick : the latter coal, which was of superior quality, was the only bed worked. The field being basin-shaped, a fitting sunk forty-four yards in the centre drained the entire. Owing to bad management, the coal then cost 5s. 6d. per ton, but, he says, it could be raised for 3s. 4d. to the bank, and paying 9d. royalty, and 1s. carriage, could be placed on quay at Lough Allen for 5s. 1d. per ton.

The mountains, which form the northern portion of this district, do not present such favourable pictures as that last described. The thick beds of coal have not as yet been traced upon them, and indeed some features in their structure render it improbable that they exist ; several thinner beds have, however, been found; and a further examination is desirable. The eastern portion of the district, separated from the last by the River Owenmore, consists of one mountain group, Slieve-a-Nie-ran (the Iron Mountain). Its structure and stratification differ only in detail from that of the southern and western portions, and it contains also three beds of coal, of which the superficial extent is very great. The total thickness of the coal is less, however, and the strata are more broken   It has not been much worked. Indeed for a long time the southern and western divisions will fully suffice for all industrial wants.

Such are the circumstances of the coal field of Lough Allen. Although subsequent examination has sobered down the expectations of its produce which were once held, it must still be considered as capable of becoming an important centre of industry for the interior of this country. The causes which led to the failure of the iron manufacture at Arigna might have acted as forcibly in Staffordshire or at Merthyr. Those causes may be removed. The quantity of coal available is certainly sufficiently great for domestic trade, and it must be recollected, that on the surface of the hills which surround Lough Allen there is a supply of fuel, probably not inferior to that which is contained within them. I have mentioned already that Mr. Griffith considers his original estimate of thirty millions of tons as too high. An estimate given in the Report of the Railway Commissioners in 1838, may probably be considered as embodying all accurate observations made. The Lough Allen district is there stated to contain 20,000 acres of coal, equal to twenty millions tons. At present there is very little coal raised. The quantity does not exceed 3000 tons per annum.

Having described the geographical and geological conditions of the coal fields of Ireland, I shall now proceed to trace the composition of the coals they yield, and ascertain how far they are adapted for use. To represent their constitution I have given in every case the practical analysis, which shews the quantity of gas given off at a red heat, and that of the coke produced; the actual weight of coke being the sum of the ashes and of the pure coke. The heating power of each fuel was experimentally determined, and in most instances the elementary analysis has been executed.

The minute quantity of nitrogen which exists in all ordinary varieties of fuel was not separately determined in those analyses, as it does not exercise any influence on their industrial value. Its amount is therefore in all cases included in the number given for the quantity of oxygen present in the specimen of fuel analyzed.

COAL OF THE CONNAUGHT BASIN.

This coal is described by Mr. Griffith as intermediate to the open-burning or quick-blazing coal of Scotland and the caking coal of Whitehaven. Mr. Twigg called it a coking coal of good quality. I have found it moderately bituminous, burning with flame, and leaving a white ash in moderate quantity. Its only disagreeable character was a great degree of friability.

I have submitted to accurate examination four kinds of it, transmitted to me through the kindness of Colonel Jones, Member of the Shannon Commission. I shall describe the results which I obtained.

AUGHABEHY COAL.

A rich black coal, easily broken. Its specific gravity 1·274. When heated it gives off a good deal of inflammable gas, and leaves a light, porous, grey, coherent coke. Analysed in this way it was found to give from 100 parts:

Volatile matter,	23·10
Pure coke,	66·15
Ashes,	10·75
	100·00

Its economic value as a fuel was determined by measuring the quantity of oxygen it was capable of absorbing on ignition with litharge. One part of it reduced twenty-six parts of lead to the metallic state; 100 parts of it, therefore, represent seventy-seven parts of pure carbon.

CELTNAVEENA AND MEENASHAMA COAL.

These two coals are almost identical in external appearance. Their specific gravities about 1·290; when ignited, they give off inflammable gas, but do not froth; they produce a moderately dense coke, and leave, when burned away, white ashes. Their analysis was found to be, in 100 parts:

	CELTNAVENA.	MEENASHAMA.
Volatile matter,	19·10	18·90
Pure coke,	65.87	61·46
Ashes,	15·03	19·64
	100·00	100·00

Ignited with litharge, one part of Celtnaveena coal gave twenty-six of lead, and one part of Menashama coal twenty-five of lead. Hence, 100 parts of Celtnaveena coal corresponded to seventy-seven. and of Meenashama to seventy-three of pure carbon.

ROVER COAL.

This coal is rather brown in aspect; and has a remarkable tendency to split into cubical fragments. Its specific gravity is 1·287. When ignited it gives out gas, but does not froth. Its coke is porous, slightly coherent. It contains less foreign matter than any of the other kinds. On analysis, its composition was found to be

Volatile matter, ...	17·70
Pure coke	74·89
Ashes	7·41
	100·00

One part of it gave, by ignition with litharge, 28·4 parts of lead, hence 100 parts of the coal correspond to 84 of pure carbon.

The prices of these coals, as given in a notice attached to the specimens, are

Rover coal, ...	4s. 9d. per ton.
Meenashama, ...	5 6 ,,
Celtnaveena	5 6 ,,
Aughabehy, ...	6 4 ,,

The Aughabehy and the Rover coal being the most important of this district, I thought it interesting, in addition to the more practical kind of analysis given above, to determine their actual elemental composition, which I found to be as follows :

	AUGHABEHY.	ROVER.
Carbon, ...	79·69	81·04
Hydrogen, ...	6·24	4·91
Oxygen, ...	3·32	6·64
Ashes, ...	10·75	7·41
	100·00	100·00

It is thus seen, that the Aughabehy is a much more bitumi-

nous coal than the Rover, which approaches nearer in its character to the anthracites of the south. I do not know whether
in the geological relations of the district there is anything
capable of explaining the fact. The Celtnaveena and Meenashama coals have an intermediate quality.

COAL OF THE TYRONE BASIN.

This coal burns rapidly, and gives out intense heat. It
cakes but little, and strongly resembles Ayrshire coal. My
colleague, Mr. Davy, examined the Braghaveel coal from Coal
Island, and the Kingarrow coal of Dungannon. The former
had specific gravity of 1·266, and gave 65·9 per cent. of coke
containing 29·4. The latter had specific gravity of 1·307, and
gave 66·9 per cent. of coke, containing 37·0 of ashes. The
following analyses by myself give the composition and properties of specimens of coal from the new Drumglass colliery,
and from the pits of Messrs. Caulfield at Coal Island.

COAL FROM DRUMGLASS NEW COLLIERY.

It is brilliant, black, friable, frequently mixed with the
pyrites, which oxidize on exposure to the air; its ashes consequently usually reddish. On ignition it gives off much gas,
froths, and gives a light porous coke. It was found to be
composed of,

Volatile matter, ...	48·70
Pure coke, ...	34·00
Brown ashes, ...	17·30
	100·00

One part of it gave with litharge 22 parts of lead, hence 100
parts correspond to 65 parts of pure carbon.

COAL FROM THE COAL ISLAND PITS.

This coal has a slaty structure, is dull coloured, but tolerably pure. Its specific gravity is 1·267; when ignited it gives off
much gas, tumesces, and leaves a very porous coke. Its
practical analysis gave,

Volatile matter, ...	38·96
Pure coke, ...	49·39
White ashes, ...	11·65
	100·00

It is, therefore, much purer than the Drumglass coal.   One part of it gave, with litharge, 26·5 of lead; hence 100 parts correspond to 78 of pure carbon.

To illustrate further the composition of the coal of this basin, its ultimate constitution was determined: it was as follows:

Carbon,	69·08
Hydrogen,	5·86
Oxygen,	13·41
Ashes	11·65
	100·00

COAL OF THE ANTRIM DISTRICT,

I found the coal of Ballycastle dull, black in colour, its specific gravity 1·279.   On ignition it gave out much gas, frothed very much, and left a porous coke.   It consisted of,

Volatile matter,	36·96
Pure coke,	45·94
Ashes,	17·10
	100·00

One part of it gave 25 of lead; hence 100 parts of it correspond to 71·4 of pure carbon.

Of the economic relations of these coals nothing need be said. They are applicable to every use in industry, to which coal is applied in England.   The remaining kind of coal, the anthracite of the South of Ireland, will require more consideration in that respect.

A remarkable feature in the coal fields of the South of Ireland is the large quantities of iron pyrites which are associated with the coal, and which, evolving sulphurous fumes when burned, renders much of it totally unsuited for domestic use, and even for many purposes in the arts.   The thicker beds are, however, free from this objection, and it is to the pure anthracite that I shall apply the following observations.   The composition of anthracite is very uniform.   From its not caking or burning with flame it is very generally termed mineral charcoal, and considered to be pure carbon mixed only with ashes.   Hence its composition is generally expressed as in the following instances. Mr. Griffith, in his valuable report on the Leinster district, gives the composition of the

FIRST BED OF SLATE COAL.

Carbon, ...	92
Ashes, ...	8
	100

FOUR FOOT COAL.

Carbon, ...	96·25
Ashes, ...	3·75
	100·00

The specific gravity of the four foot coal was found to be 1·591.

What is here termed carbon, is really the whole combustible and volatile material of the coal. This will appear from the following examination of the Irish anthracites which I made for the purposes of this work.

The specimens which I analysed were from

The Rushes coal, Queen's County, Leinster district.
The Pollough coal, Castlecomer,   ,,   ,,
The Sweet-vein, Kanturk, Munster district.

The anthracites have no tendency to froth or cake in coking. They give off little or no inflammable gas on being ignited, but usually the masses break up quite small, especially if the heat be suddenly applied. The ashes are almost always red, owing to oxide of iron remaining after the combustion of the pyrites, which the anthracite usually contains.

By the practical mode of analysis these coals yielded :

	RUSHES.	POLLOUGH.	SWEET-VEIN.
Volatile matter, . .	9·85	10·40	10·35
Pure carbon, . . .	86·42	79·71	81·13
Ashes, ...	3,73	9·89	8·52
	100·00	100·00	100·00

The results of ignition with litharge was, that one part of the

Rushes anthracite gave 31.8 of lead.

Pollough   ,,   ,, 26·7 ,,

Sweet-vein ,,   ,, 29·0 ,,

Hence they correspond respectively,

100 parts of Rushes   to 93·5 of pure carbon.

100   ,,   Pollough to 73·5   ,,   ,,

100   ,,   Sweet-vein to 85·3   ,,   ,,

I determined the elementary composition of these three varieties of anthracite, and found it to be as follows:

	RUSHES.	POLLOUGH.	SWEET-VEIN.
Carbon, ...	90·04	81.36	86·37
Hydrogen, ...	3·50	2·41	3·71
Oxygen, ...	2·73	6·34	1·40
Ashes	3·73	9·89	8·52
	100·00	100·00	100·00

Of these coals, the Sweet-vein was perfectly free from sulphur; the Rushes contained very little, but the Pollough a good deal. As this sensibly affects the determination of the carbon in the above analyses, I determined the exact quantity in this last coal, and found it to be 6·18 per cent., and hence the true composition of the Pollough coal was:

Bisulphuret of iron, ... 11·58

Ashes without iron, ... 2·19

Pure anthracite, ... 86·23

                                  100·00

The pure anthracite thus considered separate from ashes or sulphur consisted of,

	RUSHES.	POLLOUGH.	SWEET-VEIN.
Carbon, ...	93·53	92·37	94·39
Hydrogen . . .	3·63	2·40	4·05
Oxygen, ...	2.84	5·23	1·56
	100·00	100·00	100·00

Hence these coals, when pure, differ principally in the amount of hydrogen; the Sweet-vein containing most, and the Pollough least. The Rushes may be considered as representing the usual composition of this kind of coal.

The anthracite is thus shewn to be by no means mere mineral carbon; it contains a sensible quantity of hydrogen and a trace of oxygen. But these elements are not present in such proportion as admit of flame or smoke in burning, or the production of bituminous vapour or gas by distillation at a red heat.

This peculiar composition of anthracite affects its use as a fuel in the arts in an important degree, being the source of many advantages and of some defects, which, together with their remedies, it is necessary to describe. In consequence of its density and closeness of texture, anthracite is difficult to burn, except when in large masses, and it conducts heat but slowly. For this reason also it is liable to splinter up into small fragments. These peculiarities are easily accommodated in practice. One much more important to consider arises from the fact that it contains very little volatile combustible material, but consists almost entirely of dense, solid carbon, and produces, in good draft, a most intense heat, which is, however, almost confined to the immediate neighbourhood of the fire. Thus, if anthracite be used as the fuel under a steam boiler, the heat in the fire-place may become so great, as to melt away the bars of the grate, and to burn out the bottom of the boiler, and yet the air passing into the flues may not be of such temperature as to produce an evaporation by any means economical. In such case we must call in the aid of science to free our fuel from this disadvantage. It is at once done by passing the vapour of water through the mass of red hot anthracite; the water is decomposed; its oxygen combines with carbon, and forms carbonic oxide; its hydrogen is set free. These mixed combustible gases pass into the flues, and inflaming in the excess of air which enters, give a sheet of flame which I have seen to extend for thirty feet under and through a boiler. The anthracite is thus converted into a flaming coal. There is no loss of heat; there is no gain of heat either, as some persons have supposed to occur, but the action, beneficial in its result, is to absorb, in the first place, the excessive heat which was doing local injury, and to distribute it over the entire surface of the flues, where its maximum of good can be obtained. The principle of this method has been long known. Its application has been patented in England, but such patents can only stand for the particular mode of applying the watery vapour therein described, if even for so much.

Anthracite burning without smoke, and giving an intense though local heat, assimilates itself to coke, the most costly of our fuels, and hence it is interesting to inquire whether it can be used in what is now the principal employ of coke, in the fires of locomotive engines. On this point but little has as yet been experimentally ascertained. In England it is not of much importance; but one trial has been made which gives promise of its being perfectly successful in that use. I extract from the Mining Journal, quoting a report to the Directors of the Liverpool and Manchester Railway.

"In the first instance the engine ran out with a load about six miles, and the coal was found to do very good duty, without any difficulty being experienced either with the tubes or the getting up of the fires. The engine brought back a load of coal waggons from the Heyton Colliery, and acquired, thus loaded, a speed of twenty-one miles an hour. Another trial was made in the evening with the same engine for the whole distance to Manchester, taking five loaded waggons. The journey was accomplished in an hour and twenty-five minutes. The consumption of anthracite was only $5\frac{1}{2}$ cwt., although a large portion was wasted, from the fire bars being too wide apart for the economical use of this fuel. The engine would have used upwards of $7\frac{1}{2}$ cwt. of coke for the same journey with the same load."

Should this result be confirmed by experiments continued for a longer time, it may exercise important influence on the railway economy of this country.

The heating power of anthracite is very great. I have found, and my results confirm those of Berthier, that it is capable of reducing to the metallic state, from 28 to 32 times its weight of lead. Pure carbon gives 35 parts of lead. The bituminous fuels give from 25 to 30. Now the economic value of a fuel, the quantity of water it can boil, or the quantity of iron it can melt, will be found proportional to these numbers, and hence, where the other conditions are rendered suitable for the employment of anthracite, it must be considered one of the best fuels.

Before entering on the history of our coal strata, I noticed some of the more ancient rocks on which they rest, and which I shall fully describe when examining the circumstances of our metallic veins. Above the coal formation, there are also extensive series of rocks, the new red sandstone, the oolite, the lias, and the chalk, which occupy in England large portions of the surface, but with us are developed only in the north-eastern corner of the island, forming the County Antrim and part of Derry, and overtopped by these masses of igneous rocks, the trap, and basalt, which chiefly characterize the locality. Some details of special industrial applications of these rocks may hereafter require notice, but I shall now pass from them in order to describe a very peculiar deposit of fuel, more recent than the coal—the Lignite of Lough Neagh. Encompassing the southern half of the lake from Washing Bay in Tyrone, to Sandy Bay in Antrim, this deposit consists of alternations of white, brown, and bluish clay, with white sand and beds of lignite or wood-coal; and, on the margin of the lough, of the silicified wood for which that lake is so celebrated. In some parts of this deposit the lignite is so abundant, that pits are sunk to raise it when other fuel is scarce. The vast quantity of lignite may be judged from a boring at Sandy Bay, described by Mr. Griffith. In seventy-six feet of depth there occurred three beds of lignite, one of twenty, one of twenty-five, and one of fifteen feet thick, giving a total thickness of strata of fuel of sixty feet; the remaining sixteen feet were clay. Elsewhere the beds of lignite are not so much developed, but as the area of this tertiary basin extends over one hundred square

miles, the quantity of fuel therein contained may be considered
of much public interest.　The clays of this basin are analogous
to those of Bovey, where pipe-clay is obtained, along with lignite; whether good pipe-clay can be had in the basin of Lough
Neagh has not as yet been tried.

The lignite has been already described as intermediate between wood and coal.　This is shewn in its composition, given
in the following analyses from this district.

The lignites examined retained all the structure of wood,
and were of a deep brown colour.　When ignited they gave off
gaseous matter, which burned brilliantly, and left a dense
black charcoal.　In this way they were found constituted of,

	No. 1.	No. 2.
Volatile matter, ...	57·70	53·70
Pure charcoal, ...	33·66	30·09
Ashes, ...	8·64	16·21
	100·00	100·00

By ignition with litharge, No. 1 gave 19·6 times its weight
of lead, and No. 2 gave 16·7 times its weight.　Hence,

100 parts of No. 1, correspond to 58 of pure carbon.

100　　,,　　No. 2,　,,　　,,　　50　　　,,

Their elementary composition was found to be as follows:

	No. 1.	No. 2.
Carbon, ...	58·56	51·36
Hydrogen, ...	5·95	7·35
Oxygen, ...	26·85	25·08
Ashes, ...	8·64	16·21
	100·00	100·00

The economic value of the lignite appears from those analyses about two-thirds that of average coal.　The heat which it
produces is more diffused than that from coal, and less intense.
Indeed in all respects as to application to industrial uses, the
position of lignite is between those of coal and wood.

The last of our sources of fuel that I shall proceed to describe, is of comparatively modern formation, and is considered
most specially characteristic of this island; it is our turf.　Our

bogs may become, under the influence of an enlightened energy, sources of industry eminently productive. It is a fuel of excellent nature. We see it in ordinary use spoiled by its mode of preparation. It is here my duty to point out how it can be properly prepared, and economically used. Its importance to Ireland will, I trust, justify me in entering into some detail as to its nature, its composition, and its preparation. The excessive moisture of this climate, and the tendency to the growth of certain mosses, are the primary causes of bogs. The process of their formation is well described by Captain Portlock, in the Memoir of the Ordnance Survey of Londonderry :

"In the production of bog, *sphagnum* is allowed on all hands to have been a principal agent, and superabundant moisture the inducing cause. To account for such moisture, various opinions have been advanced, more especially that of the destruction of large forests, which, by obstructing in their fall the usual channels of drainage, were supposed to have caused an accumulation of water. That opinion, however, cannot be supported,—for, as Mr. Aher remarks in the 'Bog Reports,' 'such trees as are found have generally six or seven feet of compact peat under their roots, which are found standing as they grew, evidently proving the formation of peat to have been previous to the growth of the trees'—a fact, which, in relation to firs, may be verified in probably every bog in this parish, turf from three to five feet thick underlying the lowest layer of such trees. It is, indeed, so strongly marked in the bog, which on the Donegal side bounds the road to Muff, that the turf-cutters, having arrived at the last depth of turf, find timber no longer, though formerly it was abundant, as is proved by their own testimony from experience, and by the few scattered stumps which still remain resting on the present surface. Not so, however, with oaks, as their stumps are commonly found resting on the gravel at the base, or on the sides of the small hillocks of gravel and sand, which so often stud the surfaces of bogs, and have by Mr. Aher been aptly called 'islands.' He further adds, that in the counties of Tipperary, Kilkenny, &c., they are popularly called 'derries,'—a name deserving

attention, whether viewed as expressive of the existing fact,
or as resulting from a lingering traditionary remembrance of
their former condition, when, crowned with oaks, they were distinguishable from the dense forest of firs, skirting the marshy
plains around them. The strong resemblance to ancient watercourses of the valleys and basins which now contain bog, and
the occurrence of marl and shells at the bottoms of many, naturally suggest the idea of shallow lakes,—a view of the subject adopted in the 'Bog Reports,' by Messrs. Nimmo and
Griffith. Such lakes may have originated in the natural ine-
qualities of the ground,—or been formed by the choking-up of
channels of drainage by heaps of clay and gravel,—or they
may have been reduced to the necessary state of shallowness
by the gradual wearing away of obstacles which had dammed
up and retained their waters at a higher level. Mr. Nimmo
describes the mode in which the basin of a bog has been banked
in by the alluvial deposits of a river (during freshets), and, in
a similar manner, numerous examples might be adduced of
bogs separated by banks of clay and gravel, owing to rivers
running at their base, and below their level.

" In some cases also clay, which is so frequently found spread
over gravel at the bottom of bogs, has produced a kind of pud-
dle, which, by retaining the waters of floods or springs, has
facilitated the formation of muddy pools.

" In all such cases the process may be thus stated:—A shallow pool induced and favoured the vegetation of aquatic plants,
which gradually crept in from the borders towards the deeper
centre. Mud accumulated round their roots and stalks, and a
spongy, semi-fluid mass was thus formed, well fitted for the
growth of moss, which now, especially *sphagnum*, began to
luxuriate: this, absorbing a large quantity of water, and continuing to shoot out new plants above, while the old were de-
caying, rotting, and compressing into a solid substance below,
gradually replaced the water by a mass of vegetable matter.
In this manner the marsh might be filled up, while the central,
or moister portion, continuing to excite a more rapid growth
of the moss, it would be gradually raised above the edges,

until the whole surface had attained an elevation sufficient to discharge the surface water by existing channels of drainage, and calculated by its slope to facilitate their passage, when a limit would be in some degree set to its further increase. Springs existing under the bog, or in its immediate vicinity, might indeed still favour its growth, though in a decreasing ratio; and here—if the water proceeding from them were so obstructed as to accumulate at its base, and to keep it in a rotten, fluid state—the surface of the bog might be ultimately so raised, and its continuity below so totally destroyed, as to cause it to flow over the retaining obstacle, and flood the adjacent country.

"In mountain districts the progress of the phenomenon is similar. Pools, indeed, cannot in so many instances be formed, the steep slopes facilitating drainage,—but the clouds and mists, resting on the summits and sides of mountains, amply supply their surface with moisture, which comes too in the most favourable form for vegetation—not in a sudden torrent, but unceasingly and gently, drop by drop. The extent of such bogs is also affected by the nature of the rock below them. On quartz they are shallow and small; on any rock yielding by its decomposition a clayey coating, they are considerable—the thickness of the bog, for example, on Knocklaid, in the county of Antrim, which is 1685 feet high, being near twelve feet. The summit bogs of high mountains are distinguishable from those of lower levels, by the total absence of large trees."

The total area of Ireland is twenty millions of acres. The total area of bog is estimated at 2,830,000 acres; nearly one-seventh of the entire surface of the island. Of these bogs there are 1,576,000 acres of flat bog; the remaining 1,254,000 acres are mountain bog. The former is spread over the central portions of the great limestone plain; the latter is principally distributed through the hilly country which ranges along the coast. In an industrial point of view, it is the central district of bogs which deserves attention. Some special circumstances which affect certain localities may require consideration in a different point of view; at present the subject must be considered under its general relations as to the constitution and application of this fuel.

An idea of the amount of area occupied by bog, and of its geographical distribution, sufficiently exact for the general consideration of industrial problems, may be deduced from the accompanying map, in which the localities and extent of the larger bogs, surveyed by the Bog Commissioners, have been laid down. It will be seen that the district west of the Shannon contains by far the greatest proportion, and that a chain of bog passes almost from Dublin to that river through the central counties. In Leitrim, Kerry, and in Antrim, there is also a large extent of bog. This map does not include such small patches of bog as are scattered through various parts of Ireland, but which, although useful as sources of fuel to the inhabitants of the district, are totally without interest with regard to industry.

As turf includes a mass of plants in different stages of decomposition, its aspect and constitution vary very much. Near the surface it is light coloured, spongy, and contains the vegetable remains but little altered. Deeper, it is brown, denser, and more decomposed; and finally, at the base of the greater bogs, some of which present a depth of forty feet, the mass of turf assumes the black colour, and nearly the density of coal, to which also it approximates very much in chemical composition. The amount of ash contained in turf is also variable, and appears to increase in proportion as we descend. Thus in the section of a bog forty feet deep at Timahoe, those portions near the surface contained $1\frac{1}{2}$ per cent. of ashes ; the central portions $3\frac{1}{4}$ per cent., whilst the lowest four feet of turf contained 19 per cent. of ashes. In the superficial layers it may also be remarked, that the composition is nearly the same as that of wood, the vegetable material being but little altered; and in the lower we find the change into coal nearly complete. Notwithstanding these extreme variations, we may yet establish the ordinary constitution of turf with certainty enough for practical use, and on the average specimens of turf selected from various localities, the following results have been obtained.

Turf, in Ireland, is usually sold by measure, not by weight, and as our results refer to weight, it is necessary, in comparing cost, to ascertain the density of average turf, as sold. The specific gravity of the light surface turf is about 400, water being 1000, and from this it increases, with the compactness of the structure, to nearly the density of coal. A cubic yard of good turf, packed close in sods, weighs about 900℔. The densest turf well packed will go so far as 1100℔ per cubic yard; but the light turf, of which so much is burned, may not weigh more than 500℔. The density of the turf, which these numbers illustrate, affect many of its technical uses, as shall be hereafter shewn. For comparison I may mention, that the cubic yard of solid coal weighs nearly a ton; but the coal in fragments as sold and burned weighs but 13 cwt. per cubic yard: it is, therefore, about twice as dense as average turf. Furnaces, to burn the same weight of coal and turf, should require double the capacity for the latter.

By means of the following analytical results, the general practical qualities and the chemical composition of turf may be considered to be established. The specimens were selected from Cappoge in Kildare, and Kilbeggan in Westmeath, on different sides of the great Bog of Allen, and from Kilbaha in Clare, where an extensive district of bog exists.

When ignited, the turf gives off inflammable gas, much water, and leaves a light, easily combustible charcoal. I found the specimens analyzed to yield,

| | LIGHT TURF. | | | DENSE TURF. | |
	CAPPOGE.	KILBEGGAN.		KILBAHA.	CAPPOGE.
Volatile matter, .	73·63	75·50	.	72·80	70·10
Pure charcoal,	23·82	22.67	.	19·14	23·66
Ashes, . . .	2·55	1·83	.	8·06	6·24
	100·00	100·00		100·00	100·00

By ignition with litharge it was found that

One part of Cappoge turf gave 13·0 of lead.
,,   Kilbeggan   ,,   14·2   ,,
,,   Kilbaha   ,,   13·8   ,,

Hence 100 parts corresponded

Of Cappoge turf to 37 of pure carbon.

Kilbeggan   ,,   41   ,,   ,,

Kilbaha   ,,   40   ,,   ,,

I determined also the elementary composition of these turfs: the results were as follow:

	CAPPOGE.	KILBEGGAN.	KILBAHA.
Carbon, ...	51·05	61·04	51·13
Hydrogen, ...	6·85	6·67	6·33
Oxygen, ...	39·55	30·46	34·48
Ashes, ...	2·55	1·83	8·06
	100·00	100·00	100·00

Turf contains much less nitrogen than coal. Hence the liquor obtained in distilling turf contains no free ammonia. On the contrary it is acid from acetic acid, but even of this it yields so little that it cannot become, as occurs in the case of wood, an object of manufacture.

The calorific power of dry turf is about half that of coal. It yields, when ignited with litharge, about fourteen times its weight of lead. This power is, however, immensely diminished in ordinary use by the water which is allowed to remain in its texture, and of which the spongy character of its mass renders it very difficult to get rid. There is nothing in the industrial economy of this country which requires more alteration than the collection and preparation of our turf. Indeed I may say, that for practical purposes this valuable fuel is absolutely spoiled, as it is now prepared. It is cut in a wet season of the year; whilst drying, it is exposed to the weather; it hence is in reality not dried at all. It is very usual to find the turf of commerce containing one-fourth of its weight of water; although it then feels dry to the hand : but let us examine how that affects its calorific power. One pound of pure, dry turf will evaporate six pounds of water; now in one pound of turf, as usually found, there are three-quarters of a pound of dry turf, and one-quarter of a pound of water. The three-quarters of a pound can only evaporate four pounds and one-half of water. But out of this it must first evaporate the quarter of a pound contained in its mass, and hence the water boiled away by one pound of such turf is reduced to four pounds and a quarter. The loss is here 30 per cent.; a proportion which makes all the difference between a good fuel and one almost unfit for use. When turf is dried in the air, under cover, it still retains one-tenth of its weight of water, which reduces its calorific power 12 per cent.; one pound of such turf evaporating five and one-third pounds of water. This effect is sufficient, however, for the great majority of objects. The further desiccation is too expensive and too troublesome to be used, except in some especial cases, of which the more important shall be hereafter noticed.

The characteristic fault of turf as a fuel is its want of density, which renders it difficult to concentrate within a limited space the quantity of heat necessary for many operations. The manner of heating of turf is, indeed, just the opposite to that of anthracite. The turf yields a vast body of volatile inflammable ingredients, which pass into the flues and chimney, and thus distribute the heat of combustion over a great space, whilst in no one point is the heat intense. Hence for all flaming fires, turf is applicable; and in its application to boilers it is peculiarly useful, as there is no liability to that burning away of the metal, which may arise from the local intensity of the heat of coke or coal. If it be required, it is quite possible, however, to obtain a very intense heat with turf, as I shall notice when speaking of the manufacture of iron.

I have already noticed the area over which turf may become available for industry. It comprises the central limestone plain, extending also over Galway and Mayo, with parts of Clare and Kerry. The cost at which turf may be consumed in the immediate neighbourhood of the bogs, I consider to be, from pretty numerous inquiries, not above 3s. 6d. per ton, but in our subsequent calculations I shall take 4s., in order that the error, if any, may be in excess of cost. I shall consider, however, that the turf is dried in the air under cover, which, if our industry ever becomes active, and our fuel economized, must be the ordinary practice. Its economic

value may then be practically assumed as 44 per cent. of that
of ordinary coal.   The turf at 4s. per ton costs as much to
give a certain heat as coal at 9s. 1d.

The removal of the porosity and elasticity of turf, so that it
may assume the solidity of coal, has been the object of many
experimenters, who have proposed mechanical and other processes for the purpose.   Amongst those we may mention Lord
Willougby D'Eresby, whose anxiety to improve the condition
of the industrial classes deserves the highest praise.   Lately
with us Mr. Charles Wye Williams has brought into use various preparations of turf, and has given considerable impulse
to the utilization of this kind of fuel.   It has been found, that
the elasticity of the turf fibre presents great obstacles to com-
pression : and the black turf which is not fibrous, is of itself
sufficiently dense.   The only modes that present promise of
successful issue, are those invented by Mr. Williams.   One of
these consists in drying the turf well, and then impregnating
it with tar, which renders it waterproof, as it were, besides
augmenting its calorific power.   Turf so prepared has no tendency to re-absorb moisture, which is the serious failing of
turf that has been perfectly dried, and the expense of thus
bitumenizing the turf is, I understand, very trifling.   It is said
to be manufactured for from 6s. to 8s. per ton, and from the
trials that have been made with it upon a very considerable
scale, it appears to have a calorific power little inferior to coal.

All of those machines which have been invented for pressing
turf, sod after sod, by manual labour, become ultimately too
expensive to allow of their being profitably used.   It is only
by operating on a great scale, and with powerful machinery,
in fact, only by manufacturing compressed peat largely for
sale, that the operation can be made to succeed practically.
This is what Mr. Charles W. Williams has so well effected at
Cappoge.   The turf, when fresh cut, has its fibre broken up
as far as possible, and is then placed between cloths, and
pressed by a hydraulic press of great power. The condensation
is to about one-third of the volume, and it loses about two-
fifths of its weight, by the water, which is forced out in the
pressing, and subsequently dried out.   The sods of turf so

prepared, even when formed of the very upper and spongiest stratum of the turf, are denser than wood. They have little or no tendency to grow damp, and it is found that including all labour, wear and tear, and original cost, this compressed peat can be delivered at the works for 5s. per ton. When this compressed peat is carbonized it gives a fine coherent coke, which contains very little ash, and amounts to about 30 per cent. of its weight, when the coking is properly carried on. The density of this coke is greater than that of wood charcoal, being found to range from 913 to 1040; the turf from which it was made having a specific gravity of from 910 to 1160. Its cost when manufactured does not exceed 20s. per ton.

The employment of turf as a source of heat in industry is extending; already it supplies exclusively the steam boats on the Shannon and a great number of distilleries and mills. From the numerical facts that have been given, the economy of its use may be inferred and compared with that of other fuels.

Not merely may we utilize turf in its natural condition, or compressed, or impregnated with pitchy matter, but we may carbonize it as we do wood, and prepare turf charcoal, the properties of which it is important to establish. The methods of carbonization are of two kinds. 1. By heating the turf in close vessels; by this mode loss is avoided, but it is expensive, and there is no compensation in the distilled liquors, which do not contain acetic acid in any quantity. The tar is often small in quantity, and the gases are deficient in illuminating power. Hence the charcoal is the only valuable product. Its quantity varies from 30 to 40 per cent. by weight of the dry turf. The products of the distillation of 1157℔ of turf, were found by Blavier to be:

474℔ charcoal or	41·1	per cent.
226℔ watery liquor or	19·3	,,
7℔ tar or	6	,,
450℔ gaseous matter or	39·0	,,
1157	100·0	

The quantity of tar is very variable; thus the turf used in

the iron furnaces at Voitoumra gives, when coked in close
vessels :

Charcoal, ...	40·25
Tar, ...	24·50
Watery liquor, ...	14·00
Gaseous matter, ...	21·25
	100·00

The economical carbonization of turf is best carried on in
heaps, in the same manner as that of wood. The sods must be
regularly arranged, and laid as close as possible : they are the
better of being large, fifteen inches long by six broad and five
deep. The heaps, built hemispherically, should be smaller in
size than the heaps of wood usually are. In general 5000 or
6000 large sods may go to a heap, which will thus contain
1500 cubic feet. The mass must be allowed to heat more than
is necessary for wood, and the process requires to be very carefully attended to, from the extreme combustibility of the charcoal. The quantity of charcoal obtained in this mode of carbonization is from 25 to 30 per cent. of the weight of the dry
turf.

The charcoal so obtained is light and very inflammable. It
possesses nearly the volume of the turf. It usually burns with
a light flame, as the volatile matters are not totally expelled.
This is shewn by the composition of a specimen analysed with
the following result :

Carbon, ...	89·90
Hydrogen, ...	1·70
Oxygen and nitrogen, ...	4·20
Ashes, ...	4·20
	100·00

This charcoal is usually very light and friable. It is hence
peculiarly fitted for the manufacture of gunpowder, and Mr.
Derust, Pyrotechnist to Vauxhall, who experimented with it
at the request of Mr. Williams, reported that it stood the
several tests, and was 20 per cent. more combustible than
wood charcoal.

For many industrial uses, the charcoal so prepared is too light, as, generally speaking, it is only with fuels of considerable density that the most intense heat can be produced; but by cokeing compressed turf, it has been already shewn, that the resulting charcoal may attain a density of 1040, which is far superior to that of wood charcoal, and even equal to that of the best coke from coal. The importance of this result in the metallurgic relations of this fuel I shall hereafter notice. As to calorific effect, turf charcoal is about the same as coal cokes and little inferior to wood charcoal. This is shewn in the table, page 47, and it has been found to give from twenty-six to thirty parts of lead by its reducing action upon litharge. It is peculiarly important in the preparation of the charcoal from turf, that the material should be selected as free as possible from earthy impurities, for all such are concentrated in the coke, which may be thereby rendered of little comparative value. This is remarkably shewn by observing the composition of the coke from the four varieties of turf, the analyses of which are given in page 34. Thus the cokes consisted in 100 parts of

| | LIGHT TURF. | | DENSE TURF. | |
	CAPPOGE.	KILBEGGAN.	KILBAHA.	CAPPOGE.
Pure coke, ...	90·3	90·6	70·4	79·1
Ashes, ...	9·7	9·4	29·6	20·9
	100·00	100·00	100·00	100·00

Hence the coke from surface turf contains not 10 per cent. of ash, whilst that of the dense turf of the lower strata contains from 20 to 30 per cent. This latter quantity might altogether unfit it for practical purposes.

Such is the description of our sources of fuel, as far as I have been able to collect facts regarding them. I have been anxious to remove exaggerated ideas of opposite characters which have been entertained. Although destitute of the grand development of mineral fuel which has rendered the sister kingdom the centre of the industrial arts, we yet possess several coal districts of considerable extent, and yielding large supplies of fuel, and moreover, there is in our bogs amassed a quantity of turf, which, if the peculiar characters of that fuel be suitably attended to, may become of eminent importance to the country.

All the applications of fuel depend, however, on its cost, and the amount and consequences of the cost of fuel in Ireland shall form the next subject of inquiry.

CHAPTER II.

NECESSITY FOR DETERMINING THE INFLUENCE WHICH THE
COST OF FUEL EXERCISES ON THE COST OF POWER, AND THE
MEANS OF ECONOMIZING IT. GENERAL PRINCIPLE OF STEAM
POWER. EVAPORATIVE POWERS OF DIFFERENT KINDS OF
FUELS. COMPARISON OF ANTHRACITE WITH BITUMINOUS
COAL. UNIT OF STEAM POWER. CONSUMPTION OF COAL WITH
ORDINARY STEAM BOILERS. ECONOMY OF FUEL OBTAINED
WITH CORNISH BOILERS. MODE OF EMPLOYING STEAM IN CORN-
WALL. PRINCIPLE OF EXPANSION. MONEY VALUE OF COAL
IN IRELAND. COST OF STEAM POWER, WITH NATIVE AND
IMPORTED COALS. EMPLOYMENT OF TURF AS FUEL. ITS
ABSOLUTE AND RELATIVE COST. RESULTS OF PRACTICAL
TRIALS. PRACTICAL RESULTS OF THE EMPLOYMENT OF TURF
IN THE STEAMERS ON THE SHANNON AND UNDER FIXED EN-
GINES. COST OF THE HORSE POWER OF STEAM WITH COAL
AND TURF IN DIFFERENT DISTRICTS IN IRELAND AND IN ENG-
LAND. INFLUENCE OF THE COST OF FUEL ON THE FINAL
COST OF THE PRODUCTS OF MANUFACTURE. STATISTICAL
ANALYSIS OF THE DIFFERENT ELEMENTS OF EXPENDITURE,
BESIDES STEAM POWER, IN THE COTTON TRADE, IN THE WOOL-
LEN TRADE, IN THE FLAX TRADE. FINAL CONCLUSION AS TO
HOW FAR THE COST OF FUEL NECESSARILY AFFECTS INDUS-
TRY IN IRELAND. ELEMENTS OF CALCULATION FOR EVAPO-
RATIVE STEAM POWER.

THE distribution, amount, and composition of the fuels of
Ireland having been described so far as information could be
obtained upon the subject; it remains to examine the cost at
which by their means the more important mechanical operations
can be effected.

It is possible that to some, who are already habituated to
the consideration of such topics, the details, with the discussion
of which the present chapter will be occupied, may appear
unnecessary, as such persons, knowing the price of fuel as
already given, may follow out from their own experience all
the practical consequences of importance to which it leads.
But comparatively few persons are in so favourable a position.
Misconceptions of very varied, but of serious character, are
entertained of the degree in which the price of fuel influences

the industrial arts, and it is of great importance to remove those erroneous impressions. I shall, therefore, endeavour to exhibit, in as definite a form as the nature of the subject admits, the degree in which the price of fuel is an element in the cost of the final products of manufacture, and to illustrate the mode in which the greatest economy can be secured in its application.

In giving motion to machinery, fuel does not act directly, but through the medium of water, which when heated is converted into vapour, increasing enormously in bulk, and exercising a pressure on the containing vessel which is capable of overcoming the greatest resistance, provided the heat be supplied to a sufficient extent. It is thus that the steam engine, that wonderful creation of the highest mechanical genius, transfers the power originally resident in the fuel to the most remote elements of a complicated system of machinery. The power transferred is, generally speaking, proportional to the fuel burned, and thus the cost of power identifies itself for the most part with the cost of fuel. It is not my purpose to describe the steam engine. There are published special works in which all the details of its history and construction are given, but in order that the question of fuels may be placed in a proper point of view, it is necessary to notice some of the more important features of its action.

In the complete steam engine there are two distinct parts, which involve totally different scientific conditions. The motive agent is a certain bulk of steam. Now the first problem in working the engine is to generate that bulk of steam with the least possible expense, and the second is, having obtained the steam, to apply it under the mechanical conditions most favourable for its final result. According to the degree of attention to these points is the ultimate cost of power, and it is hence absolutely necessary for us to endeavour to realize them.

The unit of power assumed in all mechanical questions in these countries is the horse power. The word does not now by any means signify the actual work a horse could do, but is understood to mean a force sufficient to elevate 33,000℔ of water one foot per minute. That is about 884 tons of water raised one foot in an hour. Now as the increase of water in bulk when converted into steam at the ordinary boiling point is just 1700 times, and that its pressure is then 15℔ on each square inch, this force of a horse power will be brought into play when water is vaporized at the rate of 0·54 of a cubic foot per hour; very little more than half a cubic foot. This makes no allowance for loss of fuel, friction of machinery, &c. It is the purely theoretical result, to which all practical results must be applied as to a measure of their economy. We shall now proceed to examine some of the results of practice, pursued according to various methods, which shall be thereby contrasted.

From an extensive series of trials made by Peclet, Parkes, and others, we may deduce the following numbers as expressing the absolute heating power of fuels, and as they will be of frequent reference I shall insert them here.

One pound of each fuel evaporates in pounds of water :

Hydrogen, ...	46·8	Average coal, . . .	12·0
Pure charcoal, . .	14·6	Best turf, ...	6·0
Coke, ...	13·0	Dry wood, ...	7·0
Best turf coke, . .	12·8	Wood not dried, . .	5·2

The economic value of coal is so well determined by the experience of English engineers, that I shall hereafter assume their results without going into any detail, but as the use of turf is still a subject of doubt and discussion in this country, I shall notice some examples of its present employment, and endeavour to deduce from them its economy. It may be easily understood that the evidence collected is not from England; the superabundance of coal there causes a neglect of all other fuels, and it will hence be necessary for us in this, as in many other instances, to take our examples from countries equally unfortunate with ourselves, where the paucity and dearness of fuel render its economy important, and where the high state of scientific education renders their results satisfactory and attainable.

The numbers given above, as to the evaporative power of

coals, are for the usual bituminous coals, represented in this country by those of the Lough Allen basin which are the least, and those of Tyrone which are the most bituminous. As so much of the coal of Ireland is anthracitous, and as this variety has been but very little employed in practice in England, it will be useful, as more firmly establishing the grounds of future conclusions, to notice what the practical results of its use have been in some cases where accurate numbers have been recorded. Dr. Fyfe in Edinburgh published the results of some experiments which he carried on to compare the evaporative power of the anthracite with that of bituminous coal. The result was, that with the same furnace 1℔ anthracite evaporated 7·94℔ of water, whilst the coal evaporated 6·62. The composition of the two he found to be:

	ANTHRACITE.	BITUMINOUS COAL.
Moisture,	4·5	7·5
Volatile matter,	13·3	34·5
Fixed carbon,	71·4	50·5
Ashes,	10·8	7·5
	100·0	100·0

Dr. Fyfe concluded from his experiments, which were continued for a long time, and were very carefully conducted, that in any fuel the heating power is proportional to the quantity of fixed carbon, that is, pure coke, which the fuel yields. This would make the practical value of anthracite about one and a half times that of ordinary bituminous coal. This, however, can occur only where the volatile parts of the coal are not well burned, as certainly occurred in Dr. Fyfe's experiment.

It has been shewn that average coal will evaporate, when perfectly consumed, and the heat perfectly economized, twelve times its weight of water. The heating effect of anthracite is too local to allow of its being fully utilized if merely burned on an ordinary grate, but if the flaming character be given to it by means of a current of steam in the manner described in page 29, the economy of heat is much increased, although its absolute amount is not altered. In experiments carried on with an anthracite furnace, of which the furnace bars dipped in water troughs, and thus furnished steam to the fuel as patented by Mr. Kymer, it was found that in an engine boiler working under twenty-eight pounds pressure to the square inch, 117℔ of anthracite evaporated 1118℔ of water, that is, one pound to nine pounds and a half. It is hence evident that the anthracite is as least fully as effective as the average bituminous coal, and consequently in future it is not necessary to make any distinction between them under this point of view.

One of the most eminent mechanical engineers of the present day, Mr. Scott Russell, has given the following as the working conditions of the evaporation of water and generation of power.

One cubic foot of water evaporated per hour, is a horse power.

11℔ of coals evaporate a cubic foot of water.
1℔ of coals evaporates 6·6℔ of water.

Here the quantity of water necessary to generate a horse power of steam, is nearly double the purely theoretical result, and the quantity of coal necessary to evaporate the water is also nearly double that which has been indicated (page 47), as the proper duty of average coal. This enormous difference originates in the peculiar construction of the most usual form of steam boilers, which, having been invented in a country rich in fuel, and where its economy was, then at least, unimportant, produces a waste of the source of power very necessary for us to avoid.

If you enter the engine house of a factory in Lancashire or Lanark, unless it be of quite novel and peculiar construction, you will observe the steam boiler to be of that kind so well named waggon-shaped; under it are situated great fires, the flues from which winding round the boiler pass into a chimney, from the aperture of which are emitted vast volumes of dense black smoke. The fire-man has but two cares, to keep his boiler full of water, and his fire-place full of coals. These he throws in with astonishing good will; they are so cheap. In these waggon boilers the relation which the heated portion of the boiler bears to its entire surface seldom exceeds one-half; and

E

it has been found by Mr. Parkes, from experiments of a very precise character, that with such boilers the highest evaporative effect that can be obtained is 8·86℔ of water for one pound of coals. In those districts where fuel is so cheap, the waste is often even greater; thus Mr. Parkes values the average consumption of the best engines in Manchester at one hundred and a half of coals per horse power per day; that is fourteen pounds per hour. We may consider, therefore, that with the common waggon boiler, and ordinary steam engine, the horse power is represented by a cubic foot of water evaporated per hour, and that this requires the combustion of at least ten pounds of coals.

We in Ireland are not by any means the only people who are badly off for fuel. In one of the most industrious districts of England, in Cornwall, in the midst of its mineral wealth, there is want of fuel for steam power to drain the mines. The engineers in Cornwall, therefore, could not shovel in coals like their brethren in the North. They had the problem distinctly set before them,—how much work can be got out of a bushel of coals? and certainly their results have been surprising. The facts were denied for a long time by the Lancashire engine makers; the reports of duty of the Cornish engines were quoted as a mechanical romance; but that is now all past, and as our condition is nearly the same as that of the Cornish men, I shall describe what they have effected.

In place of the waggon boiler already noticed, there is used a long cylindrical boiler, perforated by one, two, or even three flues; so that although on a greater scale it is not very unlike the tubular boiler of a locomotive engine. Sometimes the fire-place is in the centre flue, at others, under the boiler. The flue passes also round the boiler, so that a far greater surface of water, in proportion to its mass, is presented to the action of the heat than in the waggon form. The result is found to be, that, by Mr. Parkes's trials, one pound of coal in a Cornish boiler will evaporate twelve pounds of water, thus fully giving the result I have taken as the standard. The evaporation of a cubic foot of water from a Cornish boiler should take 5·2℔ of coal; little more than one-half of what the waggon boiler in average requires, even when well worked. Hence, where fuel is dear there should be no question of waggon boilers. The manufacturer who burns two pounds of coal where one pound should be sufficient, pays twice as much as is necessary for his power, which must of course be deducted from his profits.

But the improvements in the Cornish steam engine are not restricted to a better construction of the boiler. Another is still more remarkable, inasmuch as its principle is much more latent. We have seen that to generate the steam, the elastic force of which represents the horse power, we must evaporate 0·54 cubic foot of water. Now this weighs 33¾lb, and, avoiding minute fractions, we may consider that it might be evaporated in a Cornish boiler by three pounds of coal. In place of fourteen pounds as given by Parkes, or eleven pounds as taken by Scott Russell, for practice, the theoretical result becomes three pounds. This, however, allows no loss for friction in machinery; no loss of motion in transmission through the parts of the engine; no waste of steam. Yet all these are sources of loss, and nevertheless they are compensated for in the Cornish engine, and a duty or performance obtained in practice, which, when reduced to the horse power, becomes three pounds of coal burned per hour; and even in some instances falls below it, so that the work really done with all friction of machinery, is greater than that indicated by theory without loss or friction.

In the ordinary way of working a condensing engine, the steam is let on the piston fully throughout its course, and we may assume the working pressure at fifteen pounds per square inch. This pressure is to be multiplied by the length of the stroke to obtain the effective power. Let us take the stroke at forty-eight inches. The force exerted will therefore be, per square inch,

$$15 \times 48 = 720.$$

Now an engine of forty-eight inch stroke, and consuming the same quantity of steam, is worked differently in Cornwall. The steam (for example) is generated at a pressure of sixty pounds per square inch that is of four atmospheres.

It is let on the piston until this has moved through one-fourth of its stroke, that is through twelve inches. The valve is then closed, and the steam allowed to move the piston by its own elasticity through the remaining space. The steam hence expands so as finally to fill the whole cylinder, and in so doing gradually lessens its elasticity, so that at the end its pressure is fifteeen pounds, the same as it was all through in the first example. Let us calculate what is the difference of result. The working pressure, when the steam enters the cylinder, is sixty pounds, and at that pressure it moves the piston twelve inches. The supply is then cut off; the steam expands to double its volume, and moves the piston through another twelve inches. By expanding, however, it reduces its elasticity to one-half, that is to thirty pounds; and its mean pressure through this space is to be reckoned at forty-five pounds. Continuing to expand, it moves the piston through another twelve inches, but its pressure is then reduced to twenty pounds, and hence the mean pressure through this portion of its course is twenty-five pounds; and finally, when the piston has been pushed to the end of the cylinder, and the steam quadrupled in volume, its effective pressure is reduced to fifteen pounds to the square inch, and the mean pressure during the last twelve inches of movement has been seventeen pounds and a half. Now let us sum up these results. The piston moved

In first period through 12 inches with a constant pressure of 60℔ = 720
In second „   „   12 „   with an average pressure of 45℔ = 540
In third   „   „   12 „   „   „   „   of 25℔ = 300
In fourth „   „   12 „   „   „   „   of 17¾lb= 210
                                                    Total, 1770

Which is the measure of the effective power, being two and a half times that given by the same quantity of steam used without the expansive action. These numbers would require small corrections to be made quite accurate; so great a pressure as sixty pounds is also not used in practice, but for the object of popularly illustrating the principle of expansion on which the Cornish engines are worked, it is quite sufficient.

The great economy of fuel which is effected in Cornwall, depends thus on the form of boiler, and on the use made of the steam. These are two points to which our attention must be steadily devoted, for the difference between burning fourteen pounds of coal per hour, and burning three pounds, is all important in industry.

Now it must be remarked here that a fault, to which every steam engine is liable, is most developed in the Cornish engine, that is, an inequality in the velocity of the piston. In a common engine, the action of the steam being constant tends to give the piston an accelerated velocity, and in the Cornish engine, the force of the steam being variable, gives a velocity of piston also variable within wide limits. This is partly obviated by the crank and the fly-wheel, the mass of which serves to regulate the motion, but some disadvantage still remains. It affects the application of the steam engine to many delicate operations, and I shall return specially to the subject when I come to speak of another source of industrial power.

These explanations regarding boilers and steam engines, Cornish and common, being premised, it is now possible to discuss the question—what is the expense of steam power in Ireland? The horse power is to be taken as the unit. The cost of 100 horse power is of course 100 times the cost of one.

I have already noticed the prices of coals in the coal fields of Ireland, but I shall give them here in a tabular form for comparison.

	LARGE COAL.	SMALL COAL.
Leinster coal field, ...	11s. 6d.	4s. 0d.
Tipperary ,, . . .	12 0	4 0
Tyrone ,, . . .	12 0	5 0
Connaught, ,, from 4s. 9d. to 6 4		

Now for generating heat, a mixture in equal parts of large and small coal may be very conveniently burned. Indeed small coal almost alone might be used, but I do not wish to push an ideal economy so far. In the immediate neighbourhood of the pit mouth, therefore, the cost per ton of fuel adapted to all heating purposes, may be taken as averaging 8s. per ton. In carriage to a distance, it may be assumed that 3d. per ton per mile is a sufficiently high charge, and taking the radius of sup-

ply of a pit at twenty miles, the price should be at the extreme
limit 8s. + (3d. $\times$ 20) = 13s. per ton. Hence the average price
of such coal (mixed large and small) in the district should be
10s. 6d. per ton, and I shall take it at 12s. per ton, in order to
be on the safe side.

It has been shewn that with the waggon boiler and ordinary
condensing engine, the horse power of steam is generated by
the combustion of ten pounds of coals per hour. This is 120℔
per working day of twelve hours. Now as one ton (2240℔)
costs 12s., 120℔ will cost 7$\frac{3}{4}d$. Thus, in the interior of the
country, within the distance of twenty miles from the coal pits,
the cost of fuel for steam power may be taken at 7$\frac{3}{4}d$. per
horse power per day.

None of our coal districts come near enough to the coast to
meet the competition of British coal. Round the island, therefore, and for some ten or twelve miles inland, and also along
the course of the navigable rivers, we must consider steam as
generated by the combustion of coal brought from England.
From this we may except the upper and middle Shannon, which
however, does not influence the result we seek. The price of
English, and especially of the Welsh and Scotch flaming coals,
which answer excellently for industrial purposes, has lately
fallen very much in this country, owing principally to the reduction of freight from the want of other occupation for a great
number of ships, in the recent depressed state of trade. The
price may rise somewhat, but not materially, and we may consider the average of native coal consumed at 12s., to represent
also the price at which furnace coals may be laid in on the eastern
coast, and some distance up the rivers which open into it. On
the western and southern coast, the cost of carriage should be
higher, but not materially to affect the price; for in Limerick,
which is the only locality where the question becomes important, the concurrence of Arigna coal and the abundance of
turf would prevent much alteration. I shall hence take the
cost of fuel for a horse power as being the same, 7$\frac{3}{4}d$. per
working day, burning English coal within range of the coast.

In the central counties, where the vast tubaries of the limestone plain supply abundance of fuel, the cost of it will vary

very much according to its mode of preparation. I shall put out of question here the compound fuels proposed by Mr. Williams, and even compressed peat; not that I am insensible of their value, but that I am anxious to place the question of cost on the basis most easily realized. I suppose, therefore, that the turf has been only well dried. In this case its heating power, when perfectly dry, is one-half that of coal. But under ordinary circumstances it retains so much moisture, that it may be practically taken at somewhat more than two-fifths. That this result is founded on sufficient data may be judged from the following evidence.

I have been favoured with returns of the work and consumption of a condensing engine of thirty-four horse power, which is employed to grind corn in one of our central counties, and under the boiler of which the turf of the vicinity is burned. The result is found to be, that in twelve hours there are consumed fifty boxes of 280℔ each; that is, thirty-four pounds of turf per horse power per hour. Now as we may consider a cubic foot (62·5℔) of water evaporated per hour as the measure of a horse power, it results that the turf in this instance does not evaporate quite twice its weight of water. In fact it is used damp; it is badly managed in the furnace, and I notice it only as an instance of what we shall require to correct. In this mill the box of turf costs 6d., which is just 4s. per ton. The cost of fuel is 9d. per horse power for the day of twelve hours. This we shall hereafter find to be excessive.

Mr. Purdy, by whose exertions our mineral industry has been so materially benefited, has furnished me with a note of the performance of turf under a steam engine erected for draining a lead mine at Derrynoos in Armagh, formerly worked by the Mining Company of Ireland. The district is very unfavourably circumstanced as to fuel. Coal, whether from Coal-Island or Newry, could arrive only after a land carriage, which alone costs 10s. per ton. The turf was black mountain turf, giving much ash; its cost, reduced to weight, was 6s. 10½d. per ton. In this the locality was exceptional. The work of the turf was compared with the work of average Cardiff coals in the same engine and under the same circumstances.

1℔ coal raised 365,591℔ water one foot high.

1℔ turf raised 121,489℔   ,,   ,,

Reduced to the bushel (94℔) it becomes:

A bushel of coals raised 34,365,554℔ water one foot high.

A bushel of turf   ,,   11,419,966℔   ,,   ,,

Hence the effect of the turf is one-third of that of average coal. This was inferior turf, and yet the effect is much greater than in the former case, where much better turf was used.

The engine burned per horse power per day, twenty-four pounds of turf, and for the day of twelve hours the cost of fuel per horse power was 10½d.

Now it must not be forgotten, first, that the fire places of those engines were not constructed for turf but for coal, and that consequently they could not burn turf in a suitable manner; and second, that the turf is prepared without suitable desiccation. Hence the proportionally greater cost of power.

The high price of fuel in Cornwall has led not only to the wonderful economy produced by the principle of expansion, but also to endeavours to replace the imported coal by the native turf of that district. Mr. Wickstead has given an account of an engine with which comparative trials of these fuels were made. The engine, working five horse power, consumed in twenty-four hours three bushels and one-third of coal (310℔). In the same time and doing the same work it burned three cubic feet of turf, which cost 8½d. I think that in the volume of the turf, an error has crept into Mr. Wickstead's paper, which prevents my estimating the weight of turf consumed, but the cost enables us to judge. At 10s. per ton the coals should cost 17d., and hence the turf did the same work for just half that price.

This result was so decisive, that Mr. Grout, on one of whose engines the trial was made, is getting the fire-places of all his engine boilers altered, that turf may be exclusively burned in them.

Mr. Burstall of Bristol has published the results of his use of turf with a high pressure engine. The steam was of thirty pounds pressure, and there were consumed seventy-four pounds

of turf (which he describes as bad) per hour. The quantity
of water evaporated from the boiler per hour was in average
360℔. The turf consequently evaporated nearly five times its
weight of water. This result approximates to what theory
leads us to expect, but the turf certainly was not bad, although
it is so described by Mr. Burstall.

In the factory of Garnier at Beauvais, the turf of Breles is
burned under a twenty horse power high pressure engine.
This turf is black; it contains 7 per cent. of ashes, and gives
40 per cent. of coke. The turf necessary was double the
weight of the coal previously employed. Its cost was one-
fourth.

The following results, as to the comparative effective power
of turf and coal, are derived from the working of the Lansdowne, one of the steamers of the Inland Navigation Company
which ply upon the Shannon with goods and passengers. They
have been kindly placed in my hands for my present object, by
Mr. C. W. Williams. Before the use of turf was introduced,
there was burned in a week, which comprises forty-nine hours
of work, twenty-four tons of coal, which costing in average at
Killaloe, 15s. per ton, amount to £18, or 7s. 5d. per hour. To
do the same work at present, burning nothing but turf, there
are consumed per week 315 boxes of turf, which at 7d. per
box costs £9 12s. 7d., or 3s. 11d. per hour of work,—but a
shade more than half the cost with coal. The engines of the
Lansdowne are condensing, of thirty-eight inches and a half
diameter, and three feet and a half stroke. The usual velocity
is twenty-five strokes per minute.

The box of turf contains twenty cubic feet; not very closely
packed. It weighs about three cwt. and a half; so that the
ton weight of turf costs about 3s. 6d. The weight of 315 boxes
is hence fifty-five tons and a quarter, and the practical value
of the turf is to that of the coal as 24 to $55\frac{1}{4}$, or as 43 to 100.
Almost exactly the same as calculated in page 39, from the
average composition of good turf. It is interesting to consider
the influence which the substitution of turf for coal in the
Shannon steamers has on the population residing near its banks.
In the year 1839, there was no turf burned, and the coals con-

sumed on board the Company's boats amounted to 3108 tons. In 1843 there were burned but 724 tons of coal, although the amount of trade was much increased. The quantity of turf consumed was upwards of 7000 tons, which at 3s. 6d. per ton gives an expenditure of more than £1200 distributed in wages of labour, by which almost the entire cost of the turf is made up. The equivalent quantity of coals would have cost above £1800, so that at the same time the Company saved £600 a year.

Those remarkable facts are well exhibited in a letter written by Mr. Williams to the Board of Admiralty, which is subjoined, as it illustrates some additional circumstances. Mr. Williams' estimate of the saving is greater than mine, for in the preceding analysis of the results, I have taken coal at a lower price than is assumed in his letter. The reason is, that it has fallen since those results were obtained, and I have calculated from what the price is, whereas he calculated from what it was at the time quoted.

(*Copy*).

"*Admiralty*, 12*th July*, 1843.

" SIR,—My Lords Commissioners of the Admiralty having received a proposition to cut peat at the Falkland Islands, for the service of such of H. M. steam vessels as may proceed to the Pacific, I am commanded by my Lords to request that you will favour my Lords with some information as to the proportionate duration of turf to coal in the Dublin Steam Packet Company's boats, which ply up the Shannon from Limerick.

" I am, Sir,

" Your most humble Servant,

" SIDNEY HERBERT.

" *To the Secretary of the Dublin Steam Packet Company, Eden Quay, Dublin.*"

(*Copy*).

" 6, *Princes-street, Cavendish-square,*

" *July* 21*st*, 1843.

" SIR,—I have had the honour to receive your letter of the 12th Inst., addressed to the Secretary of the City of Dublin

Steam Packet Company, inquiring, for the information of the Lords Commissioners of the Admiralty, the proportionate duration of turf to coal in the Company's boats which ply up the Shannon from Limerick, to which I beg to give the following reply, derived from experience of the boats on that river.

"1. The Landsdowne, a steamer with two engines 38½ inch cylinders, at 3 ft. 6 in. stroke, consumed upon an average 120 tons of coal per month, running daily (except Sunday) a distance of forty-six miles, at 18s. per ton, covering expenses, ... £108 0 0

"The same duty is done with 1419 boxes of turf of twenty cubic feet, about 250 ton weight, at 7d. per box, ... 41 7 9

Difference in the cost of the fuel per month, £66 12 3

"2. The difference in weight is, therefore, as two of turf to one of coal, and on the Shannon the difference in price is less than one-half that of coal.

"3. Its proportionate duration may be estimated by the quantity required, compared with coal, to perform the same duty, that being double its weight its duration in the furnace is half that of coal.

"4. From recent experiments with turf in the experimental boiler in the Company's yard at Liverpool, it is found that turf can only be profitably used when it is of the quality that is obtained in good seasons. If bad or damp, its evaporative power is reduced one-third and more. To improve the evaporative power of this fuel, however, results have shewn, that an addition of 40 per cent. of a preparation of turf by an improved method which I have been engaged upon for some years, will render it cheaper than coal used with bad turf, or than coal burned alone; and that the same per centage of this prepared fuel added to good turf, greatly increases its evaporative power with a very trifling addition to the cost.

"From these facts it is evident that turf may be used advantageously in localities where it abounds, and where there is an absence of coal. Care, however, must be taken that the furnace bars are lowered, not only to admit a greater bulk of fuel, but also to prevent too great a volume of air passing in the ash-pit, and then through the bars. I may add also, that in burning turf it is highly essential that air be admitted in the air chamber behind the bridge, in consequence of the rapidity with which the gases from this kind of fuel fly off. If it be excluded there upon the common furnace principle, the weight and bulk of fuel will be increased, the evaporative power reduced, and the cost proportionably greater.

"It will give me much pleasure to furnish you with any further information in my power.

"I have the honour to be, Sir,

"Your obedient, humble Servant,

"C. W. WILLIAMS.

" To Sidney Herbert, Esq.,

" Admiralty."

I have already noticed, that from my own inquiries the best turf may be had in the turf districts for 3s. 6d. per ton, and as it is a fuel that will never be drawn far for any industrial use, we may take 4s. per ton as the practical value of turf well dried within the range of the central counties. At this price, and allowing to it 44 per cent. of the calorific effect of coal, the horse power should cost 6d. per day, that is one-fourth cheaper than coal. Mr. Williams, using the same sort of fuel as is employed at the corn mill noticed page 55, and paying 6d. per box, but drying it well, found that, with a large working waggon boiler, there were 3.87℔ of water evaporated per pound of turf, and that it cost 3s. 7d. to evaporate 100 cubic feet of water. Now this is at the rate of $5\frac{1}{4}d.$ per horse power per working day. When the turf was burned in the furnace without Mr. Williams' peculiar mode of effecting perfect combustion, the cost per horse power was $6\frac{1}{4}d.$, coinciding with the result which I have derived from other sources.

From all these examples, it may be decisively concluded, that in Ireland the horse power of steam costs per day in fuel :

Using coals, whether British or native, $7\frac{3}{4}d.$

    Using turf properly dried, ... 6*d.*
    Using turf in Mr. Williams' mode, . 5¼*d.*

This is when the waggon boiler and the ordinary non-expansive engine are employed.

Now without entering into details which any person can deduce from what has been already said, I may lay down the distinct principle, that using the Cornish system, both as to boiler and mode of using the steam, the fuel per horse power is reduced to one half. Therefore the cost in Ireland becomes:

    With coals for 12 hours, 3⅞*d.*
    With turf   ,,   ,,   3*d.*

That is to say, that any mechanical operation, grinding or sawing, or weaving, spinning, or threshing, or any other, which requires the same labour as to raise 1000 tons of water ten feet high, can be effected in almost any part of Ireland by the consumption of a quantity of coals, costing 3¾*d.*, or by turf, costing 3*d.*

How utterly unimportant is the cost of fuel in these mechanical operations.

It may be said, however, that small as this cost is when so described, it becomes very serious when taken for a year of 300 working days, and for an 100 horse engine. It is then found, in fact, that the fuel at 3¾*d.* per horse power per day, costs £484 7*s.* 6*d.* per year, and for the other estimates in proportion. So that in England, where fuel is very abundant and cheap, the horse power is had for half the money; and thus in the article of coals a difference of £500 a year may exist, ruinous to the manufacturer in Ireland. It is necessary to examine how far this can operate.

In some parts of Lancashire, coals are sold at the pit mouth for 3*s.* 10*d.* or 4*s.* per ton. About Bury they are from 5*s.* to 5*s.* 3*d.* In the north of Lancashire they are from 6*s.* 3*d.* to 8*s.* From personal inquiries I am informed that furnace coal is never had in Manchester under 8*s.*, and Dr. Ure, in his Philosophy of Manufactures, states facts from whence it results, that he assumes the cost of coal in Manchester to be 12*s.* 4*d.* per ton.

Mr. Henwood, who has calculated the total quantity of coals raised in Lancashire and their price, gives as the resulting average cost per ton, 10s. 10d.

We may take Lancashire as the example of the other manufacturing parts of England. In none is coal materially cheaper, and we shall certainly not be far wrong if we assume as the average price of coal in English industry, two-thirds of what we have assumed for the cost in Ireland, that is two-thirds of 12s., or 8s. per ton.

But in order to estimate the cost of a horse power per day, we must see what is done in England. The cheapness of fuel there leads to an excessive waste of it, so that hitherto only in Cornwall was economy attended to; and even now improvement in that respect is but slowly taking place. According to Dr. Ure the consumption of coal in Manchester is twelve pounds per hour; according to Mr. Parkes it is fourteen pounds per hour. Mr. Fairbairn, in his Report on the Bann Reservoirs, also considers twelve pounds as the usual consumption. Mr. Scott Russell's estimate for standard performance is eleven pounds. Now taking as an average twelve pounds, the horse power costs per working day, $6\frac{1}{4}d$. We have seen that by ordinary attention with the waggon boiler, ten pounds per hour suffices, and this in Ireland costs $7\frac{3}{4}d$. The difference in favour of England from the cheap fuel is therefore but $1\frac{5}{8}d$., being nearly balanced by the waste which the idea of cheapness encourages.

If the Cornish system be employed, and that both English and Irish be anxious to save fuel, the result is also nearly to equalize, as the saving of money is more on the Irish side than on the English. Thus five pounds of coal per hour per horse power are burned; this costs for twelve hours in England $2\frac{1}{2}d$.; in Ireland it should cost $3\frac{3}{4}d$.; the difference is $1\frac{1}{4}d$. But this economy will not be practised in England. It is not important enough to make them change their system, but it is highly important to us, as we have still our industrial system to organize, and there is no principle more essential to our future prosperity, than a clear and profound perception of the means of economizing fuel.

Mr. Baynes of Blackburn, whose locality is, however, very favourably circumstanced for fuel, considers that at 6s. per ton for coal, the horse power costs per week 2s. 4d., including warming the mill. This is at the rate of twelve pounds per hour. But it is a mill of the largest size, and is admirably managed. I shall refer to its details again. The daily cost per horse power with him is but 4½d.

We must recollect, however, that it is not steam power that is to be sold: it is but an agent in subsequent operations, of which the final product is to be brought to market. The true question is, whether the greater cost of steam power in Ireland than in England seriously affects the manufactures in which it is employed. I shall proceed to exhibit some facts which will throw light upon that point.

Mr. Baines, of Leeds, in his excellent history of the cotton manufacture, gives an analysis of the elements of its value for the year 1833, which has been allowed by all judges to be correct, and although the absolute value of the manufacture may have altered since, we may safely assume that its elements remain in the same proportion to each other. His numbers are:

The value of the cotton wool employed was altogether £8,244,693.

The total value of the manufactured cotton goods was £31,338,693.

The capital employed in the manufacture was £34,000,000.

This branch of industry supported altogether 1,500,000 persons. The number of operatives receiving wages was 487,000.

The amount paid in wages to those operatives was £10,419,000.

The power employed was 44,000 horse, consisting of

Steam power 33,000 horse power.

Water power 11,000   ditto.

From these data the elements of cost may be calculated. For the cost of power:

Suppose the whole 44,000 horse, all steam power, and each burning twelve pounds of coals per hour. Then in a year of

300 working days of twelve hours, the total coals consumed
is 636,900 tons, and at the average of 8s. per ton this costs
£339,680.   Hence the elements of cost of the manufactured
cotton are,

Cotton wool, . . .	£8,244,693 or per cent.	26·27
Wages, ...	10,419,200	,,	33·16
Interest on capital, .	3,400,000	,,	10·84
Coals, ...	339,680	,,	1·08
Rent, taxes, insurance, other charges and profit, ...	8,935,320	,,	28·65
	£31,338,693		100·00

As so much of the capital of mechanical industry is invested
in machinery, not merely liable to rapid injury and wear, but
also constantly thrown out of use by the pressure of new improvements, I have considered 10 per cent. of interest on it to
be fairly allowable.   We may also deduce from these numbers,
that in 1833, Mr. Baines assumed the average rate of wages
in the cotton manufactnre to be 6s. 6d. per week.   These results are, however, but collateral.   What we have now to do
with is the fact, that in manufacturing cotton by steam power,
the cost of fuel is scarcely more than one part in 100 of the
value of the manufactured article.   Wages make up 33 per
cent., a third of the entire; the raw material a fourth of the
entire; rent and taxes also a large proportion.   Now in Ireland
wages are lower, rent is lower, taxes are lower, and there is a
difficulty about coals, of which the increased cost is not more
than a half per cent., which may be obviated by attention to
economy, or which is neutralized by a difference of average
wages of 1d. per week.

I shall notice some other examples, but without entering
into so much detail.

An eminent woollen manufacturer, one to whom industry
both in England and Ireland is under great obligations, favoured me with the following statement.

Coals at his factory in Leeds cost 3s. 4d. per ton.   A forty
horse power engine burns three tons per day, which costs

£200 per year. The wear of engine, oil, and engineer's salary are £310, making total expense of power £510. The wages paid are £14,000 per year, and the total value of the produce £50,000.

In Dublin coals are four times as dear, but the other charges of the engine being the same, the total cost of power for a similar factory is £1310. The total cost of power in Leeds is thus 1·2 per cent. of the value of the product, and in Dublin 2·62. The difference is more than balanced by the wages in Dublin. In Leeds wages form 28 per cent. of the value of the produce.

In the Irish Railway Report, Messrs. Mulholland of Belfast give an account of their excellent flax mill, one of the largest factories we possess in Ireland.

The engines are (nominal) 100 horse power. They consume weekly 90 tons of coals. There are employed 800 persons, who receive weekly £200 in wages. The coals include a supply of Cannell coal for gas works on the establishment, but although thus placing the result in the most unfavourable view for my argument, I shall charge the entire as the source of power. The price of coals in Belfast at the time was 13s. per ton.

The cost of coal for the year was £3042. The sum paid in wages £10,400. The value of the manufactured produce £80,000. The coals for power and gas make 3·8 per cent.; the wages paid are 13 per cent. of the price of the products.

Change this factory to England, the average price of coal being 8s. Its cost becomes 2·3 per cent.; saving 1·5. The average rate of wages, from 5s. at Belfast, becomes at least 6s. 6d., and makes up 16·9 per cent., losing 3·9 per cent.; £22 10s. per week saved in coals, and £60 per week lost in wages. Such should be Mr. Mulholland's great factory in England. The disproportion is, I am satisfied, much greater in fact, as perhaps not two-thirds of the coals should be really charged to the steam engines, unless they do a great deal of night work.

Since 1833, when Mr. Baines' estimate was formed, wages have risen in England, as we find that Mr. Symons, in his ex-

F

cellent work, Arts and Artizans at Home and Abroad, concludes the average of Lancashire to be 10s. 6d. This was in 1839. Now Mr. Farey, describing the organization of a cotton mill, states that a factory employing 750 persons will be driven by an engine of 100 horse power.

The wages per week in such a factory, taking Mr. Symons' average, are £393 15s.

The engine requires fuel, which at 8s. per ton, costs £19 per week. At 12s. per ton it costs £28 10s. Thus a difference of one-fortieth in the average rate of wages compensates for whatever difference can arise in the cost of fuel from the prices in Ireland and in Lancashire.

I have already noticed the cost of fuel in Mr. Baynes' mill at Blackburn, which is £26 15s. per week, for an engine working 233 horse power. I shall enumerate the machinery driven by this engine, in order that it may be seen to be a factory of the largest size.

22,500 self-acting spindles.
5,400 throstle spindles.
800 power looms.
3 blowing machines.
3 cap machines.
120 single carding engines.
16 drawing frames.
600 slubbing spindles.
1,800 roving spindles.

Mr. Baynes does not give the number of persons employed in his mill, but from its size it cannot possibly be under 800. Taking Mr. Symons' estimate of wages, 10s. 6d., the amount paid weekly in such a mill is £420; the cost of coals for power being £26 15s. In Ireland the coals might cost half as much more, but by how much less might the wages be?

In concluding this department of my subject, in which I have probably wearied many of my readers by those columns of figures and per cents., I shall subjoin some numerical illustrations taken from Mr. Symons' work already noticed. They exhibit, on the authority of eminent English manufacturers, the numerical proportions of outlay in factories such as now occupy us.

The cost of erecting a power loom factory of 500 looms, calculated to weave good calico, should be about £18,000.

Its annual produce should be 150,000 pieces of twenty-four yards at 6s., £45,000, which cost as under:

Interest of capital and wear of machinery,	£1,800
Steam power, oil, tallow, keeping up machinery, utensils, &c.,	2,000
Yarns and flax,	32,000
Wages to workmen,	7,500
Profit,	1,700
	£45,000

Probable expense of a spinning cotton mill, with hand-mules to produce No. 40, would be £23,000. With self-actors £2000 more.

The produce annually, taking the present prices of cotton, should be £25,000.

Cost of which as follows:

Interest of capital and wear and tear of machinery,	£2,300
Cotton,	14,000
Steam power, oil, tallow, gas, and general expense of keeping up utensils and machinery, and repair,	1,800
Wages to workmen,	5,400
Profit,	1,500
	£25,000

The produce is taken at 10,000℔ weekly.

Now what is to be considered in these estimates is the fact, that coals, or even steam power altogether, is not an important item, but is only inserted along with oil and tallow, gas, repairs, &c., all of which together amount in the first instance to 4½ per cent., and in the second to 7·2 per cent. of the value of the products.

In order to exhibit the proportion which the cost of fuel

bears to the other elements of manufacture in Ireland, as well
as in the sister kingdom, I have been favoured with the following return from a factory for spinning and weaving cottons,
which is situated near one of the large cities on the eastern
coast, and uses coals and cotton, both imported from England.

The value of cotton as bought in Liverpool for a year, was
£11,177 9s. 6d. The freight and other expenses of carriage
to Ireland was £332 5s. The average number of hands employed was 273, and the total amount of wages paid in the
year was £4832 8s. The coals consumed were 1669 tons;
of these about one-fifth was for heating and drying purposes,
but as this use, although not for steam power, is still for the
manufacture, there need not be any distinction drawn. The
coals cost rather under 12s. per ton, but that sum may be
taken, and hence there was paid for the coals £901. The
total value of the manufactured article was £24,099 17s.

Now from these data it follows :

That the value of the raw material was .   46·4 per cent.
The charge on its carriage to Ireland,   .   1·4   ,,
The wages of labour, ...   20·0   ,,
The fuel for steam power and for drying
    and heating, ...   2·7   ,,

of the cost of the manufactured article. Now the difference
in the cost of fuel is, as has been already shewn, but about 4s.
per ton in favour of Lancashire, and this one-third of 2·7 forms
not one per cent. of the value of the final product of industry.

The average rate of wages paid is found to be 6s. 9d. per
week. The average in Lancashire is 10s. 6d. How much
more important does this difference appear to be than that of
fuel. It is however, not possible to compare them directly.
It is a topic which will require some explanation in a future
chapter.

Besides the two steam engines of twenty-five horse nominal
power, there is on this concern a breast wheel which is employed whenever water is available. It is not large, and could
not in any material degree modify the above result. I have,
therefore, not taken it at all into account.

From all that has been described, I conclude that there is

no locality in Ireland where fuel for industrial purposes may not be had, either native or imported; and that the cost of that fuel may not exceed, by more than half, the average cost of fuel in the manufacturing districts of England, and certainly need never be the double. That the cost of fuel to generate steam power bears so small a proportion to the value of the products of mechanical industry, as to be totally unimportant, in comparison with money-wages and raw material, regarding which this country labours certainly under no natural disadvantage, and that finally, by attention to the mode of burning fuel and using steam, the difference in price of coal may even in itself be compensated for, and other specially favourable circumstances may be rendered available to the success of industry in Ireland.

I have noticed at such length the question of the cost of fuel and of steam power, not from my own opinion of its ultimate importance, but that we might at once break down that barrier to all active exertion, which indolent ignorance constantly retreats behind. The cry of, "what can we do; consider England's coal mines," is answered by shewing that we have available fuel enough. The lament that coals are so dear with us and so cheap in England, is, I trust, set at rest by the evidence of how little influential the price of fuel is. However, there are other sources of power besides coals; there are other motive powers than steam. Of the 83,000 horse power employed to give motion to mills in England, 21,000, even in the coal districts, are not moved by fire but by water. The force of gravity in falling water can spin and weave as well as the elasticity of steam; and in this power we are not deficient. It is necessary to study its circumstances in detail, and I shall, therefore, next proceed to discuss the condition of Ireland with regard to water power.

In finally passing from the subject of fuel and steam power, I shall subjoin, for convenience of reference, a tabular comparison of the peculiarities of the ordinary and of the Cornish steam boilers, taken from Mr. Scott Russell's work on the steam engine :

CONDITIONS.	ORDINARY STANDARD.	CORNISH BOILERS.
Area of fire grate in square feet, . .	1	2
Area of heating surface in do., . . .	15	60 to 70
Circuit of heat, ...	60 ft.	150 ft.
RESULTS.		
Fuel per horse power per hour, . . .	10℔.	5¼℔.
Fuel consumed per hr. per ft. of grate,	10℔.	2⅜℔.
Water evaporated by each ℔ of coal,	6℔.	11¾℔.

To the statement made in this chapter of the cost of power from various sources, it may be added that practical mechanists and engineers habitually value the cost of steam power on the east of Ireland within a range of seven or eight miles from the coast, at one shilling per horse power per day, which includes wages, interest, repairs, and every other expenditure, as well as fuel. This estimate fully agrees with that of the cost of fuel deduced from my own results.

CHAPTER III.

OF THE WATER POWER OF IRELAND. MODE IN WHICH IT ORIGI-
NATES. AMOUNT OF RAIN AND EVAPORATION IN DIFFERENT
PARTS OF IRELAND. AVERAGE ASSUMED. INFLUENCE OF
THE NATURE OF THE SURFACE ON EVAPORATION. ELEVA-
TION ABOVE THE SEA OF THE SURFACE OF IRELAND. LIME-
STONE PLAIN OF THE CENTRE. MOUNTAINOUS DISTRICTS OF
THE NORTH AND SOUTH. AVERAGE ELEVATION ASSUMED AS
THE AVERAGE HEIGHT OF FALL OF WATER FROM THE LAND
TO THE SEA. TOTAL AMOUNT OF MECHANICAL FORCE THUS
GENERATED; ITS DISTRIBUTION. ARRANGEMENT OF THE
PRINCIPAL RIVERS BY WHICH THE SURFACE OF IRELAND IS
DRAINED. DRAINAGE OF THE CENTRAL DISTRICTS BY THE
SHANNON AND ITS ADJUNCTS. WICKLOW AND WEXFORD.
DRAINAGE BASINS OF THE BLACKWATER AND THE LEE.
BASIN OF LOUGH NEAGH, OF LOUGH ERNE, AND THE FOYLE.
RELATION OF THE EXTENT OF SURFACE DRAINED TO THE
MECHANICAL FORCE. WATER POWER OF THE SHANNON; OF
THE LEE AT CORK; OF THE UPPER BANN; OF THE CON-
NAUGHT LAKES. DESCRIPTION OF THE MOST IMPORTANT
WATER ENGINES. DIFFERENT FORMS OF WATER WHEELS.
OF THE WATER PRESSURE ENGINE. REACTION MILL. OF
THE TURBINE. PRINCIPLE OF ITS ACTION; ITS ECONOMY;
CONSTANCY OF ITS POWER. DISADVANTAGES OF WATER
POWER. NECESSITY FOR ECONOMIZING THE WATERS OF
FLOODS. EXAMPLES OF THE POWER OF FLOODS. FORMATION
OF RESERVOIRS TO SECURE UNIFORMITY OF WATER POWER.
RESULTS OF THOSE ERECTED ON THE UPPER BANN AND ON
THE SHAW'S WATER AT GREENOCK. THE DODDER. LOUGH
ENNEL AND THE BROSNA. ESTIMATES OF THE COST OF WATER
POWER. RELATIVE VALUE OF WATER AND STEAM POWER
AS MOVERS OF MACHINERY. EXTENT TO WHICH WATER
POWER IS ECONOMIZED IN ENGLAND AND IN IRELAND. COM-
BINATION OF STEAM WITH WATER POWER. APPLICATION
OF THE FORCE OF THE TIDE TO MECHANICAL PURPOSES. PE-
CULIAR ADVANTAGES OF THE TURBINE AS A TIDE MILL. AD-
VANTAGEOUS SITUATION OF MANY POINTS ON THE COAST FOR
EMPLOYING THE TIDE AS A SOURCE OF MECHANICAL POWER.

THE land being placed on the surface of our globe at a level
superior to that of the ocean, by which its coasts are washed,
there is produced continually by atmospherical conditions, a
circulation of the mass of water, which, evaporating from the

surface, ascends as vapour to the higher and colder regions of
the air, where it is condensed into clouds. These float until
the electrical condition which characterizes their peculiar molecular state being dissipated, they fall as rain, as hail, or snow,
and the water thus regaining the solid or liquid form, tends
continually by its gravity to a lower level, until it joins the
general mass of ocean, from whence it had been originally derived. The rain or snow thus falling in the interior and elevated districts of the country, forms at first rivulets, then
streams, finally rivers, and the force of the descending water
is capable of application to give motion to machinery: it is
the source, best known and most simply applicable, of water
power.

If all the water which falls upon the surface of a country, as
rain, passed regularly to the sea, and that the average height
through which it passed, as well as its weight, were capable
of being determined, it should be a simple problem to calculate
the entire mechanical force thus brought into play. But there
is no country in which these data are absolutely known; with
us, at least, such inquiries are but in their infancy; and although the importance of the subject will not allow me to pass
from it, without endeavouring to obtain at least an approximation to its value, yet I can only discuss in a general point of
view the circumstances which affect the water power of this
country, and having brought forward the imperfect materials
that I have been able to collect, endeavour to excite others to
a sense of what still remains to be done.

It is but lately that observations of the quantity of rain that
falls in Ireland have been made with accuracy over a number
of points. Exposed to the first brunt of the Atlantic storms,
a vast body of rain is carried to these islands by the southerly
and westerly winds. In average, half as much more rain falls
in England than on the Continent of Europe. Here there is
probably not more actual rain than in England, but there is
more damp. Long since Arthur Young noticed the difficulty
of drying agricultural produce in this country, and assigned to
this humidity the rapid vegetation which clothes our surface
with natural herbage, even where there is scarcely a trace of

soil. It is hence that this island has been called the Emerald set in the ring of the sea. The moisture of the air in Ireland is thus greater than in England, and the quantity of rain that actually falls is in average certainly not less. The results that have been obtained up to the present time, by various observers, are as follows:

In the table are given the name of the observers, the localities, and the mean quantity of rain deduced from observations of a certain number of years.

LOCALITY.	STATED BY	QUANTITY.	AVERAGE OF
Dublin,	Apjohn,	30·87	Six years.
Belfast,	Portlock,	34·96	Six years.
Castlecomer,	Aher,	37·80	Eighteen years.
Cork,	Smith,	40·20	Six years.
Cork,	Roy. Inst.,	36·03	Six years.
Derry,	Sampson,	31·12	Seven years.

It is thus seen that Dublin is one of the dryest, and Cork one of the wettest places where observations have been made. Indeed both here and in England a great difference exists between the quantities of rain which fall on the eastern and western coasts, but our west coast has not hitherto been in such a social condition as admits of consecutive scientific observations. There is no doubt, however, but that the amount of rain falling on the west coast equals the highest number given above (that of Cork); and we shall certainly not exceed if we value the average quantity of rain that falls over the entire surface of Ireland at thirty-six inches.

If all the rain that falls on the surface of Ireland in a year were collected, it should thus cover the island to the depth of thirty-six inches; and as the area of Ireland amounts to 20,808,271 square acres, containing 100,712,631,640 square yards, there are hence this number of cubic yards of water precipitated on the surface of Ireland every year. Of this a quantity, which we shall now seek to determine, becomes available for industrial purposes. All this mass of water does not reach the sea. The spontaneous evaporation which is carried on by every point of surface that is not absolutely dry, raises again into the atmosphere a large proportion of it. This proportion is difficult to determine, indeed impossible to determine, with accuracy: it may still be approximated to in the following manner.

Mr. Dobson made experiments at Liverpool, to ascertain how much water evaporated in a year from a surface of water. The mean quantity of rain was 37·48 inches. The mean quantity of water evaporated was 36·78. Hence, if there was no dry land the rain and evaporation should balance; but the soil evaporates much less than a surface of water, and a rocky surface or dry ground scarcely evaporates at all. The illustrious Dalton carried on experiments, in conjunction with Mr. Hoyle, in Manchester, on this point. He had a box filled with soil, and tried how much less water came off from it than from a rain guage, the difference of course was due to evaporation; the rain was 33·56 inches; the evaporation was 25·16 inches. The evaporation from water was at the same time forty-four inches.

That the evaporation from a surface of water is in these islands so low as the results of Dobson and Dalton indicate, is due to the moisture of the climate; our atmosphere being already more or less loaded with vapour, and thereby preventing any further increase. This is seen in the great amount of the evaporation from a surface of water in the continental states removed from the ocean. Thus, at Manheim, the evaporation is seventy-three inches, whilst the rain is but twenty-one.

Dr. Thompson values the average evaporation from the surface of Great Britain at thirty-two inches. As the evaporation from soil is less (twenty-five by Dalton's result), and from shallow soil or rocky surface still inferior, we cannot be far from the truth in considering the quantity of rain that is not returned to the atmosphere from the surface, to be one-third of that which falls. The conclusion to which Baron Dupin arrives in discussing, for France, a question similar to that which occupies us here, is ultimately the same, although some of the principles from which he calculates cannot, as I conceive, be considered as applicable to this country, as the extent of evaporation is affected to an important degree by the geographical contour of the surface, by the neighbourhood of the ocean, and by the prevailing winds.

We have, in fact, considered the evaporating surface to be as the surface receiving the rain, horizontal and equal. But in nature such does not occur. Take the instance of a valley, bounded by sloping hills, clothed with a scanty verdure. It is evident that during rain the water flows rapidly down the sides of the hills, and collecting in the valley, converts its tranquil rivulet for a time into a mountain torrent. The water is here removed from the surface of the hills before it has time to evaporate. It is accumulated under an area of probably not one-tenth of that on which it fell, and its tendency to evaporate is reduced in the same degree. That such condition is not merely the fancy of a theorist, but is considered as real by the best practical authority, is fully shewn in the admirable report on the proposed reservoirs of the Upper Bann; drawn up by Mr. Fairbairn. After general observations, nearly similar to those I have now made, he says: "in the case of the Deer Meadow Lake, bounded by mountains whose ridge forms a rain guage of 1802 acres, with an average height of 500 feet above the reservoir, of which the area is 215 acres. Here the basin is to the reservoir as 1802 to 215, or 8 to 1; and as there can be but little evaporation, except from the reservoir, the loss is very small in proportion with the supply." Under these circumstances he considers five-sixths of the rain that falls represents fairly the supply running into the reservoirs. We shall hereafter see that the quantity of water rendered available by those reservoirs even exceeded Mr. Fairbairn's expectations.

Without more circumstance, I shall therefore assume, that out of the thirty-six inches of rain that annually fall in Ireland, twelve inches finally arrive at the sea, and in its course may become available to industry with a force proportional to the height through which it falls. This height requires also an approximate determination.

The limestone plain which occupies the central districts of the country rises to an elevation of about 300 feet, which is the height of the summit levels of the canals by which it is traversed. The mountainous districts of the north and south raise the average of the island much beyond this number, and we may arrive at a very tolerable approximation to the truth from the following considerations, which are based upon measurements conducted by the officers of the Ordnance Survey, and very kindly placed in my hands for the present object, by Captain Larcom, the distinguished officer under whose local direction the operations of that important work have been so ably carried on in Ireland.

The total area of Ireland being 32,509$\frac{4}{5}$ square miles, it is found that there are,

Between sea level and 250 feet of vertical height, } . . . .   13,242$\frac{2}{3}$ square miles.

Between 250 and 500 feet of height, .   11,797$\frac{1}{4}$,,

  ,,   500 and 1000   ,,   .   5,797$\frac{7}{8}$,,

  ,,   1000 and 2000   ,,   .   1,589$\frac{4}{5}$,,

Above 2000 in vertical height   .   .   82$\frac{2}{3}$,,

Now if we consider the average elevation of these zones to be the arithmetic mean of the extremes, and that the average of the last term be 2500, which, although not, perhaps, absolutely true, cannot be far from the truth, it results that the surface of Ireland is, in average, elevated above the level of the sea, to a height of 387 feet.

Calculated on similar principles, the average elevations of the provinces are,

Leinster, ... 378 feet.

Ulster, ... 432 ,,

Connaught, ... 266 ,,

Munster, ... 453 ,,

The number for Leinster is very materially influenced by Wicklow, of which the average elevation is 823 feet. Without Wicklow the average of Leinster is reduced to 327 feet.

The distribution of the surface at these various elevations above the sea, is graphically represented in the accompanying map, in which the proportionate space occupied by the ground less than 250 feet in height, is left unshaded, whilst the areas between 250 and 500, between 500 and 1000, and between 1000 and 2000 are distinguished by shadings of different and proportionate intensities. The areas of more than 2000 feet in height, being but a few points, principally in Wicklow and in Kerry, are not represented, as on a map of such scale, they could not be rendered sufficiently distinct, without danger of their areas being exaggerated.

The relation of the watercourses to the vertical elevation of the surface, is by this map rendered very evident. The height of the districts in which the rivers take their rise, and the direction of the lines of greatest elevation which separate the catchment basins of the different rivers, can be estimated by its means. The exact outlines and other characters of the catchment and drainage basins are, however, precisely marked on another map, that on which the extent and localities of the principal bog deposits are shewn. To this map reference will be again made.

A comparison of the map of elevations with the geological map, will at once shew how uniformly the limestone occupies the country under 500 feet, and how instantly it is replaced by other rocks, where a greater elevation is obtained.

By calculations founded on such principles, we arrive at the conclusion, that the average elevation of the surface of the country being 387 feet, the water which flows in our rivers to the sea, has an average fall of 129 yards, and now finally we may calculate the total water power of Ireland. We had for the total quantity of rain falling in a year 100,712,031,640 cubic yards; of this one-third flows into the sea, that is 33,237,343,880 cubic yards, or for each day of twenty-four hours, 91,061,216 cubic yards, weighing 68,467,100 tons. This weight falls from 129 yards, and as 884 tons falling twenty-four feet in twenty-four hours is a horse power, the final result is, that in average we possess, distributed over the surface of Ireland, a water power capable of acting night and day, without interruption, from the beginning to the end of the year, and estimated at the force of 3227 horse power per foot of fall, or, for the entire average fall of 387 feet, amounting to 1,248,849 horse power.

But mechanical power is never thus unintermittingly driven, and if we reduce this force to the year's work of 300 working days, of twelve hours each, we find it to represent 3,038,865 horse power: that is more than three millions of horse power. Of course much of this enormous quantity of force exists in localities where other circumstances may prevent it becoming useful. The perfect economy of the water for mechanical power may be inconsistent with other equally important objects. Thus the drainage of the districts for agricultural purposes, or the maintenance of navigations, may require constant discharge and loss of a certain quantity of water. The various water machines also incur a certain loss of force in working, which may be estimated at a third. But still it may be considered as decisively established that there is derivable from water power, of which I have here noticed only one source, an amount of mechanical force sufficient for the development of our industry on the greatest scale.

The manner in which this force is geographically distributed may be inferred from the position of the principal rivers, the structure of the country through which they flow, and the areas of catchment basins from which, through their tributaries, they derive their supply of water.

The great central limestone district may be considered as transmitting its waters to the sea, by means of the

> Shannon, whose total basin is 4544 square miles.
> Barrow, Nore, and Suir. ,, 3400 ,, ,,

And partly also by the
Galway waters (Loughs Corrib and
> Mask), whose basin covers . . . 1374 square miles.
Moy, ,, ,, ,, . . . 1033 ,, ,,
Blackwater in Meath, and Boyne, . 1086 ,, ,,
Liffey, Dodder, and Tolka, . . . 568 ,, ,,

But these rivers derive a great deal of their supply from the mountainous districts of Wicklow, Tipperary, Cavan, and Connemara, by which the limestone plain is bounded.

The eastern flank of the Wicklow and Wexford mountains is drained principally by the

      Slaney, from a basin of 815 square miles.
      Avonmore,   ,,   200   ,,   ,,
      Avoca River,   ,,   281   ,,   ,,

The southern counties of Munster supply the waters of the large rivers, which flowing in parallel valleys, east and west, discharge into the ocean on the south-eastern coast. These are:

      Blackwater, Waterford, from a basin of 1219 square miles.
      Lee,   Cork,   ,,   ,,   735 ,,   ,,
      Bandon River,   ,,   ,,   228 ,,   ,,

In the north of Ireland there are three principal outlets for the waters; by Lough Erne at Ballyshannon; by the Lower Bann at Coleraine, and by the Foyle at Derry. The areas from which these rivers and their tributaries collect their waters are:

      Erne, ... 1585 square miles.
      Foyle, ... 1476   ,,   ,,
      Bann, Upper and Lower, and the
        Main, ... 1266   ,,   ,,
      Blackwater, Armagh, . . . 526   ,,   ,,

Moreover, the littoral counties pour into the sea a large portion of their drainage waters, by means of a number of rivers of short course, and individually of trifling area of basin; of these may be taken as examples the Lagan at Belfast, draining 227 square miles; the Roughty at Kenmare, from 475 square miles; the Main and Inney at Killarney, from 511 square miles; the Feale and Gale, which unwater the south-western portion of the Munster coal district and discharge into the sea near Listowel, from a basin of 479 square miles.

The relation of these areas from whence the rivers derive their supply of water, is rendered evident by inspection of the map, where it will be seen that the districts through which the various rivers flow, are separated from each other by marked lines, which run along the crest of the highest intervening ground, so that the rain falling on opposite sides of such line must flow in opposite directions, and the drainage be consequently conducted to a different outlet, by which its waters may escape to the sea. The area thus enclosed and penetrated by a river will form the catchment basin of that river, and the watercourses provided must be of sufficient capacity and of sufficiently rapid descent to carry off all the water that may fall within that area, otherwise the district will be exposed to floods, and the surface being kept wet and cold, the soil may become marshy and unfit for profitable agriculture.

The area of catchment basin, and the vertical height of fall are thus the primary elements in relation to water power. The capacities of the various watercourses are also involved in the important questions of drainage and of inland navigation.

Now from the consideration that in average there passes to the sea from the surface twelve inches of water, which from the entire area of Ireland, 32,513 square miles, is capable of generating 3227 horse power per foot of fall, it follows that it requires the drainage of just ten square miles to give water for an average horse power per foot of fall; and on this principle the force capable of application from the waters of the individual rivers may be estimated. Of course it will be understood, that the force of a tributary, or of the upper portions of the river itself, will not be that derivable from the total catchment basin, but from the portion of the basin which actually supplies water to the point where the power is required.

For most of the estimates of areas of drainage basins given above, I am indebted to the kindness of Mr. Mulvany, Commissioner of Drainage

In some, though few, instances, I have obtained values for the water power of certain localities, which may give rather more special interest to the subject, after the general discussion that has just closed.

The Shannon, that great river, which, penetrating the in-

terior of Ireland, navigable from the ocean to its source, rising
in one coal formation, emptying itself through another, and
washing the banks of our most fertile counties, delivers into
the sea the rain collected from an area, which, according to
Mr. Mulvany's estimate, embraces 3613 square miles of country, north of Killaloe. This noble river, which at Lough Allen,
near its source, is but 146 feet above the level of the sea,
passes slowly along, falling but fifty feet in 150 miles, until it
arrives at Killaloe, where its waters rush down the great
rapids towards Limerick, and in a space of fifteen miles present a difference of level of ninety-seven feet, of which the
available power may be estimated, at least with tolerable approximation, from the returns and reports published by the
Commissioners for the improvement of its navigation.

In the geographical character of the basin of the Shannon,
we find all the conditions for great evaporation fulfilled. The
country, whose waters it receives, is flat, its streams sluggish,
the soil upon its banks either deep and retentive clays, or extensive bog. Expanding into numerous lakes of considerable
size, often overflowing the lowlands on its banks, it may be
considered as almost in the condition of presenting a true water
evaporating surface. Still the quantity of water it carries to
the sea is of extraordinary power. It has been observed that,
in wet weather, the level of the water in Lough Derg often
rises two or three inches in twenty-four hours; and has been
known to rise twelve inches. As the area of the Lough is
30,000 statute acres, this extent of water weighs 3,000,000
tons for each inch, and hence, so much as 36,000,000 of tons
have accumulated in a single day and night.

The average difference between summer and winter level of
the Shannon at Killaloe, where narrowing from Lough Derg,
it reassumes the river form, is about six feet, but the total of
the rises of the water during the year are found, from a discussion of the observations of three years, to be eleven feet.
The rising of the waters occupied in average seventy-seven days:
in falling to the summer level they occupied 107 days. The
quantity of water thus accumulated in the great natural reservoir of the Lough was 532,554,096 cubic yards, or 403,416,600

tons, which is discharged in 107 days at the rate of 155,926 tons per hour. By this, a force continuous day and night of 177 horse power per foot of fall may be produced. An equal force is of course available whilst the river is rising, and thus through 184 days, or six months of the year, this enormous power is in action, independent of the ordinary discharge which goes on when the waters are at the lowest.

When the river is high, the motive force available is far greater than that just now mentioned. An example furnished to me by Mr. Mulvany will shew this sufficiently. " On the 2nd of December, 1836, when the water was 13 feet on the upper sill of Killaloe lock, the observed discharge was 882,450 cubic feet per minute, and on the 10th of that month, the height was 14 ft. 1 in., on the 18th 14 ft. 4 in., at which height it continued until the 25th, with of course a *greatly increased discharge ;* on the latter day it began to descend gradually. During the period mentioned, the whole lake rose four inches between the 3rd and 4th, and five inches in two days, between the 5th and 7th, and two inches in other days. These grand rises, at that height of water, extended over the flooded lands as well as the lake, that is, over a surface of from 36,000 to 38,000 statute acres." Now the discharge for the month of December, 1836, may certainly, from the description above given, be taken at one million cubic feet per minute, that is, one and two-third million of tons of water per hour, capable of producing 1885 horse power per foot of fall.

The minimum discharge of the Shannon at Killaloe has been estimated by Mr. Mulvany, in the dryest summer, so low as 100,000 cubic feet of water per minute. This is equal to a force of 188 horse power per foot of fall. At this minimum, however, the flow is kept but for a very short time, certainly not more than a month in the year, which is also the duration that may be allotted to the maximum elevation of the waters.

Although it is not possible to deduce from these returns the actual average force exerted by the waters of this river, yet I consider from all the facts I have been able to collect, regarding its discharge at various seasons, that the mean cannot fall below 350 horse power per foot of fall. For as the summer

level of the river, for which the minimum discharge is taken,
does not last more than two months, and that during the six
months of the rising and the falling of the waters, the force is
at least 188 + 177 horse power per foot of fall, and finally,
that the maximum delivery at winter level, lasts at least a
month, there are nine months of which the force per foot of fall
are

2 months at 188, ...	376
6 months at 365, ...	2190
1 month at 1885, ...	1885

Which give an average of 495 horse power. The other
three months are certainly not below the six months of rising
and falling, but in order that the final results may not be possibly liable to any suspicion of exaggeration, I shall take the
average force of water available per foot of fall, at 350 horse
power, which gives for the ninety-seven feet of fall between
Killaloe and Limerick, a total of 33,950 horse power in continuous action, day and night, throughout the year.

This, however, is by no means the whole power of the river,
for although in the upper portion of its course it flows through
a district unusually level, there is yet between Lough Derg
and Lough Allen a total available fall of forty-six feet six
inches. We may consider, that at the several points on the
river, the supply of water will bear the same proportion to that
at Killaloe, as exists between the respective areas of their
catchment basins, and this is shewn to be a very legitimate
assumption, since at Carrick, where the area of basin is about
350 square miles, the minimum quantity of water passing in
summer through the bridge has been determined by Mr. Mulvany to be 10,000 cubic feet per minute. This is just a tenth
of the minimum at Killaloe, the basin at which is ten times the
area of the surface drained at Carrick.

The distribution of the falls on the upper and middle Shannon will be, when the improvements now in progress are completed, as follows. The area of catchment basin of the river,
at each fall, and the average resulting horse power continuous,
is given in the accompanying column of the table.

	AREA OF BASIN.	HEIGHT OF FALL.	TOTAL HORSE POWER.
Mouth of Lough Allen, 146 square miles	13 feet .	199
Jamestown, . . . 400	,, 6 ,, .	252
Rooskey, ... 650	,, 3½ ,, .	239
Tarmonbarry, . . 780	,, 8 ,, .	656
Athlone, ... 1321	,, 8 ,, .	1109
Meelick, ... 2657	,, 8 ,, .	2232

The total continuous power is, therefore, 4,717 horse, which, added to that of the river from Killaloe, 33,950, gives a force existing between Limerick and Lough Allen of 38,667 horse power, supposed in constant action.

The vast inequality of force at different seasons is the most remarkable disadvantage of water power. It can be perfectly and economically compensated for, as shall be seen hereafter.

To judge of the evaporation which goes on in the basin of the Shannon, we must compare those practical results with what theory indicates.

The area of the basin of the Shannon above Killaloe is 3613 square miles, and as thirty-six inches of rain give 0·3 continuous horse power per foot of fall for every square mile of basin, the total power of the Shannon, without evaporation, should be 1084 horse power per foot of fall. Its average is found to be about 350, and hence the Shannon transmits annually to the sea 11·6 inches of water collected from its extensive basin, a result remarkably in accordance with that of twelve inches (one-third of the rain), which I have taken as the average of Ireland.

If we pass more to the south we shall find a river in which different circumstances prevail. The Lee, rising amidst the picturesque solitudes of West Muskerry, passes by a direct and rapid course through mountainous country to Cork, where it joins the sea. I have calculated the area of country, above Cork, drained by the Lee at 562 square miles. The average rain should, therefore, produce 169 horse power per foot of fall. Some measurements were made at my request by a most intelligent friend, at a period when the river was very low, and admitted of greater accuracy than at other times. He found that there passed through the river in twenty-four hours, 442,800

tons of water. This is at the rate of twenty-one horse power
per foot. The water passing to the sea was, therefore, just
one-eighth of the rain. This is in summer. The average
delivery of the River Lee is certainly more than treble this.
The power calculated from the average for Ireland of one-
third of the rain, should be fifty-six horse power per foot of fall.
But the rain in the west of Cork is above the average; the course
of the river is direct, and the slope of its basin precipitous.

A river in the north of Ireland, concerning the practical
efficiency of which we possess numerical data, is the Upper
Bann; it rises in Down in the mountains of Mourne, and
falls into Lough Neagh, near Lisburn. This river is the most
fully economized in Ireland; its banks present a picture
of industry, of comfort, and intelligence, which I am glad to
hold up as a pattern to other districts. The natural supply
of the river was not enough for the demands of its industrious
occupiers; and Mr. Fairbairn, employed to examine how its
capabilities could be increased, made a report to which I have
already had occasion to refer. I have calculated the total
available catchment basin of the Upper Bann to be 256 square
miles. Hence, without evaporation, and with the rain at
thirty-six inches, which coincides very closely with the fact,
in that locality, the horse power per foot of fall is seventy-
seven. Now Mr. Fairbairn had estimated the force obtainable,
when the water was fully brought into play, at eight working
horse power. It has resulted, from even the partial execution
of his plan, that the river is capable of increase, even beyond
that, and ten working horse power per foot is what appears
may be calculated on. Now this ten working horse power cor-
responds to fifteen horse power on the theoretical standard I
have assumed, which supposes there is no loss of force, and hence
the water practically available is exactly one-fifth of the rain.

Such are the few facts regarding the actual water power of
certain localities which I have been able to collect. It shews
how much remains to be done in this department of practical
science. If it in any way indicates the route; if among my
readers some may be induced by these explanations to occupy
themselves, whilst in the provinces, in those operations, really

simple, only requiring care, by which the sectional area and
the velocity of the current in a river are determined, the country will be positively benefited; for such determinations are
at the basis of all investment of capital for industrial objects,
and the want of them has often occasioned considerable loss of
time and money.

Before quitting this subject I may mention, that Mr. Bald
has published some estimates of the water power of certain localities. He considers that eighteen inches of rain pass to the
sea. This is certainly above the truth. Consequently all his
numbers are too high.

Mr. Henessy, who has recently published an estimate of the
total water power of Ireland, supposes, that four-fifths of the
rain become available for industry. This proportion, although
it may exist in certain mountainous districts, where the water
collects rapidly in basins of small area, and passes with a short
course to the sea, is certainly too large for an average estimate, and he has not attempted to support his views upon any
definite numerical results. But Mr. Bald's measurement of
the areas of the basins, and of the heights of fall of localities
of water power in the west of Ireland, are very valuable, and I
have from them calculated the available horse power of the Connaught lakes, which, together with the area of catchment basin,
and the mean height of fall, is given in the following table:

LAKES.	CATCHMENT AREA.	FALL.	HORSE POWER.
Conn and Cullin,	900 . . .	27	. . . 2430
Mask, ⎰	. . . 1374 . .	36 ⎱	. . . 6850
Corrib, ⎱		14 ⎰	

Total horse power, 9280

We have now sufficiently discussed the manner in which the
water power of Ireland originates, its distribution, and, so far
as our materials allow, its amount. We cannot, however, part
from the subject without describing, though briefly, its practical application. It is not my purpose to discuss the mechanical details of water engines. This is done by special
mechanical writers. Some engines are fitted for some uses and

for some localities, others for different conditions; and it is essential to the connexion of our subject that a certain analysis of the economic efficiency of each should be given here.

We may reduce the water engines to four classes. In the first the water acts by its weight; of this kind is the overshot water-wheel. In the second the action is by impulse, as in the undershot wheel. In the third it is by pressure, as in the water pressure machine. In the fourth, it is by reactive pressure, as in Barker's mill; and similarly reactive impulse gives origin to the horizontal wheel or turbine.

The overshot water-wheel is the most important engine of water power. It is applicable under a great variety of circumstances, and from its inertia it serves as a regulator as well as a producer of the velocity of machinery placed in connexion with it. Its construction requires considerable mechanical skill that its powers may be brought fully into play; the form of the buckets; the quantity of water let into each bucket; the point of the circumference at which the water is to be let on; the exact centreing of it, so that its motion may be absolutely uniform; all these are points to be carefully executed, as the injurious results of a fault in the prime mover might be very serious. When an overshot water-wheel is well made, and well proportioned to the supply of water, we may consider that there is absorbed by the machine one-fourth of the power of the water, and that three-fourths are delivered capable of producing useful effect. In some wheels 80 per cent. of useful effect is obtained, but this seldom occurs.

Wherever the supply of water is moderately large, and that the height of available fall lies between fifteen and fifty feet, the overshot wheel is certainly the engine to be adopted under ordinary circumstances. It is not liable to injury; it is easily repaired; and its prime cost, in relation to its power, is not considerable. In order to derive from it all its power, it must be recollected, however, that the water should act only by its weight; the principle on which its maximum action depends being, that the water should enter the wheel without impulse, and should leave it without velocity. To fulfil this condition, as far as possible, should be the object of the engineer.

In level countries, where, though the quantity of water may be large, the height of fall may be but a few feet, the under-shot wheel is often employed. The water acquiring a velocity from rushing down an inclined race, strikes the float-boards near the bottom of the wheel, and communicates to the machinery a portion of its own motion. The float-boards are generally set radial; but sometimes they make an angle of 20° with the radius. In the latter case the water acts slightly by its weight; but there does not appear to be much difference in the practical results. Now this undershot wheel must be understood to be an inperfect machine. In the overshot wheel the theoretic value of the water is equal to its weight multiplied by its height of fall, and of this force three-fourths are actually available in practice. In the undershot, on the other hand, the theoretic power is but half the weight of the water multiplied by its height of fall, and of this but two-thirds are availble in practice. Hence, the final performance of the undershot wheel is but one-third of the total theoretic power of the water expended. This machine should, therefore, never be used where any other is practicable: it is the least economic. Still in the level districts of Ireland numerous positions occur, where a large quantity of water falls through a height of from two to six feet. Here one-third of the power may be economized by an undershot wheel, and may suffice for all the industrial wants of that particular locality. Beyond six feet, however, I consider this machine not to be recommended. From six feet to fifteen feet of fall, the interval between the effective limiting height of water for the undershot and overshot wheels, a form of wheel intermediate to those, indeed compounded, as it were, of them, is most advantageously employed; this is the breast wheel.

The breast wheel has float boards like the undershot, but instead of moving in an open race, it revolves in a carefully constructed channel, the sides of which are so closely fitted to its frame, as with the float boards to form in some degree a set of buckets. The water is let on somewhat below the axis, and entering the channel with some velocity, it acts at once by weight and impulse. The power of the breast wheel is intermediate to those of the wheels already noticed. It is in fact compounded of the two, and in the words of Barlow: " The effect of the breast wheel is equal to that of an undershot whose head is equal to the difference of level between the surface of the reservoir and the point at which it strikes the wheels, added to that of an overshot whose height is equal to the difference of level between the point where it strikes the wheels and the level of the tail water." Now this gives for the breast wheel a theoretic power of 83 per cent. of the whole effect of the water. In practice about a third of this is absorbed by the machine, and hence the available working effect of the breast wheel may be taken at 55 per cent., rather more than half of the calculated force of the water.

M. Poncelet has proposed to form the breast wheel still more on the model of the overshot, by giving to the float boards a curved form, that they may act more effectually as buckets. He considers also that the principle of the overshot should be used in letting on the water, that is, that it should enter without impulse and leave without velocity. A model wheel constructed on his plan gave a useful effect of 74 per cent. of the total power, and working wheels, of which many of large size have been erected in France, are found to economize from 70 to 60 per cent. below which none have fallen. They may be considered as giving in average two-thirds of the total power of the water, and are hence better than the breast wheels of ordinary construction.

In conclusion I add in a tabular form, the proportional available power by each kind of wheel and the heights of fall within which its use may be recommended.

WHEEL.	ECONOMY OF POWER.	LIMITS OF HEAD.
Overshot, . . .	75 per cent.	15 to 50 feet.
Breast, . . .	55 ,, ...	6 to 15 ,,
Undershot, . . .	33 ,, ...	2 to 6 ,,
Poncelet, . . .	66 ,, ...	6 to 15 ,,

A question may naturally be asked by those not practically conversant with those matters, "why then ever use one of those inferior wheels? if you have a fall of twelve feet, why use a breast wheel of thirty feet which economizes but two-thirds of the power, and not an overshot of fourteen feet, which might economize three-fourths." It is that there is a great practical advantage in large wheels. The motive force acts to more advantage at the extremity of a longer lever. The angular velocity becomes small, which is one of the conditions necessary to a maximum economy, and the mass of the wheel acts as a fly wheel, and by its inertia preserves a regularity of movement which is of the highest importance in practice. Hence the wheels should always be as large as the mechanical circumstances of their locality admit, and thus the practical limits above assigned are fixed.

It will be seen from the numbers now given, that the average performance of breast and overshot water wheels, taken together, is close to two-thirds of the calculated power of the water they expend. On this is founded a practical estimate of the power of mill streams, frequently employed by engineers, and which it is useful to know. It is that twelve cubic feet of water falling one foot per second is a horse power available. Now this is 720 cubic feet per minute, and as the cubic foot of water weighs 62 5lb, the weight is 45·000lb falling a foot per minute. This is four-thirds of the theoretic horse power, as I have stated at page 42, and thus one-third additional power is assumed as expended in transference to the machines.

The water-pressure engine is a machine but little known in this country. In fact, borrowing as we do our mechanical ideas from England, a country, generally speaking, so rich in fuel as to render the economy of water power unimportant, water engines do not fix the attention of mechanists as they deserve. In mechanism the water-pressure engine is essentially the same as a steam engine, usually single acting. The valves and passages are large, as water cannot be wire-drawn like steam. A main-pipe from a reservoir at a distance brings the water to the valve box, through which it enters the cylinder, which, raising the piston, it gradually fills: the entrance valve closes, the water is let off by the opening of an exit valve, and the piston falls by the weight of the machinery with which it is in connexion. Some engines are made double-acting, in which case they are absolutely constructed as the simple high pressure steam engine, but they use cold water in place of steam.

Now as to the mechanical power of these engines. The water acts, not by its weight or impulse, but by its pressure. The height of head to give this pressure must, therefore, be considerable, but the quantity of water consumed may be very small. In a mountainous district, a reservoir is formed among the hills. From it the water is conducted, not by a costly embankment, but by a pipe of a few inches diameter. The machine is erected at the most convenient locality. For every thirty-five feet of head, the pressure is one atmosphere on the piston; fifteen pounds to the square inch. A head of 350 feet gives, therefore, ten atmospheres, and in mining districts, where such elevation is often available, those engines are peculiarly suitable. With such a head and a piston of a square foot of surface, moving with a mean velocity of two feet per second, there should be produced a force of seventy-eight horse power, and as the engine is found to deliver in practice 70 per cent. of the theoretical amount, the working efficiency of such an engine should be fifty-four horse power. The expenditure of water would be 120 cubic feet per minute.

The expenditure of the same water, acting by the same head, on an overshot wheel, would give seventy-three theoretic horse power, and in practice fifty-five horse power. The efficiency of the water pressure engine is, therefore, a little less than that of the overshot wheel, but it is to be remarked, that a head of 350 feet could not be made use of with any wheel. A wheel cannot be practically used over fifty feet, and hence 300 feet of fall should go to waste, five-sixths of the entire power, all of which is economized with the water-pressure engine.

On the Continent the employment of water-pressure engines is very general. At Freyberg, one of the deepest silver mines, the Altemord Grube is drained by an engine working with two single acting cylinders, which is fixed itself 360 feet below the surface. Its effective duty is seventy per cent. of the calculated power. In Bavaria, where the water-pressure engine has received its most remarkable improvements, from the hands

of Reichenbach, the brine, from the salt mines of the neighbourhood of Salzburg, is transmitted over the mountains, 1200 feet
high, for a distance of seven miles, by means of a series of nine
engines, that the evaporation may be carried on in a district
where fuel is cheap.   The effective duty of these engines is
from 60 to 72 per cent. of the theoretical force.   In France in
various localities they are erected.   One at Huelgoat in Finis-
terre, which works with a column of water, sixty-five yards
high, and draws up the waters from the lead mines from a depth
of 305 yards, delivers 64 per cent. of the theoretical force, and
when it is placed in connexion with the deeper pits, for which
it was constructed, is expected to increase its efficiency to at
least 70 per cent. of theory.

These machines are now also being introduced into Cornwall.   Mr. Fairbairn and Mr. Darlington have erected water-
pressure engines in the mines of that country.   One erected
by the latter engineer has two cylinders of fifty inches diameter and ten feet stroke.   It is worked by a column of water
thirty inches diameter and forty-four yards high.   It works
four to six strokes in the minute.   The blow produced by the
valve is almost totally gotten rid of by peculiar mechanical
arrangements invented by Mr. Darlington, but which need not
be described here.   The power of this machine calculated by
the principles given above, from its dimensions and the supply
of water, should be 166 horse power, which at 70 per cent.
becomes 116 horse power of practical efficiency.

I must remark, however, two disadvantages of this machine,
1st. The water flowing with a constant pressure into the cylinder, imparts to the piston an accelerated motion, so that
finally the stroke is terminated by a shock from the inelastic
water, whilst in the steam engine, the steam acts as an elastic
cushion, by which the piston is brought to rest, and injury to
the machinery prevented.   To remedy this, in the water engine, many plans are devised; an air vessel on the cylinder;
springs under the working beam ; a cavity containing air in
the piston. By means of such provisions this disadvantage is
removed, and although the motion is not regular enough for
certain delicate uses, yet for draining mines, and numerous

other purposes, it is most effectual. The second disadvantage is, that its parts, being like those of the steam engine, are somewhat complicated, and require more repair and attention than those of water wheels. But in this it is not more troublesome than the steam engine, which nobody faults on that account.

The machine which is popularly known as Barker's mill, and in which water issuing from an orifice gives motion to machinery by its reactive force, is not one with which I need occupy attention. Its theory indicates the maximum effect to be but one-half the true power of the water, and as in practice further deduction must be made, it is likely that not one-third is really economized. It is hence one of the worst water engines, and I only name it here because a modification of it by Messrs. Whitelaw and Skerrit of Glasgow has lately been brought forward, said to economize power in as great a degree as the overshot wheel. In the new form the horizontal arms are curved in such a manner, that the water, when passing from the centre, moves in a straight line, the arms by their curvature retreating as it advances. In this way the centrifugal force of the water, which, in the old straight arms, partly acted against the reactive force, is obviated; indeed as it is exerted along the axis of the tube, it is added to the power generated by the reaction. The results of the use of this engine published by the patentees are highly favourable to it, but I understand, that in many instances it has not fulfilled expectation. Without intending, therefore, at all to disparage this improved form of the reaction mill, I may observe that more extended practical knowledge of its power is required before we can rank it with those useful machines already noticed.

Finally, I have to describe a water engine of quite modern invention and of remarkable efficiency, the turbine, invented by M. Fourneyron. Coals being abundant, the steam engine is invented in England; coals being scarce, the water-pressure engine and the turbine are invented in France. It is thus the physical condition of each country directs its mechanical genius. The turbine is a horizontal wheel furnished with curved float boards, on which the water presses from a cylinder which is suspended over the wheel, and the base of which is divided by curved partitions, that the water may be directed in issuing, so as to produce upon the curved float-boards of the wheel its greatest effect. The best curvature to be given to the fixed partitions and to the float boards is a delicate problem, but practically it has been completely solved. The construction of the machine is simple; its parts not liable to go out of order, and as the action of the water is by pressure, the force is under the most favourable circumstances for being utilized.

The effective economy of the turbine appears to equal that of the overshot wheel. But this economy in the turbine is accompanied by some conditions which render it peculiarly valuable. In a water wheel you cannot have great economy of power without very slow motion, and hence where high velocity is required at the working point, a train of mechanism is necessary, which causes a material loss of force. Now in the turbine, the greatest economy is accompanied by rapid motion, and hence the connected machinery may be rendered much less complex. In the turbine also a change in the height of the head of water alters only the power of the machine in that proportion, but the whole quantity of water is economized to the same degree. Thus if a turbine be working with a force of ten horses, and that its supply of water be suddenly doubled, it becomes of twenty horse power; if the supply be reduced to one-half, it still works five horse power : whilst such sudden and extreme changes would altogether disarrange water wheels, which can only be constructed for the minimum and allow the overplus to go to waste.

Mr. Rühlman, who has published a very full report on the theory of this machine, and on the practical performance of the more important of those erected on the Continent, concludes, that it is certainly wrong to suppose that turbines can altogether do away with the use of vertical wheels, and that the economy of 80 per cent. of the theoretical effect, obtained by Fourneyron with some wheels, cannot be expected in all cases; but that certainly in practice from 60 to 70 per cent.

may be depended on. As to the choice between turbines and vertical wheels, his decision is, that where there is a fall of a certain height, which may be economized by means of an overshot wheel, such is to be preferred to the turbine, for when carefully arranged, the overshot wheel economizes more than 70 per cent. of the theoretical power; the only exception to this may be in those cases, where, as in corn mills, the horizontal motion of the turbine may be directly utilized, or where the engine must work against considerable backwater, in which case the effect of the turbine is but very little affected, though the ordinary wheel loses considerably in power.

But in all cases of very high or very low falls, Mr. Rühlman, as well as all other engineers who have written on the subject, gives decided preference to the turbine, and considers, that their universal application to such circumstances can only be retarded by want of foresight and of knowledge of their actual performance.

The extreme conditions under which the turbine will act, are shewn very satisfactorily by the result of one erected at St. Blasien, and by which is driven the machinery of a cotton mill, containing 8000 spindles, with carding machines, beaters, and all other necessary engines. The flow of water was one cubic foot per second, but a height of 332 feet was available. On a fifty foot overshot wheel, this quantity of water would give but five and three-fourths theoretical, and but four and one-fourth practical horse power; but the water, being collected at a distance of two miles, is brought to St. Blasien by a metal pipe eighteen inches diameter, and delivered to the turbine with all its pressure available. The wheel of the turbine is but one foot diameter, and it makes about 2250 revolutions in a minute. Its theoretical force is thirty-eight horse power, of which nearly three-fourths or twenty-eight horse power is delivered in practice.

Contrasted with this machine, are the great turbines erected at St. Maur, near Paris, to grind corn. The wheel of each turbine is six feet in diameter; its paddles ten inches high. The head of water averages 11 ft. 9 in., and the discharge is thirty-four cubic feet per second. Each turbine drives ten pair of millstones, with all accompanying cleansing machinery, and in twenty-four hours grinds fifteen tons of corn. The theoretical power of each turbine equals forty-five and a half horse power; the practical efficiency is thirty-three. In another case where the height of the fall of water to a turbine was but thirteen inches, the economy in practice was 55 per cent. of the theoretical power.

Having thus considered the machines by which water power is rendered available to industry, it remains to examine some circumstances affecting it, which are not of inferior importance.

The worst feature of water power is, that its production does not depend upon the will of the person who employs it. Originating in cosmical laws, which, from their complexity, have as yet totally defied the predicting power of science, the amount of water flowing along any given river cannot be estimated for any time in advance, and hence the manufacturer has open to him one or other of but two courses, each of which is beset with disadvantages, which I shall endeavour to enumerate. In the first place, having estimated the smallest quantity of water that is available in summer, he may proportion his machinery, and work to that amount of power. But by doing so, he sees pass by him through the greater portion of the year, power many times as great as that which he economizes. The forces of nature flow by his door, but he knows not how to control them. The powers which could execute in a day that which occupies his factory for a week, are running to waste, but the intelligence which might arrest them in their course, and make them pay tribute, is not possessed by the manufacturer whose case we have taken, and hence he drags along an existence dull and unprofitable, until some turn of commercial circumstances seals his ruin. The alternative course by which the machinery is constructed of power sufficient for the employment of the average quantity of water, is accompanied by not less evils. In fact, in the dry season, industry is arrested; there is not water enough to work the mill: workmen unemployed, their families possibly without food, a prey to discontent, are consequences sufficiently se-

rious; whilst orders remaining unexecuted, contracts unful-
filled, may entail loss of the most serious kind upon those whose
capital is invested in such works. In addition we must consider, that upon a river, factories, by which its water is economized, present great obstacles to the flowing of the current,
and hence in case of sudden floods, by the arresting of the
stream at the mill works, the lands higher up are rendered
liable to inundations, which may be destructive to property
and even life. Thus the employment of water power is liable
to interruption, and may be productive of injury, affecting not
merely the interests of the workmen and the capitalists who
share in its advantages, but also of those at a distance who
derive no benefit from its use.

I believe that the disadvantages to which water power is
liable, are fully expressed in the above statement. Now I do
not hesitate to say, that they are all capable of being removed.
If we give to the conditions of water power the same care that
is bestowed upon the circumstances of steam power, those disadvantages disappear, and we obtain from water, during the
year, a steadiness of supply, and a regularity in work, that
leave nothing to be desired.

In fact, as we have under the earth vast deposits of coal,
the source of steam power, from which we draw, at desire, the
necessary supply, so is it necessary to organize on the surface
vast depositories of water power to be made available at our
will. In place of wretched mill ponds, by which a stock of
water is scarcely secured for a week, there should be a basin
so capacious, that the floods of an entire winter might be received, and thus invested for most profitable expenditure in
summer. This is the course actually pursued where industry
is most active and enlightened. I shall proceed to detail the
circumstances of one or two such cases, in order that they may
serve as examples of what may be done.

The quantity of mechanical force that is brought suddenly
into existence by the waters of a winter flood, and which, for
want of sufficient reservoirs, is altogether lost in almost every
case, may be exemplified by considering the quantity of water,
which, during a few days of the winter of 1840, accumulated in

Lough Derg. The depth of water on the upper sill of Killaloe lock on the respective dates were :

November 15th, ...	9 feet 8½ inches.
,, 16th, ...	9 ,, 9 ,,
,, 17th, ...	10 ,, 9 ,,
,, 18th, ...	11 ,, 1 ,,
Stationary until,	
December 8th, ...	10 ,, 9 ,,
,, 9th, ...	11 ,, 0 ,,
,, 10th, ...	11 ,, 6 ,,
,, 11th, ...	11 ,, 11 ,,

In the twenty-four hours of the 16th and 17th November, the water rose twelve inches, and in the three days and nights of December, 8th to the 11th, it rose fourteen inches. Now each inch of water on this lake amounts to 3,000,000 of tons in weight. These floods, therefore, brought down, first in one day, 36,000,000, and then in three days, 42,000,000 of tons of water, over and above the vast discharge constantly going on at the orifice of the lake. Now if these masses of water could have been, by suitable engineering arrangements, preserved from immediate and useless expenditure; if their discharge could have been spread over the entire year, these two quantities alone, of twelve and fourteen inches of rise of surface, the fruits of four days and nights of winter flood, would be able to generate, on the fall of the river below Killaloe, a force acting throughout the entire year, night and day, of 967 horse power.

The mill owners on the Upper Bann were exposed to all the disadvantages above stated. Floods drowning their mills in winter; drought stopping their works in summer. Mr. Fairbairn was employed to survey the district, and proposed the formation of three reservoirs. the circumstances of which I shall briefly describe in his own words.

" Lough Island Reavy, which is the best situated reservoir, is a natural lake bounded north and south by land of considerable elevation. It has good feeders, which, with the overplus waters of the River Muddock, would give ample supplies, and fill the reservoir one or twice in the year. The present area

of the Lough is ninety-two and a half statute acres. On this
is to be raised thirty-five feet of water, and drawn to a depth
of forty feet under that height. The area thus enlarged will
be 253 acres, equal to 140 acres thirty-five feet deep, and 113
acres fifteen feet deep, making a total of 287,278,200 cubic
feet of water.

"The Deer's Meadow, embanked to 100 feet above the level
of the river, will flood 215 acres to twenty-four feet average
depth, having 224,769,600 cubic feet of water. The feeders
are uncertain, being but the drainage of 1802 acres. This
reservoir should, therefore, be the last executed.

"Corbet Lough is a valuable auxiliary to the other two. It
has excellent feeders, and controls every mill from its outlet
to Lough Neagh. It may be raised eighteen feet above its
summer level. It should then cover seventy-four and a half
acres, and contain 46,783,440 cubic feet of water. The supply
is from the flood waters of the Bann by a canal cut and land
feeders.

"The sum of the three reservoirs:

	CUBIC FEET.	ACRES.
Lough Island Reavy, .	287,278,200	covering 253
Deer's Meadow, . . .	224,769,600	,, 215
Corbet Lough, . . .	46,783,440	,, 74¼
Cubic feet of water,	558,831,240	542¼

"This total amount, at sixty cubic feet per second, will
afford a constant discharge for 108 days, or for 216 days,
working twelve hours; and as twelve cubic feet per second
falling a foot, is a working horse power, the reservoirs alone
give five horse power per foot of fall for 216 days in the year.
Now as there are 350 feet fall, this is a total on the Bann, of
1750 horse power, and, adding the water of the river course,
the power may be considered as equivalent to 2800 horse
power."

The above is extracted from Mr. Fairbairn's Report; he proceeds to some estimates of the cost of these reservoirs. The
total expenditure he values at £32,000, and deduces, that the
annual cost of delivery of water should be £1860, arranged as

below, and that each reservoir gives for a shilling expense, the
following number of tons of water :

	TOTAL EXPENSE.	GIVES FOR A SHILLING
Lough Island Reavy,	£700	33 tons water
Corbet Lough, . . .	260	12 ,,
Deer's Meadow, . .	900	14 ,,

Mr. Fairbairn calculates that steam power to do the same
work should cost £9050, and hence the water power should
produce a saving of £7191 per annum.

Such was Mr. Fairbairn's plan; I was aware that it had not
been all carried into execution, but that such parts of it as
were carried out had produced even greater effects than he had
estimated. Through the kindness of Mr. Bergin I was enabled
to communicate with Mr. Bateman, who was Mr. Fairbairn's
colleague in the execution of the works, and received from him,
in answer to certain queries, replies which I subjoin.

" Of the works authorized by Act of Parliament, the Lough
Island Reavy Reservoir has been completed, and been in operation for upwards of three years.

" The land for Corbet Lough Reservoir is purchased, and
the Deer's Meadow Reservoir abandoned.

"Previous to the construction of the Lough Island Reavy
Reservoir, the River Bann, where most closely occupied by
mills and bleach works, had not water power more than equal
to one or one and one-half horse power upon each foot of fall,
during the dry periods of the year, for months together.

" The lowest power *now* is about five horse power to a foot
of fall, being a gain, by means of the reservoir, of about three
and one-half horse power per foot, and the regular full quantity is uniformly maintained.

" Should the Corbet Lough Reservoir ever be completed, the
minimum power of the river, below its outlet, will be brought
up to about ten horse power per foot of fall.

" In dry seasons, when the river has fallen to its lowest volume, the discharge may probably be equal to from seventy to
one hundred cubic feet per second. In floods it amounts to
3 or 4000 cubic feet per second.

" Below the Lough Island Reavy Reservoir there is a fall of 124 feet upon the River Muddock, partially occupied by small corn and flax mills.

" On the River Bann, from its junction with the Muddock to the Corbet Lough Reservoir, there is a fall of forty-four feet and a half, at present occupied by limited establishments, which are capable of great improvement. The regular power *now* is never less than about five horse power per foot of fall.

" Below Corbet Lough to the last mill on the river there is a fall of 168 feet; on this portion the more extensive establishments are situated,—the whole fall being occupied. The river is now equal to about five horse power per foot of fall, and by an outlay of of between 2 and £3000 on Corbet Lough may be increased to ten horse power per foot.

" The mills have been gradually increasing since the improvement of the river, but few are yet enlarged to the extent they may be.

" The annual rate levied upon the river for the cost of the improvement is £10 per foot of fall, which will diminish as the works increase in value, and the river is more extensively occupied. As the measure of a river, when no other assistant power can be applied, must be taken at its minimum, the gain already acquired is about three and one-half horse power per foot, which, at the present rate, is equal to a cost per horse power per annum of under £3. The cost of the same power by steam in that district would be from £20 to £30 per annum.

" Should the full scheme be developed by the completion of the Corbet Lough Reservoir, the cost of the additional power will be little more than 20s. per horse power per annum.

"J. F. BATEMAN."

We here see how fully the so called natural disadvantages of water power are obviated. I shall in addition notice an instance taken from Scotland, where the result has been, not merely the increase in amount and steadiness of power previously existing, but absolutely the creation of a vast water power, where none had been deemed to exist before.

The inhabitants of Greenock had long suffered from a want

of water for domestic use. Several engineers had reported, that the circumstances of the locality did not allow of any copious supply of this necessary element of cleanliness and health; but at last Mr. Thom, having examined the surrounding country, astonished the people of Greenock by asserting, that not merely water sufficient for domestic and municipal purposes might be brought in, but that water power might be made available for mechanical purposes to a very considerable amount. His scheme has been carried into effect. His calculations have been more than borne out, and the rapid rise of Greenock as an emporium of commerce and industry is, in no small degree, due to the bold foresight of the engineer of the Shaw's Water Works.

I shall extract a few notices of these works from an account of them printed some years since, and now extremely rare.

" The distinguishing characteristics of *this scheme* are the following :—Instead of erecting works on natural waterfalls, on the banks of rivers, in remote and almost inaccessible places, where immense capital must, in the first instance, be expended in forming roads and houses for the work people, as well as a heavy and perpetual charge for carriage to and from the seat of trade,—the water is carried, by an aqueduct, from the river and reservoirs, to a populous sea-port town, with a redundant unemployed population, where roads, harbours, piers, and every thing requisite for the most extensive trade and manufacture, are already formed. Besides, by thus forming artificial waterfalls on advantageous grounds, every inch of fall, from the river or reservoir to the sea, is rendered available; whereas, by the former mode, only a very small part of the fall could, in general, be employed. In the present case a fall of 512 feet has been made available, of which not more than twenty was formerly occupied, or thought capable of being usefully employed. But, besides the immense advantage thus gained by increasing the fall, a still greater advantage is obtained from the greatly increased, and perfectly uniform, supply of water; by the adaptation of the various reservoirs, aqueducts, basins, and self-acting sluices—as will be seen by the description of the parts which they respectively perform.

" The embankment of the great reservoir, which is sixty feet high from the bottom of the rivulet, is now very nearly, and in a few months will be entirely, finished.

" This reservoir contains two hundred and eighty-four millions, six hundred and seventy-eight thousand, five hundred and fifty (284,678,550) cubic feet of water; and covers two hundred and ninety-four and three-fourths imperial acres of land.

" The compensation reservoir contains fourteen millions, four hundred and sixty-five thousand, eight hundred and ninety-eight (14,465,898) cubic feet of water ; and covers about forty imperial acres. Its embankment is twenty-three feet high from the bottom of the rivulet.

" The auxiliary reservoir, No. 3, contains four millions, six hundred and fifty-two thousand, seven hundred and seventy-five (4,652,775) cubic feet of water ; and covers about ten imperial acres.

" The other auxiliary reservoirs, Nos. 1, 2, 4, 5, and 6, are now about to be formed, and will contain something more than six millions cubic feet of water.

" Thus, the reservoirs already formed, contain three hundred and three millions, seven hundred and ninety-seven thousand, two hundred and twenty-three (303,797,223) cubic feet; and when the other five auxiliary reservoirs are finished, the whole will contain above three hundred and ten millions (310,000,000) cubic feet of water."

Anxious to obtain information as to the actual condition and performance of these remarkable water works, and unable personally to visit Scotland, I have to thank one of the most eminent men that country has presented to the practical sciences, for a note descriptive of the power that is now produced by the water so economized. Mr. Scott Russell replied to my inquiries in the following words :

" MY DEAR SIR,—I had hoped to have been able to get a full and very satisfactory account of the Shaw's water drawn up for you by a competent engineer, resident on the spot; but I find that so many delays are occurring to prevent this, that I now write to beg you will not calculate upon it: had my own time permitted I should have done so myself, but now just when I might have hoped for leisure, I am taken from home.

"I have, however, procured a copy of a *now* scarce pamphlet, printed some thirteen or fourteen years ago, *before* the works were finished, giving some account of them *as proposed.* I may now add for your information, that every thing *predicted* has been satisfactorily and fully accomplished; that the Company now divide a fair per centage on their capital, even though at present only one-half of the capabilities of the reservoir are employed. There has in all years been an abundant supply.

"I may also add, that the sole supply of water here obtained is from the fall of rain, and that the artificial lake has been created in a place where formerly there were only slender mountain rivulets.

"The guaranteed and realized supply of water amounts to 2500 cubic feet per minute during 310 days per annum. The total fall is about 500 feet; the total power thus *created* is, therefore, as follows, in round numbers :

> 2500 feet of water.
> 60℔ weight.

> 150,000
> 500 feet fall.

50,000)75,000,000(1500. Steam engine mercantile horse power.
Or about 2000. Bolton and Watt's estimated horse power.

"Thus then a power has been created and brought six miles and a half to the suburbs of populous towns, equal to the power of thirty steam engines of fifty horse power; being equivalent to the creation of wealth or *productive capital* to the extent of £75000; and the annual effect of which, when fully employed, will be something like the employment of 7000 people, and the annual distribution of something like £300,000 per annum in wages in a single town; besides the supply of ample store of water for the use of the town.

"Such, my dear Sir, is a hurried sketch of what has been accomplished: the accompanying pamphlet will tell you something about the details. What further may be necessary for your purpose let me know, and I shall try and send it you.

"J. Scott Russell."

The greater number of Irish rivers are more or less anal

gous to the Shannon, in having lakes either at their origin or on their course, and hence present facilities for the accumulation of water power of the highest interest to the mechanical engineer. The concentration of the waters of a district in such reservoirs, by appropriate embankments, may be, and in most cases must be connected with another operation of the greatest importance to the agriculture of this country, the drainage of the surface. As an example of how both objects may be at the same time secured, and how well the physical circumstances of the country lend themselves to their accomplishment, I may notice the relations of Lough Ennell, near Mullingar, to the River Brosna, by which its waters are carried to the Shannon. The facts are taken from Mr. Mulvany's Report.

The catchment basin of the Brosna discharges almost altogether into the lake, the waters flowing directly to the river course being comparatively trifling. The difference of winter and summer level is but two feet, yet by this a great extent of land is flooded. Mr. Mulvany proposes to deepen the channel of the lake and river by these two feet, by this means relieving the flat lands, and rendering the winter accumulation of the water available for the supply of the mills upon the river during the dry summer seasons.

The area of Lough Ennell is 3603 acres, and at two feet in depth it should discharge 314,000,000 of cubic feet. As in the case of the Dodder, this supply would probably be available twice in the year, for the midsummer floods, though not so great as those of winter, will be in all cases sufficient to replenish such reservoirs. Hence, as the difference of level of the Brosna issuing from Lough Ennell, and where it joins the Shannon, is 154 feet, a force continuous through half the year of 692 horse power, or four and one-half horse power per foot of fall, should be made available.

The River Dodder, although trifling in magnitude, is yet of much interest to us, from the amount of industry which it sustains in the immediate neighbourhood of Dublin. There are situated on its banks at present twenty-eight mills occupied with various manufactures, as paper, flour, woollens, cloth, &c. This stream, passing by a highly inclined channel from the

flanks of the Dublin mountains to the sea, is liable to very great
fluctuation in the amount of its discharge. It frequently has
done great damage to the lands and edifices along its banks,
by sudden floods, and in summer its waters fall so low, that
the mills may be considered as being kept idle half time for a
period of three months in the year.

At present the occupied fall upon the Dodder is 370 feet.
The total horse power which is now precariously available, is
estimated at 926, which is two and a half horse power per foot
of fall. The question of rendering the supply of water more
uniform, and of economizing a larger proportion of its force,
has been recently taken up by the Board of Works, at the request of the mill-owners upon the river, and an accurate survey
has been made, and a Report drawn up by Mr. Mallet, whose
union of scientific and practical skill is so well known.

Mr. Mallet proposes to form, by means of an embankment
about 2000 feet long, and 100 feet high at its centre, across
the head of Glenismaul, a reservoir with an area of 162 statute
acres, and capable of containing 228,000,000 of cubic feet of
water. The catchment basin of this reservoir should have an
area of 6070 acres, chiefly mountain bog, and from the quantity
of rain which falls in that hilly district, Mr. Mallet calculates,
that the reservoir should be filled at least twice in the year,
and hence a total annual quantity of water of 456,000,000 of
cubic feet obtained, which Mr. Mallet values as equivalent to
1387 horse power in constant operation.

On the construction of this reservoir, it appears by Mr.
Mallet's Report, that the total force of the river should become
practically equivalent to 2038 horse power. This is five and
a half horse power per foot of fall; more than double that now
irregularly in operation. The probable cost of these improvements may taken at 86s. per annum per foot of fall, or 23s. per
additional horse power. That is, the expense is just one-tenth
that of the corresponding steam power, or one-seventh that of
the mere coals for a steam engine.

As I discussed the question of the cost of power so fully
when speaking of the production of steam, it will suffice to notice briefly the circumstances of water power as to cost. It is

only necessary to contrast it with steam power. It is certainly much cheaper, not merely in Ireland, but in all places where it is available. An eminent manufacturer in Leeds said to me, that water power is cheaper than steam at the mouth of the coal pit. All evidence bears this out. In Mr. Fairbairn's Report, and Mr. Bateman's letter, this point is decided, as regards the Upper Bann. Even at present it may be taken at £3 per annum per horse power,—steam costing from £20 to £30; it may thus be averaged at one-eighth. But Mr. Bateman considers, that when the reservoir system is worked out, the horse power will be had for 20s. per year, not one-twentieth of the cost of steam.

Regarding the Shaw's Water Works we also have money estimates, which are highly valuable, as they place the relative cost of power by water and steam in contrast, not merely for Ireland, where steam is dear, but for the banks of the Clyde, where coal is at its lowest price. Mr. Thom thus describes the system followed in Glasgow, which is different from anything here. With us a builder speculates only in houses, in Glasgow he speculates in cotton mills.

"I have stated the cost of steam power at £30 for each horse power. Let us see its market price in Glasgow: there it is customary to provide a house for the manufacture, with the steam engine, great-gearing, and steam-pipes,—and keep the engine going twelve hours a day, and heat the work,—for £50 for each horse power.

" The cost of erecting a mill or factory, capable of containing machinery for the cotton manufacture to the extent of thirty horse power, with the great-gearing and steam-pipes, but exclusive of steam engine and engine-house, may be taken at £4200. Allow the landlord 8 per cent. on this sum, £336, and for heating the house by steam, £84, together £420; which is a fair return for every thing except the steam power. But the landlord draws for the whole a rent of £1500; which leaves for the *power* a rent of £1080: divide this by 30, the number of horse power, and it gives for each £36 annually.

" The average water rent for each horse power at Greenock is £3; the average rent for two acres of land, to be fued along with each mill site if required, is £16. The work being of fifty horse power, take one-fiftieth of this sum (6s. 5d.) for each horse power. Interest on £2000, the cost of a water wheel, arc, trows, &c., for a work of fifty horse power, £100; one-fiftieth of which is £2, making the whole cost of water power, for one horse power, at Greenock, £5 6s. 5d.

" Thus each horse power, by water at Greenock, costs upon the whole £5 6s. 5d., being £30 13s. 7d. less than the cost of one horse power by steam at Glasgow. Besides, this calculation includes the rent of two acres of land for each mill at Greenock, whereas at Glasgow no land is taken into the account, except the spot on which the work stands. Were the same quantity of ground given to the mill at Glasgow, at the rate it brings there, it would throw the balance still more in favour of Greenock.

Thus, whether we take Mr. Bateman's value, which is for the bare supply of power; or Mr. Thom's value, which includes the delivery of the power in a working form, we see that the cost of water power is not more than one-tenth of the cost of steam. Why then is steam so much used? In the first place, water power is available only in certain localities, where other more influential circumstances may forbid the introduction of manufactures; and secondly, the influence of the cost of power is generally so small in mechanical industry, that the question of saving in regard to it is swallowed up in more important questions. Still, wherever water power is to be had, it is always employed in preference to steam, as I shall, in fact, shew; but it is first necessary to notice an objection to water power, of a very absurd kind, which, however, requires refutation, because it is held by many persons in Ireland, otherwise well informed, and exercises very considerable influence upon public opinion as to the manufacturing circumstances of the country. This idea is to the effect, that there is an inherent defect in water power that must prevent its being ever extensively used in industry, to wit, that the water soaking into a water wheel at night renders whichever side is then undermost the heavier, and this preponderating afterwards, gives an unequal and jogging motion which unfits the wheel for any delicate work.

I shall transcribe, in order to preclude further misunder-
standing on this point, one passage from the article "Steam
Engine," in the Encyclopædia Britannica. The article is
written by Scott Russell.

"Mr. Lucy had constructed at Birmingham a flour mill
driven by steam; and it had been his object to obtain perfection without any limitation of expense. He had got one of
Bolton and Watt's best steam engines, and yet he found that
his mill neither produced such perfect flour, nor moved so
smoothly as mills driven by water. On the contrary, it was
found that the irregularity of the motion produced a larger
quantity of coarse than of fine flour, at a mercantile loss to the
owner; and it was likewise found that the irregular propulsion
a tergo intervening with the uniform motion, towards which
the millstones tended by their own momentum, produced a
clanging reciprocation along the whole line of toothed gearing,
which was most injurious, and rapidly destructive to the toothed wheels. When we visited the spot in 1838, the ruins of former wheels, most unequally worn and totally destroyed, were
strewed about the yard. The usual plan of increasing the
weight of the fly-wheel was resorted to without success; and
Mr. Lucy applied to Mr. Buckle to propose a remedy for the
evil. This remedy Mr. Buckle found in the very simple con-
trivance of a pneumatic pump.

"So perfect was the action of this mechanism, that the fly-
wheel had been wholly removed, and the engine and the whole
mill-work were moving in the most smooth and effective manner. It was found that the change enabled them to give all
the grinding stones a greater velocity than formerly, so that
the quantity ground was greater, in the proportion of 56 to
52, and the quantity of the finest or first flour, from the same
wheat, was likewise much increased; so that, both by quantity
and quality, the owner of that mill was now able to command
the market.' The same motion has subsequently been applied
to cotton mills with perfect success; the quality and the quantity of yarn produced being much improved."

Now it may be observed that Mr. Russell does not proceed
to explain that water power may be employed, but to describe

the endeavours of engineers to render the steam engine as regular and as useful for delicate work, as the water wheel is found to be. In fact, cotton spun by water-power bears, and has always borne, a higher price than cotton spun by steam power. Moreover, if we analyze the power employed in England in the spinning and weaving factories, we shall have very conclusive evidence on the point. In the estimate of the state of the cotton manufacture in 1833, drawn up by Mr. Baines, and of which the principal items are given in page 64, he considers that of the 44,000 horse power employed, there are

Steam power, 33,000.
Water power, 11,000.

But we have much more complete and more accurate numbers given in the Returns of the Factory Inspectors for 1839, of which the following is a summary.

The total mill power in factories subject to inspection in England was 83,264 horse power.

Of these there were

62,846 horse power, steam;
20,418 ,, ,,   water;

coinciding with Mr. Baines' general view of three-fourths steam; and one-fourth water.

In Lancashire, where coals are so cheap, we might suppose that nobody would use water, but we find:

Total mill power inspected in Lancashire is 36,446 horse power:

Consisting of,

Steam, 32,123 horse power.
Water, 4,323 ,,   ,,

Thus, one-ninth of the total mill power of Lancashire is water power. But in order to estimate how far water power is valued, we must learn, not merely how much is used, but how much is left unused. Now I have endeavoured to calculate, on the same principles as I adopted for the surface of Ireland in the beginning of this chapter, the theoretical water power of Lancashire; I have found that it is represented by 72,600

horse power, taken as working continuously. Now the 4323
horse power economized, makes 6 per cent. of the entire; and
as there are in Ireland a million and a quarter of such horse
power, it follows that if we economized our water all over Ireland, in the same degree as water power is actually economized in Lancashire, we should have at work a force of 75,000
horse power, that is to say, almost equal to the mill power of .
England returned by the factory inspectors.

This shews how water power is valued in Lancashire. In
fact, advantage is taken of every possible situation. The River
Irwell, which passes by Bolton and Manchester, and washes
the heart of the factory districts, is the hardest worked stream
probably in the world. It has, from its first mill at Bacun to
Prestolee near Bolton, a fall of 900 feet, of which 800 are actually economized by mills. I do not know another example
of such complete application of water power as in that place,
where coal is on all sides available. We may, therefore, pass
away from this question, of whether water power answers for
mechanical purposes, which I should not have at all noticed,
but that the public often receive a bold statement from a public man, without troubling themselves to examine whether it
be likely that he understands what he talks about.

Contrast with this the actual economy of water power in Ireland. By the returns of 1839, there are employed in Ireland :

Steam, 1503 horse power.
Water, 2147 ,,   ,,

It has been found that to give to water power its full economy
and value, it is necessary to secure its steadiness of supply by
the construction of reservoirs, in which such quantity of water
may be retained as shall suffice for the average performance of
the machine during the entire year. Another mode of compensating for the deficient supply of water in dry seasons remains
to be described. This consists in having also a steam engine
of such power as to be supplemental to the water wheel, and
according as water fails, to work the engine, so that the mechanical force exerted by the steam engine and water machine
together, may be constant. This mode is actually adopted in

many localities. In the factories of Messrs. Malcolmson at
Portlaw in Waterford, two engines of a hundred horse power,
and two overshot wheels, of nearly equal force, thus work
together. There is no mechanical difficulty in the co-adapta-
tion of these prime movers. Where circumstances prevent the
formation of great reservoirs, which, indeed, must perhaps
always require the co-operation of several manufacturers, and,
therefore, become practicable only in certain localities, the
union of steam power with water power, so as to combine the
economy of the one with the convenience of the other, presents
probably a result beyond which industry need not go.

I have so far described the amount and the application of
water power, as it is derived from the residual rain water
flowing down the declivity of the country to the sea. This is,
in fact, all that is popularly understood by water power; yet
it is far from being the only source of mechanical industry
which is derived from water. Another of great interest remains to be considered.

From the observations hitherto made it appears, that around
the coasts of Ireland the tide rises through a height, which
may in average be taken at twelve feet. Our tides are derived, that is to say, they result from the action of those vast
masses of water in the great oceans, which being raised above,
or depressed below their proper level by the attractive forces
of the sun and moon, force, in regaining their position, into, or
draw from, the narrow seas and channels, such as ours, quantities of water, which thereby form true currents, as much so
as the current of a river, and are equally available to produce
mechanical effects. Hence the motion of the tide becomes a
source of power, and tide mills form an important variety of
water mills. In England they are scarcely used, coals being
so cheap, but to us, by proper application, I am convinced they
may become an important basis of industry. In order that the
force available from the tide may be properly understood, it
not being much noticed in mechanical books, I shall proceed to
describe the principles of its application more in detail, than
otherwise I should deem necessary.

If we conceive a reservoir situated near the shore, and separated from the sea by a narrow canal, and that at low water the reservoir is dry, we will have the conditions necessary for the economy of motive power. Let the canal be provided with a sluice, and waiting until the tide has risen to a certain height, say two feet, let the sluice be opened, and the water let in, in such quantity that it shall rise in the reservoir as rapidly as the tide rises outside. Hence, through the period of the influx of the tide there will be a current through the canal, with a head of two feet. Finally, the reservoir fills to the same height as the sea outside. Then let the sluice be closed, and remain closed, until the tide has fallen two feet. On opening the sluice the water of the reservoir flows out with a head of two feet, and will continue until the tide is out; the reservoir will then empty itself, and be ready for repeating this operation the next tide.

Now let us consider how this is circumstanced as to time. We may take the duration of a tide as twelve hours twenty minutes, and as the tide in average rises and falls twelve feet in that time, the mean rate of motion of the tide, in height, is found to be one foot in thirty-one minutes. We may take half an hour to a foot without sensible error. Now the tide being out, the sluice must be closed for an hour, in order to allow the water outside to get the head of two feet, with which it has to work. On opening the sluice, it will then flow into the pond, and so continue for five hours, when the tide will be fully in. The reservoir being then allowed to fill completely, for which there is ten minutes available, with additional sluices, the canal is to be closed for an hour, until the sea outside shall have fallen two feet. On opening the sluice the water will issue for five hours, with a two foot head, and then, by the extra sluices, the remaining water of the reservoir may be got rid of in ten minutes, so that it shall be ready to begin again.

The current is thus, with two feet head, for five hours on the rise, and five hours on the fall of each tide ; that is for twenty hours out of the twenty-four. Let us now calculate the theoretical power of this current. As a standard reservoir we shall take the area of an acre. When the tide is fully in, the water in the reservoir shall be as deep as the tide rises, that

I

is twelve feet. Of this, however, the two feet that entered
last is supposed not to have been mechanically employed. The
water of the reservoir which may be used as power is, therefore, ten feet deep. The acre contains consequently 435,600
cubic feet of water. This quantity passes in twice, and passes
out twice in every twenty-four hours; that is, in the twenty-
four hours there are available, 48,400 tons of water falling
through two feet. Now as 884 tons falling twenty-four feet in
twenty-four hours is a horse power, it follows, that the theoretical power of the tide, used with two feet fall, is four one-
half horse power for each acre of reservoir, in which the depth
of the water is equal to the height of rise of the tide. Hence,
ten acres of reservoir should give a theoretic force of forty-
five horse power for twenty hours out of the twenty-four.

Now if this were as in an ordinary stream, nothing could be
more simple than the erection of an undershot wheel, which,
economizing one-third of the theoretic power, should deliver
one and a half working horse power for each acre of reservoir.
But it is easy to observe two circumstances which render the
construction of tide-mills more complicated, and their application more difficult. In fact, the current of water changes its
direction every six hours, as the tide runs in and out. This,
however, is easily met by mechanical contrivances of various
and simple kinds, by which the direction of action of the current is altered, when its own direction changes, so that the
motion transmitted to the machinery remains the same. This,
therefore, is not a real difficulty, although it introduces some
additional mechanism. But it is more important to consider,
that as the level of the tidal water is continually changing, at
the rate, indeed, of two feet in height per hour, the machinery
capable of acting at the lower levels of the tide, should be
totally submerged at the upper; particularly if in place of
the average rise and fall, which we have taken at twelve feet,
we consider the rise and fall at springs, which we may estimate at eighteen feet upon our coasts. From this comes
the greatest difficulty in managing tide-mills. It is, however,
surmounted in either of two ways, which I shall but briefly
notice.

In the first the force of the water is applied to bear up the wheel itself, so that it shall constantly float, rising and falling with the tide. This object has been effected, by letting the pressure of the water act on a water-tight frame, within which the whole mechanism of the wheel is contained. It has been also done by making the extremities of the axle of the wheel rest on the pistons of an hydrostatic press, into which water was injected by the wheel itself. All these means are quite practicable; they are not expensive, but they are troublesome, and the necessity for them has probably been the principal cause of the neglect into which the tide-mill has fallen. The second means of compensating for the change of level in the water consists in employing peculiar forms of wheels, of which many kinds have been proposed, which work even submerged, or, at least, admit of being partly submerged without their power being all destroyed. Such wheels have been described by Belidor, Barlow, and other writers, but I shall not delay upon them. They have the merit of turning round when almost drowned, but they have the fault of not being able to do any important proportion of work. The loss of power in such wheels is so great as to negative their practical employment.

It is thus easily seen, that I do not strongly recommend those tide-mills, which are at present known, whether they work nearly submerged at a constant level, or that they change their level by the aid of complex machinery. I should not, in fact, direct attention to the tidal waters as an important source of power, but that there has been recently invented a machine, which, I conceive, renders them truly available. It is the turbine, already noticed under another point of view. The acting force in the turbine is proportional to the difference between the pressure of the water inside and outside of its cylinder. It is no matter how deep it may be under water, provided this difference is kept up. It works with the same effect; delivers out in practice the same per centage of the theoretic power; and hence realizes absolutely the conditions necessary for the perfect utilization of the motive power of our tides. If, returning to the example of canal and reservoir, which I already employed, there was placed behind the sluice a turbine, and the water let on at the head of two feet, the turbine would deliver out practically two-thirds of the calculated force, at least, and continue to do so all the time that the rise or fall of the waters continued. The mechanical arrangements for the change of direction of rotation, for conducting the water to and from the top and bottom of the machine, are such as will present themselves to the mind of every mechanical engineer, and would be of too purely technical a character for me to notice here.

The turbine is, therefore, peculiarly the machine for economizing tidal power. For each acre of reservoir it may be expected to give at least three horse power, working twenty hours out of the twenty-four. In average for thirty-three acres of reservoir, on which the flood rises in average twelve feet, a working efficiency of 100 horse power may be calculated on.

Now let us consider how many situations on our coasts there are, where flats left bare by the retreating tide, and covered many feet deep with water on its return, are utterly useless in their present state, but only require an embankment easily and cheaply constructible, to be converted into reservoirs for setting tidemills at work. How many places are there, especially on our eastern coast, where reservoirs of vast size appear, indeed, as if presented by nature to tempt man to enterprize, leaving but little for him to do. Ballyteigue, Tacumshane, and the adjacent bays on the Wexford coast are examples of such inlets; narrow at the mouth; capacious inside; formed as if laid out by a skilful engineer. But in some such cases the tides, being complex from local causes, counteract the advantages of their form. The inlets along the shores between Dublin and Drogheda present also many similar cases, though not so curiously affected in adaptation. The areas included between the Kingstown Railway and the shore, may serve to exemplify the facility of embanking such reservoirs, and the tidal currents by which they are filled and emptied. I shall not attempt to calculate the mechanical power that might be created in those situations; I shall leave it as a useful exercise to those, of whom I hope there are many, who may be led by what I have now stated, to think and examine for themselves, and to apply the bases of calculation which have been given in this and the preceding chapters to those instances, and to such others as their own observation may bring before them.

CHAPTER IV.

IMPORTANCE OF IRON IN THE ARTS. ANCIENT MANUFACTURE
OF IRON IN IRELAND. ORES OF IRON. MAGNETIC IRONSTONE.
HEMATITES. BOG IRON ORES. CLAY IRONSTONE OF THE COAL
DISTRICTS. DISTRIBUTION, PROPERTIES, AND COMPOSITION
OF THE IRONSTONES OF THE LEINSTER COAL FIELD. CON-
NAUGHT COAL DISTRICT. IRON ORES OF ARIGNA AND SLIEVE-
A-NIERAN; THEIR ABUNDANCE; THEIR COMPOSITION, COM-
PARED WITH THE BRITISH AND SCOTTISH ORES. SKETCH OF
THE PROCESS OF IRON SMELTING, AND ANALYSES OF THE ELE-
MENTS OF ITS COST IN STAFFORDSHIRE AND IN WALES. PRO-
BABLE COST OF MAKING IRON AT LOUGH ALLEN. EFFECTS
OF THE HOT BLAST ON THE IRON MANUFACTURE IN SCOT-
LAND. ITS POSSIBLE INFLUENCE IN IRELAND. OF THE SMELT-
ING OF IRON BY ANTHRACITE IN WALES AND PENNSYLVANIA.
ITS FEASIBILITY IN THE LEINSTER COAL FIELD. CONVERSION
OF PIG INTO BAR IRON. ANALYSIS OF THE COMPARATIVE
COST IN ENGLAND AND AT LOUGH ALLEN. EMPLOYMENT OF
TURF IN THE MANUFACTURE OF IRON IN GERMANY AND
FRANCE. ANALYSIS OF THE COST OF PRODUCTION OF IRON
BY TURF. REFINING OF IRON WITH TURF: ITS SUPERIOR
QUALITY. INFLUENCE OF THE COST OF FUEL ON THE IRON
MANUFACTURE. RECENT PROCESSES FOR ECONOMIZING THE
WASTE HEAT OF IRON FURNACES. UTILIZATION OF FUELS
OF INFERIOR QUALITY.

IN the preceding chapter I have endeavoured to establish the
conditions, under which are found in Ireland two elements, essential above all others to the prosecution of manufacturing
industry, fuel and power, and to analyse the relation, which
the cost of motive power in mechanical operations, bears to the
other circumstances. There remain for examination, however,
other subjects of not inferior interest or importance, and of
these one will specially require a detailed notice, as it affects the
industrial arts almost in an equal degree with the cost of fuel.
I shall, therefore, endeavour to represent in the following notice, the circumstances under which this country is placed with
regard to the supply and manufacture of *iron*. This metal is,
indeed, indispensable to an advanced condition of the arts. If
we employ fuel to give motion to our machinery, we as inevita-

bly employ iron in the construction of the machine. Its various properties adapt it to our uses in an unparalleled degree: as we require massive strength or delicacy of form, whether we wish our material to be rigid or highly elastic, hard or soft, iron is that which satisfies our wants; fusible in one condition, infusible, but highly plastic in another, it is capable of being moulded, welded, turned, ground, and polished; whilst by the wise economy of nature, fortunately for man, being found in every country, and available at a small expense, its supply is practically unlimited. Its use has hence become at once the cause and measure of material progress. A nation without iron cannot emerge from the condition of semi-barbarism. Its chiefs may be magnificent in gold and jewels; its warriors may be armed with shields and swords of bronze, on which the labour of long practised workmen may bestow a finish, admirable even at the present day; but the rarity and cost, as well of material as of artificer, deprive the general population of all power to render those precious metals available to their domestic comfort. It is only where iron is obtainable; where, cheap and abundant, it places within the reach of all, the means of constructing the various tools and instruments by which the arts and agriculture are so materially advanced, that civilization can become firmly grounded amongst a people. If we consider how each succeeding step in industry places the elements of material domestic comfort more cheaply in the power of a people; that by this greater cheapness and facility of procuring the means of animal existence, there is afforded time for mental cultivation, and growing out of that, by proper discipline, a sounder morality, a love of peace and justice, we may well recognize in coal and iron, agents of civilization and of intellectual happiness to man, of whose powers, astounding as they appear, we trace but the infant energies—of whose final results we can no more apply a measure, than could the savage, who, sensible of the value of the tool, barters his golden ornaments for a knife, estimate the industrial and educational movements of the present day.

The variety of properties which fits iron so wonderfully for its uses in the arts, is the foundation also of a variety in its

money value, which I shall here notice, as it will be found to
affect, in a very material degree, the circumstances of this
country as to its manufacture. In fact, so cheaply is the metal
itself obtained, that its subsequent adaptation to different uses
demands a degree of mechanical skill and labour which over-
shadows totally the cost of the iron employed; and hence, in
the following table, selected from results given by Babbage
and Friedenberg, the increase of value is for the most part
made up of the cost of labour bestowed upon the article in the
various processes it passes through.

The quantity of cast iron worth £1 sterling becomes worth
the following sums, when converted into

Ordinary machinery, ...	£4
Larger ornamental work, ...	45
Buckles, . Berlin work, ...	660
Neck chains, ,, ,, ...	1386
Shirt buttons, ,, ,, ...	5896

The quantity of bar iron worth £1 sterling becomes, when
formed into

Horse shoes, worth	£2 10s.
Knives (table), ...	36 0
Needles, ...	71 0
Penknife blades, ...	657 0
Polished buttons and buckles, ...	897 0
Balance springs of watches, ...	50,000 0

Some centuries ago Ireland presented a picture of manufacturing industry, such as we would now find, perhaps, in the
interior of Russia, or the mountainous districts of northern
Spain, but which the progress of the arts has banished from
Britain and from central Europe. Covered with forests, and
possessing iron ore, as we shall hereafter shew, of the highest
purity in great abundance, Ireland was sprinkled over with
small iron works, in which the wood charcoal was employed,
and thus iron manufactured of excellent quality; in fact, such
as we now import from Sweden and Russia for all the finer purposes of cutlery and mechanism. Such kinds of iron furnaces
may be considered as now belonging but to the history of art;

yet in an historical point of view it is not uninteresting to extract some particulars of this industry amongst ourselves, from
the remarkable work on the natural history of Ireland, written
by Dr. Boate two centuries ago.

" Of the iron mines there are three sorts in Ireland, for in
some places the oar of the iron is drawn out of moores and
bogs, in others it is hewen out of rocks, and in others it is digged
out of mountains: of which three sorts the first is called bog-
mine, the other rock-mine, and the third with several names,
white-mine, pin-mine, and shell-mine.

" The first sort, as we have said, and as the name itself doth
shew, is found in low and boggie places, out of the which it is
raised with very little charge, as lying not deep at all, commonly on the superficies of the earth, and about a foot in thickness. This oar is very rich of metal, and that very good and
tough, nevertheless in the melting it must be mingled with
some of the mine or oar of some of the other sorts : for else it
is too harsh, and keeping the furnace too hot, it melteth too
suddenly, and stoppeth the mouth of the furnace, or, to use
the workmen's own expression, choaketh the furnace.

" The second sort, that which is taken out of rocks, being a
hard and meer stony substance, of a dark and rustie colour,
doth not lye scattered in several places, but is a piece of the
very rock, of the which it is hewen : which rock being covered
over with earth, is within equally every where of the same substance ; so as the whole rock, and every parcel thereof, is oar
of iron. This mine, as well as the former, is raised with little
trouble, for the iron-rock, being full of joints, is with pick-axes
easily divided and broken into pieces of what bigness one will :
which by reason of the same joints, whereof they are full every
where, may easily be broke into other lesser pieces ; as that is
necessary, before they be put into the furnace.

" Of this kind hitherto there hath but two mines been discovered in Ireland, the one in Munster, near the town of Tallow, by the Earl of Cork's iron works; the other in Leinster,
in King's County, in a place called Desart land, belonging to
one Sergeant-Major Piggot, which rock is of so great a compass, that before this rebellion it furnished divers great iron
works, and could have furnished many more, without any nota-

ble diminution; seeing the deepest pits that have been yet made in it, were not above two yards deep. The land, under which this rock lieth, is very good and fruitful, as much as any other land thereabouts, the mold being generally two feet and two and a half, and in many places three feet deep.

" The third sort of iron-mine is digg'd out of the mountains in several parts of the kingdom; in Ulster, in the county of Fermanagh, upon Lough Earn, in the county of Cavan, in a place called Doubally, in a dry mountain; and in the county of nether-Tyrone, by the side of the rivulet Lishan, not far from Lough Neagh; at the foot of the mountains Slew-galen, mentioned by us upon another occasion, in the beginning of this chapter; in Leinster; in King's-county, hard by Mount-mellick; and in Queen's-county, two miles from Mountrath; in Connaught; in Tomound, or the county of Clare, six miles from Limerick; in the county of Roscommon, by the side of Lough Allen; and in the county of Leitrim, on the east side of the said lough, where the mountains are so full of this metal, that thereof it hath got in Irish the name of *Slew Nerin*, that is, mountains of iron: and in the province of Munster also in sundry places.

" This sort is of a whitish or grey colour, like that of ashes; and one needs not take much pains for to find it out, for the mountains which do contain it within themselves, do commonly shew it of their own accord, so as one may see the veins thereof at the very outside in the side of the mountains, being not very broad, but of great length, and commonly divers in one place, five or six ridges the one above the other, with ridges of earth between them.

" These veins or ridges are vulgarly called pins, from whence the mine hath the name of pin-mine; being also called white-mine, because of its whitish colour; and shell-mine, for the following reason; for this stuff or oar being neither loose or soft as earth or clay, neither firm and hard as stone, is of a middle substance between both, somewhat like unto slate, composed of shells or scales, they which do lie one upon another, and may be separated and taken asunder very easily, without any great force or trouble. This stuff is digged out of the ground in lumps of the bigness of a man's head, bigger or less, according as the vein affordeth opportunity. Within every one of these lumps, when the mine is very rich and of the best sort (for all the oar of this kind is not of equal goodness, some yielding more and better iron than other), lieth a small kernal, which hath the name of hony-comb given to it, because it is full of little holes, in the same manner as that substance whereof it borroweth its appellation.

" The iron coming of this oar is not brittle, as that of the rock-mine, but tough, and in many places as good as any Spanish iron."

It would be difficult at the present day, independent of chemical analysis, to furnish a better description than that given two centuries ago by Boate, as just quoted, of the bog-iron, which is found in patches in almost every part of this island, and of the ironstone, of which the very rich quality of Lough Allen, and that of the Leinster district, was even then recognized. I shall return hereafter to the question of their composition, but before leaving Dr. Boate I shall extract his account of the financial condition of the iron trade in Ireland, as it will shew the difference between the cost of manufacture then, and in the present day.

" To speak somewhat more particularly both of the charges and profits of these iron-works, we shall instance the matter in one of the works of the said Sir Charles Coot, namely that which he had in the lordship of Mountrath, in Queen's-county. At that work the tun (that is twenty hundred weight) of rock-mine at the furnace head came in all to stand in five shillings and six-pence sterling, and the tun of white-mine, which he had brought him from a place two miles further off, in seven shillings. These two were mixed in that proportion, that to one part of rock-mine were taken two parts of white-mine : for if more of the rock-mine had been taken, the iron would not have been so good, and too brittle ; and being thus mixed, they yielded one-third part of iron : that is to say, of two tuns of white-mine, and one of rock-mine, being mingled and melted together, they had one tun of good iron, such as is called merchant's iron, being not of the first, but second melting, and hammered out into bars, and consequently fit for all kinds of use.

" This iron he sent down the river Oure (by others called
the Nure) to Rosse and Waterford, in that kind of Irish boats
which are called cots in that country, being made of one piece
of timber : which kind of ill favoured boats (mentioned also by
us above) are very common throughout all Ireland, both for to
pass rivers in, and to carry goods from one place to another ;
and not only upon shallow waters, such as the aforenamed
river is, in the greatest part of its course, but even upon the
great rivers and loughs.

" At Waterford the iron was put aboard of ships going for
London, where it was sold for sixteen, otherwhiles for seventeen pounds sterling, and sometimes for seventeen and a half;
whereas it did not stand Sir Charles Coot in more than betwixt
ten and eleven pounds sterling, all charges reckoned, as well
of digging, melting, fining, as of carrying, boat-hire and freight,
even the custom also comprehended in it.

" In most of the other places did a tun of the iron-mine or
oar come to stand in five, five and a half, and six shillings sterling at the furnace head ; and it was an ordinary thing, as well
where they used white-mine, as where they mixed rock-mine
with it, to have a tun of good iron out of three tuns of oar : in
some places, where the mine was richer, they would have a tun
of iron out of only two tuns and a half of oar.   Nevertheless
few of them gained more or as much as Sir Charles Coot, because they had not the same conveniency of transportation ;
and he himself did not gain so much by his iron works in Connaught, as by that near Mountrath, although the mines there
afforded a richer oar, and that the tun thereof, did cost him but
three shillings at the furnace, because that Lough Allen,
whereunto the same mines and works are contiguous, gave
him the opportunity of carrying the oar by water from the
mine unto the work, and that in boats of forty tuns.

" The Earl of Cork, whose iron works being seated in Munster, afforded unto him very good opportunity of sending his
iron out of the land by shipping, did in this particular surpass
all others, so as he hath gained great treasures thereby : and
knowing persons, who have had a particular insight into his
affairs, do assure me, that he hath profited above one hundred
thousand pounds clear gain by his said iron works."

We thus see that two hundred years ago iron was an article of export from Ireland to London.

In fact, as well in Ireland as in England, where, at the same time, the same processes of manufacture were followed, the vast quantity of wood consumed, to make charcoal for the iron works, gradually stripped the country of its forests, and with the supply of fuel, of course the working of iron was abandoned. Similar causes are at the present moment in operation on the Continent of Europe, and limit the economic manufacture of iron by means of wood, to those countries in which a thinly scattered population admits of large tracts being occupied in growing timber. The wonderfully fortunate destiny of England, however, intervened at that very time, when her iron trade was in process of rapid annihilation. The energy and genius of one man, to whose name the deserved honour has never yet been paid by England, rescued her from becoming a mere dependant for iron on the north of Europe, and by inventing the process of reducing iron by means of coke, made the first step in the path of technical discovery which rendered that country the industrial sovereign of the world. It would not be difficult to shew, that had not Dudley substituted coke for charcoal in smelting iron, the conditions of industry which gave field for Watt and Arkwright, could scarcely have existed. In Ireland there was no man like Dudley. The iron manufacture in England assumed a new and enlarged existence. The iron manufacture of Ireland rapidly declined, and finally, a century ago, in Kerry, the last charcoal furnace was extinguished, when they had burned out the last remaining wood.

It is necessary now to examine, with all the aid which modern science, and the experience of other countries, may afford us, how the materials necessary for the manufacture of iron are circumstanced with us.

The ores of iron that are actually employed as sources of the metal are of three kinds, the anhydrous peroxide, or specular iron; the hydrous peroxide, including hematite and bog ore; and the carbonate of iron, to which the clay-ironstone of the coal formations belongs.

Of the first kind of ore, there is but one locality in which it has hitherto become of industrial importance, the island of Elba, which has been celebrated from the earliest ages for the goodness of its iron and steel, obtained by the working of this ore. It is the richest ore of iron that is known, containing 70 per cent. of metal; but as it cannot be smelted on the spot, it has been rendered unimportant by the superior economy of working inferior ores in more suitable localities, and the celebrity of Elba as a source of iron is now but a fact in history. To us this ore is not without interest nevertheless. It has been found, and in some quantity, in the south of Ireland. I possess excellent specimens from the Cosheen mines at Skibbereen, and from the Glandore mines in Carberry. It is there associated with ores of copper and of manganese, which being of far greater value, the iron ore is not looked after: but it might be of considerable use to mix with the poorer ores of other districts, should circumstances ever justify the practical development of iron working in Ireland.

The second kind of ore is of more practical importance, being probably the most extensively diffused of all the compounds of iron. It presents itself under a great variety of forms, according to the rocks with which it is associated, and the circumstances under which it has had its origin, and hence furnishes to the mineralogist a number of species, the detailed description of which I need not enter upon. When quite pure this ore is a hydrate of the peroxide of iron, in which the oxide contains twice as much oxygen as the water, having the formula, $2 Fe_2 O_3 + 3 HO$, and containing:

Iron, ...	60·0
Oxygen, ...	25·6
Water, ...	14·4
	100

Various forms of it support the majority of the iron furnaces of France and Germany. In England it is not employed, except to bring up, by its richness of produce, the poorer ores of the coal districts, to the standard at which their working becomes most easy. The forms of it require notice as to their composition and distribution in Ireland. These are the brown nodular hematite, and the ochrey or bog iron ore. In the pure state it is but rarely found, and is then associated with the specular iron, and with other ores in the rocks of the older formations. It is hence not smelted by itself.

The brown iron ore is found in abundance associated with the beds of coal and fire-clay, and the ordinary ironstone, in the coal district of Tyrone. I have examined specimens of it, not picked, but taken at random from heaps of it thrown out of the pits, and which may, therefore, represent its usual quality. It is the variety termed popularly *eagle-stone*, and forms globular masses of a deep brown colour, which are generally hollow, and contain a kernel of a lighter colour than the exterior, with which, however, it agrees in constitution. The specimens I analysed yielded:

Peroxide of iron, ...	80·79
Water, ...	11·97
Magnesia, ...	0·27
Insoluble matter, ...	5·81
Oxide of manganese, ...	1·16
	100·00

This ore should hence have given by appropriate treatment 57 of iron per cent., or from 35 cwt. of ore a ton of iron.

Of the similar ores actually employed upon the Continent, there are scarcely any materially richer than this. The following numbers shew the composition of the principal French and German ores of this class:

	FRANCE.		GERMANY.	
	L'AUDE.	ALLEVARD.	STYRIA.	CARINTHIA.
Peroxide of iron, . .	82·8	79·6	78·5	77·5
Oxide of manganese,	3·6	3·5	1·9	2·7
Lime and magnesia,	0·7	1·0	9·6	1·7
Insoluble matter, . .	3·2	4·8	0·9	3·6
Water, ...	9·7	11·1	9·1	14·5
	100·0	100·0	100·0	100·0

Although we do not know exactly the causes which led to the formation of these concretionary masses of hydrated oxide of iron, it is quite certain that these causes are now in operation, and that the production of considerable quantities of this material is actually going on. We find in almost every deep morass, beds of it, sometimes a foot thick. It is hence called bog iron ore. This ore supported the majority of the small iron furnaces formerly scattered over the surface of this country. It appears as a brownish clay, which dries to a mass, sometimes dense and hard, at others friable, and becomes much darker in colour when it dries. Its origin appears to be connected with the former existence of tribes of minute animals, of which the fossilized remains may be detected in it by the microscope. This also explains a fact in its composition which seriously affects the quality of the iron obtained from it, the presence of phosphoric acid, and there occurs also black oxide of manganese, sometimes in such quantity that it might as well be called an ore of manganese as of iron.

The bog iron ore of Ireland has not yet been analysed, but I annex the composition of three foreign specimens, in order that the nature of this mineral may be shewn.

	SCHLESWIG.	DAMMEROW.	POMERANIA.
Peroxide of iron, . . .	62·92	23·24	56·45
Oxide of manganese, . .	4·18	20·40	2·60
Phosphoric acid, . . .	3·44	2·01	1·75
Water, ...	18·40	21·85	22·60
Silica, ...	7·06	7·75	12·20
Vegetable matter, . .	,,	0·10	0·10
Sand, ...	,	24·65	4·30
Alumina, ...	4·00	,,	,,
	100·00	100·00	100·00

These bog iron ores are smelted with the greatest ease. They are at once very fusible and easily reduced. They produce a metal which runs very thin and congeals slowly, so that it is proper for the manufacture of cast iron articles which do not require much strength. As all the phosphorus of the ore passes into the metal, this is sometimes very fragile. The Berlin ornaments, which as specimens of casting, and as objects of art, excite so much admiration, are made of iron smelted from the bog iron ore of the vast morasses of the east of Prussia: analyses of two of these ores are amongst those just now given I have not been able to ascertain the extent to which this ore of iron may now exist within our bogs; nor do I consider it a question of much importance, as it will be hereafter seen, that ores of much richer character, and yielding a purer metal, are so abundant, as to render the bog iron ore merely an object of curiosity to us.

The substitution, by Dudley, of coal coke for charcoal in the manufacture of iron, created a revolution, not only in the kind of fuel, but in the kind of ore employed, and indeed in the localities where the manufacture could advantageously be carried on. Before that time, the minerals employed were the various kinds of hematites, more or less pure, such as we have in Tyrone, and the bog iron ores; but it was found, that in almost every coal district there occurs an ore of iron, quite different from those, and which is now known as clay-ironstone. The richness of this ore varies vary much, but being found in immediate proximity to the fuel, and still more the coal beds presenting various other mineral materials of use in the manufacture, it was found more advantageous to smelt it than to bring either richer ores from a distance to the fuel, or the fuel any distance to the richer ores, and hence the iron manufacture was located, and has since remained, in the coal districts of Great Britain, which the superior economy of its processes and of its materials will probably maintain as its head quarters for numerous ages to come.

In fact, the manufacture of iron requires a variety of materials, which it would be very expensive to bring together, did their sources lie at considerable distances, and hence the cost of the metal produced should be considerably higher, and thereby its extent of use and of manufacture limited in proportion. But by an organization of nature, of which it is impossible to exaggerate the wisdom and the importance to mankind, the coal measures rest upon, and contain beds of hard and infusible sandstone, of which the most refractory portions of the furnaces may be built. The coal rests usually on clay, of which the best fire-bricks may be formed; dispersed in layers through the slate which covers the coal, is found in abundance the iron ore, whilst the limestone necessary as a flux, lies on the edges of the coal basin, where the underlying calcareous strata come to the surface.

Now this combination of sandstone for hearths, clay for crucibles and for bricks, lime for flux, ore and coal for smelting, is not restricted to any one coal district. The same is found in England and Wales, the same in Scotland, and in fact, were any one of those materials absent or difficult to be procured, the economic manufacture of the metal would be impossible.

A knowledge of these circumstances is necessary, that we may compare the means which we possess in Ireland for making iron, with those of other countries. That there is ore is certain, that there is fuel is certain, but if the ore, the fuel, the clay, and all the other conditions do not conspire, the economic manufacture becomes impossible, and an attempt would only ruin those who unadvisedly engaged upon it.

The clay ironstone which has thus become almost the exclusive source of iron to Great Britain, occurs in great abundance in this country, in the coal districts of Leinster and of Connaught; it is not of the same quality or appearance in both, and as the difference is not without importance in its application, it will be necessary to notice each in turn.

It will hence be easily understood, how, in order to trace the localities of the clay ironstone, it is necessary to revert to the description of the coal formations given in a former chapter, and indeed to complete their history by an account of the ores of iron which they contain. I shall, however, only enter into detail with regard to two of those districts, those of Connaught and of Leinster, as the other coal districts do not appear to me to present any features sufficiently promising in relation to iron to render them important.

In the Leinster district a succession of beds of slate, sandstone, and clay, are associated with the coal, according to an order which has been very perfectly illustrated by the Reports of Mr. Griffith already noticed. The clay ironstone occurs abundantly in nodules disseminated through the layers of slate, from which they separate spontaneously by weathering, or are easily detached. The total thickness of this slate is estimated at 239 feet, distributed in eight beds. Its characters are represented by those given in the following words of Mr. Griffith's description of the second bed from below. Its thickness was thirty feet.

"Spheroidal slate-clay, containing balls of clay ironstone frequently one foot in thickness. By spheroidal slate-clay is meant a species of hard slate, which on being exposed to the atmosphere, divides into large flattened spheroids; on being struck the outer coat comes off, and leaves a smaller spheroid, which being again struck, a second concentric coat is separated, and so on until the nucleus is met with, which sometimes is composed of hard claystone, and sometimes of clay ironstone. The ironstone contained in this bed is very rich, and in many places remains of ancient excavations are still visible where this bed has been wrought in search of ironstone, and indeed some of the iron furnaces may be seen."

All the other beds assimilate to this in character. The quantity of ironstone present is of course in proportion to that of the rock in which it is disseminated; its quantity may be inferred from the results of borings given by Mr. Griffith. Thus in a deep bore-hole at Massford, down to the four foot coal, where the total depth was sixty-eight yards, the layers of pure ironstone amounted to thirty-eight inches, and the strata were found to be constituted of

Sinking to rock, ...	8 yards.	
Sandstone, ...	31 ,,	
Slate-clay, ...	25 ,,	
Ironstone, ...	1 ,,	2 inches.
Coal and kelve, ...	3 ,,	
	68 yards.	

In a boring at Moneen Roe, near Massford, which extended eighty-four yards, six feet nine inches of pure ironstone were found. The strata consisting of

Sinking by pit, ...	16 yards.	
Sandstone, ...	32 ,,	
Slate-clay, ...	31 ,,	
Ironstone, ...	2 ,,	9 inches.
Coal and kelve, ...	3 ,,	
	84 yards.	

It is necessary to describe more specially the properties and composition of this ironstone. Specimens presented to me by Mr. Wandesford, from his collieries at Castlecomer, gave the following results:

The colour is dark gray when fresh, but becoming rust coloured by long exposure to the air. The specific gravity is about 3·250. When ignited it loses 29 per cent. of its weight, and the residue is strongly attracted by the magnet. Two different specimens analysed, gave the following results:

	No. 1.	No. 2.
Protoxide of iron, ...	51·08	48·03
Lime, ...	·16	1·51
Magnesia, ...	1·05	4·24
Alumina, ...	1·86	1·45
Insoluble matter, ...	13·92	16·17
Carbonic acid, ...	31·93	28·60
	100·00	100·00

Of these ores No. 1 contains 39·7 per cent. of iron, and No. 2 37·6. As they were not selected for analysis on account of any apparent superiority to other specimens, they may probably represent the ordinary run of the ironstone of the Leinster district.

The supply of the iron ore in this district is not limited to the clay slate lying deep among the coal strata. The other sources of it are thus described by Mr. Tighe in his Survey of the county of Kilkenny : " We have already seen that the slate covering the collieries contains nodules of iron ore, and this ore is very heavy and rich, but some of the best iron mines lie open to the surface, and form the upper strata of entire hills. Hills of this kind run in a north-east direction from Lady Ormond's demesne towards the colliery. On the lands of Aghamucky is a hollow road cut to a great depth through a rich mine of iron; from this place the ore was formerly carried to be smelted at Mountrath, in the Queen's County, as long as the timber lasted in that neighbourhood." The richness of these ores may be inferred from the account of Boate, that when the ore was good, two and a half tons of it gave a ton of iron, but in common, one ton for three was expected.

The abundance of ironstone found in the Connaught coal district gave origin to several works for the reduction of the metal at that early period, when the extensive woods supplied charcoal for the furnaces; and almost without intermission, since the invention of the method of smelting by means of coal and coke, attempts have been made at various times, and by different individuals, to carry on iron works in that locality. These attempts have hitherto failed, owing to circumstances, of which most were of a nature purely personal, and cannot be noticed here. Other sources of failure were connected with the conditions of the manufactures and of the locality itself, and it will be in another place important to trace and illustrate those, in order that we may judge whether the difficulties, before which so many have sunk, are in themselves really insurmountable.

It is necessary first to describe the composition and distribution of the ore.

On the eastern shore of Lough Allen rises the Iron Mountain (Slieve-a-Nierin), a hill of considerable elevation. It consists of alternate beds of sandstone and slate-clay resting upon the basis of the upper limestone. The great bed of slate-clay varies from 300 to 500 feet in thickness; others are of different but lesser magnitude. In this clay the nodules of ironstone are disseminated in abundance; and the rains, washing away the softened and decomposing clay, the balls of ore are carried down to the shore of the lake, whence, and from the beds of the rivulets, they are collected by the peasantry and brought to the works for use. At the base of this mountain, on the eastern side of the outlet of the lake, lies Drumshambo, where this ore was formerly smelted. I shall hence designate this ore from the eastern side of the basin as Drumshambo ore. In purity it is somewhat superior to that which is found on the western side.

The southern and western division of this coal field is popularly known from the River Arigna, which is its northern boundary, and whose name became notorious by the iron works established on its banks, the history of which has so fatally influenced industrial enterprize in Ireland.   The stratification of the mountain is similar to that of the opposite side ; resting on the limestone of the surrounding country, occurs the great bed of slate-clay, 600 feet in thickness, and containing numerous beds of ironstone, from half an inch to two feet in thickness.   Their number is, as Mr. Griffith mentions, almost incredible, but the most important occur from 200 to 300 feet above the limestone.   The same eminent geologist describes the thin beds as being in most cases the best, but that of Altagowlan, which is a foot thick, was amongst the richest ironstone Mr. Griffith ever saw.   The usual form is that of nodules, in size from an egg to that of a bull's head ; but it forms also strata, or sheets of considerable extent.   In many places the bed of the River Arigna in its whole breadth is formed of a flag of ironstone, which is often many perches in length.   On this side of the lake also, owing to the weathering of the slate-clay, the nodules of ironstone are deposited in vast quantities in the beds of the mountain streams.   Were the ore employed this source would soon become exhausted, and of course the beds of ironstone should then be worked *in situ*, as they are elsewhere.

Mr. Twigg, whose observations on the Arigna district are the most recent, thus speaks, in his Report made to the Directors of the Arigna Company in 1830: " The ironstone mines have been examined, and the result found extremely favourable. A greater variety of ironstones I never met with, from which, by a proper admixture and proper management, I have no hesitation in saying, that pig-iron of best marks, and fit for foundry work of every kind, may be obtained. The iron mines begin in Rover, and continue for two miles and a half. I measured several of the beds to more than two feet thick, in some places laid bare in the ravines, and in the bed of the Arigna river we can get any quantity at the shortest notice. There is enough to last two furnaces for 250 years."

In quantity there is no doubt but that the ironstone of this district is practicably inexhaustible. In order to ascertain its quality, I have effected accurate analyses of numerous specimens of it, obtained from different portions of the district. Their detailed characters and composition follow:

CLAY IRONSTONE NODULES FROM ARIGNA.

	No. 1.	No. 2.	No. 3.
Protoxide of iron, . . .	53·65	54·42	51·52
Lime, ...	,,	2·23	0·69
Magnesia, ...	,,	2·02	1·55
Alumina, ...	1·00	1.43	,,
Insoluble clay, ...	12·43	8·65	15·50
Carbonic acid, ...	32·92	31·25	30·74
	100·00	100·00	100·00

Of these ores, No. 1 lost 31·5 per cent. in roasting, and contained 41·7 per cent. of iron; No. 2 lost 30·9 per cent. by roasting, and contained 42·3 per cent. of iron; No. 3 lost 30·7 per cent. by roasting and contained 40 per cent. of iron.

Of the veins of ironstone, two specimens were analysed taken *in situ.* They gave:

	No. 4.	No. 5.
Protoxide of iron, ...	47·28	49·94
Lime, ...	1·26	3·75
Magnesia, ...	2·23	3·79
Alumina, ...	1·59	0·87
Insoluble clay, ...	18·46	9·08
Carbonic acid, ...	29·18	32·57
	100·00	100·00

No. 4 lost by roasting 32·14 per cent. of its weight, and contains 37·7 of metallic iron.   No. 5 loses 29·80 per cent. of its weight, and contained 38·8 per cent of iron.

In Nos. 2, 3 and 5 there existed traces of manganese, too minute, however, to be numerically stated. Nos. 1 and 4 were absolutely free from that impurity.

As none of these were picked specimens, the average of all of them may be fairly calculated as the material available on the large scale at Lough Allen, and the mean of the above five analyses gives:

Protoxide of iron,	51·36
Lime,	1·59
Magnesia,	1·92
Alumina,	0·98
Insoluble clay,	12·82
Carbonic acid,	31·33
	100·00

And this contains 40 per cent. of metallic iron.

The loss by calcining, the iron remaining as protoxide, should be in average 31·33 per cent., and the calcined ore should consist in 100 parts of,

Iron,	58·2
Oxygen,	16·6
Lime and magnesia,	5·1
Clay,	20·1
	100·00

It is not enough thus to have determined the composition of the ironstones of the Leinster and Connaught coal fields, but in order to ascertain how far they may become of use, we must compare them with the ores employed in the principal seats of the iron trade in the sister kingdom.

MM. Dufresnoy and Berthier have analysed the ores of iron worked in Staffordshire and in South Wales.   Their results are briefly the following.

In Staffordshire the thick, rounded nodules, having a blackish grey fracture, are called *gubbins ;* these are rare. The usual ore is in thin flattened veins, bluish grey in colour, and is called *blue-flat*. These consist, in 100 parts, of

BLUE-FLAT.

Protoxide of iron,	36·25
Lime,	2·50
Insoluble residue,	31·50
Carbonic acid,	29·75
	100·00

This ore gives 28 per cent of iron.

GUBBIN.

Protoxide of iron,	52·50
Lime,	2·66
Insoluble residue,	12·66
Carbonic acid, &c.,	32·18
	100·00

This ore gives 40·5 per cent. of iron.

Every thing which gives more than 20 per cent. of iron is reckoned as ore, but the price depends on the quality. Thus the gubbins are worth more than twice as much as the blue-flats.

The following analyses give in a similar manner the composition of the rich and usual kinds of the Welsh ore:

	USUAL ORE.	RICH ORE.
Protoxide of iron,	41·4	54·1
Lime,	6·0	,,
Insoluble residue,	22·8	8·4
Carbonic acid,	29·8	37·5
	100·0	100·0
Yield of iron,	31·4	42·1

The ironstone of the coal field of Lanarkshire is well known for its richness, and has been, indeed, the foundation stone of the commercial prosperity of Glasgow. A series of accurate analyses of those ores has been made by Dr. Colquhoun, of which the most important are subjoined.

CROSS BASKET RONSTONE.

Protoxide of iron, ...	42·15
Lime, ...	4·93
Magnesia, ...	4·80
Silica, ...	9·73
Alumina, ...	3·77
Bituminous matter, ...	3·12
Carbonic acid, ...	31·50
	100·00

MUSHET'S BLACK BAND.

Protoxide of iron, ...	53·03
Lime, ...	3·33
Magnesia, ...	1·77
Silica, ...	1·40
Alumina, ...	0·63
Peroxide of iron, ...	0·23
Bituminous matter, ...	3·03
Moisture and loss, ...	1·41
Carbonic acid, ...	35·17
	100·00

The latter ore, the richest known, except some Welsh specimens, yields 41 of metallic iron per cent. The Cross Basket ore, which may be taken as the usual run of the ores of the Clyde district, yields 31·6 per cent of iron.

I shall now compare more directly the contents in metallic iron of the native ores, and of the English, Scotch, and Welsh. 100 parts of ore give of metal:

	NATURAL STATE.	ROASTED.
Richest Arigna ore, ...	42·3	61·4
Poorest ,, ,, ...	37·7	53·2
Average ,, ,, ...	40·0	58·2
Common Staffordshire ore, . . .	28·0	40·4
Richest ,, ,,	40·5	60·0
Ordinary Welsh ore, ...	31·4	44·7
Richest ,, ,, ...	42 1	60·0

	NATURAL STATE.	ROASTED.
Ordinary Glasgow ore, ...	31·6	45·8
Mushet's black band, ...	41·0	63·1
Average Kilkenny ore, ...	38·7	55·3

There is hence no doubt but that the ores of the Leinster and Connaught coal fields are equal, and even in average superior, to those generally employed in Great Britain. The ironstone of Kilkenny is but little inferior to that of Arigna, whilst the ores of Lough Allen attain a richness in iron, only equalled by the black band ironstone of Glasgow.

It is necessary, however, to trace further the conditions of the iron manufacture in these districts, for, as has been already mentioned, such is the economy required in this department of industry, that unless there be upon the spot all the materials to be used, the cost of obtaining them would be too high. Now in order to smelt and work iron, there are required building materials for the furnaces, which must be formed of infusible sandstone and of the most refractory bricks, for which fire-clay is necessary. These substances are found abundantly interstratified with the slate-clay and coal; their detailed description will be given elsewhere, but their properties are such, as may be now assumed to present no obstacle to the manufacture. To flux the earthy material of the ore, lime must be added. This is in all cases accessible, as the whole coal field rests on limestone, which presents itself on every side within short distances. Finally, the coal necessary for the smelting of the ore is derivable from the same formation; but as our coal beds are thin and limited in size, and hence more difficult to work than the larger beds of the British coal fields, it becomes a question whether the greater price of the coals in Ireland is not prohibitory to the manufacture. In order to appreciate how far this acts, it is necessary to trace somewhat in detail the conditions of the smelting process, and the proportions of the materials used.

The smelting of iron from the ore is accomplished in furnaces of great size, generally termed high furnaces. Their dimensions vary; the height is usually from forty to fifty feet; the external form is that of a massive tower, the interior is divided into four portions, of different forms, and acting differently in the smelting process.   The lowest is the hearth or crucible, formed of the most refractory sandstone of the coal field, built as a rectangular prism, and widening at top into the second portion, which is built also of sandstone. From this the dimensions of the cavity rapidly expand, forming the lower body, or *boshes ;* this part of the furnace is conical, with its base upwards, on which the body of the furnace rises, constituting about two-thirds of the entire height, and extending to the top, where it supports a chimney of about ten feet high.

Near the bottom of the furnace are formed apertures, by which the pipes from the blowing machines are introduced, to force air into the furnace.   These apertures are termed *tuyeres.* On one side of the hearth is the arrangement for opening, so that the melted metal may be run out as soon as a suitable quantity has collected, and also that the slags formed in the process may be discharged as they come down.

Such being the structure of the furnace, the process followed is easily understood.   The ore contains oxide of iron ; the fuel contains carbon ; when these are heated together the oxygen unites with the carbon, and the iron is set free.   The iron itself combines also with some carbon, so that it assumes the state of metal or cast iron, in which, being fusible, it melts, runs down to the bottom, and accumulating in the crucible, is run off at certain intervals into moulds prepared on the floor of the apartment in sand, where solidifying, it forms the masses commercially termed *pigs.*   It may have been remarked, however, that the ore contains from 10 to 20 per cent. of foreign materials, such as silica, alumina, magnesia, and that the fuel employed contains ashes from 5 to 15 per cent of the same materials.   These, at a high temperature, would react on the oxide of iron, and interfere with its reduction; and also forming difficulty fusible clinkers would impede the descent of the fuel and ore, and disturb the progress of the operation.   All this evil is avoided by the use of a certain quantity of lime. This, uniting with the silica and alumina, forms an easily fusible slag, a kind of glass, which runs down into the crucible, where it floats upon the liquid iron, and as it accumulates, is run off through an aperture temporarily opened for the purpose.

Before placing these materials in the high furnace, there are two preliminary operations performed. First, the calcining of the ore, and second, the cokeing of the coal. For these processes, as they involve the expulsion of a large body of volatile matter at a low heat, would, if carried on in the high furnace, produce such a cooling effect as might retard, if not stop, the work entirely. The mineral is broken into small pieces, and being mixed with some coal, this is set on fire and allowed to burn slowly. About 30 per cent. of the weight of the ore is thus driven off, consisting of carbonic acid, and of any water that it contained

The loss which the Irish ores suffered by calcination has been described already. It may be mentioned, however, that when the roasting takes place in the air, the iron is partially converted into peroxide, whilst, when it has been effected in close vessels, the residue contains the iron as black magnetic oxide, and carbonic oxide is evolved

The cokeing of the coal for the purposes of the iron furnaces is accomplished by a partial combustion in great heaps, by means of such a limited supply of air, that little but the volatile portions of the coal is driven off. The quantity of coke produced varies, according to the quality of the coal and the care with which the process is conducted, being from 50 to 65 per cent. of the weight of the coal. The quantity and quality of the coke obtained from the different varieties of Irish fuel have been given already.

Such being the general conditions of the process of smelting iron from the ore, it now remains to trace the elements of its money cost, and to apply the experience and results of other districts to the circumstances which prevail in Ireland. I shall, therefore, first briefly describe the estimates of cost of fabricating pig-iron in Staffordshire and Wales. The facts and numbers I shall give are derived from the Voyage Metallurgique en Angleterre, published in 1837, by a commission of the most eminent French engineers. The market price of iron has changed very much since that period, but the cost of production has altered but very little: certainly not in any degree to affect the conclusions we may draw.

From an examination of the work of six high furnaces in the vicinity of Dudley in Staffordshire, it results that the average materials necessary to produce a ton of good pig-iron are:

Coal, ...	3 tons, 16 cwt.,	60 ℔.
Ore, ...	2 tons, 18 cwt.,	100 ℔.
Flux, ...	13 cwt.,	100 ℔.

The coal for roasting the ore, as well as that for making coke, is included; but it is necessary to add the small coal used in the engine to drive the blowing machine. This may be taken at ten cwt. Now the prices of these materials are,

Small coal, from 2s. to 3s. per ton. Coal for coke, from 6s. to 7s., per ton. It may be taken at 6s.

The ores vary from 4s. to 10s. per ton, seldom falling below 7s., which may be taken as the average.

Finally, it has been found, from an experience of several years, that the sundry expenses of labour, superintendence, interest, &c., incurred in producing a ton of pig-iron, are from 22s. to 23s. The cost of production is, therefore, as follows:

Coal for roasting and cokeing at 6s. . . .	£1	3	0
Ore ,, ,, at 7s. . . .	1	0	8
Limestone for flux, at 6s.	0	3	11
Small coal for engine, at 3s.	0	1	6
Labour and general expenses, ...	1	2	6
	£3	11	7

Mr. Aikin has given an account in the Technical Repository of the proportions used in Shropshire, which are, in order to form a ton of iron,

2 tons, 16 cwt. of ironstone;

Or, 2 tons of roasted ore.

12 cwt. of coal for the roasting.

4 tons, 10 cwt. of coal for the furnace;

Or, 2 tons, 4½ cwt., coke.

10½ limestone for flux.

There is here much more coal used than in Staffordshire,

where it is dearer. Mr. Aikin does not give the pecuniary estimate of the process.

In Wales the iron works are on a much larger scale than in Staffordshire, and most of the iron is made for refining into bars. These circumstances affect very materially the proportions of the materials, and the cost of production of the metal.

At the great iron works of Cy-fartha, near Merthyr, belonging to Mr. Crayshaw, the proportions and cost of the materials, and other expenses for producing a ton of iron, were, when the French Engineers wrote, as follows :

	£	s.	d.
3 tons 10 cwt. coal, at 4s. per ton, . .	£0	14	0
3 tons mineral, at 10s. per ton, ...	1	10	0
14 cwt. limestone, at 1s. 6d. per ton, . .	0	1	0
Labour, ...	0	12	0
Rent, ...	0	1	5½
Management, ...	0	0	9
Repairs, &c., ...	0	1	0
	£3	0	2½

At Mr. Hunt's of Pontypool, for the ton of metal the material required and the cost were :

	£	s.	d.
6 tons of coal, at 4s., ...	£1	4	0
14 cwt. of small coal for roasting and engine, at 1s. 6d., ...	0	1	1
3 tons, 3 cwt. of ore, at 7s., ...	1	2	1
15 cwt. limestone, at 2s. 6d., ...	0	1	10
General expenses and interest, ...	1	1	0
	£3	10	0

The coal used in these works is of bad quality, and hence the large quantity consumed.

Finally, the following estimate shews the cost of production of iron at Abersichan, where, however, it must be remarked, the cost of materials is but the mere cost of raising the ore and coal from the pit, as the mines are on the works themselves.

Labour, ...	£0	7	5½
Carriage of materials, ...	0	1	7½
Coal, 3 tons, 2 cwt., at 2s. 5d., ...	0	7	6
Ore, 2 tons, 17 cwt., 99℔, at 3s. 6d., .	0	19	3½
Limestone, 19 cwt., 42℔, at 3s. 6d., . .	0	3	4½
Repairs, ...	0	0	8
Rent, &c., ...	0	7	0
General expenses, ...	0	1	8
	£2	8	7

The Commissioners could not obtain so accurate estimates of the cost of production of iron in the Glasgow district, as those given above; but the general calculation was, that including engine and roasting, there was used in making a ton of iron eight tons of coal. The Scotch coal is very bituminous and loses greatly in cokeing, which is one cause of the large quantity used; but another is found in its cheapness. The coal was found to cost 4s. 6d. per ton, and the mineral the same. I shall have occasion immediately to notice how fully this estimate for Glasgow has been verified by more recent inquiries.

We thus see that the quantity of materials used in making a ton of pig-iron varies within very wide limits; and of course affects the cost of production in a very considerable degree. Some of this certainly depends on the quality of the ore and fuel; some also on the peculiar quality of metal which it is necessary to produce; but much also results from the sources of loss and imperfection in the working, which are better known and guarded against in some places than in others.

In order that we may trace the probable cost of producing iron in Ireland by the analogy of those estimates, it is necessary to consider for the present only the Connaught coal field, as the Kilkenny coal, being anthracite, requires quite separate consideration. I shall first quote the estimates made by various persons of the cost of smelting iron at Arigna, and then see what alterations they may now require.

In 1800 Mr. John Grieve made a report on the performance

and capabilities of the Arigna iron works, and gave the following estimate of the cost of production of a ton of pig-iron.

5½ tons of raw coal, at 4s. 11d., . . .	£1	7	0
4 tons of raw ironstone, at 3s. 8d., . .	0	14	8
23 cwt. of limestone, at 2s. 3d. per ton, .	0	2	7
Cost of materials, ...	£2	4	3
Labour, being the sum paid in Shropshire to contractors for all work on a ton of iron, ...	0	7	7
Cost of a ton of pig-iron, ...	£2	11	10
This includes every thing except small coal for roasting the ore, and for this, and for wear and tear, take, ...	0	8	2
Total cost of a ton of pig, ...	£3	0	0

At the time of Mr. Grieve's report the coals cost on the furnace bank, 8s. 4d. per ton, but he pointed out simple means by which the cost of raising could be reduced, so as to deliver the coals for 4s. 11d., and on this value his estimate is founded. The other values are those actually paid, and the proportions are those on which the manufacture was carried on.

In 1804, Mr. Guest of the Dowlais's iron works in Wales, reported on the state of the Arigna works, and estimated the cost of production as follows. He considered that the coal of the Aughabehy and Rover collieries may be delivered at 6s. 4d. per ton, and that the ironstone, of which the greater part must be raised on the east side of the lake, will ultimately cost 6s. per ton, and the limestone 4s. Therefore:

5 tons raw coal, at 6s. 4d., ...	£1	11	8
4 tons ironstone, at 6s., ...	1	4	0
1 ton limestone, ...	0	4	0
Labour, ...	0	10	0
Rent, wear and tear, and other incidental expenses, ...	1	5	4
	£4	15	0

L

Finally, in 1818, Mr. Griffith, in his valuable Report on the Connaught Coal District, estimated as follows the cost of production. He had shewn very fully that the coal could be raised at 4s. per ton, and assuming that the ironstone should be worked from the beds he calculated the cost of 5s. per ton. As he was not himself conversant with the proportions of the process, he assumed as correct the proportions given by Mr. Guest, which had been used at the works. There were, therefore:

5 tons of raw coal, at 4s.,	£1 0 0
4 tons of ironstone, at 5s.,	1 0 0
1 ton of limestone,	0 2 0
Labour,	0 10 0
Contingencies, at 20 per cent.,	0 10 5
Cost of a ton of pig-iron,	£3 2 5

From Mr. Grieve's and Mr. Griffith's estimate it hence appears, that the cost of making iron at Arigna is not greater than in the most favoured localities of England. Mr. Guest's estimate makes it much higher, but it is easy to shew that his statement is too high. First it is not easy to see how the charge of £1 5s. for contingencies could be incurred. Neither Mr. Griffith nor Mr. Grieve admits such an expenditure, nor in any of the estimates of the English and Welsh processes, given by Dufresnoy, does so large a sum occur; and yet those latter are not speculative, being all returns of the actual working of large establishments for many months. Hence, I think it must be considered seriously overcharged. As to the price of the coal, also, it is important to recollect, that the sum he charges is the maximum. The price of the Aughabehy coal is now 6s. 4d. per ton. It is a most excellent coal, and yields two-thirds of its weight of good coke. The Rover coal, however, of which the accurate analysis (as also of the Aughabehy) is given page 21, is sold at present at 4s. 9d. per ton, and it is excellent for preparing iron, as its composition indicates, and as is also shewn by the testimony of Mr. Guest, who in his Report says: "I have seen some of the Rover coal coked and used in the cupola; it melted the iron very quick and well, which I consider is a symptom of its good quality, and, from what I could judge, have little reason to doubt its answering the purpose of making iron." He might have no doubt about it; analysis shews that it is constituted as the best Welsh coal, and gives 82·3 per cent. of coke.

In 1827, the review of the circumstances of these works, made by Mr. Twigg, at the request of the Arigna Company, which has been already fully quoted with regard to the conditions of the collieries, led to an estimate of the cost of manufacture of the iron, which I now subjoin:

5½ tons of best raw coal, at 7s. 10d. per ton, the supposed average price of 25 years, ...	£2	3	1
3 tons 4 cwt of ironstone, at 4s. 10d., .	0	15	5
1 ton of limestone, at 3s., ...	0	3	0
Workmen's wages for making No. 1 pig-iron, as now paid to English workmen,	0	13	3
Cost of engine sleck, agency, and all incidentals of furnaces, &c., ...	0	11	0
	£4	5	9
If limestone be supplied by a railway, deduct 1s. 11d. per ton, ...	0	1	11
Final cost of a ton of No. 1 pig, . . .	£4	3	10

There are two cardinal errors in this estimate of Mr. Twigg's. First, that the price of the coal is overcharged. The best Aughabehy coal is now sold for 6s. 4d. per ton. The Rover coal is sold for 4s. 9d.; and how can arise an average cost of 7s. 10d. ? The second is that the richness of the ironstone is much undervalued. He takes the ore at 30 per cent. of metal, whereas it contains in average fully 40 per cent.; therefore, the quantity of ore should be two tons and a half, and it costs, at 4s. 10d., only 12s. 1d. In fact, all these estimates by English writers are in that respect faulty, that they do not take into account at all, differences in the composition, either of the ore or fuel, but reckon down all in the same proportion as they have been habituated to in the routine of their own immediate locality, beyond which their knowledge, in very few cases, indeed, is found to extend.

Since the periods of those Arigna estimates, the quantity of materials necessary to produce a ton of iron has been diminished by improvements in the mode of treatment, and if we consider that the Irish ore is far superior to the average Welsh, the coal not inferior, and that for the blowing machine, &c., there is water power in abundance, the cost of production, and the quantity of materials required, may, as I consider, be fairly estimated as follows :

4 tons of coal, at 4s. 9d., ...	£0	19	0
3 tons of ironstone, at 5s., ...	0	15	0
15 cwt. of limestone, at 2s. per ton, . .	0	1	6
Labour and general expenses, ...	1	2	6
	£2	18	0

The last item is taken the same as at Dudley, where it is given by Dufresnoy as higher than elsewhere in England and Wales. Labour is not likely to be dearer at Arigna, and although we shall require to distinguish carefully hereafter between nominal and real dearness of labour, for illustrating which, indeed, this very subject will supply examples, we may, by adding 5s., certainly cover all contingencies, and leave the estimated cost of pig-iron at Arigna £3 3s. sterling per ton.

These estimates are founded on the mode of preparing iron, until late universal, in which the furnaces were blown with air at ordinary temperatures. A vast revolution has, however, been produced in this manufacture by the plan invented by Mr. Neilson of Glasgow, of blowing the furnaces with hot air; working, as it is termed, with the *hot blast*. It is necessary to describe the changes this method has made in the English and Scotch iron manufacture, in order that its influence upon our own industry may be estimated.

In 1829 it occurred to Mr. Neilson, Manager of the Gas Works in Glasgow, that there would be an advantage gained in previously heating the air with which the blast furnaces of the iron works are supplied, and having carried on some experiments, in conjunction with Mr. Mackintosh and Mr. Wilson, at the Clyde Iron Works, they became satisfied of the accuracy of the idea, and took out a patent for the process. The mode of heating the air now generally in use, consists in passing it through a contorted iron tube around which the flame of a small furnace plays. The tube having numerous turns, a great surface is exposed to the action of the heat, so that the air attains a temperature, such as the worker wishes it to possess. The effect of the introduction of this process has been, 1st, very materially to diminish the quantity of coal employed; 2nd, to enable raw coal to be used in place of its being previously coked; 3rd, to increase the work of the furnace; and 4th, to enable a smaller quantity of flux to suffice. These consequences are shewn by the following numbers, published by Dr. Clark, deduced from the working of three furnaces at the Clyde Iron Works.

In 1829 with cold air, the three furnaces gave per week 111 tons of iron with 403 tons of coke from 888 tons of coal.

In 1830, with air at 300° Fah., they gave 162 tons of iron with 376 of coke from 836 of coal.

In 1833, four furnaces gave 245 tons of iron with 554 tons of coal.

Throughout, the power of the blast was the same. The yield of iron was doubled from the same furnace. It was trebled from the same fuel.

In 1829, 1 ton of iron required 8 tons, 1 cwt., 1 qr. coal.
In 1830,   ,,   ,,   ,,   5 tons, 3 cwt., 1 qr. ,,
In 1833,   ,,   ,,   ,,   2 tons, 5 cwt., 1 qr. ,,

The charge for the furnace was in

	1829.	1333.
Coke, ...	5 cwt., ...	Coal, 5 cwt.
Roasted ironstone,	3 cwt. 1 qr. 14℔, .	,, 5 cwt.
Limestone, . .	3 qrs. 16℔, . . .	,, 5 cwt.

The effect of this enormous alteration may easily be imagined. The iron trade of Scotland received an impulse of the most healthful and permanent kind, and the use of the hot blast has since been extending into all the other iron districts; subject, however, to some conditions which must be noticed.

The great economy of fuel which arose in Scotland was, in part, derivable from two sources independent of the hot blast. First, that the iron manufacture had previously been badly managed there, and a great deal of fuel wasted; and second, that the coal employed being highly bituminous, it lost, when employed as coke, more than half its weight. Thus, the coal of the Clyde Works gives but 45 per cent. of coke.

Now in Staffordshire the coal gives 65 per cent. of coke. Consequently, the 8 tons, 1 cwt. of Scotch coal represent but 72 cwt. coke, whilst the 3 tons, 16 cwt., 60℔, of Staffordshire coal used to make a ton of iron, represent 50 cwt. coke. The excess in Scotland was, therefore, in reality, but 50 per cent. of available fuel in place of 110 per cent. as it might at first appear. Accordingly, the saving effected by the hot blast has been found to vary in different localities, according as the manufacture had been previously in a more or less perfect state, and as the coals used lost more or less by cokeing. Mr. Mushet, than whom there is no higher authority, states the savings to be per ton of iron:

On Scotch coals from	. . . . .	$3\frac{1}{2}$ to 4 tons.
In Yorkshire,	. . . .	$2\frac{1}{2}$ to 3 ,,
Staffordshire,	. . . .	2 to $2\frac{1}{2}$,,
Gloucestershire,	. . . .	1 to $1\frac{1}{2}$,,
South Wales,	. . . .	$\frac{3}{4}$ to $1\frac{1}{2}$,,

Two tons of Merthyr-tydvil coal give as much coke as three tons of Scotch coal, which may be considered 67 per cent.

The coal of Plymouth Works give 83 per cent. of coke, and at Dowlais's 66 per cent.

It has been shewn that the coals of Arigna all belong to the moderately bituminous family. The per centage of coke being:

Aughabehy coal,	. . . . 76·9
Celtnaveena,	. . . . 80·9
Meeneshama,	. . . . 81·1
Rover,	. . . . 82·3

Hence no such difference could arise as to the consumption of coal at Arigna from the use of hot blast, as was found to occur in Scotland. It is more likely that the saving of fuel would not exceed what has been found to occur in South Wales, which may be averaged at a ton of coal per ton of iron. This would, of course, be a saving of 4s. 9d., and also a saving of time and labour in the previous cokeing.

It may, therefore, be concluded, that the difference between hot and cold blast in the iron district of Lough Allen, cannot be of such importance as to affect the other conditions of its success or failure; and finally, that from the various estimates drawn up by those who have inspected the locality, as well as from the analysis of the cost of production of iron in Scotland, England, and Wales, there remains little doubt, but that cast iron of the best quality can be obtained at Arigna, at an expense of production, probably falling sensibly under, but certainly not exceeding, £3 3s. sterling per ton.

We shall now pass to the examination of the conditions of the manufacture of iron in the coal districts of Leinster.

Until very lately, the smelting of iron by means of anthracite was looked upon as impracticable, although from the vast deposits of that kind of coal in many countries, experiments had frequently been made upon it. These experiments were all failures as to the use of the anthracite alone. The condition of the process will be exhibited, by the following extract from the Report of M. Perdonnet on the manufacture of iron in France. He says:

I will now speak of some experiments made with a curious combustible substance, called anthracite,—a kind of pure carbon, without any mixture of bitumen, compact, igniting with great difficulty, and giving out such a heat, when once in a state of combustion, that it is very difficult to procure materials for the construction of the blast furnaces which will not melt. It has been ascertained that cast-iron cannot be made with anthracite, except by excessive care, and that the furnace will not work regular unless three parts of coke be mixed with seven of the anthracite; and indeed, by reason of its burn-

ing so slowly, it has been found more advantageous to use
them in equal quantities.

"The cast-iron obtained with these different proportions of
anthracite has always been of excellent quality. This may
cause surprise, as the combustible used without preparation as
it comes from the mine always contains a large quantity of
sulphur."

The trials in England took place in Brecknockshire, and are
described by Mr. Scrivenor as follows:

"Nearly twenty years back a patent was taken out, and
a furnace erected on the borders of Brecknockshire, for the
smelting of iron with stone coal (anthracite); many experiments were made with different proportions of the stone coal
and bituminous coal used together. The iron produced was of
good quality, but the object being to use the anthracite in its
raw state, which could not then be effected, the furnace, after
a few months' trial, was blown out."

Such having been the results in England and in France, it is
interesting to do justice to a fellow-countryman, who appears,
from Mr. Tighe's Survey of Kilkenny, to have succeeded in
the attempt long before. Mr. Tighe's statement is:

"It has been said that this coal will not answer for smelting
iron, but Finlan did actually smelt the iron ore of Castlecomer
with it, in a small furnace before mentioned, and said that the
quality of the iron was good. If the coal always answers to
Mr. Kirwan's analysis, the iron could not be injured by it, except where it contained any martial pyrites, which should be
carefully separated But it is objected to this coal, that igniting slowly, and consuming without flame, it does not bear
the operation of a blast furnace, nor can its heat be rapidly
increased; and to remove this difficulty Finlan suggested the
expedient of mixing it with charred or dried turf, or any other
fuel that would open and separate its parts. For the purposes
of cementing steel, it seems peculiarly calculated, as it does
also for potteries, and almost every other manufacturing purpose; and that it should not be applied to these purposes at
Castlecomer, where materials for earthen ware are to be found,

and where iron mines of the best quality lie, as it were, above ground, seems a national loss."

Very recently attempts have been again made, and with more success, so that at present there are at work in South Wales, furnaces in which anthracite is used with the air blast at ordinary temperature; but the final and perfect solution of the problem of smelting iron by anthracite, has been established by Mr. Crane of the Yniscedwin Iron Works, by whom the process has been patented. The improvement which he has made consists simply in the application of the hot blast to the anthracite coal, and the result shall be briefly stated in his words, extracted from the account read by him to the British Association at Liverpool, and the facts contained in which have been fully verified by continued working since.

When he used bituminous coal the ton of iron had required in his furnaces the coke produced from a quantity of coal, varying from four to five tons. The average consumption of anthracite has been found to be, per ton of iron, twenty-seven cwt.

The work of the furnace with coke from bituminous coal had been from twenty-two to twenty-four tons of iron. On using the anthracite this was raised so as to vary from thirty to thirty-six tons, and once to thirty-nine tons. With respect to quality, Mr. Crane considers, that the iron made with the anthracite is superior to any he ever made before, and his works have always ranked high for the quality of iron they produced.

Referring to the analyses of the ironstone of the Leinster district, it will be found to contain in average 38·7 per cent. of iron. It is, therefore, much superior to the average ore worked in Wales, and the cost of the fuel per ton of iron, assuming that the consumption should be thirty cwt. per ton of iron produced, should not exceed, at the pit mouth, where, of course, if any where, iron works should be established, 13s. 6d. If we consider all other expenses to be the same as they are estimated to be in Wales, by Dufresnoy, and as we have taken them at Arigna, the ton of cast iron manufactured with anthracite, in the Leinster or Tipperary coal fields, should not

exceed £2 10s , and should certainly fall below £2 15s. Further, should the development of this branch of industry, leading to an increased demand for coals, be the means of introducing better systems of working the collieries, so that the
cost of raising the coals may be materially diminished, there
may result a diminution of the cost of fuel, though with an
increased profit to the coal owners, by which again the manufacture of the iron should be rendered still more economical.

Such, as far as I am able to represent them, are the circumstances under which this important branch of industry may be
placed in Ireland.   But I am far from believing that it would
be prudent in any person now to enter upon this branch of manufacture.   We are not yet ready for it, nor is the time fitting.
The iron trade of England and Scotland has been for some
years in an exceedingly depressed state.   The prices of pig-
iron are from £2 15s. for Clyde iron, to £3 15s. for No. 1 Welsh
iron, on which it may be at once calculated, from the estimates
already given, there can be but little profit.   Now this is not
the sort of trade in which it would be proper to disturb our
fortunate neighbours.   The present paroxysm of railway enterprize promises to cause some improvement in the iron trade,
but it will be of too ephemeral a character to justify any attempt at manufacturing here at present.   If other circumstances, stimulating our industrial energies, and increasing our
domestic wants, determine an increased demand for iron in
Ireland, where all charges, risks, and trouble of freight and
transport, should tell against the imported metal, it will be
important for our capitalists to recollect, that the ironstone of
Arigna is equal to the celebrated black band of Glasgow, and
that, taking all circumstances into account, iron can be made
as cheaply and as good in Ireland as in any other portion of
the empire.

The iron produced by the operations which alone have
hitherto been noticed, is in the form of metal, which, from its
fusibility, adapts itself to so great a variety of purposes; but
the preparation of malleable iron from the pig metal requires
additional processes, and the subject would remain imperfect

were not the circumstances of these further branches of the manufacture of iron noticed.

The change of pig-iron into bar requires three operations, viz., refining, puddling, and balling. This last is not universally practised; but it is best to consider it here as being employed. The refining is conducted in a small blast furnace, with a shallow rectangular crucible. The crucible is filled with coke, the pigs of metal are laid on it and covered up with coke, and the fire being lighted, and the air let on, the metal fuses, runs down into the crucible, and much of its carbon is disengaged as carbonic oxide gas. Some slags from other operations are added to save the crucible from being cut up, and often scoriæ of iron from the forges, or hæmatite, or oxide of manganese, is added, which favour the elimination of the carbon from the metal, and diminish the loss which occurs. When the treatment of the metal has been completed, the *fine metal* is run out on a level surface of sand, so that it forms a thin plate, which is cooled rapidly by throwing water on it, and it is then broken and transferred to the puddling furnace.

As an example of the proportions of expense of this process, the following abstract of the work at Verteg in South Wales may be taken; it does not differ materially from Staffordshire. To produce a ton of fine metal it took

	£	s.	d.
1 ton, 2 cwt., 1 qr. of pig at £3 6s., . .	£3	13	5
14 cwt. of coal, at 4s. per ton, ...	0	2	10
Cost of cokeing the coal, ...	0	0	4
Cost of labour, made up of,			
Weighing, 0s. 3d.			
Refining, 1 7	0	2	4¼
Carriage, 0 6¼			
Blast and Management, ...	0	0	9
Cost of 1 ton of fine metal,.	£3	19	8¼

The fine metal is transferred to the floor of reverberatory furnaces, where it is fused, and whilst liquid carefully agitated It appears to burn, the carbon which gave it its fusibility is gradually worked out, and it becomes less liquid, and finally breaks into granules like sand. On increasing the heat, these agglutinate, and the workman, kneading them together with suitable tools, gradually works the entire into a mass, which taken from the furnace is already plastic and malleable. It is rolled into bars by being placed between grooved cylinders, made to revolve by a powerful engine, and these bars, if the iron be wanted of superior quality, are balled, by being heated in a reverberatory furnace still more intensely than in puddling, and many bars being welded together, and drawn out again by the roller, the highest degree of purity and homogeneity is given to the material.

The total cost of these processes, as carried on in Staffordshire, was found by the French Commission of Inquiry to be, in the period from 1828 to 1837 :

To produce a ton of fine metal:

	£	s.	d.
22¼ cwt. of pig, at £3 12s., ...	£4	0	1
3 packs of coke, ...	0	4	1
Workmen, ...	0	1	4
Blast and management, ...	0	1	1
Repairs and sundries, ...	0	0	11
Cost of a ton of fine metal, ...	£4	7	6

To convert this fine metal into *mill bar iron* by puddling and rolling, there is for a ton of product:

	£	s.	d.
22 cwt. of fine metal as above, ...	£4	16	3
20 cwt. of coal, ...	0	5	6
10 cwt. of slack for engine, ...	0	1	4
Labour, viz., Puddling, 7s. 8d., Rolling, 2s. 1d., Weighing, 7d.,	0	10	4
Repairs of furnaces and machinery, . .	0	3	0
Management, &c., ...	0	1	10
Cost of a ton of mill bar, ...	£5	18	3

To form from this the common merchantable bar iron, there is required:

22½ cwt. of mill bar as above, ...	£6	14	1
12 cwt. of coal, ...	0	3	6
10 cwt. of slack, ...	0	1	6
Cost of rolling, ...	0	5	0
General expenses, ...	0	5	6
Total cost of a ton of iron bars, . . .	£7	9	7

It is now interesting to add all these various processes together, and see how this final cost of the ton of bar iron is distributed throughout the entire manufacture. On doing so in suitable proportions it is found that there is paid for

4 tons, 9 cwt. of ore at 7s., ...	£1	11	3
8 tons, 6 cwt. of coal at 6s., ...	2	9	10
1 ton, 16 cwt. of slack at 3s., ...	0	5	6
Limestone per ton, ...	0	5	6
Labour, management and repairs, . .	2	17	6
	£7	9	7

The total quantity of fuel consumed is therefore just ten times the weight of the bar iron produced, and makes 40 per cent. of the entire cost. It is hence easily intelligible how the iron manufacture naturally limits itself to the coal district.

It must be recollected that the above estimates are derived from Staffordshire, where the cost of making iron is high, and were taken some years ago, when the cost of labour and materials was much greater than at present. Thus the merchant bar iron would now be sold for about £6 per ton. And if we take a final estimate at the prices for which it has been already shewn that pig iron can be made at Arigna, considering labour and superintendence to be the same as in Staffordshire:

4 tons of ore at 5s., ...	£1	0	0
10 tons of coal at 4s. 9d., ...	2	7	6
1 ton of limestone, ...	0	2	6
Labour and general expenses, ...	2	17	6
	£6	7	6

Thus merchant bar iron can be made at Arigna at the same price as it is now made in Staffordshire, and indeed cheaper, as

the quantity of ore is calculated from the average of Staffordshire, of 30 per cent., whilst Arigna ore yields 40 per cent. of
ron. H nce 5s. might have been taken from the above estimate of cost.

It is now necessary to pass to a branch of this subject which
is of considerable importance to Ireland. The refining of iron
by means of turf or turf charcoal. A few words will briefly
point out its bearings. The iron which is smelted by means of
pit coal always preserves a degree of impurity of constitution
which reduces its strength and deteriorates its structure, so
that for the finer purposes of machinery and of cutlery England is indebted for much iron to Russia and Sweden, as in
these countries, the smelting and refining being carried on by
means of wood, the metal is obtained in absolute purity. Hence
the great difference of price between the British and foreign
iron; common English bar being sold at £6 per ton; whilst
Swedish and Russian iron bars will cost £15, £25, or even
£35 per ton, according to their quality. Now we possess in
Ireland the means of preparing those irons of superior quality
and of replacing, if not the finest, at least the ordinary sorts
of Baltic iron. The elements necessary to produce such metal
are ores of great purity and a vegetable fuel of proper kind.

The ores we have already seen to be abundant. The vegetable fuel is found abundantly in our turf.

In England it can be easily understood that the manufacture
of iron by turf is not thought worthy of notice. On the Continent, however, where the promotion of native industry is an
object of primary importance, and where the limited development of the coal districts obliges them to economize every
source of fuel, it has been not merely tried, but is extensively
carried on at present in France, in Prussia, and in Bavaria.
These countries resemble our's in their relations to fuel, and it
is by observation of what they do, that we may learn how to
economize our own resources. I shall accordingly proceed to
describe how turf is applied in the manufacture of iron abroad,
and then endeavour to apply their results to the peculiar circumstances of Ireland.

At Ransko, in Bohemia, there is an extensive iron work
consisting of high furnaces for the smelting of pig-iron from

the ores; of cupolas for the remelting of pig and making castings, and the reverberatory furnaces and machinery for the
manufacture of bar and plate. The ore that is employed is
the clay ironstone, and is of very moderate quality. For fuel,
is used a mixture of turf and charcoal. The turf is light, it is
dried in the air, but not in any way prepared or pressed. The
cubic metre of it weighs 225 kilos, and costs 1·34 franc. This
is at the rate of 5s. per ton. The furnaces are blown with hot
air at the temperature of 280° Fah. The proportions of materials and products that are given from an average of long
experience, is, that to make a ton of iron, there is consumed
34 cwt. 3 qrs. of turf, which costs 8s. 9d., and 30 cwt. of charcoal, costing 24s. 7d. The fuel for the smelting costs, therefore, 33s. 4d., and the other expenses bring the total cost of
the pig iron to £3 15s. per ton. The fuel used in the cupolas
and furnaces is the same, and the quality of iron is of the very
highest character.

At Königsbrunn in Bavaria, are iron works peculiarly
worthy of attention, as from the report of the French engineers
sent to examine them, it appears, that "they execute with
turf alone the puddling and second fusion, reheating and rolling, finally, all the operations which are effected with coal in
the English furnaces."

The turf employed is prepared with unusual care, as, owing
to the excessively high price of fuel, every economy is important. It is not pressed, but is dried perfectly in stores of
various kinds, of which two deserve especial notice. The first
kind of store is heated by a fire-place belonging to itself. The
other mode of drying the turf consists in an arrangement by
which the waste heat of the various puddling and reheating
furnaces is economized.

The turf, as finally delivered at the furnace, is charged at
the rate of 13s. per ton. It is of an average quality. Berthier
found it to consist of

Volatile matter,	70·6
Carbon	24·4
Ashes,	5·0
	100·0

and to give by ignition with litharge 14·3 times its weight of lead.

The furnaces employed in these works all require peculiarities of construction, arising from the bulk of the fuel being so much greater in proportion to its weight than when wood or coal is used. These peculiarities it would, however, be tedious to describe here. They can be found on reference to the original memoirs and drawings; it is only the results that are of importance to the immediate object of this work.

It is found that in order to deliver a ton of puddled iron, there are required twenty-two and a half cwt. of pig, and there are consumed thirty and a quarter cwt. of turf, for which the densest is always selected. Of this puddled iron twenty-four and a half cwt. are reheated and rolled, with the consumption of thirty cwt. of dense turf, and the produce is a ton of small bars of iron of fine quality.

The cost of manufacturing the fine bar iron by this turf is therefore, per ton:

$27\frac{1}{2}$ cwt. of pig-iron, which is charged at £6 13s. per ton, that being the selling price. £9 1 4

Turf, at 14s. per ton:

37 cwt. for puddling, ⎫
30 cwt. for reheating, ⎬ 2 7 6

Labour and general expenses, . . . 0 10 10

Cost of fine bars per ton, £11 19 8

Such are the financial circumstances of the manufacture of iron in a country, where there is really a scarcity of fuel, and where the introduction of English iron is practically prohibited.

I may add, that the consumption of turf has been found to be—

For running a ton of iron in castings, twenty-one and a half cwt. of pig, and twenty-two cwt. of turf.

For heating and rolling a ton of sheet iron, twenty-one cwt. of flat iron and thirty cwt. of turf.

In the iron works of Ichoux, department of the Landes in France, no fuel is used in puddling but turf. The turf of moderate quality costs at the rate of 8s. per ton. The ton of puddled iron is given by twenty-two cwt. of pig, and forty-five cwt. of turf. M. Alex of Lauchhammer has substituted turf for coal in his puddling furnaces. It requires two and a half times as much turf as coal: the usual work being, that twenty-five cwt. of pig, worked up with twenty-six cubic feet of turf gives twenty cwt. of iron rolled into bars.

The perfect similarity of the charcoal of ense turf, and especially of compressed turf, to that of wood, has been mentioned in a former place. It has been tried as a substitute for wood charcoal in iron works, and with complete success. In the high furnaces of M. Muller at Wendenhammer, wood charcoal has been replaced by an equal volume of turf charcoal, and this method has been so beneficial, that the quantity of ore worked off was materially increased. In the high furnaces of Wachter at Neunhammer, when half of the charcoal of wood was replaced by turf coke, the charge of ore was raised from 386℔ to 464℔. The quality of iron produced was excellent. Finally, MM. Moser and Wagner, who have examined minutely into the various conditions of this branch of industry, conclude, that both for smelting and refining iron, the coke of turf is as good and useful as an equal weight of wood charcoal.

It is unnecessary to multiply quotations of evidence of this kind. The great fact which is to be recollected is, that turf and turf coke answer perfectly for making and refining iron, and from the quantities of materials and products, which the experience of the French and German workers has found to answer, and the cost of those materials, as we know they can be had with us, we may proceed to calculate what are the financial conditions of the subject.

To produce a ton of pig-iron at Ransko, there are required thirty-five cwt. of turf and thirty cwt. of wood charcoal. Now for the latter may be substituted the turf coke, provided it be compressed; and as the turf may be taken at 4s. per ton, and the coke at 20s., taking the ore and labour to be the same as

M

in our final estimate regarding the manufacture at Lough Allen, with coal, it becomes :

		£	s.	d.
2½ tons of ore, at 5s., ...		£0	12	6
15 cwt. of limestone, at 2s. 6d., ...		0	1	9
35 cwt. of turf, at 4s., ...		0	7	0
30 cwt. of turf coke, at 20s., ...		1	10	0
Labour and general expenses, ...		1	2	6
Total cost of a ton of pig, ...		£3	13	9

Such iron should, however, not be sold as mere pig or used in castings. Its fine quality would peculiarly fit it for being made into bars; now the Königsbrunn results enable us to see what those bars should cost in Ireland. The calculation is :

	£	s.	d.
27½ cwt. of pig made as above and costing £3 6s. 3d. per ton, ...	£4	11	1
Turf, at 4s. per ton: 37 cwt. for puddling, 30 cwt. for reheating, }	0	13	5
Labour and general expenses, for which, in order to avoid an error in deficiency, I will take double the German cost, . .	1	1	8
	£6	6	2

Hence the ton of charcoal iron in bars would be made for six guineas. Now the price of the foreign charcoal iron ranges from £15 to £35 per ton. It cannot be made in England, for the wood charcoal is £4 per ton in the Forest of Dean, where some little remnant of the manufacture lingers. They have no extensive peat deposits. If they boast of their greater extent of underground repositories of fuel, we may point to our's which lie upon the surface. We must learn, however, to employ them properly, and with economy, or else we would shew ourselves utterly unworthy of the riches with which Providence has blessed our country.

The consumption of fuel at Ransko is greater than elsewhere with charcoal furnaces. Thus in Pennsylvania, a ton of metal is obtained from forty-one cwt of ore, and between twenty-five and twenty-seven cwt. of wood charcoal. On the Continent, the ton of metal requires from thirty to thirty-four cwt. of charcoal. So that if turf coke alone can be substituted for the wood charcoal, the above estimate may have the cost of the turf removed, and the ton of pig iron should come to about £3 10s. The introduction of the hot blast into charcoal furnaces has been found attended with the remarkable saving of from one-fourth to one-third of the entire quantity of fuel. With turf charcoal a similar economy might possibly arise, but I shall retain as illustration the cost of production already calculated.

Although the iron is not prepared from the ore by means of charcoal in any part of England, yet iron bar is manufactured by a mixed process of refining with coke and charcoal, from which a product is obtained of such excellent quality as to sell for £14 per ton, and to replace for such purposes as chain cables, nail-rods, boiler plates, piston rods, &c., the iron of the north of Europe, which is now, indeed employed only for conversion into steel for the purposes of cutlery. The quantity of charcoal used in such processes of refining is about four cwt. and a half, per ton of iron. In this method of working also the charcoal from turf may ultimately be utilized.

The consumption of fuel in these processes is so great, and its cost enters so largely into the expense of the manufacture, that it becomes important to fix attention upon every mode by which any economy may be effected. The attention of chemists and engineers has been especially directed to this point upon the Continent, and now also in England it is attracting the notice it deserves.

During the work of a high iron furnace, the air which is blown into the fire escapes from the top, changed essentially in composition. Its oxygen has, of course, gone to support the combustion of the furnace, but in place of the escape of useless products, as nitrogen and carbonic acid, there is generated a large quantity of combustible gas, which takes fire on escaping, and generates that pale cone of flame by which the high furnace is so well characterized. The gaseous material thus passing off was found, on analysis by Bunsen and Ebelmen, to consist of:

Nitrogen, ...	from 63·0 to 60·2
Carbonic oxide, ...	,, 30·7 ,, 19·7
Carbonic acid, ...	,, 5·9 ,, 12·8
Hydrogen, ...	,, 0·4 ,, 7·3
	100·0 100·0

Now as the quantity of air blown in may be calculated, the quantity of the combustible gases given off may be inferred, and the conclusion finally arrived at is, that in the high furnaces a quantity of fuel is carried off under the form of combustible gases, which amounts to from 55 to 65 per cent. of the total heating value of the fuel introduced into the furnace, and also, as the gases pass off at an intense heat, they carry away thereby at least 10 per cent. of the heat produced by the combustion, so that the quantity of fuel that is really employed in producing the heat by which the iron is smelted, does not amount to more than from 25 to 35 per cent. of that which is actually consumed. This vast loss, of course, more than doubles the cost of fuel in the process, and the following means have been devised and successfully employed for utilizing it in other ways.

The upper portion of the high furnace, where the charge of ore and fuel does not be yet ignited, is lined with a cylinder of iron, sustained by stays some inches from the brick work. The great body of the gas rushes into this space, where it has not to act against the solid mass of smelting materials. Into this space horizontal flues open on each side, leading to a metal chamber, where they unite, and from which the gas is delivered by nozzles on the floor of the reverberatory furnaces, in which the puddling and reheating is carried on. The chimney of the puddling furnace gives draft sufficient to draw in all the gas.

The result practically found is, that the temperature produced by the combustion of the combustible gases of the high furnace is fully sufficient for the puddling and refining of the iron; and thus the fuel (coal, charcoal, or coke) with which the high furnace is charged, may be made to serve for the en-

tire conversion of the ore into fine bar iron. Now if we consider that it is usually taken in average, that to produce a ton
of bars requires ten ton of coals, of which four tons only are
used in the high furnace, it is evident that the economy of heat,
by the methods now described, may reduce the cost of the bar
iron per ton by the price of six tons of coal, and of course
the advantage will be proportionally greatest where fuel is
dearest.

The proportion of hydrogen in the gas evolved, depends on
the presence of watery vapour in the air blown into the furnace, and of course varies with it. On this principle is founded
another method of economy. I have mentioned, when speaking
of the modes of applying anthracite, that when the vapour of
water is passed over it at a high temperature, a mixture of hydrogen and carbonic oxide gases is evolved, by means of
which a flaming property is given to that coal: this is the
basis of Kymer's and Leighton's patent. This process is employed on the Continent, in order to economize very inferior
fuels, such as slaty coal or earthy turf. The plan was originally invented by Ebelmen, but it is now applied in many places.
A small furnace is built like an iron furnace, which may be
blown either with air or steam. The top may be closed, except at the times of introducing fuel. From near the top pass
lateral flues, which conduct the gaseous products to a chamber,
from whence they are led to the furnaces where they are to be
burned. Such a furnace is termed a generator. If it be blown
with air, the products are the same as the gases of the high
iron furnace. If it be blown with steam, the products are
similar to those given with steam and anthracite. The following analyses give the composition of the gases resulting
from a generator with very bad coal:

	BLOWN WITH AIR.	BLOWN WITH MIXED AIR AND STEAM.
Carbonic acid,	0·5	5·5
Carbonic oxide,	33·3	27·2
Hydrogen,	2.8	14·1
Nitrogen,	63·4	53·2
	100·0	100·0

In the same generator, a fire of turf blown with air in its usual condition, gave :

Carbonic acid, ... 10·79
Carbonic oxide, ... 21·04
Hydrogen, ... 9·36
Nitrogen, ... 58·81
                                    ―――――
                                     100·00

It is hence evident that even with the worst fuel, by proper arrangements, the purest fire, that of flame, can be obtained; and thus the local differences of quality of coal or turf almost obliterated by the application of suitable mechanical constructions, guided by a correct knowledge of chemical principles.

It remains to notice one further mode of economy of fuel that has been adopted with complete success, not merely on the Continent, but also in certain works in Staffordshire. It consists in conducting the flues from the puddling furnaces under and round the boilers of the steam engine, so that the water in these last may be boiled, and the steam power for rolling, &c., may be generated by the heat, which should otherwise pass up the chimney and be lost.

The results obtained at Abbainville may be taken as an example of the amount of the saving so effected. It is there found that each pound of coal burned in the puddling furnace, evaporates 3·7 pounds of water in the steam boilers. Hence, the economy is at least half of the practical value of the fuel. The steam engine is thirty horse power, and is in almost constant activity for driving the cutters, rollers, and punches.

The works contain two puddling furnaces. The produce was 1000 tons of bar iron from 487 of coal and 1137 of pig, and this proportion of fuel remained the same, whether the steam engine was driven by the waste heat, or by independent fires.

I have noticed these sources of economy, because they, and all similar ameliorations, are not merely important to be known in order that the cheapest means of manufacture may be adopted, but that they are peculiarly of vital interest to us, who labour, as compared with the sister kingdom, under a certain disadvantage in regard to fuel Every thing which diminishes the quantity of fuel, diminishes the amount of this disadvantage, and hence removes the greatest difficulty felt in the financial success of industry in Ireland. Thus if the English manufacturer have an advantage of 1s. per ton in the price of coals, and that there be ten tons of coal used to make a ton of iron bars, his advantage is 10s.; and that 10s. may enable him to send his iron to every part of Ireland, and to destroy our market. But if, by processes in which fuel is economized, the bars be made with five tons of coal, in place of ten, then his total advantage in fuel becomes but 5s., and this may not be, indeed would not be, sufficient to enable him to keep possession of the Irish market. It is evident also, that if one party adopt methods of economy, and the other party do not, the scale is at once and decisively turned in favour of the party who avails himself most rapidly of all improvements.

CHAPTER V.

GEOLOGICAL STRUCTURE OF IRELAND. GRANITIC ROCKS; THEIR
DISTRIBUTION AND COMPOSITION. MICA-SLATE; ITS EX-
TENT. CLAY-SLATE, UPPER AND LOWER; ITS MINERAL CON-
TENTS AND AREA. VEINS AND PROTRUSIONS OF QUARTZ
ROCK. SANDSTONE FORMATIONS; OLD RED AND YELLOW
SANDSTONES; CONGLOMERATES; THEIR DISTRIBUTION. CAR-
BONIFEROUS SLATE. RELATIONS OF THE LIMESTONE AND
COAL MEASURES TO THE UNDERLYING AND SUPERINCUMBENT
ROCKS. NEW RED SANDSTONE. CHALK OF ANTRIM. BA-
SALT AND TRAP ROCKS OF THE NORTH OF IRELAND.
MINING DISTRICTS OF IRELAND. COPPER MINES. ORES OF
COPPER. MINES OF THE WICKLOW DISTRICT; THEIR DIS-
TRIBUTION; MODE OF WORKING AND PRODUCE. MINES OF
THE WATERFORD DISTRICT; THEIR STRUCTURE AND PRO-
DUCE. COPPER MINES OF THE SOUTH-WESTERN DISTRICT;
THEIR GEOLOGICAL RELATIONS AND PRODUCE. COPPER DIS-
TRICT OF TIPPERARY. MINES IN THE CLAY-SLATE NORTH OF
DUBLIN. METALLURGIC TREATMENT OF COPPER ORES. ECO-
NOMY OF FUEL IN SMELTING.
OF THE LEAD MINES OF IRELAND. ORES OF LEAD. LEAD
MINES OF WICKLOW AND WEXFORD; THEIR STRUCTURE AND
PRODUCE. LEAD MINES OF THE NORTHERN AND SOUTH-
WESTERN SLATE DISTRICTS. DEPOSITS OF LEAD ORE IN THE
LIMESTONE OF IRELAND MINES NEAR DUBLIN. MINES OF
CLARE. PREPARATION AND SMELTING OF LEAD ORES. EX-
TRACTION OF THE SILVER FROM LEAD. RICHNESS OF THE
IRISH ORES IN SILVER. ECONOMY OF FUEL IN THE TREAT-
MENT OF LEAD ORES.

THE two important minerals, coal and iron, the circumstances of which have been described in the preceding chapters,
are, as has been shewn, closely associated in nature, and limited, so far as their practical extraction is concerned, almost
totally to that division of rocks, termed by geologists the coal
formation. The numerous other metallic and mineral bodies
which are required for the purposes of the arts, must be sought
in localities of other and various geological nature; and hence,
in order that a proper representation may be given, as well of
the actual mineral resources of Ireland, as of the extent to which
those resources are capable of being developed, it will be ne-

cessary briefly to enumerate the species of rocks of which the
surface of our country is composed, the mode of their arrangement, and such facts regarding their chemical composition as
bear upon technical or agricultural industry.

On looking over a map of Ireland, it may be observed that
towards the coast the surface is occupied for the most part by
mountain ranges, whilst the central portion of the island constitutes an almost uniform plane. This diversity of geographical character, is accompanied by a difference of geological
structure of the most decided character: the mountainous
country consisting of the various older or primitive rocks,
while the central plain is formed by the limestone, which has
been already described as the basis upon which the various
tracts of coal formation rest. Almost every district presents
in the mineralogical character and arrangement of its rocks,
something peculiar in detail, which should be described in a
work on the geology of Ireland, and on which many important
essays have been published by the Geological Society of Dublin; but here such details would be out of place, and I shall
only notice the mode of arrangement and constitution of those
rocks in a general point of view, and in their principal situations. In the order of formation, which is usually adopted, we
may consider the principal rocks found in Ireland, inferior to
the carboniferous limestone, to be, granite; mica-slate; clay-
slate; old red sandstone; yellow sandstone. There are also
rocks which do not appear limited to a certain position in the
above series, but present themselves accompanying sometimes
one, sometimes another member of it; of these are quartz rock,
various porphyries, and greenstones.

In order to render more easily intelligible and definite the following brief account of the geological structure of the country,
the distribution of the principal classes of rocks has been laid
down in the accompanying map. It is not intended to represent every locality of a rock, or every rock that occurs in any
locality. It should, on such a scale, in that case become too
crowded, and the parts too minute to be of any practical use,
but considering the rocks of Ireland to belong to nine principal
classes, in their usual order.

1. Granite and Gneiss.
2. Mica-slate.
3. Lower clay-slate.
4. Upper clay-slate.
5. Old red sandstone series.
6. Carboniferous limestone.
7. Coal formations.
8. Newer strata, including sandstone, chalk, and tertiary clays, which collectively occupy but a small space, and that only round the edge of Antrim.
9. Trap and basaltic rocks.

The relations of these classes of rocks to each other, and to the general surface, may be simply represented by the different shadings, as explained upon the map. The carboniferous limestone, which occupies so large an area of the country, being left unshaded for distinction sake.

The granite rises from under the other more recently deposited formations, at various points, situated mostly along the coast. There are four principal tracts of granite, that of Wicklow, of Galway, of Newry, and of Donegal. The first is the most extensive, it commences a few miles from Dublin, on the shore at Dalkey, and stretches in a south-westerly direction to near New Ross in Wexford, a distance of sixty-six statute miles. Its greatest breadth is from Kilkea to Sandiford, eighteen miles. The granitic district of Galway commences at the town and forms the entire of the northern coast of the Bay of Galway. Its northern edge passes by Oughterard to Roundstone: including the islands, its area is roughly elliptical, with axes of thirty-six miles by twelve. On the eastern coast a granite district, occupying part of the counties of Armagh and Down, constitutes the greater part of the hills of Carlingford and the mountains of Mourne, which from opposite sides give so much picturesque effect to the Bay of Newry. The extreme range of this granitic district is twenty-eight miles by twelve. The north-western coast of Donegal constitutes the fourth important locality of this rock. Intermixed with vast veins of quartz, it stretches inland about eighteen miles, and its south-eastern edge from Ardara to Glen ranges almost rectilinear for thirty-five miles.

In addition to these localities there are numerous others where the rock comes up to the surface, only in small patches. This occurs in Tyrone, in Sligo, Fermanagh, Mayo, and Cavan; in Kilkenny, and in several parts of Wexford. These smaller masses, however, are not of any industrial interest.

The rock granite is of complex constitution, being a mixture of various minerals, of which, however, three are so predominant that they are properly considered its characteristic elements. They are quartz, felspar, and mica. The granite of the vicinity of Dublin is distinguished for the whiteness of its felspar and the complete absence of hornblende. The granite of the Mourne mountains, on the other hand, contains abundance of hornblende, and the felspar is of a flesh red colour. In many places the texture of the rock is so close that it admits of being worked for artificial purposes, and when polished presents a beautiful appearance, from the varied colours and disposition of its constituent minerals. Other varieties are unfit for this use, from the rapidity with which they are decomposed on exposure to the air; thereby producing the materials of other rocks, as well as the clays of purest quality, and best adapted for the manufacture of earthenware. It is the felspar which is thus altered. This mineral is rich in potash, being composed of

Silica, ... 65·5
Potash, ... 17·7
Alumina, ... 16·8
_____
100·0

when it is decomposed, the alkali and most of the silica are carried off by the drainage water, and furnish to the cultivated soils of the lower country, those materials so necessary to the growth of their crops of grain. The alumina, with some silica, remains as clay, the uses of which will come again under our notice.

The principal lead mines of Ireland are situated in granite. Copper is also found, but not abundantly. It is the usual receptacle of the ores of tin and of the precious metals. The mines which have been found and worked in the granite districts, will be hereafter fully described.

Closely associated with the granite, and usually in contact with it, is mica-slate. This rock is not much developed in Leinster; a narrow fringe of it merely edging the granitic district of Wicklow and Wexford. In Donegal and Galway it assumes a more important character. Of the former county, by far the greatest part consists of mica-slate, which commencing at the edge of the granite, spreads over the remaining area, and passing into Derry and Tyrone, forms also in these counties the characteristic rock, until it disappears under the sandstone formation, which, ranging in a circular sweep from Malin-head to Ballyshannon on the western coast, constitutes its boundary. In Galway a large tract, ranging northward from the granitic district, is formed of mica-slate, and this rock occurs extensively also in Mayo, where, although separated by some intervening narrow strips of other rocks, it may be considered as part of the Galway district.

The chemical character of mica-slate is by no means definite or uniform; it graduates by insensible degrees into the rock, which usually lies upon it, the clay-slate, and frequently by the development in it of felspathic crystals it passes by slight gradations into that kind of granitic rock, which still preserving traces of stratification, is called gneiss. The mica-slate has no special metalliferous character, but it is important to remark that the granite is most likely to be rich in metals near its junction with mica-slate It will be seen hereafter, that the lodes or veins of ore are usually found cutting the line of junction of these rocks.

In chemical constitution, mica is very complex, and may yield to the soil, by its decomposition, a greater number of ingredients than almost any other mineral; it contains potash, lime, and magnesia, besides silica, alumina, and often soda. It is a material, however, very little susceptible of decomposition, as is seen by examining a fragment of weathered granite, where the quartz and mica will be found to remain perfectly unaltered, whilst the felspar may have totally rotted away.

The clay-slate, which usually rests upon the mica-slate, is one of the most important rocks of Ireland, as well from the area over which it extends, as from the quantity of minerals it includes. The Counties of Wexford, Louth, Down, Waterford, Cork, and Kerry, are for the most part constituted of this rock, which, however, appears at the surface in various other localities of less extent. Under the name of clay-slate, there have been, until lately, confounded two formations of very different geological character, and occupying different geographical positions. I shall call them by their simplest titles of lower and upper slate, as those names are least liable to misapprehension. Of the lower slate there are two great districts; one north of Dublin, the other south. The northern clay-slate formation commences at Drogheda, and continues along the coast, interrupted only by the granitic protrusion of Carlingford and Mourne, to near Belfast. Inland, its southern edge ranges almost due east and west until it comes near the Shannon at Longford. A line from Belfast to Longford, by Armagh and Clones, marks its remaining boundary. Within this great area, which includes almost entirely the Counties of Louth and Down, with parts of Longford, Cavan, Monaghan, and Armagh, the continuity of the clay-slate is interrupted in numerous places by the appearance of other rocks upon the surface. The only one deserving of remark, is that extending from Moynalty by Kingscourt to Carrickmacross. It is an insulated district of limestone, with millstone grit and some rocks of the coal formation, and thin veins of coal, of which the character has been mentioned in page 15. The southern district of lower slate spreads on each side of the Wicklow and Wexford granite, with which it in many places lies in contact; the usually interposed sheet of mica-slate being absent. On the eastern and southern flanks, the clay-slate extends down to the sea-shore and to the River Suir. On the west it is much less developed; forming the range of hills bounding the granite mountains along the Counties of Dublin and Kildare until it reaches the valley of Barrow near Athy.

From Wexford, the clay-slate, intersected by the valley of the Suir, crosses into Waterford, of which county it constitutes

a large proportion, extending along the coast to near Dungarvan, and westward to where it is overlaid by the sandstone
rocks, which form the crests of the Cummeragh and Mona-
vullagh mountains.

The upper slate, which is distinguished from the lower, not
merely by its relative position, but by being found to contain
imbedded fossils of specific character, of which traces of primitive organic life the lower slate appears to be nearly destitute,
occupies the greater part of the south-west of Kerry, and the
adjoining portions of the County of Cork. Its eastern limit is
from Dunmanway to near Macroom, whence, stretching towards
Mallow, it constitutes the group of the Boghra mountains,
from which the northern edge of the slate district passes due
east and west, by Mill-street and Killarney, to the Atlantic
coast at Doulus Head. The coastward boundary of the upper
slate is remarkable for the bold character of its promontories,
which, truly peninsular, project far into the ocean, and are
separated by the magnificent bays of Bantry and Kenmare.
Some of the most picturesque scenery of Ireland lies within
this field, as well as some of the loftiest mountains: Mangerton
and Macgillicuddy's Reeks, Dunloe, and Glengariff, have given
to this geographical district, a celebrity from which the opportunities for industrial enterprize which it presents, may possibly derive an extraneous interest. Independent of minor
objects, there may be signalized as belonging to it, one of the
most productive copper districts, that of Allihies and Berehaven, and in the island of Valentia, the quarries for slates and
flags, which afford so large an amount of profit and employment.

The peninsula of Dingle consists principally, its western
half exclusively, of this upper slate; although it is geographically isolated from the main portion of the rock just noticed,
by the interposition of the limestone and of the Munster coal
formation, which at Castlemain haven stretches down to the
coast.

In the other parts of Ireland the upper or silurian slate is
found in but few localities, and there developed but to a small
extent. The most remarkable is at Pomeroy in Tyrone, on
the edge of the great mica-slate district of Derry, from which

it is separated by a narrow band of granite. This patch of slate has become of much scientific importance from the study of its peculiar fossils by Captain Portlock, but it does not possess any industrial features that interest us.

I have mentioned that the quartz rock, although not itself possessing a stratified structure, is yet usually associated with those formations of mica-slate and the upper and lower clay-slates, and makes its appearance in great beds or projecting veins, frequently capping the mountain ranges, or isolated hills of the slate districts just now described. The greatest development of quartz rock in Ireland, is in Mayo and in Donegal. In Mayo the northern coast from Erris Head to Bealdarig, consists of quartz, which extends inland to near Lake Carramore, and to the south, some of the highest mountains, as Nephin, in the interior of the county, are formed of isolated masses of it. Similarly circumstanced are the Bina-bola (twelve Pins) mountains in Connemara, which, situated in the midst of mica-slate, consist of quartz.

In the north of Donegal are found vast veins of quartz, from one to three miles broad, more or less interrupted by the adjacent granite and mica-slate, and by the protrusions of green-stone and primitive limestone. The largest and most inland of these veins passes from Cullaff Bay in Innishowen, southwest by Buncrana and Ramelton, crossing Lough Swilly, and finally tapering off at Firtown near Ardara. Its length is about twenty-three miles. From this to the north-eastern coast, several parallel and similar beds occur, of which the highest mountains in the county are composed, as Muckish, from which such excellent sand for technical uses is obtained, and Errigal. The north island of Arran also is formed by a projecting rock of this material.

Proceeding south we meet with quartz in connexion with the clay-slate of Wicklow and Wexford. The peninsula of Howth, and the summits of the Sugarloaf mountains and of Bray Head, which give so much picturesque beauty to the entrance of Dublin Bay, are composed of quartz. In Wexford a great number of isolated hills are capped with it, and the district of Forth consists almost exclusively of this material;

this is the most southern point of Ireland in which quartz rock
is found.

Resting on the clay-slate, upper and lower, according to its
distribution, and occupying, in the geological series, the interval extending from the upper slate to the carboniferous limestone, occur a number of rocks, which extend over a very large
area of the country, and which, being by no means homogeneous, either in their mineral character or their chemical
composition, it is very difficult to describe without entering into
too much detail.   These rocks are usually siliceous, the grain
varying from the finest sand to large pebbles; they are hence
called sandstones, sandstone conglomerates, &c. The siliceous
material is cemented by a paste, usually aluminous, but more
or less coloured by iron, whence the trivial distinctive names,
as red or yellow, have been derived. In certain localities the
upper beds of this formation are less siliceous, and assume a
slaty structure, and hence Mr. Griffith, the highest authority
on the subject of our local geology, considers, that interposed
between the clay-slate and the limestone there may be distinguished three formations,—the old red sandstone, which is
lowest, and by far the most largely developed; the yellow
sandstone, resting on the red, and usually accompanying
it; and the carboniferous slate, which has been traced but in
one portion of Ireland, in Cork, where it occupies a considerable area.

The old red sandstone is most extensively developed in the
south of Ireland; it forms the greater part of the County of Cork,
commencing to the west at the limits of the district of the upper slate, on which it rests, and extending eastwards until it
meets the ocean, to which it forms the boundary of Cork and
Waterford along the greater portion of this coast.   Stretching northwards from Cork, almost to the foot of the Wexford
granitic ridge, the mountain ranges of Knockmeldon and Com-
meragh, and also those of the Galtees, and the Rooley mountains, are constituted of this old red sandstone: these mountain groups being only separated by the valleys of the Blackwater and Suir, into which the limestone of the central plain
ramifies.   The highest portions of these mountains generally

shew the clay-slate breaking out from under the red sandstone, and illustrating the geological order of superposition, whilst along their flanks, where they emerge from contact with the limestone, a fringe of the more recent yellow sandstone is generally to be traced.

More to the centre, a great number of isolated patches of this sandstone break through the general flatness of the limestone country, especially in Longford and Roscommon; but the greatest development of it, within that district, is in the range of mountains which, under various names of Slieve Boughta, Silvermines, Slieve Bloom, the Arra, Slieve Phelim, &c., occupies a considerable area in the counties of Clare, Limerick, and Tipperary, and in the Queen's County, extending north and south from Limerick to near Loughrea, and eastwards to near Mountmellick. The central and highest points of the several portions of these mountains are of clay-slate; the flanks and general mass are old red sandstone, whilst the edge is fringed with the newer or yellow sandstone, on which the limestone of the surrounding level country rests. Through a gorge in this mountain range, at Killaloe, the Shannon rushes, its vast waters being precipitated from the level expanse of Lough Derg down the rapids of Doonas and Castletroy towards Limerick. In the Arra mountains on the eastern side of the lake, are the well known slate quarries of Killaloe, which, together with numerous localities of mineral and metallic substances in this district, will be hereafter noticed.

Between the mica-slate, clay-slate, and quartz rocks, which form the west of Mayo, and the limestone, is interposed a large tract of old red and yellow sandstone, which from the north coast at Killala, skirts by Loughs Conn and Cullin, and reaches the Atlantic again at Westport. In Tyrone another large field of old red sandstone appears. It extends from near Cookstown to the shores of Lough Erne, about twenty miles, and its breadth is about six miles, marked by Omagh and Ballygawley, which are just on its boundary. Scattered around, and some miles from it, are several smaller patches of the same rock, and of the yellow sandstone, which, however, could not be described without entering too much into detail. This sand-

N

stone district may be considered as interposed between the great mica-slate formation of Derry and Donegal, and the more southern limestone country, of which the arms stretch up by Monaghan and Clogher to Coal Island and the basin of Lough Neagh.

The only locality in which the third member of this geological series, the carboniferous slate, is found developed, is on the south-eastern coast of Cork. There it rests on the yellow and red sandstone, and forms a band, of which the usual breadth, as from near Bandon to the old head of Kinsale, is about seven miles, and the greatest length, from Dunmanus Bay to the mouth of Cork harbour, about thirty-four miles. In the promontories of Dunmanus and Skibbereen, the central mountain ridges are of the old red sandstone, on which, at each side near the coast, rests the carboniferous slate: the newer rock, as in most instances, occupying the troughs or more level area between the bolder elevations of those lower in geological order. Several valuable mines of copper, lead, and manganese are situated in this rock.

Already, in the commencement of this work, the general distribution of the limestone rock, and also of the strata of the coal formation which rest upon it, has been noticed; and attention was directed to the great development of the millstone grit, or sandstone of the coal formation, in Leitrim and Roscommon, the circumstances of which, particularly the marine character of its fossils, induce Mr. Griffith to consider it a distinct formation lying between the carboniferous limestone, and the true coal strata. The Connaught coal field would, therefore, require, in a purely geological sense, to be distinguished from the other coal districts which are not connected with the millstone grit formation, but are more recent and superior to it, in order of superposition. These considerations are, however, of interest only in philosophical geology; they are not concerned in the practical description of our coal districts given in a preceding chapter, and hence do not require further notice. The limestone strata yield for industrial purposes a great variety of building stones and marbles. The sandstones and conglomerates are used for building, and for millstones. The most important localities for such uses will be hereafter enumerated.

The rocks superior in geological order to the coal formation, are found in Ireland to occupy but a very limited area, being confined almost exclusively to the north-eastern corner of the island, forming the county of Antrim, with some portions of the contiguous counties of Derry and Armagh. In an ascending order the rocks met with in this district are, magnesian limestone, new red sandstone, black shale, lias limestone, greensand and chalk. These rocks present themselves, however, but on the edges of the district, as the whole is covered with a thick mass of tabular trap (basalt), from which the most characteristic features of the country are derived. Viewed from a distance it appears as a high table land rising from the flat country, or from the sea. Its outline is marked by lofty precipices and barren cliffs, especially along the eastern coast, where masses of black trap from 200 to 300 feet in thickness, often columnar, surmounting precipices of chalk, of dazzling brightness, of 60 or 100 feet high, presents a series of objects, which, for beauty of contrast and picturesque effect, are seldom rivalled.

The vast flood of trap and basaltic rocks which overspread this part of Ireland, has, in many cases, so altered the mineral character of the underlying rocks as to render them very unlike the rocks which occupy the same geological position in England. Still they are completely identified by the fossil contents, and in general distribution are as follows.

The magnesian limestone is found but at Hollywood, on the southern side of Belfast Lough. It is a true dolomite, and has been exported to Glasgow to make sulphate of magnesia. In composition it is the same as the dolomites found in various other places in Ireland, of which the more important shall be noticed hereafter.

The new red sandstone, which in England covers so large an area, and is of so much industrial importance, from its being the depository of rock salt and gypsum, is with us but of very limited extent, and is totally destitute of the former valuable mineral. The sandstone, which is usually brownish red, con-

sisting of grains of quartz cemented by a paste, which, though
usually argillaceous, is sometimes calcareous, contains much
mica, and is often striped with various colours, from decomposition of its ferruginous contents.   This sandstone comes to
the surface at various points along the edges of the basaltic
field; but its principal development is in the valley of the
Lagan, which it constitutes from above Moira by Lisburn to
Belfast.   Resting on the sandstone are the gypseous marls,
which, as a source of plaster of Paris, I shall again notice. To
these succeed shales and limestones, which are of the formation termed lias, in England, and finally, the chalk, which presents all varieties of hardness, from its usually soft condition,
to that of a hard and granular, but beautifully white marble.

Some isolated patches of new red sandstone are found resting on the limestone of the more central districts, and also on
the coal district of Tyrone.   The coal strata of Monaghan,
described pp 15 and 173, are surmounted by the new red sandstone, and by marls, important for a large deposit of gypsum,
to which I shall again refer.

Strata of the tertiary epoch are found in Ireland, only at the
southern shore of Lough Neagh, where the clays containing
wood coal occur. These have been sufficiently noticed in page
31, as a source of fuel.

Finally, the igneous rocks, which, according to differences
in minute mineral character and structure, receive the various
names of trap, basalt, greenstone, &c., cover over the entire
table land of Antrim.   These rocks are remarkable for the
complexity of their chemical composition and the varieties of
imbedded minerals which they contain.   They are hence decomposed with great rapidity, and produce ochres and clays of
various and beautiful colours, of which beds of great extent
occur in Antrim.   The soil formed round the edges of this district by the mixture of the decomposing trap and subjacent
rocks is one of the most naturally fertile that is found in Ireland.

Such are the general characters of the geological structure
of Ireland.   The various groups of rocks differ remarkably in

their chemical composition, and consequently are applicable to very diversified uses. Their composition, and also the circumstances under which they have been found, and the agencies to which they have been subjected since their formation, influence materially their mineral contents, and it will be found that the distribution of the several kinds of mineral substances of use in the arts, coincides very closely with the geological arrangement of the rocks. It will be more convenient, however, for the present, to abandon all geological considerations, and merely consider how the several mineral substances of leading interest are circumstanced in Ireland

1st. OF THE COPPER MINES.

The ores of this valuable metal are found distributed thoughout the clay-slate districts in a great number of localities, more or less abundantly. In many places the indications are so trifling as not to offer any inducement to enterprize ; in others, so abundant as to have given origin to numerous extensive and prosperous mining establishments. The mines of copper at present in practical work, may be conveniently described as forming three great groups, all on the sea side. The first, in the County Wicklow, occupying the valley of the Ovoca. The second is in the County of Waterford, occupying the district of Knockmahon, and the third, occupying the southwestern angle of the island, is situated in the southern portions of Cork and in Kerry. Each of these districts deserves special examination. A number of smaller mines which are scattered through other parts of Ireland may be noticed more briefly afterwards.

Before proceeding to that subject it will be found convenient to remark, that the copper ores most usually found, and which alone become practically of importance, are three in number.

1st. The carbonate of copper, of which there are two kinds, green and blue. The green, or *malachite*, is not unusual in mines, but occurs only in small quantity. It is very rich in metal and very easily worked. It consists of carbonic acid, water, and oxide of copper in the following proportions.

Oxide of copper, ... 72·07
Carbonic acid, ... 19·82
Water, ... 8·11
                                    _____
                                    100·00

It hence yields 57·7 per cent. of copper.

This mineral, when pure, possesses a beautiful structure and colour, which renders it very valuable for ornamental uses.

The blue carbonate is still rarer than the green. It is termed *azurite*. Its composition is,

Carbonic acid, ... 25·43
Oxide of copper, ... 69·36
Water, ... 5·21
                                    _____
                                    100·00

and it yields 55·5 per cent. of copper.

2nd. The subsulphuret of copper, *grey copper ore.* This ore is sometimes found very abundantly, and is the most valuable of all the ores of copper. More commonly, however, it is only found in small pieces mixed with the ordinary ore. It consists of

Sulphur, ... 20
Copper, ... 80
                                    ____
                                    100

3rd. The ordinary or yellow copper ore, *copper pyrites.* This mineral, known by its brilliant golden yellow colour, is a double sulphuret of iron and copper, and contains, when pure,

Sulphur, ... 34·78
Copper, ... 34·78
Iron, ... 30·44
                                    _____
                                    100·00

In some of the foreign mines the grey sulphuret is the predominant mineral, but in all the Irish, indeed also in all the English mines it is the copper pyrites which forms the material produce; the other ores being but casually found and in very trifling quantity.

The copper pyrites is associated almost universally with iron pyrites, the bi-sulphuret of iron, the peculiar uses of which shall be hereafter specially noticed. The effect of this mixture is to reduce the per centage of copper, which is further depressed by the impossibility of separating, even by the most perfect machinery, all the adherent rock and veinstone from the ore. Hence copper ore, which contains 12 or 15 per cent. of copper, as sent to market, is considered very rich. The average produce of the copper mines of Cornwall does not exceed 7 per cent. The ore is of course valued according to the quantity of copper which it contains, subject to certain deductions, which it is not here necessary to explain.

Metallic ores are very rarely found disseminated through the general substance of the containing rock, indeed where they are so, they are seldom worth the trouble of extracting. A rock of which the mechanical and chemical structure is uniform, very seldom contains any important quantity of copper or other ores. These occur where a rock has been violently acted upon subsequent to its formation; its strata dislocated and its substance split up by the forcible entry of other kinds of rocks, which, penetrating its mass, form veins, ramifying in various directions, and traceable sometimes for hundreds of miles. It is in those veins, where many different materials are brought into contact, and that the forces of heat and electricity probably awakening the chemical affinities of the elements of the rocks, induce their action on one another, that metallic deposits occur: the vein rock, which is very commonly quartz or sulphate of barytes, or fluor spar, having within it or at its side a vein of ore more or less rich, but unfortunately very capricious in its distribution and in its magnitude. Usually, however, the more violent the action on the containing rocks appears to have been, the richer are its metallic contents. If several veins meet, cross, and shatter one another, the ore is likely to occur in masses or bunches at this point, and where the structure of the rock becomes regular, almost universally the metallic veins disappear. The substance of the vein rock is often termed the *gangue* or *matrix* of the ore, or the *veinstone*. The separation of the ore from it, by picking, pounding, and washing, forms an extensive series of operations, for the description of which the standard works on mining and metallurgy may be consulted.

Such being the circumstances under which metallic ores are usually found, I shall pass to the description of the districts of the copper mines of Ireland.

1st. *Of the Wicklow District.* The principal features of this district have been so accurately described by Mr. Weaver, who was for many years principal conductor of the mines, that I shall do little more than abridge his description, and add thereto such facts as I have been able to collect illustrative of their subsequent progress and their present condition.

The metalliferous clay-slate district occupies but a small space, being very narrow in breadth, and not more than ten miles long, from Croghan–Kinshela on the south, towards west Acton on the north.

Metallic substances are diffused throughout the entire space, in slight layers, in cotemporaneous veins, and in massy beds, which last are principally composed of copper pyrites and iron pyrites. The line of the excavations of the works in Connoree and Tigroney extended in 1819 upwards of 1000 fathoms. At various depths in the mass of the clay-slate occur beds of what is technically termed *soft ground*, which consists of decomposed slate of various tints, abounding in particles of pyrites of iron, and sometimes copper and arsenic, and usually accompanied by a considerable body of greyish or yellowish-white clay. When brought to the surface and exposed to the action of the air, these bodies rapidly decompose, and absorbing oxygen form alum, sulphate of iron and sulphate of copper. A similar decomposition takes place under ground, and hence the drainage water of the district contains a very sensible quantity of copper, which has been, and indeed is, economized by conveying the water as well from the lower as from the upper mines into tanks, where the muddy particles are allowed to subside. The clean water is then run into pits containing scrap iron, which causes the precipitation of the copper and dissolves in its place. An idea of the quantity of copper thus saved from waste, may be formed from the fact that during Mr. Weaver's management there were 442½ tons of impure precipitated copper sold, the value of which was £12 12s. per ton. The quantity of iron consumed was 429 tons, 14 cwt.

Each bed of soft ground contains one or more layers of copper pyrites, or mere iron pyrites, varying in thickness, and sometimes acquiring a breadth of several fathoms. Five of such beds are met with, one in Connoree, two in the old or upper mine of Cronebane, one in the new or lower mine, and one in Tigroney. That in Connoree contains a bed of ore about four feet thick, consisting of a fine-grained intermixture of galena (sulphuret of lead), grey ore (sulphuret of antimony), and blende (sulphuret of zinc), with pyrites of copper, iron, and arsenic. A similar compound occurs in the second bed of the upper mine of Cronebane. The more southern bed contains much iron pyrites, and has yielded at different periods some thousand tons of grey copper ore, which, in the greater depth of the mine, passes into copper pyrites. The third bed, in Cronebane, situated on the western side of the hill, has proved the most valuable, the greater part of its width being occupied by copper ore, which in the upper part consisted principally of grey ore, but at greater depths passed into copper pyrites with iron pyrites. The bed of solid ore has varied from one to three fathoms in breadth; no quartz or spar of any kind attend these beds. The more productive parts of the bed have, in several instances, yielded from ten to fifteen tons of merchantable ore per cubic fathom, the average produce of which has varied from five to seven per cent. of copper. The bed in Tigroney had yielded only iron pyrites when Mr. Weaver wrote.

Beds of iron pyrites, from a few feet to some fathoms in thickness, have appeared in the firm and flinty slate, as in the deep levels of Tigroney and Cronebane. In the flinty slate are found also several cotemporaneous veins of quartz, having rich copper pyrites, accompanied sometimes by azure copper ore, and whose average produce is from 10 to 12 per cent. of copper. These veins range with the slate, ramifying, and where they coalesce, forming a body sometimes twelve feet wide, with four or five feet of solid ore, but they seldom continue productive for more than thirty fathoms in length. Small veins of this description are very numerous.

The mines of Connoree, Cronebane, and Tigroney, so often

mentioned above, are situated on the north bank of the Ovoca River. The structure and circumstances of the southern side, on which are the mines of Ballymurtagh and Ballygahan, are precisely similar. It is, therefore, unnecessary to enter on a description, which should be mainly a repetition of what has been already said.

The quantity and value of the ore raised in this district at various periods, may be inferred from the following numbers.

In the twelve years ending 1799, the mines of Cronebane yielded 7533 tons of ore, containing 9 per cent. of copper.

In the twelve years ending 1811, the produce was 1934⅔ tons, containing 5½ per cent. of copper.

After this period, owing to many conspiring causes, very little ore was raised for many years.

Mr. Griffith states, that in 1826 the copper ore raised in Cronebane sold in Swansea for £12,354 14s., and the ore raised at Ballymurtagh sold for £3373. The latter was worked by the Hibernian Mining Company, on a single metallic bed, containing copper pyrites with some blende. The lode (vein) at eighty fathoms depth yielded per fathom of driving four tons of dressed ore, of 5½ per cent. produce. The ore he calculates cost the Company, when finished, £7 per ton, and certainly left little, if any, profit.

The following tables, illustrative of the actual condition of the mines of this district, have been extracted from the notes of sales at Swansea, and from notices published in the Mining Journal.

The quantities of copper ore from each mine, which was sold at Swansea, and its value, was in 1836:

MINE.	TONS.	VALUE.		
		£	s.	d.
Ballymurtagh, ...	4659	19,943	12	0
Connoree, ...	2158	10,960	10	0
Cronebane and Tigroney,	4691	23,497	10	0
Ballygahan, ...	305	1,417	0	0
	11,813	55,818	12	0

In 1840:

MINE.	TONS.	VALUE.		
		£	s.	d.
Ballymurtagh, ...	3274	6,956	2	0
Cronebane and Tigroney,	3017	12,889	8	6
Connoree, ...	158	1,250	8	0
Ballygahan, ...	198	346	5	0
	6647	21,442	3	6

In 1843:

MINE.	TONS.	VALUE.		
		£	s.	d.
Ballymurtagh, ...	1385	4,866	19	0
Connoree, ...	654	2,512	0	0
Cronebane and Tigroney,	1160	5,438	2	0
Ballygahan, ...	28	100	18	0
	3227	12,917	19	0

It would hence appear, that the quantity of ore raised in this district had very much diminished since 1836, but such is not actually the case; on the contrary, the activity of industry in those mines, as well as the profits to their undertakers, is, as I understand, steadily on the increase. The quantity of ore sold at Swansea has, however, fallen off very much, as is shewn by the above returns, owing to the copper being now extensively smelted in the neighbourhood of Liverpool, and also to the poorer ores of the Wicklow district being extensively exported to various localities of chemical manufacture, where the sulphur, as well as the copper which they contain, is economized. The true produce of this district at present may be judged by the following table of the ores raised and sold from the Ballymurtagh mine, worked by the Wicklow Copper Mining Company, for which I am indebted to the kindness of Mr. Wright.

"BALLYMURTAGH, CO. WICKLOW.

| YEAR. | PRODUCE. | | GROSS VALUE. | SOLD AT | | PAID IN WAGES. |
	COPPER ORE.	IRON PYRITES.		SWANSEA.	OTHER PORTS.	
	Tons.	Tons.	£	£	£	£
1840	4839	5334	29596	,,	29596	9927
1841	4617	18575	34493	,,	34493	16312
1842	7549	9023	29113	1256	27857	15371
1843	6555	8376	24238	5897	18341	10985

" Average produce of copper ore, 4½ per cent.

" Average number of persons employed, 700.

"W. HODGSON WRIGHT."

In this table is given the quantity of iron pyrites sold by the Company : its price is included in the gross values given.

It is here seen that the industry of this region has acquired a vast development within the last ten years.   This arose from another branch of mining industry coming into play; the trade in iron pyrites as a source of sulphur. In the Wicklow district the copper ore is associated with such vast quantities of iron pyrites, that in order to raise it, it is necessary to quarry the latter to a large amount, which very much enhanced the cost. But when there arose an outlet for the bisulphuret of iron, the mining for the copper ore became much more remunerative, and hence the vast quantities which have been sent to market since that period.

It has been seen that by the operations of the Ballymurtagh mine, about £12,000 is annually distributed in wages to about 700 persons.   Including the other mines, the total number of persons deriving employment from the mineral industry of the Ovoca district, may be considered as brought up to about two thousand.

2nd. *Of the Waterford District.*—The geological character of the slate district of Waterford has been already noticed. That part of it which includes the Knockmahon mines, is situated on the sea coast, close to the village of Bonmahon and extends from the Bay of Dungarvan on the west, to the Bay of Tramore on the east. It has been long known for its mineral treasures : many of the metalliferous veins having been worked by the ancient inhabitants. One almost insulated promontory is perforated like a rabbit burrow, and is known as the Dane's Island ; the peasantry attributing these ancient mines, like all other relics of remote civilization, to that enterprizing people. In the abandoned workings antique tools have been found, stone hammers and chisels, and wooden shovels. These workings were easily carried on, as the metalliferous veins presented themselves at the face of the cliffs on the sea shore, and they were abandoned as soon as, by the accumulation of water, or an exhaustion of the richer ores, they became difficult to manage.

Within a range of three miles, taking Bonmahon as a centre, a great number of lodes of lead and copper are distinguishable in the cliffs, some of considerable width, but others comparatively small. The direction of the principal lodes is about 20° south of east, but others vary considerably from this. The principal lodes dip towards the north. The most productive at present in course of working, occur in the clay-slate, although they sometimes penetrate through the strata of other rocks, as hornstone, which are found within the slate. In this hornstone Mr. Holdsworth has remarked the presence of several ores of cobalt, but not in quantity. The lead veins, which contained galena (sulphuret of lead), and calc spar, are not worked. The copper lodes consist of quartz, and produce native copper, sulphuret of copper, grey copper ore, and black oxide of copper. Sulphuret of zinc, carbonate of iron, and sulphate of barytes occur occasionally, and also argentiferous sulphuret of lead.

It has been seen already that there is found, in addition to the ordinary clay-slate of this district (Cambrian slate), a small deposit of the superior slate containing fossil remains (silurian), which is found so much developed further south and west. It is, however, here not of practical importance.

In the following letter from Captain Petherick, the manager of these mines, additional circumstances of their structure, as well as their actual extent and workings, are well described:

"My dear Sir,—The rock formation in which the metalliferous veins of this district occur is principally clay-slate of a light blue colour, and immediately in contact with the *productive* part of the vein it is generally in a softened or partially decomposed state.

"The veins are composed of hard compact quartz, intermixed occasionally, particularly where they prove unproductive, with angular fragments of clay-slate; the quartz is the matrix of the ore.

"Our principal vein varies in width from six inches to upwards of thirty feet, but its average size is probably from ten to twelve feet: it is, in fact, an unusually large lode; numerous smaller veins also occur on each side of it, some of which have been worked with partial success, but as far as they have yet been explored, they have uniformly become small and unproductive in depth, and at present our operations, with a few trifling exceptions, are exclusively confined to the larger vein.

"The mining ground leased to the Mining Company, extends about four miles along the coast, and nearly three miles inland.

"Grey sulphuret of copper, native copper, and the red oxide of copper, occur occasionally in the shallow workings, but in comparatively small quantities; the most abundant, and therefore the most remunerative ore, is the yellow pyrites, and in the deeper levels no other kind of ore is met with.

"The *average* per centage of the produce of these mines is 9½ to 10 per cent.

"The greatest depth we have yet worked is about 800 feet from the surface; and the greatest length of our underground workings is rather more than an English mile, in a direct line.

"The number of persons in constant employment in these mines is about 1200; and of that number 140 are females employed in cleaning the ores. No females are ever permitted to go underground.

" It is a remarkable characteristic of this district, at least I have never observed it elsewhere, that a part of the vein is composed of a conglomerate of pebbles of quartz and copper, in an indurated clay-paste. Sometimes the fragments of quartz are angular, but more frequently they occur in a rounded state; and occasionally the copper is disseminated in small particles throughout the paste. When I have an opportunity I will take the liberty of sending you a few specimens of the conglomerate, which I am sure will be interesting to you.

"Your's, very faithfully,

"JOHN PETHERICK."

The mines of this district, at present working, consist of four groups, which are held by the Mining Company of Ireland from different proprietors. They are, Knockmahon, Kilduane, Bonmahon, and Balinasisla. In the returns of ores sold, these divisions are not distinguished, and hence the following table gives only the aggregate produce, and the average value of the entire:

YEAR.	TONS.	VALUE.
1836,	 3588,	. . . . £33,166 0 0
1840,	 7875,	. . . . 63,087 0 0
1843,	 9101,	. . . . 62,956 0 0

It is seen by this table how rapidly these mines have been extended by the energies of the Mining Company, under the zealous and skilful direction of Mr. Purdy and Captain Petherick. This extension has been accompanied by some very remarkable circumstances, to which I shall hereafter direct attention.

The ores are dressed at Knockmahon by very perfect machinery, which is set in motion by overshot wheels, of which one is forty feet diameter and four feet wide: for which there is an ample supply of water. In these operations, as well as in mining, employment is given altogether to an average of 1200 persons, whose earnings fluctuate with the produce of the mine. The sum paid by the Mining Company for labour, in this district, is not less than £2500 per month.

3rd. *Of the south-western District.*—The space occupied by
the clay-slate formation in the Counties of Cork and Kerry,
has been found rich in mineral indications; but in many cases
where trials have been made, often at very great expense, the
result has been unpromising. Of these failures many may be
traced to the incompetency or imprudence of the undertakers,
but others to the peculiarities in the nature of the ground,
which could not have been foreseen. Some mines have been
remarkably productive, of which the Allihies mine, belonging
to Mr. Puxley, and conducted by Captain Read, is an excellent
example. Although indications of metalliferous veins have
been noticed in all parts of this vast district, it is especially
towards its edge, round the sea coast, where it is more or less
in contact with, or in the vicinity of, the older slate, or of the
old red sandstone, that the more important deposits are found,
and hence proceeding from east to west we may trace the series
of mining localities of greater or less importance from Skibbereen in Cork, to Kenmare and Killarney.

Between Skibbereen and Skull, at the village of Ballydehob,
a vein of copper ore was found of considerable extent upon the
surface, and of good produce. This mine was worked with
activity for about four years; it gave employment to about
200 persons, and many thousand tons of ore were shipped to
Swansea. It was found, however, that according as the workings descended below the surface the lodes became impoverished, and it was ultimately abandoned as unprofitable. It is
stated that parties are about to make new trials of this mine.

About ten miles west of Skibbereen, on the property of Lord
Audley, are metalliferous veins in great number on which
mines have been opened, known as the Audley mines, and
which, like the Arigna Iron Company, have been the means of
bringing into disrepute Irish industrial enterprizes, through
the fault of jobbing speculators in London. The district of
these mines comprises about 5500 acres. The principal lodes
are three in number, not far asunder. The first consists of
quartz, with bright yellow copper and iron pyrites, which has
been found to contain usually about 8 per cent. of copper. In
the second, which has been but little worked upon, particles of

carbonate of copper (malachite), with nodules of grey sulphuret of copper, are disseminated through the clay-slate rock. The third, the Cappagh lode, is that which was principally worked upon. It contained copper pyrites and grey copper ore. The produce was so rich as to give 55 to 65 per cent. of copper, but these indications, so favourable near the surface, diminished as the works went down, and the mines were, after some time, abandoned. It being considered that their failure in the hands of Mr. Hall, their first undertaker, arose from want of capital, the Mining Company of Ireland took them in hands, and expended £12,000 in fully examining their value. The shaft on Cappagh was sunk to 120 fathoms, and works were extended in levels 200 fathoms. The indications of the veins on the surface shewed that they should intersect at that depth, and it was hoped that, as very frequently occurs in mines, a great deposit of metallic ore should be found at the junction. On the contrary, it was discovered, that after their junction they became unproductive, and the works were abandoned. At Horse Island, similarly, the ore near the surface yielded in some cases 55 per cent. of copper, and 230 tons which were sold at Swansea, realized £2800, but on the shaft being sunk to forty fathoms, the lode, like the others, became impoverished, and the Mining Company surrendered their lease to the proprietor of the soil. A company was afterwards formed in London, which purchased at an enormous sum, upwards of £100,000, the right of working these abandoned mines, and their affairs have been in litigation ever since. The whole produce sold by this Company (the West Cork Mining Company) appears, by the Swansea returns, to have been 173 tons of ore, which realized £1601 12s. A company formed as that was could not come to good in any way, and it is to be hoped, that the future operations in this field may be executed by persons more deserving of success, and more competent to secure it.

South of the district of the Audley mines, on the shores of Roaring-water Bay, are situated the mines of Roaring-water, of Cosheen, and of Skull. At Roaring-water the lode is friable quartz and gossan, with bunches of black and grey copper ore. As the workings descend, this passes into rich yellow copper pyrites, which is described as free from iron pyrites. This is a new mine. I do not know that it has yet sent any ore to market. I trust that the indications of rich produce shewn upon the surface, may not be found to vanish further down.

Of the mines of Cosheen and Skull, the former is situated on the shore, the latter on the island of that name. The Cosheen mine was commenced in 1839 by Messrs. Connell and M'Mullen of Cork. It is advantageously situated on the side of a hill at Skull harbour. A deep adit level has been driven in, just above high water mark, for about 250 fathoms, in the course of the principal lode. This adit drains the mine, and by it the ore is extracted on a railway. The adit is now being driven farther south to cut some parallel lodes which had been superficially explored. The arrangements for working this mine have been made on an extensive scale, under the direction of Mr. Thomas. The number of hands employed is about 130, and I trust, that its proprietors will continue to receive the benefit they deserve, for an enterprize which has brought comfort to a hundred families that had previously no employment.

The ore from these mines, which are but a short time open, was, as given in the Swansea returns :

In 1840, Cosheen,	126 tons,	value,	.	£1164	2	0
In 1843, Cosheen,	360 ,,	,,	.	2605	15	0
,, Skull,	84 ,,	,,	.	134	8	0

The most important mine in this district is that conducted by Captain Read, near Ballydonegan Bay on the west side of the promontory of Bere. The existence of mineral deposits in this locality was first recognized by Colonel Hall, and pointed out by him to the proprietor, Mr. Puxley. The following particulars as to its actual state were communicated to me by its very skilful manager :

This mine was commenced about thirty-three years ago,

under the name of the Allihies mine, but as the workings are now removed from the land of Allihies, the name of the Berehaven mine has been adopted for it. In the space of three or four miles are several veins, most of which run east and west, and dip to the north. Some of these were found on trial unproductive and were abandoned, but two veins, one called the *Mountain*, being situated 450 feet above the level of the sea, on a large east and west lode, the other, the *Caminche* vein, which runs north-east, have furnished the principal workings.

In the Mountain, a great quantity of copper ore has been raised; there is still obtained about 200 tons per month, of about 10 per cent. produce. The principal working is about 760 feet in length, and 852 feet in depth. The lode is sixty feet wide in one place, but branches and narrows in other places to three or four feet. It consists of quartz and copper pyrites. It is all blasted with gunpowder. The deepest levels had been hitherto rather unproductive, but just now, ore of excellent promise has been raised from them.

The Caminche vein is worked for about 570 feet in length and 912 in depth. The engine shaft sinks sixty feet more. The vein runs north east and dips south east. It has been very productive; the ore is cleaner than in the Mountain vein; the breadth of the lode is from one to twelve feet.

There are employed in these mines about 1000 persons, as follows :

Miners,	400
Smiths and joiners,	30
Helpers,	25
Labourers,	245
Boys,	170
Girls,	130

Mr. John Read, who is engaged in this mine under the dition of his father, kindly furnished me with the following analysis of the usual quality of ore: he found it composed of

Copper, ... 10·2
Iron, ... 10·8
Sulphur, ... 14·8
Quartz, ... 63·9
Loss, ... 0·3
                                              ———
                                              100·0

A short distance from these copper veins, is a vein of lead, which was worked some years ago, and some ore raised, but as it did not promise very well, the workings were not proceeded with.

Owing to the conformation of the surrounding country, there is no command of water power at Allihies, and all the machinery for crushing and dressing the ore is driven by steam engines, of which there are five at work.

The ore raised in this mine is about the same quality as at Knockmahon, varying from 10 to 15 per cent. of copper. In the return made to the Railway Commissioners in 1837, the average annual produce is given at from 6000 to 7000 tons, valued at £9 per ton. I find by the returns of sales at Swansea, that the produce was in

YEAR.	TONS.	VALUE.
1836, ...	6418	£74,879 18 0
1840, ...	4808	40,981 2 6
1843, ...	4446	36,348 6 0

The produce has, therefore, diminished considerably in amount, and still more in richness, but it is to be hoped that this may not continue.

At Holyhill, near Bantry, workings have been executed on a vein of copper ore, but are not now in operation.

At Ardtully, near Kenmare, is a copper mine worked by the Kenmare Mining Association. The produce is the ordinary copper pyrites of moderate richness. The principal shaft has been sunk about twenty fathoms, and the levels extend about sixty. The lode of quartz and calc spar is about five feet wide: it lies at the junction of the clay-slate and limestone.

In 1843, there were sold at Swansea from this mine thirty-one tons of ore, which brought £275 18s. The workings of it are as yet but in their infancy. There are about 100 persons employed on this and the lead mines belonging to the same company and situated close by.

The Lakes of Killarney mark the line of junction of the underlying slate and sandstone rock, with the limestone which fringes the Munster coal field. Along this line, metallic indications have been found in several points, on two of which, mines were opened, which, although not now wrought, deserve some notice from the extent to which they were at one time worked, and the peculiar circumstances under which they were abandoned. These localities are Mucruss and Ross Island.

The Mucruss mine was situated near the head of the great lake, by which, and the River Laune, a complete water communication was opened to the sea at Castlemaine. The lode was five feet wide, and was worked at the depth of thirty-six fathoms on the front shaft, and about twenty by another, sunk some distance to the east. The ore was copper pyrites mixed with much iron pyrites. This mine was worked with great profit from the years 1749 to 1754, but difficulties arising from the circumstances of the European war caused its abandonment. A curious fact in the history of this mine deserves attention. There was found in great profusion a mineral of a granulated metallic appearance, as hard as stone; its colour on the surface dark blue, tending to a beautiful pink. It was not copper ore; it was thrown away as rubbish: no body knew what it was, except one workman, who recognized it to be cobalt ore (arseniuret of cobalt), a mineral of great value, from which the beautiful blue glass and smalt blue is made. This man managed to get away upwards of twenty tons of it as rubbish. Long afterwards a more candid miner, who visited the works and saw some specimens of it, told the proprietor its value; but the deposit of it had been worked out in order to explore for copper; the produce had been thrown away as useless, and it only remained for the mine owner to ruminate on the fortune he might have made, if he had possessed a proper knowledge of his business.

Ross Island, in the great Lake at Killarney, consists of limestone; the metallic lode which passes through it is parallel to that at Mucruss. It dips under the lake at an angle of 30°, which circumstance ultimately led to the abandonment of the mine, for the ore being disseminated through a large quantity of rock, the excavations were necessarily large, and the pursuit of the richer veins was pushed so near the surface, that the water of the lake broke in in such profusion as to render the effective drainage impracticable. The quantity of rock brought up with the ore was another source of loss, as the cost of dressing was thereby rendered very heavy. The quantity of ore raised whilst this mine was at work averaged 200 tons per month. It was, however, very rich. The poorest sold for £14 per ton, and the richest for £40: the average being about £20. The total value of the ore raised in four years, and sold at Swansea, was £80,000. The number of hands employed was about 500. In order to drain these mines a steam engine was put up, and that an idea may be formed of how carelessly matters were managed at that time, it may be here mentioned, that whilst every square mile of the vicinity furnished abundance of turf for the trouble of cutting it, the steam engine was supplied with coals from England at two guineas a ton.

The range of mountains which occupies the north of Tipperary, and forms the gorge of Killaloe, has been found to contain several veins of lead and copper. Of these some are now worked: others have been abandoned after trials, which were not finally satisfactory. I shall notice these mines but briefly.

These mountains consist of clay-slate, fringed in most places by the old red and by the yellow sandstone, but in others coming directly into contact with the edge of the limestone of the plain. At such a junction is situated Silvermines, deriving its name from old and profitable workings which are now exhausted. A split between the limestone and clay-slate of several fathoms wide at top, and twenty-five fathoms deep, was occupied by soft decomposing clay, with lumps of sand and limestone, cemented by various metallic substances, iron ochre and pyrites, sulphuret and carbonate of lead, sulphuret and carbonate of copper, and sulphuret of zinc. Lead was extracted from this mass, and the lead so obtained being unusually rich in silver, gave to the vicinity the name it at present bears.

In the clay-slate tract, south of Silvermines, are several metalliferous veins. In Knockeenroe a powerful vein, consisting of quartz and iron pyrites, with some galena, ranges nearly east and west, and may be traced for a considerable distance, until it sinks under the sandstone which caps the hill. In the latter part of its course it contains copper pyrites. This vein has been examined by Mr. Taylor, who, after some trials, gave it up, and then the Mining Company of Ireland, at the time when the monopoly of the sulphur trade had led to an active demand for iron pyrites, essayed to work through the great mass of sulphur ore, hoping that its sale would enable them to finally ascertain the prospects of copper ore in its interior. It was found, however, that the inland position of the mines, and the refractory nature of the rock, rendered the iron pyrites raised too costly for sale in the English market, and hence the Company was obliged to abandon the investigation without having penetrated through the vast body of sulphur ore which forms the vein. Higher on the mountain, above the junction of the sandstone and clay-slate, are three veins of smaller dimensions, they consist of quartz with sulphate of barytes, and the sulphurets of lead, iron, and zinc.

In the valley of the Newport River are situated the mines of Lackamore. The lode consists of carbonate of lime and iron, bearing rich copper ore in bunches. This mine has been long known and worked. In 1812, when Mr. Weaver wrote, the workings had extended 120 fathoms in length, at a depth of 30 fathoms. After that time they were abandoned, but have been recently brought into activity. There are now about 200 persons employed, and there were sold at Swansea from this mine, in 1840, 111 tons of ore, which produced £1153 7s., and in 1843, 260 tons of ore, which realized £2386 18s.

In the slate district north of Dublin there have been found veins containing ores of copper, which, however, were small and irregular, and have not been found in any case, as yet profitable to work. At Lough Shinny, near Rush, three veins occur, on which extensive workings have been made, and a good deal of ore raised from time to time, but the operations do not appear to be continuously carried on. On the coast at Salterstown, in Louth, veins of lead and copper appear, which were tried and abandoned by the Hibernian Mining Company. At Brownstown, in Meath, a vein of copper pyrites has been found traversing the limestone. Some superficial workings had been made upon this vein, but they have not been since prosecuted.

In Tyrone, some miles from Dungannon, a number of masses of grey sulphuret of copper have been found, some of considerable size; they were imbedded in a soft vein in the conglomerate, resting on the old red sandstone, very near the junction of the two rocks, and were coated with a film of malachite. The geological character of the ground is certainly an unusual one for a connected vein; but trial works are now being executed, and it is to be hoped that the enterprising undertakers may be successful. The ore found is decidedly very rich: specimens of it, which I examined, were pure grey sulphuret, containing 80 per cent. of copper.

Such are the general features of the copper mines that have been, or are now, worked in Ireland, so far as I have been able to discover. Indications of copper have been reported as found in several localities, that I have not noticed, as I ascertained that no real workings had been made, and that the evidence of the importance of the indications, did not appear to be of sufficient weight to justify me in inserting them in the present work.

In what has preceded it may be remarked, that I have spoken always of the quantity of copper ore raised in the Irish mines as being indicated by the returns of sales at Swansea. In fact, the facilities afforded in that locality for the economical smelting of metallic ores are so great, that it has become the centre of the copper trade; and the ores of Cuba, of Cornwall, and of Ireland, mostly converge to South Wales, in order that the metal may be extracted. In estimating the circumstances of any locality where copper ore may be found, the means of conveying it to the shore for exportation form, therefore, an important element; and fortunately almost all the districts in Ireland, in which copper mines exist, lie directly on the coast, or near our navigable rivers.

The treatment of the copper pyrites for the extraction of the metal, consists in a long series of processes, alternately of an oxidizing and deoxidizing character, which have for their object to remove the sulphur and prevent the reduction of the iron of the ore, whilst the copper may be separated in the metallic state. These processes are altogether usually eight in number, and are performed in reverberatory furnaces, at very high temperatures. Hence the consumption of fuel is very great, and its cost makes up a large proportion of the expense of the operation. I will briefly describe the nature of this process, as it is of considerable interest in a scientific point of view, and then point out the numerical estimate of its cost.

The first object in the smelting process is to roast the ore in a current of air, so that the sulphur may be burned out, and the metals, copper and iron, may be oxidized. If the ore contain arsenic, or other volatile impurities, they also are driven off. Most of the sulphur passes away as sulphurous acid gas, but some remains as sulphuric acid united with the oxides of iron and of copper. If now this mixture were at once submitted to a reducing action, the metal obtained would be a mixture of iron and copper; this is to be avoided, for such a product would be very intractable and difficult to purify. It is necessary to reduce the copper without reducing the iron, and for this, advantage is taken of the principle that the silicates of the metallic oxides are not reducible by contact with carbon. The quartz, which usually forms the vein-stone in copper mines, remains attached to the particles of ore in such quantity, as generally to constitute half its weight. Now when the roasted ore is subjected to a strong heat, the silica of the quartz unites with the metallic oxides, and forms silicates; but as it is wished to form only silicate of iron, the oxide of copper must be protected, and this is done by adding to the roasted ore, lime, or else a quantity of the slags formed in a subsequent process, and which consist principally of oxide of iron. Either of these being a stronger base than the oxide of copper, combines with the silica in preference, and there is thus formed a fusible slag containing silicates of lime and iron, and a very impure metallic copper which flows underneath. In this part of the process also, the residual sulphur is expelled, for the silica, in combining with the metallic oxides, expels the volatile sulphuric acid they had previously retained.

The mass of impure copper thus gotten, and termed matt or coarse metal, is purified by a series of roastings and reductions, which act on the principle that iron is more oxidizable than copper. The matt being melted is oxidized by the air, the iron oxidizes first, and the scoriæ of oxide which form on the surface of the molten mass are skimmed off. Sometimes sand is added, which combines with the oxide of iron and prevents any of it from being accidentally reduced by the flame. In this way the iron is gradually all worked out, and the copper assumes the characters by which it is known to be absolutely pure.

These processes are best carried on with an ore which contains from 8 to 10 per cent. of copper, and hence the advantage which a central smelting district like Swansea presents, of enabling the metallurgist to mix together ores of various origin and richness, so as to produce accurately the composition with which his process succeeds best. Thus the poor ores of Wicklow and of Cornwall serve to dilute the richer ores of Cuba, of Berehaven, and Knockmahon. Such a mixture prepared for smelting, and analysed by Mr. Richard Phillips, was found to consist of

Copper,	9
Iron,	20
Sulphur,	14
Earthy materials,	57
	100

This had been formed by mixing together equal parts of Cornish ores, of ores from Knockmahon, and of Wicklow ore from Connoree.

The fuel consumed in producing a ton of metallic copper is usually reckoned at from 18 to 20 tons. The value of the ore of course varies with the price of copper, which recently has fallen very much. At 8½ per cent. of metal the weight of ore necessary is 12½ tons, which may be considered as averaging £6 10s. per ton. The coals cost in Swansea usually 6s. per ton, 20 tons therefore cost £6 sterling, and as the ton of fine copper is now worth about £90, the cost of fuel makes up about 6¾ per cent. of its value. If the copper ore raised in Ireland were smelted on the coast, the price of fuel would be certainly double that in Swansea, and make up 13⅛ per cent. of the cost of the product. This precludes altogether the introduction of this industry amongst us, but I shall have occasion to notice certain operations to which the ore might be subjected before exportation, and from which considerable advantage might be derived.

Mr. Strom has recently directed attention to the great saving of fuel in smelting copper ores by the method followed on the Continent. This consists in roasting the ores in heaps in the open air, and then smelting them in blast furnaces, not unlike the high furnaces of the iron manufacture, but of smaller size. In this manner the fine copper is produced with an expenditure of 13½ tons of coal, almost exactly two-thirds of the quantity consumed in the reverberatory furnaces employed in England. He states also that there is actually a smaller loss of copper during the operation. The money saving by this method should be in Swansea £2, or in Ireland £4 per ton of fine copper, and it is hence a subject well deserving consideration.

In order to complete this sketch of the industrial condition of the copper mines of Ireland, I shall add the following *resumé* of their produce, as compared with that of the English mining district of Cornwall.

The total quantities and values of copper ores from Ireland sold in Swansea were in

1836, . . 21,819 tons, . .   £163,864 10 0 value.
1840, . . 19,580 ,, . .   127,910 13 0 ,,
1843, . . 17,509 ,, . .   117,625 4 0 ,,

The apparent diminution arises from the causes described in page 187, and which have principally affected the returns of the Wicklow district. The total quantity of copper ore raised in Ireland I believe to approximate, at present, closely to 25,000 tons per annum.

The quantity of copper ore raised in Cornwall was:

In 1780, . . . 24,433 tons . . worth £171,231
In 1800, . . . 55,981 ,, . . ,,   550,925
In 1820, . . . 92,672 ,, . . ,,   620,347
In 1838, . . . 145,688 ,, . . ,,   857,779

In little more than half a century the produce of the Cornish mines has been increased six-fold. It remains for us to apply the same energy and perseverance to the development of our mineral resources.

2nd. Of the Lead Mines.

Lead is even more extensively diffused through Ireland than copper, and is found in a much greater variety of rocks, so that I shall not endeavour to trace the distribution of our lead mines in any geological point of view, but describe them in the order of their practical importance, first noticing the constitution of the ores which they usually contain.

That which is pre-eminently called lead ore is the *galena* or *sulphuret of lead*. In 100 parts it contains

Lead, ... 86·6
Sulphur, ... 13·4

Its colour is bluish grey; its lustre brilliant metallic: it crystallizes in cubes, and when broken generally forms cubical fragments; but its structure varies very much.

The *carbonate of lead*, or *white lead ore*, is occasionally found in quantity, but many mines do not contain it at all. It forms white crystals or masses, which consist of

Lead, ... 77·6
Oxygen, ... 6·0
Carbonic acid, ... 16·4
                                    ———
                                    100·0

The *sulphate of lead* is, like the carbonate, white and crystalline, but is distinguished from it by not dissolving in dilute nitric acid. It contains

Lead, ... 68·4
Oxygen, ... 5·3
Sulphuric acid, ... 26·3
                                    ———
                                    100·0

This ore is of still less frequent occurrence than the carbonate. Both may be considered as only accidentally present, the lead ore, for which a mine is worked, being always the *galena.*

The granitic district of Dublin and Wicklow is intersected by a great number of veins containing ores of lead; they lie along its eastern boundary, and cross, in an oblique direction, the juncture of the granite with the mica slate. Veins have been worked along this line at Dalkey, and Killiney, on Ballycorus, at Powerscourt, Djouce, Lough Bray, Lough Dan, Glenasane, Glendalough, Glenmalur, and Shillelagh. Of these many have been found ultimately unproductive, and the only portions of this district which it is necessary to describe in detail, are those of Glendalough, of Glenmalur, and Ballycorus.

The mountains which enclose the lake and ruins of the Seven Churches consist of granite, through which run numerous veins of quartz, associated with which are found the ores of lead, and in some instances traces of copper. Their general distribution is as follows. At the head of Glenasane, a little above the junction of the granite and mica-slate, a vein of quartz six feet wide, with blende, galena, and some copper pyrites, passes nearly from east to west, and were it continuous would join the vein of Luganure. The latter, the most important in the district, runs altogether in granite. It crosses the mountain Comaderry, and has been accurately traced through a course of 900 fathoms; its ascertained depth being 180 fathoms. This vein is usually five feet wide, but in one place it expands to twelve feet. The principal vein-stone is quartz. The granite in contact with the lower surface of the vein is generally soft and decomposed to a depth of from one to three feet. This vein yielded, according to Mr. Weaver, in some portions of its course, per cubic fathom, from three to four and a-half tons of galena, which is found either in layers parallel to the walls or in disseminated masses. White lead ore is not uncommon. There are also found sulphuret of zinc, copper pyrites, and phosphate of lead. The produce of this vein usually yielded seventy per cent. of metallic lead. A few fathoms west of this is another vein in the granite; it is three feet wide, and consists of quartz with galena and white lead ore.

The Glendalough vein ranges east and west, crossing the glen obliquely. Its course is down the southern flank of Comaderry and it reappears high on the mountain of the opposite side, south of the Waterfall. Its line has been traced for about half a mile, it appears to range far into the granite on the western side, but not to penetrate much into the mica-slate. Its width varies from five to seven fathoms. The great mass of it is quartz. It contains numerous minerals, principally galena, with copper pyrites, sparry iron, and sulphate of barytes. The lead ore of this vein produces 70 per cent., and the copper ore gave from 10 to 15 per cent. of metal. In the Waterfall and ravine at the head of Glendalough are smaller veins, in which lead and copper ores have been found, but on which no workings have been carried on.

On the Luganure vein, and on some smaller veins discovered on both sides of Glenasane, and which are probably outliers from it, a number of shafts have been sunk and very extensive workings made. The old Luganure mine, as well as the Hero mine, have ceased to yield any produce, but the mine of Ripplagh, on the east, and one on the western side of the glen, lately opened at the base of Luganure mountain, are now actively worked by the Mining Company of Ireland, and yield a very fair quantity of ore. They are termed the Luganure mines.

The state of activity of their operations and their amount of produce are shewn by the quantity of dressed ore obtained which was

In 1842, ... 675 tons.
In 1843, ... 547½ ,,

The ore raised is dressed by hand labour and machinery, to which motion is given by water power derived from the rivulet which passes through the glen. To this Lough-Nahagan serves as a copious reservoir, which has been rendered fully available to the purposes of the dressing works. The dressed ore is brought on cars to the Company's smelting works at Ballycorus, where it is worked up along with ores from other sources, by processes to which I shall, after a little, return. The metallic lead is manufactured into sheet or pipe, so as to suit the markets in which it may be sold.

The lead mine situated on the hill of Ballycorus, contains two lead veins, which at the surface are nearly parallel, and cross the junction of the granite and mica-slate, which takes place on the summit. In the workings these veins have been found sometimes to diverge, and at others to coalesce, and were then in every case found to yield valuable bunches of ore. These veins had latterly, however, become unproductive, and although some limited explorations were still carried on by the Mining Company, this mine was not reckoned as being at the present time in actual work; but within the last few months, it has assumed a new interest, by the vein of lead ore being found to contain a rib of native silver, the condition of which will be described more fully, further on. In its vicinity are situated the Mining Company's smelting works, to which all their lead ores are brought for the purpose of their reduction and manufacture.

On the northern side of Glenmalur, where the granite and mica-slate join in Lugduff mountain, a powerful metalliferous vein presents itself, forming an acute angle with the course of the valley. It has been traced for above 400 fathoms, but probably extends much farther. The vein, as described by Mr. Griffith, is, on an average, fifteen feet thick, and excepting where there are bunches of ore, is divided into five parts. There are three feet of a soft slaty vein containing much talc, then a vein of white quartz, from one to three feet thick, which usually contains ore, next three feet of soft talcy matter, similar to the first, then two feet of quartz, in which most of the ore has been found, finally, a third layer of the soft talcy matter extends to the opposite wall of the lode. The lead ore of this mine is considered to be unusually free from zinc and antimony. It has yielded very abundant produce, several large bunches or masses of ore having been met with in the course of the workings. The productiveness has, however, latterly diminished. The number of persons employed on it is at present about thirty.

On the same and on the opposite side of Glenmalur, several other veins, containing indications of lead, have been discovered, but no serious trials of them have been made.

The clay-slate districts, which have been found so rich in copper, yield also abundant indications of lead, but, up to the present time, few of the mines that have been worked have yielded a profitable return. Of very few of them have there been as yet detailed examinations made, and hence it will be sufficient to notice them succinctly.

At Caime in Wexford, the clay-slate is penetrated by a vein of quartz, ramifying very much, and bearing galena, white lead ore, sulphuret of zinc, with copper and iron pyrites. This vein is of considerable magnitude; at forty-seven fathoms in depth, being twelve feet wide. Several years ago some quantity of copper ore was exported from this mine, and also large quantities of galena, but it was abandoned until a few years back, when its working was resumed by the Mining Company of Ireland, but it is questionable how far its working may be profitable at deep levels. The lode is considered to yield about three tons of ore per fathom. The quantity of dressed ore obtained was,

In 1842, ... 505 tons.
In 1843, ... 270 ,,

The ore usually contains 75 per cent. of metal, and is sent to

Ballycorus to be smelted. The number of hands employed is about 130.

In the clay-slate of the north of Ireland, which spreads over the Counties of Louth, Armagh, and Down, several lead mines have been opened. In Armagh at Derrynoos, a vein of lead was worked for several years by the Mining Company of Ireland, but finally abandoned. It yielded about 200 tons of dressed ore per annum. It was in this mine that were made the trials of turf as fuel for the steam engine employed in draining, which have been given in a former chapter. At Keady, in the same county, a vein of lead was found, of which Sir Charles Coote, in his Survey of Armagh, speaks in the following words: "This mine is on the estate of the College of Dublin, the lands are held by the Earl of Farnham; the late Earl expended large sums in sinking and working, but made no profit of it. It is rather wonderful, and indeed proves the value of these mines, that he was not a considerable loser, as he had no active partner to superintend works under ground which he never saw himself. The vein is so rich and abundant, it would be well worth the attention of the monied undertaker." This attention, as far as I can learn, has not since been given to that district.

In Down, at Clonligg, near Newtownards, is a lead mine which is at present worked to a moderate extent. At Dundrum, in the same county, a vein containing lead ore has been discovered, and superficial trials of it made.

In the slate districts of the south of Ireland, veins containing lead have been found at Ardmore in Waterford, and in several of the localities already mentioned as the depositories of copper ore. In Kenmare only is the extraction of lead ore at present actually carried on, and the circumstances are so similar to those described in page 196, for the mine of copper of the same place, that it is unnecessary to notice it further. The workings for lead carried on at Silvermines have been also sufficiently described already in page 199. There is nothing doing at present in that locality.

In Ringabella creek, on the southern coast of Cork, a vein occurs in the carboniferous slate, in which lead ore is found.

P

It has been worked from time to time by different persons. Its frequent abandonment does not speak much in its favour, but may have been due to want of knowledge or of enterprize on the part of the undertakers.

Lead ore has been met with in several localities in the granite and mica-slate district of Connemara, but no workings hitherto entered upon. In the same class of rocks in Donegal, lead veins have been found, and at Kildrum a mine was worked for some time by the Mining Company of Ireland, but it has been given up, and is, I believe, now idle.

The limestone formation affords numerous indications of metallic contents, principally lead: copper pyrites, iron pyrites, and blende, have been found in small quantities, but galena alone has been met with in such quantity as to be profitably worked. The vein stone is usually calcareous spar, accompanied by brown spar. The limestone of the centre of Ireland is, as Mr. Weaver remarks, singularly ill-calculated for the conducting of mining operations. It occupies the lowest and richest part of the country, and frequently supports a great depth of alluvial matter and soil. Hence the drainage of the mines becomes difficult and expensive, and the cost of fuel, and damage to the land, are important. The number of localities in which lead ore has been found in the limestone district is considerable, and some of the deposits have proved of value.

Near Dublin, at Clontarf, a vein of lead ore, accompanied by blende, appeared on the sea shore, where it was wrought until the tide broke in on the workings and the mine became filled up with water. In almost every direction round Dublin small veins of galena have been found in the calp, as at Dolphin's Barn, Castleknock, Kilmainham, &c., but none of them maintained their produce to any depth, or were of a magnitude which would justify any extensive trials.

In the Counties of Meath, at Beauparc and Athboy, and of Kilkenny, in several localities, lead ore has been found, but only at Floodhall was a mine ever actually worked. From it considerable profit is said to have been derived, the lead extracted having been very rich in silver. No workings are at present carried on. In Longford, close to the town, lead ore has been raised, and in Kildare, at Wheatfield, on the banks of the Grand Canal, a large deposit of pure galena was found, in connexion with a vein of calcareous and brown spars, on which extensive works were erected, but after some time the store of mineral was exhausted.

The lower limestone of the east of Clare has been found to contain several very large deposits of galena, which have been worked by Mr. Taylor with great success. From his account of them given to the Geological Society of Dublin, the following is extracted:

Milltown Lead Mine.—" The Milltown lead mine in the barony of Tully, in the County of Clare, is probably one of the oldest mines in Ireland. At one time it may be supposed, that there must have been a rich deposit, the ancient excavations being very extensive.

" The Royal Irish Mining Company took a lease of it about twelve years ago, but after partially clearing the old workings, and driving a level for a short distance into the north side of the mine, they abandoned the speculation, after raising above eleven tons of ore.

" In the year 1836, a grant of this mine was taken from the present proprietors, Anthony Colpoys and George O'Callaghan, Esqrs., by John Taylor, Esq., of London, whose name is so well known and deservedly identified with the mining interests of England.

" The ancient workings were now completely cleared, and some rude tools discovered, such as oaken shovels and iron picks, the latter of an extraordinary size and weight; also the remains of fires, which had been evidently made use of to crack and loosen the masses of calcareous spar and carbonate of lime, in which the ore of this mine is chiefly imbedded. The spar is very beautiful, being perfectly white, and much of it transparent.

" After considerable labour and expense, Mr. Taylor's agents were disappointed in the expectations they had formed of making fresh discoveries of sufficient importance. The works, therefore, were abandoned in April, 1838, after raising forty tons of ore, which, upon an average, yielded about

75 per cent. of lead, and 37 ounces of silver for each ton of ditto.

" Within half a mile of this mine, upon the estate of James Moloney, Esq., of Kiltannon, are the celebrated Tomines, or immense natural vaulted passages of limestone, through which the River Ardsullas winds a most extraordinary course. The place is extremely curious, and the stupendous masses of rock forming a gigantic roof over the river, present a scene of magnificence which can never be forgotten by those who have viewed it.

" The same river loses itself again among the cavernous strata of limestone rocks near Quin, and afterwards passing though the picturesque lake of Dromoland, falls into the Fergus, below Castle Fergus."

Kilbricken Lead Mine, in the Barony of Bunratty and Parish of Dura.—" In the year 1833, attention was awakened by the circumstance of the accidental discovery of lead ore, by persons in his employment, on the estate of John M'Donnell, Esq., of New Hall, near Ennis.

" The first specimens were found by persons while cutting the new line of road between Moriesk and the new town of Clare; after which more important discoveries were made on the farm of Moniuve, by the tenant, John Egan, while cutting a drain though his bog.

" The specimens and description of soil and calcareous spar, in which these stones of ore were discovered, having been submitted to the inspection of Mr. Taylor, in London, he determined on sending agents to examine the district, and in consequence of their report, some experienced miners were despatched from England, through whose exertions about twenty-five tons of lead ore were raised and shipped, which sold at a very high price, being found to assay for lead 76 per cent., and for silver 120 ounces per ton.

" At this time, however, the rush of water from the surrounding bogs was found to be an insuperable obtacle to further progress, without the aid of machinery, and it was then determined to stay the proceedings until a steam engine of sufficient power to contend against the difficulty, should be despatched from England. This engine was erected and put to work in 1837; operations are now going on upon an extensive scale, and great hopes are entertained of a successful result, but it is too soon to form an accurate opinion upon this point.

" This mine is situated within two and a half miles of Quin, and is about six miles from Ennis.

Ballyhickey Lead Mine, in the Parish of Clooney and Barony of Bunratty.—" This is the richest lead mine which has been discovered in the County of Clare, and is upon the estate of Hugh Singleton, Esq., of Hazelwood; in a direct line of distance it is about a mile and a half east from Kilbricken, and here lead ore was discovered nearly at the surface. Operations were commenced by Mr. Taylor's agents in the autumn of 1834, and with decisive success, so much so, that an export of 125 tons took place the following spring, and from that period to the present, not less than 2500 tons have been shipped from the port of Clare to the River Dee, averaging by assay, 77 per cent. for lead, and 15 ounces for silver in the ton of lead, and a considerable quantity of ore is still raised and shipped monthly."

" The three deposits of ore above mentioned, occur in large veins of calcareous spar which traverse the limestone rock of this country; they differ from any hitherto observed in the mining districts of England and Wales, and indeed upon the Continent of Europe. The veins of spar are of immense width; in places from twenty to thirty feet, and they run generally a little to the north of east and south of west.

" The quantities of ore found at Milltown and at Kilbricken are so small, and the masses of spar so large, that it is not easy to trace the intersection of veins or branches at the points of deposit, as distinctly as at Ballyhickey. There the bunch of ore, the richest probably that was ever seen, taking the number of tons raised, and the number of solid fathoms of ground broken into account, occurs upon the intersection of two veins. The main vein runs N. E. and S. W., and its tributary falls in the angle of 45°. At this point the mass of ore was from sixteen to twenty feet wide, in places, almost pure; in others, raised with sulphuret of copper and zinc. The total length of the rich branch was about forty feet, and it is still orey at the depth of eleven fathoms; how deep it may be worth pursuing is a question yet to be solved. The quantity of water is not considerable, although the mine is situated in the middle of a boggy piece of land. An engine, however, has been erected, for the double purpose of grinding the ores, and pumping the water. Fresh intersections of veins are still sought after, being the places at which only other deposits are expected."

The lead ore, as dressed for smelting, usually contains from 60 to 70 per cent. of metallic lead. This is combined with sulphur, and mixed with the material of the associated minerals, principally quartz, and often sulphate of barytes. The mode of extracting the metal is simple: by calcining the ore in a current of air, at a temperature just below redness, the sulphur and metal both become oxidized, and the greater part of the former is expelled as sulphurous acid gas. On then increasing the heat and excluding the air, so that the combustible gases of the fuel act directly on the roasted ore, the oxide of lead formed in the first stage of the process is reduced, and the metal separates. The smelting is usually carried on in a reverberatory furnace, by which the oxidizing and reducing processes are effected in turn, by regulating the admission of the air. The bed of the furnace is dished, so that the melted lead trickles down from all parts of its surface to the centre, and when it has collected in proper quantity, is run off by an aperture in the side of the furnace, into moulds, where solidifying, it forms the pig lead of commerce. There are two circumstances of this process which require further notice. First, the draught of the furnace carries up into the chimney a very sensible quantity of the roasted ore, which would be a source of serious loss, were it not that the chimney is provided with a considerable extent of horizontal passages, in which the fine powder of the lead ore deposits itself, and at certain intervals these flues being cleared out, the matter found there is added to the other products of the ore, and all smelted together.

Second. Although, in roasting the ore, the greater part of

the sulphur is burned out, yet a quantity of it is converted into sulphuric acid, which unites with oxide of lead and forms sulphate of lead. This is not further changed by calcination, but when the reducing fire is applied, this sulphate of lead, losing all oxygen, would reproduce sulphuret, and thus so much of the material be brought back to its primitive state. To avoid this, the smelter adds to the roasted ore a quantity of lime, which combines with the sulphuric acid and sets free the oxide of lead, which is then perfectly reduced. The lime is also useful in preventing the silica (quartz) present in the ore, from seizing upon oxide of lead and thus producing loss. It takes the silica, as it does the sulphuric acid, from being a stronger base.

The slags which are formed in this process, consist of the earthy matters of the ore, melted up with the lime which had been added. They also contain a large quantity of lead, so that they are set aside, and being mixed with the material extracted from the flues of the furnace chimney, are smelted in an operation by themselves, and the metal they contain extracted.

Third. A great deal of the success of this mode of smelting depends on a very curious reaction of that part of the ore which has been fully roasted, on that which has not been altered. It will be easily understood, that when sulphuret of lead and oxide of lead are melted together, the sulphur of the one and the oxygen of the other unite to form sulphurous acid gas, and the lead of both separates in the metallic state. Expressed in chemical symbols, $Pb\ S$ and $2\ Pb\ O$ give SO_2 and $3\ Pb$. The proportions by weight being that 120 parts of sulphuret of lead, and 224 parts of oxide of lead, give 32 parts of sulphurous acid, and 312 parts of metallic lead. A similar reaction takes place when sulphuret of lead and sulphate of lead are ignited together; all sulphur and all oxygen are evolved as sulphurous acid, and all the lead separates. The weights engaged are 120 parts of sulphuret of lead, and 152 parts of sulphate of lead, and there are produced 64 parts of sulphurous acid gas, and 208 parts of lead. In chemical formulæ: $Pb\ S$ and $Pb\ O\ SO_3$ give $2\ Pb$ and $2\ SO_2$. Now these processes of reduction are independent of the consumption of fuel. The surface of the ore having been suitably roasted, so as to generate oxide and sulphate, it is mixed thoroughly with the unaltered mass beneath, and the reactions occurring, metallic lead separates in abundance, and sulphurous fumes pass off.

In order to afford an idea of the influence which the cost of the fuel used in the smelting processes exercises on the value of metallic lead, I shall add the numerical results, which have been obtained at Lord Grosvenor's Works at Holywell in Flintshire, and at the Works of the Mining Company of Ireland at Ballycorus, near Dublin.

The ore smelted at Holywell averages 71 per cent. of metal, and is found to yield, by the process above described, in practice, 66 per cent., so that the loss is but 5 per cent. The combustion of coal during the process is half a ton per ton of ore, which amounts to 15 cwt. 17℔ for each ton of metallic lead.

At Ballycorus, where the lead ores from the mines worked by the Mining Company of Ireland are smelted, and the lead wrought into sheet and pipe, litharge and shot, the quantity of ore worked up in the year 1843 was:

From Luganure mines, ... 547½ tons.
From Caime mine, ... 270 ,,

Which delivered 10288 pigs of lead, weighing 588 tons, 4½ cwt., equivalent to 72 per cent.

The total fuel consumed in the smelting operations was 551 tons of coal and eight tons of coke, making together nineteen cwt. of fuel per ton of lead. The pig lead being now sold at £17 per ton, the coals at 12s., make up 3½ per cent. of the cost of the reduced metal.

The quantity of fuel given, as consumed in smelting the lead at Ballycorus, includes that employed in a process not performed at Holywell, which is the extraction of silver from the metallic lead. This is now practised to a very considerable extent. In noticing the lead mines of Clare, the fact of their yielding silver has been mentioned, and almost all the Irish galenas are argentiferous. So remarkably is this the case, that formerly the lead smelted in Ireland was so hard and brittle, that it was accounted inferior to the English in our own market, and would not be bought, but was sent over to England and to Holland to be refined. This purification consisted in removing from it the silver which it contained, and then it was sent back fitted for its proper uses, and was sold at a higher price. These processes are now all carried on at Ballycorus, and so perfectly as to leave nothing to be desired as to economy of method and purity of product. It is conducted as follows:

The lead having been obtained by the ordinary smelting process, it is remelted, and the concentration of the silver effected by the very ingenious plan invented by Mr. Pattinson. This is founded on the fact that an alloy of lead and silver is more fusible than pure lead. Hence, the lead being melted, is allowed to cool very slowly, until it begins to solidify. What becomes solid contains no silver, and by removing the grains of lead as they form, with a perforated ladle, the silver is concentrated in the portion which remains liquid, so effectually, that ultimately, after several repetitions of the process, the whole quantity of silver is obtained united with about one-tenth of the lead, whilst the remaining nine-tenths of the lead is free from silver and is sent to market.

The rich portion of the lead is then cupelled. A shallow crucible, or capsule, is formed of bone dust and ashes; in this the lead is melted, and then a strong blast from a bellows is blown across its surface; the lead is oxidized, and the oxide of lead is partly absorbed by the porous cupel, partly blown off over the edge of the cupel, and being collected forms the litharge of commerce. This process is continued until all the lead is oxidized, when the dull film, which had throughout covered the melted metal, passes off, and the pure silver remains. It is allowed to solidify in the cupel, and removed from it when cold. The old cupels are broken up, and smelted with the slags to extract the oxide of lead they had absorbed.

The quantity of silver contained in the lead ores of Ireland, so far as it has been experimentally ascertained, is as follows:

The proportions of silver to a ton of lead are generally found to be :

From Luganure mine, Wicklow, . . . 3 ounces.

From Caime mine, Wexford, ... 12 ,,

From Ballyhickey mine, Clare, . . . 15 ,,

From Kilbricken mine, Clare, ... 120 ,,

From Tollyratty mine, Strangford, Down, 10 ,,

The average produce of silver extracted from the lead ores of the mines worked by the Mining Company of Ireland during 1843 was seven ounces and a half to the ton of lead, and the total quantity was 4261 ounces, which sold for £1157 10s. 8d.

The precise localities of the more important deposits of copper and lead ores, are marked on the map which represents the distribution of bog and the catchment basins of rivers.

CHAPTER VI.

GOLD MINES OF WICKLOW; THEIR SITUATION AND PRODUCE.
NATIVE SILVER. MINES OF MANGANESE, ANTIMONY, COBALT.
MINERALS OF ZINC, NICKEL, AND TIN. SULPHUR TRADE OF
WICKLOW. IRON PYRITES. DEPOSITS AT SILVERMINES. DE-
COMPOSABLE PYRITES OF THE COAL FIELDS. MEANS OF MANU-
FACTURING COPPERAS AND ALUM. NATIVE ALUMS OF CLARE
AND KERRY. VARIETIES OF CLAY FOUND IN IRELAND. PORCE-
LAIN CLAY OF BALTINGLASS AND TULLOW. PIPE-CLAY OF
CAHIR AND ROSCOMMON. CLAYS OF COAL ISLAND, KILKENNY,
ARIGNA, AND HOWTH. FLINTS AND QUARTZOZE SAND. MA-
NUFACTURE OF GLASS AND EARTHENWARE. BUILDING STONES
OF IRELAND; THEIR VARIETIES AND QUALITIES. ROOFING
SLATES OF KILLALOE, VALENTIA, ROSS, AND WICKLOW. MI-
NERALS OF BARYTES AND OF MAGNESIA. LIST OF VARIETIES
AND LOCALITIES OF MARBLES.

OF THE GOLD MINES OF WICKLOW.

TOWARDS the close of the last century native gold was accidentally found to occur, disseminated in the bed of the streams
which descend from the northern flank of Croghan Kinshela;
a mountain which lies on the confines of Wicklow and Wexford, and at the junction of the granitic ridge with the clay-
slate. Considerable quantities of gold were collected by the
people. It occurred in massive lumps, and in small pieces,
down to the minutest grain. One piece weighed twenty-two
ounces; another eighteen ounces; others nine and seven ounces.
The gold was found accompanied by other metallic substances
dispersed through a kind of stratum, composed of clay, sand,
gravel, and fragments of rock, and covered by soil, which
sometimes attained a very considerable depth (from twenty to
fifty feet) in the bed and banks of the different streams.
Shortly after the discovery of the occurrence of gold, the
business of its extraction was taken up by the Government,
under the management of Mr. Weaver and some others. The
method followed was that usual in gold mining districts, of
washing the clay or soil in vessels with water; the metal, from

its great density, settles down, and the lighter earthy impurities are decanted. The valuable material is thus concentrated by a succession of washings, until finally the operators are enabled to pick out the particles of precious metal. The further operation of dissolving out with mercury the particles of gold too fine to be recognized by the eye, was, in some instances, had recourse to.

The total quantity of gold collected by the Government workings, in about two years, was 945 ounces, which was sold for £3675; but the cost of the workings, and of various trials made in search of the original deposit of the gold, exceeded this return, and the workings having been interrupted, were not again resumed by Government. It has been calculated that at least £10,000 was paid to the country people for gold, collected before the Government took possession of the works.

This native gold is of a rich yellow colour, soft, and malleable. Its specific gravity is 19. An assay of 24 grains of it, effected by Mr. Weaver, gave pure gold 22·58, and silver 1·43. Another assay of it, by Mr. Alchorn, Assay Master in London, gave, for 24 grains, 21⅝ fine gold, 1¼ silver, and three-eighths of a grain of an alloy of copper and iron.

The localities that have yielded gold in the largest quantity are Ballinvally, Ballintemple, and Killahurler, all situated in the same valley. The gold is associated with magnetic iron-stone, sometimes in masses of half a hundred weight; also iron pyrites, brown and red hematite, wolfram, manganese, and fragments of tin-stone in crystals, together with quartz. From the nature of these attendant minerals, of which most are known to occur in the quartz veins of the adjacent mountain, it was hoped that by tracing up the rivulets to their sources, and laying bare in various directions the underlying rock, the metalliferous veins might be discovered, from the disintegration of which the sand and soil of the bed of the streams had been produced. All such trials proved useless, and the question as to the source from whence the gold of those streams in Wicklow has been derived, remains still unanswered.

A few years since this district was leased to a London Company, under whose directions some workings were carried on, in a very imperfect and trifling manner, up to a short time since, when they were finally abandoned. Neither the intelligence nor the energy necessary for success in such undertakings appears to have been applied. It is questionable whether under any management this source of mineral wealth could be rendered profitable, and mines of the precious metals are certainly those which this country can best afford to do without.

In other localities in Wicklow particles of native gold have been found, as at Croghan Moira, at Ballycrea, and Ballynacapogue, but the quantities were too trifling to be an object of practical working.

There is no doubt but that sources of native gold were known to the Irish at a very remote period. The abundance of gold ornaments and weapons, which are so peculiar to this island, and for which no source by importation can be assigned, is sufficient evidence of this, as well as the testimony of our ancient writers, descriptive of the use and manufacture of this precious metal. That it was much more abundant here than in England is shewn by the fact mentioned in Delarnes' History of Caen, that when, after the Norman conquest of the British Islands, treasure was exacted from both to the exchequer of Normandy, the tribute exacted from England was 23730 marcs of silver, but from Ireland 400 marcs of silver, and 400 ounces of gold, an enormous quantity for those times.

Native silver has also been found in Wicklow in a bed of iron ochre in the upper ground of Cronebane. The particles were seldom so large as to be visible to the eye, but the silver was extracted by fusion with lead, and subsequent cupellation. It was auriferous, containing thirty grains of gold in each ounce. This deposit has been long since exhausted.

Since the publication of the first edition of this work an event of considerable interest to mining in Ireland has occurred,—the discovery of native silver associated with the lead ore in the mine of Ballycorus (page 207). The native silver, which is quite pure and filamentous in structure, forms a rib in some places half an inch in thickness, but usually thinning out from that and lying quite close to the thin vein of galena, for which some workings had still been carried on by the Mining Company of Ireland. The quartz rock around is impregnated with silver in minute particles to a considerable distance. The economy of working this native silver is, however, by no means yet decided. The great hardness of the rock in which it is contained, and the irregularity of its distribution, render it a question of much uncertainty. The Mining Company are, as I understand, about to erect and carry on the necessary works with their usual energy and prudence.

The occurrence of *tinstone* in Ireland is of very considerable importance, as this metal, indispensable in the arts, and of high price, is one of the most valuable elements of mineral industry. Hitherto it has been found, however, only disseminated through the auriferous soil of Wicklow; no veins or workable deposits of it having been met with.

Of the remaining metals of practical importance many have been found, and in some cases their mines have been worked in Ireland, but they have not attained much development hitherto. The oxide of manganese occurs at Howth in the vicinity of Dublin, in Wicklow, but more especially at Glandore, on the southern coast of Cork, where considerable quantities of the ore have been raised. In the Glandore mine, the principal variety of ore is the true peroxide; the hydrated sesqui-oxide is also found. The ore occurs associated with veins of quartz. The rock of the locality itself is the upper clay-slate, of which so much of the mining district of the south of Ireland is composed. The earthy hydrated peroxide of manganese is of very common occurrence, but I do not know any locality in which its quantity or its quality would require special notice.

An ore of antimony is found in Clare associated with the lead ore of the mines described in page 211, which is of interest as a source of that important metal, and also that in composition it differs from the usual ores, being a new mineral, and named Kilbrickenite by Dr. Apjohn, who analysed it. It consists of sulphuret of antimony united to sulphuret of lead, and it is remarkable, that the two metals are here naturally united in the same proportions as they are in manufacturing printing types, so that this ore, when smelted, should give a natural type metal.

The ordinary ore of antimony, the grey suphuret, has been found near Clontibret in Armagh, where it forms a vein about four inches thick, with a bedding of quartz, in the clay-slate rock of the district. Some desultory attempts have been made to utilize this deposit of antimony ; shafts had been sunk, one of fourteen yards deep, with several lateral drifts, but these trials have been, so far as I understand, without much profit.

The curious history of the occurrence of *Cobalt ore* at Killarney, has been given in page 197. No where else has it been found in quantity, though traces of it occur in all the mining districts. The minerals of nickel, chrome, arsenic, and bismuth, have been found, but have not been hitherto the objects of industrial enterprize. One of the *ores of zinc*, the sulphuret, or *blende*, is a common associate of the veins of lead and copper ore, and is intermixed sometimes in large quantity with the iron pyrites, worked in the Wicklow district for the manufacture of sulphur and sulphuric acid, but no deposits of the zinc ore, sufficient in extent and purity to enable the metal to be extracted, have been as yet found, though the circumstances of this country lead to a confident expectation of their being yet discovered. From the impure blende of the Wicklow district could be easily prepared the sulphate of zinc or white vitriol. The process consists in roasting the mineral in kilns or furnaces, for which its own combustion supplies nearly the necessary heat. The product is lixiviated with water, and by treating successive quantities of mineral with the same portion of water, the liquor may be obtained so concentrated, that it requires very little evaporation to enable it to crystallize.

SULPHUR ORE OR IRON PYRITES.

It has been mentioned in the general description of the Wicklow clay-slate district, that the copper lodes are associated with vast beds of bisulphuret of iron, which rendered the extraction of the more valuable ore difficult and expensive. This iron pyrites, which, when pure, is of a very pale yellow colour, is so hard as to strike fire with steel, and crystallizes in cubes and octohedrons ; it consists in 100 parts of

Iron, ...	46·67
Sulphur, ...	53·33

When it is heated in close vessels it gives off a third of the sulphur which it contains, and the residue, which is dark grey, and is called magnetic pyrites, consists of

Iron, ...	56·76
Sulphur, ...	43·24
	100·00

This residual sulphuret, when exposed to the air and moisture, rapidly decomposes, absorbing oxygen and forming sulphuric acid and oxide of iron, so that on washing it, a solution of green sulphate of iron (copperas) is obtained, from which the salt may be had in crystals.

If the iron pyrites be heated in a current of air, all the sulphur which it contains may be burned out as sulphurous acid gas, and the iron will remain in the state of red oxide. As the mineral is itself combustible, it may be burned in a kiln, the exhausted portions being extracted from the bottom, and the fresh ore introduced at the top. In this way the sulphur contained in it may be made available in the manufacture of oil of vitriol, and indeed in every case where ordinary sulphur would be burned.

To all these uses the iron pyrites had long been devoted in the north and east of Europe, but in this country it had been considered not merely valueless, but absolutely an impediment to the working of the copper mines. About eight years since, however, the mineral suddenly became important. The Government of Naples placed an exorbitant price on the sulphur, with which the manufacturers of England had previously been supplied from the volcanic districts of Sicily, and they being driven to obtain a substitute at a cheaper rate, had recourse to the deposits of iron pyrites in Wicklow.

The mines which produce the iron pyrites, are those of Ballymurtagh, Ballygahan, Tigrony, Cronebane, and Connoree; they all contain the same sulphur course, as it is termed by the miners, which traverses them in a north-eastern and south-western direction. This mineral occurs immediately at the surface, and is raised in large quantities down to the depth of fifty feet, the lode varying in width from four to thirty-six feet, and in bunches according to the purity of the ore.

The iron pyrites is indeed seldom absolutely pure ; besides an intermixture of clay-slate or other rock in various proportions, it is associated with other metallic sulphurets in small quantity, and frequently with the arseniuret of iron or arsenical pyrites. These impurities influence the value, and the products, of the sulphur ore in a very sensible degree. Thus the presence of copper renders it more valuable. Mr. Barnes, in his letters on this district, shews, that the sulphur and copper ores are in no way distinct, but graduate insensibly into each other. Thus the copper ore of Ballymurtagh contains at least 30 per cent. of sulphur ore, and the greater part of the pyrites workings in the same mine contains about $2\frac{1}{2}$ per cent. of copper. The presence of from $\frac{1}{2}$ to 1 per cent. of copper in the sulphur ore of commerce is not unusual. When this ore is burned in the kilns for the manufacture of sulphuric acid, the sulphuret of copper passes, by oxidizement, to sulphate of copper which may be extracted by lixiviating the slags with water, and either crystallized, or, as is more usual, decomposed by fragments of old iron, and the copper precipitated in the metallic state. When the ore contains sulphuret of zinc, this forms by the roasting, sulphate of zinc, which may be similarly extracted and crystallized. The presence of the arsenical iron is very injurious, for owing to the volatility of the arsenic, which accompanies the sulphur in all its stages of manufacture, the iron pyrites becomes unfit for the preparation of sulphur or sulphuric acid, wherever those bodies are to be applied to form medicinal substances, or that they are required pure for chemical uses; but it is yet perfectly applicable for all manufacturing and technical uses, and although the price of the Sicilian sulphur has now fallen very low, the pyrites trade has by no means diminished in proportion.

During the interruption of the Sicilian trade, the quantity of pyrites annually exported from the Wicklow district is considered to have reached 100,000 tons. It is now, however, considerably less.

The returns given in page 188 for the produce in copper ore and pyrites of the Ballymurtagh mine enable a general idea to be formed of the present extent of this branch of mining. It is highly gratifying, that the favourable position in which the mines of the Avoca valley were placed by the force of the sulphur monopoly in Naples, has been sustained up to the present day by the judicious enterprize of the proprietors, and the steady improvement of the produce.

Mr. Roper states the number of persons employed in this district to be about 2000, and that from 500 to 1000 carts are daily employed in bringing the ore to Wicklow and to Arklow for exportation.

I have mentioned that when the bisulphuret of iron is heated to redness, one-third of its sulphur is given off, and the iron remains as magnetic sulphuret, which by exposure to the air absorbs oxygen and forms green copperas. This application of pyrites is of extensive use on the Continent of Europe. It may be carried on in a variety of ways. The pyrites may be distilled in retorts of earthen ware, like those used in some gas works, or the ore may be burned in kilns, to which only a limited supply of air is admitted, so that one part of the sulphur being burned, the heat evolved suffices to distill off the rest, and the sulphurous flames being conducted into large brickwork chambers, the sulphur is deposited, whilst the sulphurous acid gas passes off to the vitriol chamber, where it also is economized. Where this process has been tried in this country, much disappointment has occurred from not using pure pyrites, and from the belief, that the pyrites should lose half its sulphur,

whilst it really gives off but a third. A ton of pure iron pyrites gives by distillation 3·6 cwt. of sulphur. But if a ton of
the good sulphur ore of commerce be taken, which does not
contain more than 75 per cent. of the pyrites, the produce of
sulphur, on distilling it, will be only 2·7 cwt., and the impure
ore requires a higher temperature, causes more loss of apparatus, and leaves a much more intractable residue. Hence this
process can only be profitably carried on, where the pyrites
available is found almost absolutely pure.

In speaking of the copper and lead district at Silvermines in
Tipperary, I have noticed the immense vein of iron pyrites
which is there found, but the inland situation of which prevented its being worked by the Mining Company of Ireland.
In the case of our domestic industry becoming active, the sulphur ore of that locality, from its proximity to the Shannon,
may be available throughout a very extensive range of country.

The bisulphuret of iron is met with in another and totally
different geological position, that of the coal formation, where
it occurs so abundantly intermixed with the coal, and in the
shales above, as to prove often seriously detrimental to the
quality of the fuel. This pyrites oxidizes much more rapidly,
on exposure to the air, than the pyrites of the primitive clay-
slate or other older rocks, so much so, that the masses of it become, in a short time, coated with a crystalline covering of green
copperas. In the Drumglass collieries, Tyrone, this oxidizable
pyrites is peculiarly abundant, and there, as well as in the
collieries of the Leinster district, it would only be necessary,
in order to manufacture copperas from it, to collect the pyrites
into a heap, and in dry weather to wet it occasionally. The
liquor which would drain off being conducted to a tank, should
be allowed to digest on some old iron to neutralize the excess
of acid, and by a moderate evaporation, the salt could be obtained crystallized. This is the plan adopted in England and
Scotland, where copperas is manufactured, and there is nothing
to prevent the same process being successfully carried on with
us. In the Munster coal field there is also abundance of this
oxidizable pyrites, which by its spontaneous decomposition in

many places, impregnates the waters with iron. The reaction of these products on the soft slaty rocks of the coal strata gives origin to other bodies, of which some are of considerable practical importance, as they afford the materials for the manufacture of alum, and of these it will be necessary to speak with some detail.

Alum is manufactured in England, either naturally, as it is termed, or artificially. The latter is a process which consists in decomposing pure clay with sulphuric acid, and adding then the alcali, which may be either potash or ammonia. The alum so made is crystallized in the usual way. The only objection to this process is, that the sulphuric acid has to be first manufactured, which is costly. The natural alum is made at Whitby, where the shales of the lias formation contain pyrites in abundance, together with some coaly matter. This *alum slate*, as it is termed, is formed into great heaps with brushwood, and the whole set on fire. A very slow combustion is kept up for some weeks, the sulphur of the pyrites reacts on the alumina of the clay, and on lixiviating the roasted mass sulphate of alumina dissolves. The alcali is then added, and the crystallization of the alum is effected in the usual manner. Near Glasgow, the alum is made similarly from the soft pyritic shales of the exhausted coal pits, the process followed being absolutely the same in all its general features. Now there is no requisite for the preparation of alum on the other side of the channel, which we do not possess here in those localities of oxidizable pyrites, which I have just enumerated; but it is remarkable, that we are even more favourably circumstanced, for a formation of true alum slate presents itself on the western coast of Ireland, more extensive than that in Yorkshire, indeed, as Mr. Ainsworth says, the most extensive that is to be found in Europe.

This slate forms the upper layers of the great Munster coal formation, the superficial extent of which has been already noticed. Its section, presented to the Atlantic for a distance of forty miles from Ballyvoughan in Clare, to Ballybunion in Kerry, offers a series of frowning precipices and deep caverns. The softness of certain portions of the rock allows the ocean, which on that coast rages in all its vigour, to undercut the cliffs, and work out from between the layers of harder strata, passages and caves, which present scenes of singular beauty and grandeur. Along this coast the pyrites with which these shales abound produces, by gradual oxidizement, copperas, and by its action on the material of the rock, native alum. Mr. Ainsworth, who published a very full account of one of the most curious localities on this coast, the caves of Ballybunion, describes the structure of the alum cliffs, in words of which the following may serve as an example: "In Dune Bay, the upper stratum of the cliff is composed entirely of very anthracitous alum-slate in thin laminæ, which are divided by parallel and transverse veins of crystallized alum, the same mineral occurring in nodules, efflorescences, and in loose powder, in the more decomposed beds, often contaminated by shades of yellow and red. In the small cave beyond, copper pyrites abounds, accompanied by arsenical iron, and in the cavities another combination of alum with sulphuric acid, and a mineral alkali."

Mr. Ainsworth found at Ballybunion, and along the coast, various aluminous minerals, which he describes as follows:

True alum, in powdery and capillary efflorescences, and in globular concretions.

The basic alum, or aluminite, in abundance.

The iron alum, or hair salt, similar to that found in the alum pits at Hurlet, near Glasgow.

Sulphate of iron and sulphate of copper were found in efflorescences on the surface of the rocks. Iron pyrites exists in abundance in the generality of the cliffs and rocks. Copper pyrites were found, and also, but rarely, arseniuret of iron.

It is possible that the enthusiasm of Mr. Ainsworth has given a colouring to his descriptions of these aluminous shales, of which some of the very brilliant tints may become sobered under more practical examination. Certainly, although profoundly scientific in his phraseology, the chemical nature of the bodies he describes cannot be considered as independent of future analyses; as Dr. Scouler has ascertained that a mineral, which Ainsworth announced as a new kind of alum, is nothing more than common gypsum, sulphate of lime. Nevertheless, the general characters of this district are decisive as to its capabilities for all branches of the manufacture of alum and copperas. The abundance of turf and coal makes fuel cheap, whilst the Shannon, by which it is intersected, gives it communication with the interior of the country, and affords the most favourable means of access to foreign and domestic markets. Nearly two centuries ago, alum and copperas were manufactured at Tralee and elsewhere in this district by Petty, Blennerhasset, and others, and the soft slate containing copperas, was administered as a medicine, and is described by many old medical writers, under the name of "*Lapis Hibernicus.*"

VARIETIES OF CLAY, AND SAND.

Clay in its purest form, and in the chemical sense, is produced from the gradual decomposition of the felspar contained in the various granitic rocks, by the action of water and of the atmosphere. The composition of the felspar has been stated in page 171. The potash which it contains is washed out in combination with the greater part of the silica, and there remains a fine light powder, which is pure clay. Its colour is perfectly white, which it preserves when most intensely ignited. It is absolutely infusible. These qualities identify the pure porcelain clay. In England the granitic district of Cornwall is the source of the pure clays used in the potteries of Staffordshire; in France, the granitic rocks of Limoges; in Germany, those of the Riesengebirge. The composition of the porcelain clay, or as it is often called by its Chinese name, *Kaolin*, may be expressed by the chemical formula, $3\,Al_2\,O_3 + 4\,Si\,O_3 + 6\,HO$, which gives:

Silica, ...	47·0
Alumina, ...	39·2
Water	13·8
	100·0

The clays of different localities vary very sensibly from this standard. They are mixed with traces of the undecomposed rocks and minerals which affect their composition ; thus most clays contain traces of potash from felspar, of which the decomposition has not been complete. Traces of lime and of iron arise from minerals accidentally present, which are very detrimental to the subsequent value of the clay, and often an excess of silica from the cotemporaneous degradation of the quartz, which is a principal ingredient of the granitic rock.

In all the granitic districts of this country, beds are found where the felspar has been so completely decomposed, as to have produced clayey deposits. I possess masses of decomposed granite from Mourne, perfectly similar to that of the china-claystone of Cornwall. The agricultural soil of extensive tracts of Wicklow, Carlow, and Wexford, has been produced by this weathering of the granite; and at Kilranelagh, near Baltinglass, kaolin of fine quality has been obtained. At Tullow, also, in Carlow, porcelain clay, not absolutely free from iron, however, exists in considerable quantity. It is not to be expected, however, that fine porcelain clay is to be found presenting itself on the surface of our granitic districts. Its preparation in Cornwall is strictly artificial. The blocks of decomposed granite are crushed and washed with water. The liquors, loaded with the fine particles of clay, are made to flow into reservoirs where this material is deposited, the clear water is run off, and the clay so obtained brought into commerce. No person has yet essayed the manufacture of china clay in this country; the materials for it appear from all evidence to exist abundantly.

In other places extensive deposits of clay occur, which, though not pure enough for the manufacture of fine porcelain, are yet excellently adapted for other uses. Mr. Griffith describes an extensive district of such clay occurring in Tipperary, between Cahir and Clonmel, which he considers equal to the pipe-clay of Bovey. It burns purely white, and in the extreme heat of a porcelain furnace only acquired a very slight buff tinge. Large quantities of this clay have been exported to England, but no use has ever been made of it at home. This clay, though on the edge of the coal district, lies in the cavities of the lower limestone ; and just similarly circumstanced are several deposits of very pure clay which occur in Roscommon, some along the shores of Lough Ree, especially near St. John's Point, and others more inland, as at Kellymount. This clay has given origin to a local manufacture of tobacco pipes, of which from 500 to 1000 gross are made weekly. The whole-sale price of these pipes is about one penny per dozen; they are very rudely formed, owing to the imperfect instruments used. If suitable tools, and some instructed workmen from Dublin, were to assist those local efforts, a considerable trade might be created, for the quality and colour of the clay are fully equal to any that we import, or that is used in the sister kingdom.

Although up to the present time no beds of absolutely white clay have been found in the tertiary formation of Lough Neagh, yet it is probable that future examinations will reveal such. The beds at Annaghmore, and in other places, of not less than seventeen feet in thickness, are found to become but slightly coloured on being calcined.

In an industrial point of view, however,, there are no clay deposits more important than those of the coal formation, the necessity for which, along with the ore and fuel, for the manu-facture of iron, has been already noticed (page 130). In all our coal fields the beds of coal rest on strata of clay of excel-lent quality, to the particular description of which I shall now proceed.

The Tyrone coal field contains numerous beds of clay, of that quality which, being infusible, is denominated *fire-clay*. In the Annagher colliery, each of the four coal beds worked, rests on a bed of clay, from four to six feet thick; but deposits of similar clay occur nearer the surface, and it is obtained for the purposes of the brick and coarse pottery manufacture of Coal Island, by pits of about thirty feet in depth. It is very strong adhesive clay, fawn coloured, and burning reddish yel-low. It is absolutely infusible, and makes fire-bricks, tiles, and crucibles, of the best quality. It is, as well in appearance as in properties, and in geological position, perfectly analo-gous to the clay of the Staffordshire district, so well known as Stourbridge clay. In order that the nature of the Coal Island

clay may be decisively established, I made an accurate analysis of it, of which the following are the results, and for comparison I annex the composition of the two clays most esteemed
for the manufacture of crucibles for making steel, and for
fire-bricks, in England.

CLAY OF	COAL ISLAND.	STOURBRIDGE.	STANNINGTON.
Silica, ...	46·2	46·1	43·0
Alumina, . . .	30·8	38·8	40·9
Peroxide of iron,	8·4	,,	Traces.
Lime, ...	,,	,,	1·3
Magnesia, . .	,,	,,	0·1
Potash, . . .	0·4	,,	,,
Water, . . .	14·2	15·1	14·7

The analyses of the English clays are taken from a valuable
Memoir on the Manufacture of Steel in England, by M. Le Play,
published in the Annales des Mines.

The presence of the oxide of iron in the clay of Tyrone gives
the wares formed of it a buff or brown colour, which must
always limit its use. The analyses shew that it contains just
the same silica as the Stourbridge clay, and the sum of the
oxide of iron and alumina is just equal to the alumina of the
other.

In the Lough Allen coal field, beds of fire-clay are found, of
which that forming the seat of the Crow coal varies from a
few inches to three feet in thickness at the edges. In the val-
vey of the Arigna this bed was found uniformly three feet
thick, and of excellent quality, the whole of the bricks used at
the iron works by the original proprietors, having been made
of it ; and comparative experiments, described by Mr. Weld,
as having been carried on in the Laboratory of the Royal Dublin Society, between it and Stourbridge clay, having shewn it
to be not inferior. Under the three foot coal lies another and
similar bed.

Near Lough Allen, on the western base of Benbo mountain,
are found clays of various colours, red, yellow, black, and

whitish, produced by the decomposition of the rocks. Considerable quantities of a whitish clay have been raised and used as fuller's earth. It feels soapy, and resembles decomposed steatite. It is mixed with iron pyrites.

In the Leinster coal field the coal beds rest on strata of clay, which I have found to contain a great deal of very finely comminuted mica, and some sand. When freed from these admixtures, it is a very pure, strongly adhesive clay, which burns almost perfectly white, and was infusible in the strongest heat of a wind furnace. Of this clay Mr. Griffith says: "This fire-clay is of very fine quality, and is, in my opinion, superior to that of Stourbridge in Worcestershire; excellent fire-bricks have been made of it, but no manufacture to any extent has been attempted." Mr. Tighe, whose Statistical Survey of Kilkenny is so rich in facts, describes more fully the proporties of this clay. He says:

"The *seat* of the coal has properties which appear worthy of attention; it has been long used at Castlecomer for backs of grates, and is known to stand fire in a peculiar manner. Mr. Finlan, the late director of the steam engines, constructed by means of it a small reverberating furnace, in which he smelted iron, and made crucibles of it which stood the heat of the strongest fire. Mr. Whitmore Davis, the architect employed in building the new barracks at Castlecomer, made some experiments upon it which he communicated to the Dublin Society last year. He formed fire-bricks of it, of the very best quality, and he observes, that 'by pulverizing the coal seat, and making it into mortar, nothing can better stand the fire and answer all purposes for fire works, as the more fire it gets, the harder it grows.' This he affirms from repeated trials, and says he is convinced from the handsome colour it assumes, ' it will not only answer every purpose in earthen ware, but he hopes also, that of pots for glass-house purposes; and being convinced of the great utility of the coal seat in the fire, he made trial of it also in water, and found that when properly prepared, it would answer every purpose of terras; he made trials also of its utility as to external incrustation on walls, where it set firmly, and has every reason to think will answer well. The best bricks made by Mr. Davis consisted of two parts of coal seat, and one of olay: a sixth part of sand being added, made them run too much: the coal seat which he used in building a brick cistern, was first calcined in a lime-kiln and then pulverized; it held water immediately in the most perfect manner. The coal seat in its natural state burned in a strong fire becomes white, and as hard as many silicious stones. Mr. Davis sent specimens to Dublin, which were examined by Mr. Higgins, who returned it as part of his opinion, that the coal seat 'would answer for porcelain, as one of the ingredients. Its uses under water appear more doubtful, for though pieces of it found in the stream of Castlecomer had become very hard in the water, they were also brittle, and perhaps would rather crack than set like terras, whose property of swelling in water depends upon the quantity of iron it contains, which becomes oxygenated by combining with the oxygen of the water. The coal seat appears to contain no iron, or a very trifling quantity: finely powdered and digested in marine acid, it did not lose quite a grain in an hundred of its weight: the solution gave no precipitation with volatile alkali, a very slight one indeed with prussiate of potash; but with pure potash it gave a little precipitation; by which it appears to contain a small quantity of calcareous earth: the remainder consisted, as near as it could be analized, of 54 per cent. silex and 44 argill; and the colouring matter appeared to be carbon, in a small proportion. One hundred grains digested repeatedly in concentrated sulphuric acid, left forty-eight grains of silicious sand, with a little carbon: the solution gave a white precipitate with volatile alkali; none with prussiate of potash. By another analysis one hundred grains appeared to contain 61 per cent. of silex, 36 of argill, the remaining three grains were carbon and calcareous earth, with an almost imperceptible quantity of iron. On the whole then it appears to contain a larger proportion of silex than of argill, and not enough of any other mineral to effect its qualities."

I have not myself analysed this clay of the Kilkenny coal beds, but the composition given by Mr. Tighe above, is remarkable, as being identical with that of pure Stourbridge clay, when dried. The proportions given in p. 233, when calculated without the water, are, silica 54·3, and alumina 45·7, practically identical with Mr. Tighe's of 54 and 46, and hence proving the excellent quality of the material.

Deposits of clay, which, though inferior in quality to those above described, are available for the manufacture of coarse pottery, of flooring and draining tiles, and of bricks, occur in almost every county in Ireland. Several in Kilkenny, along the edge of the coal district; in Wexford, near Gorey; in almost every parish of Tyrone; at Knock, in Meath; in Mayo; in Tory Island, off Donegal; near Celbridge, in Kildare.

Of a quality much superior to the common sort are whitish clays found near Cloyne, and at Youghal in the county of Cork, and at Calinafersy in Kerry. These are light coloured, strongly absorbent, and have been used by the peasantry as fuller's earth; when calcined they become a light yellowish red, and are very suitable to the manufacture, not merely of tiles and common pottery, but also of an excellent description of coloured earthenware. At the south side of Howth, associated with the limestone and dolomitic rocks, are extensive deposits of a very excellent clay, which burns nearly quite white and resists the most intense heat. It contains some fine quartz sand, fragments of disintegrated felspar, and a little mica. From these it is separated by washing, and is then soft and ductile, strongly adherent, and very plastic. It has been analyzed by Mr. Robert Mallett, and was found composed of,

Silica, ...	67·96
Alumina, ... , . .	23·20
Lime, ...	3·23
Magnesia, ...	·63
Oxide of iron, ...	1·19
Water and loss, ...	3·79
	100,00

This clay is worked into crucibles by Messrs. Mallett, for the various operations of their extensive foundry, and is found equal to the clay of Stourbridge; its quality is such as would render it excellent for delft and stoneware, to which objects, however, it has not been applied.

I shall terminate this notice of the clays of Ireland, by reference to the mode of preparing them for their various uses, to which but very little attention has been hitherto paid. These clays, as dug up from the ground, contain, universally disseminated through their mass, portions of organic matter, and also frequently iron pyrites. When such clay is calcined, these foreign matters are decomposed, and evolve gases, by which bubbles and cracks are formed in the clay, and the soundness of the ware deteriorated. To avoid this, the potter in other countries stores up his clay for many months, or perhaps a year: he cuts it up and mixes it frequently, and exposes fresh surfaces to the air; the clay ferments, exhales a fœtid odour, and at last all these organic and sulphury impurities become decomposed and pass off, and the clay is found very much improved in quality. The clay, as used in Ireland, is, on the contrary, injured by bad management. Clays of different beds are imperfectly mixed together; sand and pebbles are left intermixed with the clay, and hence, when bricks or tiles so made, are burned, they contract unequally, and become deformed in shape. Some parts vitrefy, whilst others remain unburned, and thus from clays which might produce excellent products, articles of very inferior value and low price alone can be obtained. In other countries the clay is diffused through water, and the sand and gravel having settled, the thick liquid is run into reservoirs, where the clay gradually deposits. This purified clay is worked in a pug mill, so that its quality becomes absolutely uniform, no matter how many different kinds may have been originally taken, and thus the articles fabricated acquire a soundness of quality, and uniformity of texture, by which their price and the advantage to the artizan is materially enhanced.

Immediately in connexion with the clays, stand the other materials of the earthen-ware, china and glass manufactures: silica, in its various forms of flint, quartz, and sand. The chalk of Antrim contains abundance of flints. The great masses of quartz of Donegal and Mayo, the patches of it which appear in other places, forming Howth and Bray Head, and capping various mountains, afford unlimited supply of it, and though the general mass of the quartz rock is usually tinged by iron, yet veins of perfect whiteness occur sufficiently abundant for industrial uses.

The weathering of the quartz rock of the Muckish mountain in Donegal, has given origin to a species of sand of singular character. It is perfectly white, in rather large grains, and is chemically pure. If the approaches to that mountain were more easy, and that this kind of sand were brought into the market upon fair terms, there is no doubt but that it would be preferred to the sands of the south of England, none of which can at all compete with it in purity of colour and composition. In several of the bays of Donegal, the sand thrown up by the Atlantic storms is of great purity, and fully equal to that in ordinary use amongst glass manufacturers. Fine crystalline sand occurs at Lough Grana and at Lough Coutra, which is highly valued for the purposes of polishing and whetting.

The quantity of fuel consumed in the burning of porcelain and earthen-ware, and in the melting of the materials of which glass consists, might appear to many persons to present a serious obstacle to the introduction of such occupations amongst us. Such is in reality not the case. The establishment of the potteries in Staffordshire, and the great development of the manufacture of earthen-ware in England, arose, not from the mere price of fuel, but from the energy and artistic taste of the illustrious Wedgewood. In fact, Staffordshire is very badly placed with regard to the materials of the ware, all of which are more important than the fuel. The china clay, the quartz, and granite, are brought from Cornwall, the second rate clay from Devon and Dorsetshire; the flints from Kent and Antrim. I have not been able to procure accurate returns of the cost of the coals employed in making the different kinds of earthen-ware, but I am satisfied, from the analysis of the elements of the manufacture, that its influence must be comparatively small. Even in making glass, where certainly much more fuel is consumed than in forming the same value of stoneware or china, the proportion which it bears to the other elements of cost is not considerable.

From numerical facts of the circumstances of this trade, which were given to me by an extensive and intelligent manufacturer, I have calculated, that to produce a ton of finished flint glass, there are required thirty-one tons of coal. The glass may be considered as selling in average, duty included, for 1s. 3d. per pound, and the ton is hence worth £140. The coals, at 6s. per ton, cost £9 6s., and hence the fuel makes up 6⅔ per cent. of the value of the manufactured article. In Ireland, the cost of fuel being double in proportion, the cost should be 13½ per cent. Now articles so liable to injury by carriage as earthen-ware and glass are peculiarly adapted for local manufacture. The additional freight from England or Scotland, here certainly counterbalances the advantages of 6⅔ per cent. in fuel, the dearness of which cannot, therefore, be considered as negativing the introduction of those branches of industry, in which taste and artistic skill are elements of cost as influential as the raw materials and rough labour.

BUILDING MATERIALS AND MARBLES.

A very laborious and truly useful inquiry has recently been instituted by Mr. Wilkinson, superintending architect of the Poor Law Commission, into the qualities of the various kinds of stone used for building purposes in Ireland. The results to which he arrived, were embodied in a memoir read to the Geological Society, to the economic museum of which institution he presented the collection of specimens upon which he had experimented, and which becomes thereby a standard of reference for the properties of almost every important quarry in the country, accessible to every individual. The stones which he submitted to trial were altogether 600 in number, and included all the known varieties of each kind of rock found in Ireland. They were examined under three different points of view. First. That of the tendency to absorb water, which determines principally the decomposing action of the atmosphere upon them. Second. As to their capability of resisting transverse fracture, which was essayed by loading a square piece of twelve inches by three, supported at each end, till it broke in the centre. Finally, their capability of resisting a crushing force, which was tried by pressing on an inch cube of the stone, by means of a lever, loaded until the stone gave way. It is to be hoped, that for the benefit of those engaged in building and practical architecture, the details of those experiments may be published. The general results, with a few examples of the extreme cases can only be stated here.

The ordinary limestone of Ireland weighs in average per cubic foot 170℔. The extremes of weight were 159 and 180℔. The average weight of water, which it absorbed by immersion, was one-fourth pound; the greatest absorption was one-half pound of water. The chalk of Antrim weighs 160℔ per cubic foot, and absorbs three pounds of water. The impure shaley calp weighs 160℔, and absorbs from one to four pounds of water per cubic foot.

The average weight of sandstone is 145℔ per cubic foot, the extremes are 123 and 170℔. The absorption varies from nothing to upwards of ten pounds, the average being five and a half pounds.

Granite averages per cubic foot 170℔. Its extreme weights were 143 and 176℔. The granite of Newry and of Kingstown absorbs one-fourth pound, that of Carlow from one and a half to two pounds, that of Glenties in Donegal four pounds.

Basalt weighs from 171 to 181℔ per cubic foot; the average is 178℔. It absorbs less than one-fourth pound of water per cubic foot.

Clay roofing slate weighs from 174 to 179℔, in average 177 ; the absorption is less than one-fourth pound. The soft clay-slate from Bantry absorbs about two pounds.

In resisting fracture it was found, that the slate rocks were the strongest, and of these some were stronger when the pressure is applied on the edges of the cleavage planes than on the faces. The basalts are next in strength : then the limestones, then the granite, and the weakest are the sandstones.

Considered in relation to a crushing force, the basalts are found to be the strongest stones, next the limestones, and successively the slates and sandstones. In th different varieties of limestone, some of the larger crystalline stones and the compact hard calp are the strongest. The light coloured crystalline stones of Ardbraccan, and those around Cork are the weakest. The Connemara white marble or primary limestone, is the strongest that has been found. The strongest sandstones are the red rocks of the south, and the hard quartzoze grits of the north of Ireland. Among the weakest are the County Down quarries, and the sandstones in Antrim, and around Clonmel, and some of the coarse quartzoze sandstones of Donegal. From trials of the slates, Mr. Wilkinson found those of Valentia to resist pressure less effectually than those of Killaloe, and those of Mr. Synge's quarries in Wicklow are about intermediate. From the experiments on granite, with regard to crushing force, no positive conclusion can be as yet drawn, but Mr. Wilkinson finds it not to possess any superiority over many of the stones in ordinary use.

It is observable in these experiments, that the denser stones are generally those which absorb least water, and which would therefore, be best fitted for resisting the weathering influence of our climate; also that the power of resisting transverse fracture, and of resisting a crushing force, are by no means connected. A rock, as clay-slate, may rank high under one, and very low under the other point of view, Hence, in different parts of a building, it may be proper for the architect to employ stones of diverse nature, and from the tables of numerical results, which Mr. Wilkinson has obtained, the magnitude of a pillar or transverse beam, to support a given weight, or bear up a transverse load, may be now, for the first time, calculated for the various building materials of our country. It would not suit the general object of this work, to enter into the detail of this subject, especially as all the particulars of these experiments will be published by Mr. Wilkinson in an independent form, and that by visiting the Economic Museum of the Geological Society, which is liberally thrown open to the public, the specimens themselves may be examined, and the documents regarding them referred to, with the assistance of Mr. Oldham, the able Curator of the Society's Museum.

The clay-slate rocks in various parts of Ireland have been

quarried for slates for roofing purposes, and for flags, to a
very considerable extent in several localities. In Wicklow,
near Rathdrum, and at Glanmore, where Mr. Synge is now
carrying on operations on a considerable scale, giving employment to upwards of 100 persons, and bringing into the market
slates of a quality and appearance fully equal to those imported
from Bangor, with the slate of which, indeed, the district in
which Mr. Synge's quarries are situated is geologically identical. I may remark, that it is found in all slate districts,
that the more superficial strata are soft, and of a very inferior
quality, and that to obtain first rate slates, it is necessary to
sink to a considerable depth. It arose from this, that when
various individuals first brought Irish slates into the market,
their quality was very universally condemned, and a prejudice
arose against their use, which is even yet not quite extinct.
However, the workings in Wicklow and elsewhere have fully
now brought into play strata of excellent nature, and this
source of domestic industry, it is to be hoped, may be considered as well established.

The most extensive slate quarries in Ireland are near Killaloe. They were for many years worked by the Mining
Company of Ireland, but when that Company removed its
operations, in order to concentrate on the productive copper
mines of Waterford, the slate quarries passed into the hands
of an English company, by which, under the name of the Imperial Slate Company, they have been since worked with considerable success. The slates are of the very finest quality,
and can be had of almost any magnitude; there are some in
the Museum of the Royal Dublin Society of ten square feet
area. The stone is, for building purposes, one of the best in
Ireland.

This district of slate rock is upwards of twenty square miles
in extent, but the operations of the Company have been latterly confined to the two most important quarries, the Big Pit
and Cunaghbally. These have been thoroughly drained, and
the soft bad rock blown away, and in 1842 an acre of pure
slate rock was laid bare in Cunaghbally quarry. In the Big
Pit all the veins and strata proved to be continuations of Cunaghbally, and a vast extent of beautiful slate rocks from eight

to ten feet in length have been exposed. These two quarries produce about 10,000 tons of manufactured slates per annum, and if a greater demand occurred, the Water and the Spout quarries could be put into immediate operation. By the operations of this Company, employment is given to more than 700 men and boys, and all who visit the district are equally struck with the unexpected size and magnificence of the quarries, as with the good order and appearance of the men, whose steady industry and comfortable mode of living, in a district which some years ago existed only as a desert mountain, may serve as an encouraging example to the starving and semi-barbarous agricultural population by whom they are surrounded.

The island of Valentia, consisting of the upper or silurian slate, is also a locality in which this rock is worked for industrial purposes. It cannot be split so delicately as to serve for the finer roofing slates, but its great strength, and evenness of texture, render it most useful as a building stone, and for flags, of which a very large quantity is annually sent to London. Slabs of Valentia slate are easily attainable thirty feet long, four or five feet wide, and from six to twelve inches thick, so that of it, without any intermediate bearing, the floors and ceilings of large rooms might be constructed. In the quarries of Valentia, about 200 individuals usually obtain employment.

The carboniferous slate of the south-east of Cork has been quarried in several places, and has yielded roofing slate of good quality, the produce having been found exceedingly light and durable. The principal quarries were at Clonakilty and the Old Head of Kinsale.

At Bradford in Clare near Killaloe, slate quarries had been opened many years ago, and are still worked to a certain extent. The clay-slate of Westport in Mayo was also worked some years ago, but its quality was not such as to stand the competition of slates imported from other sources.

At Ross in Waterford quarries of roofing slate have been opened. The slates are greenish grey, rather softer than those of Killaloe; they are obtained of very considerable size.

The limestone districts of Ireland contain numerous beds, which the closeness of texture, and the purity or variety of colour, render available for ornamental purposes, as marble. I shall only enumerate the localities in which the most remarkable marbles are found. There is no county which does not afford specimens of greater or less excellence.

The principal quarries of black marble are those at Kilkenny and near the town of Galway. These are both in the upper limestone. The Kilkenny marble takes a beautiful polish, and, when first cut, is quite black, but the organic matter to which its colour appears to be due, gradually passes of, and ultimately white marks of fossils, of varied and interesting forms, present themselves upon its surface. The Galway marble quarries are situated along the verge of Lough Corrib; they supply a large quantity of marble annually to London and New York, but are capable of almost indefinite development.

Near Armagh is found a marble, which, from the excellence of its surface, and the variety of red, yellow, and brown tints which it shews, possesses great beauty. It contains abundant fossil remains of fishes. A similar marble, elegantly variegated with yellow and purple, occurs at Churchtown, in Cork, which county is indeed rich in this material, there being found

Black marble, at Churchtown and Donerail.

Purple and white, and blue and white marbles, also at Churchtown.

Ash-coloured, gray, and dove-coloured marbles at Carrigaline, and Castlemary.

Pale brown marbles at Kilcrea.

In Kerry, there are black and white variegated marbles near Tralee; and in the islands in the River Kenmare, near Dunkerron, marbles of various colours, black and white, purple, white, and yellow, and some specimens of a purple colour, veined with dark green, resembling bloodstone.

At Craigleath, in Down, at Lyons and Ballysimon in Limerick, at Westport in Mayo, 'and at Castlebegs in Tipperary, are quarries of black marble. At Clondeslough in Clare, a fine bourdella marble. Near Shannon Harbour, on the Galway side, fine sienna and dove marble. At Clonmacnoise, King's County, and Dromineer in Tipperary, are fine gray marbles, variously tinted and peculiarly sound and useful. At Killarney occurs a very beautifully striped white and red marble; and a brownish red, mottled with gray of various shades, at Ballymahon, in Longford.

The primitive limestones of Connemara and Donegal, supply white marbles, which in Galway is often absolutely pure in tint, but in Donegal is more frequently of a grayish cast. The Galway white marble has been already noticed, page 241, as the strongest of limestones, when used for building.

The west of Galway and Mayo is also remarkable for the serpentine rocks, which afford the beautifully variegated green and white marbles, so deservedly esteemed. The most valuable quarries of this remarkable mineral are situated near Clifden, on the estate of Mr. Darcy. This marble is exported in considerable quantities.

The sandstone rocks, as well of the older as of the newer geological formations, have furnished not merely building stones and flags of good quality, of which the principal sources are in Carlow, and at Kilrush and Moneypoint, in Clare, but also grindstones and millstones, which latter, especially those of Cuilcagh mountain at Lough Allen, and Drumdowney, in Kilkenny, were formerly much esteemed. Their manufacture has ceased, but certainly not owing to inferiority in the material.

MINERALS OF BARYTES AND MAGNESIA.

The sulphate of barytes, a mineral, which, ground to fine powder, is extensively used as a pigment, either by itself or mixed with the more expensive white lead, occurs very abundantly in various parts of Ireland. In Ulster it is found in veins in different parts of the old red sandstone districts. The lead mines situated in the granitic ridge of Leinster have this mineral usually as the vein-stone of the ore, and it might be hence obtained in large quantity. In Wexford, several large veins of it present themselves on the sea shore, and in the vicinity of Youghal it is found similarly circumstanced

The earth barytes, extracted from this mineral, by processes into the detail of which it would not be suitable to enter here, is employed extensively in the potteries of Staffordshire, where the sulphate is itself also used in some quantity. The composition of the sulphate of barytes is in 100 parts,

Sulphuric acid, ... 34·4
Barytes, ... 65·6

The earth magnesia, and its sulphate, popularly known as Epsom Salts, which are so extensively employed in medicine and the arts, are prepared from a mineral, of which there exists vast quantities in Ireland, the magnesian limestone or dolomite. This stone is distinguished from common limestone, by its drab or fawn colour, its greater density, and its dissolving but slowly, and with gentle effervescence, in dilute acids. It occurs as a substantive rock but in one locality, at Holywood, on the south side of Belfast Lough, where it forms a stratum of about sixty feet in thickness. It has been raised there, and exported to Glasgow, to be used in the manufacture of Epsom Salts, although no use has been made of it at home. Veins and smaller deposits of dolomite occur in different parts of the limestone districts, particularly where that rock comes into contact with, or near to, other formations. The composition of this rock is perfectly definite, it consists of an equivalent of carbonate of lime, and an equivalent of carbonate of magnesia, and, when pure, contains in 100 parts,

Magnesia, ... 22·1
Lime, ... 30·3
Carbonic acid, ... 47·6

But the beds or veins of dolomite are usually rendered impure by intermixed sandy or clayey materials, and the earthy carbonates are often associated with a certain quantity of carbonates of iron and manganese. It is seldom, therefore, that the produce in magnesia equals that given above, and the following analyses of specimens from various localities in Ireland, will shew the usual composition.

	KILKENNY.	DOWN.	DUBLIN.	SLIGO.
Lime, ...	30·13	30·26	30·2	30·3
Magnesia, ...	21·43	18·25	20·6	22·1
Oxides of iron and				
manganese, . .	0·95	3·10	1·5	0·6
Silica, ...	5·74	,,	1·5	,,
Carbonic acid, . .	46·65	47·26	46·2	47·0

These are by no means all the localities in which this mineral is found, but they are sufficient to mark its usual practical composition. It would be out of place to advert here to the modes of extracting the magnesia from it, for which reference must be made to works specially devoted to chemistry.

I have endeavoured in these chapters to present such an account of the metallic and other minerals of Ireland, as, without entering needlessly into mining or metallurgic details, should indicate the localities of those rocks, which, by the analogy of other countries, we may expect to be rich in metallic ores, or other substances useful in industry. I have also endeavoured to represent, as faithfully as the materials available by an individual would admit, the actual condition of our mines, the amount of produce which they yield, and of the employment which they afford to the people.

It results from these inquiries, that by far the greater portion of this island is constituted of mineral formations, analogous to those of the principal mining districts of England and of the Continent of Europe. That in almost every quarter valuable deposits of the more important metals, rocks, and minerals have been found, and the quantity of ores raised and sold is annually on the increase. In many cases, mines and quarries, formerly abandoned, are now being worked with advantage, owing to increase of economy and skill, and it should not be a source of discouragement for the future prospects of our mineral industry, that numerous unsuccessful trials are made, for it must be recollected, that by such trials only, can

the really valuable mines be ultimately found, and that localities and enterprizes, of which we now appreciate the final
success, shew us but the result of numerous and toilsome
searches, under which the first adventurers were too frequently
depressed.

The precise localities of the more important metallic and
other minerals described in this chapter are marked on the
map of the distribution of bog and of river drainage.

CHAPTER VII.

OF THE AGRICULTURAL INDUSTRY OF IRELAND. ITS IMPOR-
TANCE AS AN OCCUPATION. RELATIONS OF AGRICULTURE TO
MANUFACTURES. NATURAL FERTILITY OF THE SOIL OF IRE-
LAND. STATISTICAL VALUATION OF ITS PRODUCE. DISTRI-
BUTION OF THE SURFACE OF THE COUNTRY. OFFICE OF
PLANTS. CORRELATIVE FUNCTIONS OF THE MINERAL, VEGE-
TABLE, AND ANIMAL KINGDOMS. COMPOSITION OF PLANTS.
ORIGIN OF THE SOIL. CONNEXION BETWEEN THE FERTILITY
OF THE SOIL AND ITS COMPOSITION. EXAMPLES OF FERTILE
DISTRICTS. NATURE OF THE SOILS OF VARIOUS PARTS OF
IRELAND. COMPOSITION OF SUBSOILS. ORGANIC ELEMENTS
OF THE SOIL. MECHANICAL AND PHYSICAL OFFICE OF THE
SOIL. OF DRAINAGE; ITS IMPORTANCE TO IRISH AGRICULTURE.
ACTION OF PLANTS ON THE SOIL. OF EXHAUSTION. COMPO-
SITION OF THE MOST IMPORTANT CROPS. OF MANURES.
COMPOSITION AND PROPERTIES OF THE MOST IMPORTANT
NATIVE MANURES. OF LIME AND LIMESTONE; MARL; SEA
SAND; CORAL SAND, ITS NATURE. VALUE OF THOSE SANDS
DREDGED UPON THE NORTH AND SOUTH COASTS. OF GYP-
SUM; OF SEA-WEED; OF BONES; FARM YARD MANURE; ITS
COMPOSITION AND RELATIVE POWER. IMPORTANCE OF ITS
PRESERVATION AND SUITABLE ECONOMY TO PRACTICAL AGRI-
CULTURE.

ALTHOUGH I have considered it of great importance to fix
attention on the facilities which this country presents for pro-
secuting the various departments of mechanical and chemical
manufacture, of which the essential circumstances and materials have been described in the preceding chapters, I am far
from being forgetful of the fact, that the support of the great
body of the people is, and must continue to be, derived from
the soil; that the manufacture most extensive and most indispensable, is the production of food, and that agriculture, in
its proper sense, is the most important of the various sources
of industry which the country contains, and which it is my
duty to describe. There is no country in which a very large
proportion of the people is not supported by, and occupied
with, agricultural pursuits. In Great Britain alone they do
not constitute the majority of the population, and even there

it appears, from the Census returns of 1831, that of 100 families, there were

Employed in agriculture, ... 28·2
,, in trade and manufactures . . . . 42·0
,, otherwise, ... 29·8

In this country a very large majority of the people depend on the produce of the land for subsistence. Thus in 1831 it was found, that of every 100 males above 20 years of age, there were supported:

By agriculture, ... 65·7
By trade or manufacture, ... 17·4
Otherwise, ... 16·9

The more accurate, as well as more recent, classification of the Census of 1841, gives for the occupations of the people of Ireland:

In agriculture . . . 5,406,743 or 66·1 per cent.
In trade and manufac-
 tures, ... 1,953,688 or 24·0 ,,
In other pursuits, . . 813,535 or 9·9 ,,
         ——— ———
Total population, . . 8,173,966 100·0

From the cultivation of the soil, therefore, there are at present means of subsistence to be sought for two-thirds of the entire population, and it may well be conceived, that the inquiry as to the actual nature of the soil, its productiveness and its extent, the means of increasing its fertility, and of economizing its produce, so as to give the greatest possible amount of employment and support, presents topics for discussion, important, not merely in relation to chemical or botanical philosophy, but to the gravest problems that can occupy the minds of the philanthropist or legislator.

The point of view under which the subjects of this chapter are to be considered, is different from that in which the preceding topics have been placed. Dazzled by the wondrous facilities for industrial activity which the structure of the sister kingdom presents, we had gradually sunk under a stupefying impression, that Ireland was not suited for any manufactures;

and the phrase currently ran : " We are an agricultural population, the English a manufacturing people; our soil and climate fit us for producing corn and cattle, whilst her mines of
coal and iron, the sources of her machine power, make her the
workshop of the world. The position of the two islands is,
therefore, correlative, and mutually advantageous; she sends
us clothing, and we send her food; from her crowded factories
we receive all the products of complex manufacture, and in return she takes our corn and cattle, the raw productions of our
soil." These ideas, every way prejudicial to the true interests
of the people, it was necessary to oppose. That we are not
destitute of the means of considerable manufacturing industry
has been, I trust, already shewn, and the propriety of availing
ourselves of such resources, of passing, where it is possible,
from occupations yielding little employment, to those which
create most demand for labour, needs, as I believe, no argument, in a country of which the heaviest calamities arise from
a population able and willing to work, for which the land does
not afford employment, and to which no other industrial occupation has been as yet presented.

The distinction which is drawn between an agricultural and
a manufacturing population, is, indeed, much more one of social condition and of civilization, than of geographical character. Man, in his first escape from barbarism, attaches himself
to the soil, becomes a shepherd, and next a farmer : as his
wants become more numerous, his agricultural operations become more complex, his ingenuity increases, and the assistance
he derives from the machines for abridging labour is more important. From watching cattle he passes to manufacturing
food, the earth becomes a portion of his machinery, he cleans,
prepares, and sets it into action, restores the worn out portions, adds such as are deficient under the form of manures,
and in all the general characters of his operations resembles a
manufacturing chemist, except that his product is a palateable
food instead of soap or oil of vitriol. So far from there being
aught antagonistic between agriculture and manufacture, the
former can only be carried on, with its best effect, where the
industrial arts are in a flourishing condition. The farmer re-

quires for his clothing the produce of various manufactures, and for his protection a house made comfortable by the labours of various artizans. His plough, his machines for winnowing and threshing, have been invented for him by ingenious mechanists. On the other hand, the manufacturer must be fed. The produce of the farm finds its quickest and readiest sale in the neighbouring manufacturing town. The risk of transport to a distance, of sales to strangers, of change of markets, are all avoided where domestic industry provides for the farmer purchasers in his own country. Moreover, besides food, the manufacturer takes from the agriculturist various materials, as flax and hemp, wool and hides, which form a large part of the value of his farm produce, and yet derive their greatest value from the subsequent processes of manufacture to which they are submitted.

The two great branches of human occupation, manufacturing and agricultural, so far from being opposed or inconsistent, are thus really bound together by the strongest ties. The same principles of science regulate the operations of both, and afford similar means of amelioration. The products of both are equally necessary for the subsistence of a civilized people, and each depends for the disposal of his stock on the capability of the other to purchase and to pay for it. No population that is exclusively devoted to the one or to the other mode of existence, can have a healthy organization, or be considered as in a natural state. It is, therefore, important to seek for the means of advancing both together, and as I have already described the relations of this country to manufacture, I shall now pass to the circumstances under which agricultur exists in Ireland.

It will, I trust, be understood, that I do not contemplate entering into any detailed description, either of the actual condition of agriculture in Ireland, or of the various methods and systems of cultivation and improvement which have been proposed, and are now, in many cases, being actively discussed. Such a task would be totally foreign to my immediate object, as well as inconsistent with the necessary limits of this work. I shall only endeavour to fix attention on the general circumstances of this department of industry, the relations which it bears to other sources of employment of the people; the great features of those applications of chemical science to agriculture, which promise to benefit so materially its condition; and finally, endeavour to direct the notice of those engaged in such pursuits, to certain branches of agricultural manufacture.

Ireland has been considered as peculiarly adapted to agriculture, from the fertility of the soil, to which all travellers or writers, who were competent to judge, have borne testimony. It may, however, be useful to adduce some such evidence, and without referring to any of older or more dubious authority, I shall briefly notice the statements of M'Culloch, of Arthur Young, and of Wakefield. In the Statistical Account of the British Empire, Mr. M'Culloch says: "A large proportion of the surface of Ireland is covered with bogs and mountains, but notwithstanding this deduction it contains a great deal of most excellent land. The luxuriance of the pastures, and the heavy crops of oats that are every where raised, even with the most wretched cultivation, attest its extraordinary fertility. This is the more singular, since, as has been already observed, the soil is generally thin." Mr. Wakefield, who was himself an agriculturist of long experience, and on a great scale, in England, notices, in his elaborate account of Ireland, published in 1812, the soils of Ireland as follows: "A great portion of the soil of Ireland throws out a luxuriant herbage, springing from a calcareous subsoil without any considerable depth. This is one species of the rich soil of Ireland, and is found throughout Roscommon, in some parts of Galway, Clare, and other districts. Some places exhibit the richest loam I ever saw turned up with a plough; this is the case throughout Meath in particular. Where such soil occurs, its fertility is so conspicuous, that it appears as if nature had determined to counteract the bad effects produced by the clumsy system of its cultivators. On the banks of the Fergus and Shannon, the land is of a different kind, but equally productive, though the surface presents the appearance of marsh. These districts are called caucasses: the substratum is a blue silt deposited by the sea, which seems to partake of the qualities of the upper stratum, for this land can be injured by no depth of ploughing.

" In the Counties of Limerick and Tipperary there is another kind of rich land, consisting of a dark, friable, dry, sandy loam, which, if preserved in a clean state, would throw out corn for several years in succession. It is equally well adapted for grazing and tillage, and I will venture to say, seldom experiences a season too wet, or a summer too dry. The richness of the land in some of the vales may be accounted for by the deposition of soil carried thither from the upper grounds by the rains. The subsoil is calcareous, so that the very richest manure is thus spread over the land below, without subjecting the farmer to any labour."

Again, he says : " In the north the quantity of rich soil is not very considerable, yet valleys of extraordinary fertility are found in every county, and I was not a little astonished, amidst the rocky and dreary mountains of Donegal, where there was hardly a vestige of cultivation, to find myself drop all at once into a district where the soil was exceedingly fertile." "Independently of the caucasses, the richest soil in Ireland is to be found in the Counties of Tipperary, Limerick, Longford, and Meath. Some parts of the County of Cork are uncommonly fertile, and upon the whole, Ireland may be considered as affording land of excellent quality, although I am by no means prepared to go the length of many writers, who assert, that it is decidedly, acre for acre, richer than England."

Arthur Young, by whose exertions as Secretary to the Board of Agriculture, and by his publications, the extension of agricultural knowledge in England had been so powerfully aided, says of Limerick and Tipperary : " It is the richest soil I ever saw, and such as is applicable to every wish. It will fatten the largest bullock, and at the same time do equally well for sheep, for tillage, for turnips, for wheat, for beans, and, in a word, for every crop and circumstance of profitable husbandry, You must examine into the soil before you can believe that a country, which has so beggarly an appearance, can be so rich and fertile."

Besides these general statements, we are enabled to form more definite ideas of the actual amount of produce from the soil of Ireland, by means of a very elaborate inquiry instituted by Mr. Wakefield into the usual weights of the more important crops in the various parts of Ireland. He divides the country into nine agricultural districts, but as these divisions were not founded on any geological or other natural principle, having regard only to the circumstances of his tour, they need not be specially described. The averages of the numbers of all nine, shewing the average crops of the cultivated land of Ireland generally, are given in the following table, per statute acre:

Of Wheat, from 142½℔ of seed, . 1300℔ of corn.
Of Bere, ,, 132½ ,, . 2148 ,,
Of Barley, ,, 145 ,, . 1820 ,,
Of Oats, ,, 196 ,, . 1734 ,,
Potatoes, ,, 1404 ,, . 13669 produce.

The largest amount of produce for each kind of crop, as given by Mr. Wakefield, and which may be taken as shewing the capability of the best land, is as follows:

Wheat, in Waterford, ... 4200℔
Bere in Limerick, ... 4480
Barley, in Kildare, Carlow, and Meath, . . 4480
Oats, in the East of Derry, ... 4032
Potatoes, at Athboy, in Meath, ... 72100

From a statute acre of ground.

In order to render our ideas more distinct, I shall here annex the statements made by some of the most eminent authorities in British and Scotch agriculture, as to the average and maximum produce of the various crops noticed above. In his valuable Treatise on Agriculture, Professor Low estimates the weight of the various kinds of crops to be, for Great Britain generally, per statute acre:

Wheat, ... 1380℔
Barley, ... 1872
Oats, ... 1200
Potatoes, ... 17920

Professor Johnstone, in his excellent Lectures on Agricultural chemistry and Geology, estimates the average crops, and the greatest recorded crops to be:

		AVERAGE.	MAXIMUM.
Wheat,	. . . .	1440℔	4200℔
Barley,	. . . .	1768	4160
Oats,	. . . .	1480	4000
Potatoes	. . . .	13440	67200

It hence appears, that the quantities which Mr. Wakefield concluded, from very extensive inquiry, to be the usual produce of the cultivated land of Ireland, and also the quantities which were the greatest obtained in the localities where the circumstances were most favourable, are almost absolutely the same as those given by the best and most recent authorities, as the usual, and as the most abundant produce of Great Britain Yet Mr. Wakefield's work was printed in 1812, and Messrs. Johnstone and Low's in 1843. The mode of farming was, in Ireland in 1812, such as made it a matter of wonder that any crop at all should be obtained. It must therefore, be concluded, that the naturally high fertility of the soil compensated for the ignorance of the farmer, and brought the final result of Ireland in 1812, and Great Britain in 1843, to the equality of production which has been just illustrated.

Further confirmation of this superior fertility of the soil of Ireland, may be derived from the results to which M. Moreau de Jonnes has arrived, after an elaborate examination of the agricultural condition of the British Islands, and has published in his Statistique de la Grande Bretagne et de l'Irlande. He considers the average crops for a Hectare (2·47 statute acres), measured in Hectolitres (2·8 bushels), to be :

		ENGLAND.	SCOTLAND.	IRELAND.
Wheat,	. . . . . .	18	16	20
Rye,	. . . . . .	10	12	32
Barley,	. . . . .	21	12	21
Oats,	. . . . . .	16	16	16
	Mean,	16	14	17½

I have more than once stated the area of Ireland to be 20,808,271 statute acres. The precise mode of distribution of this surface requires to be now noticed. It appears from the Census inquiries of 1841, that there are :

STATUTE ACRES.

Of arable land, ...	13,464,300
Uncultivated ground, ...	6,295,735
Plantations, ...	374,482
Under towns, ...	42,929
Under water (lakes and rivers), . . .	630,825

The uncultivated land includes bogs and mountains. It has been already shewn, that the area of bog is 2,833,000 acres, of which almost all is capable of reclamation, and of being adapted to productive husbandry, if not required as repositories of fuel. Of the mountainy land also, comparatively little is beyond the domain of agricultural enterprize. The average elevation of Ireland above the sea is not more than 387 feet, as shewn in a former chapter; very little ground indeed lies above the elevation of 600 feet. In fact, there is no district in Ireland sufficiently elevated to thereby present serious impediments to cultivation, and scarcely an acre to which the name of incapable of cultivation can be applied. It has been calculated that of the land at present waste, 4,600,000 acres are really available for agriculture, and from my own investigations, I am inclined to consider that estimate as certainly not exaggerated.

Such being the circumstances of the soil, it would be desirable to possess an estimate of the quantity of food which the island generally affords for the support of its inhabitants and for exportation. This, however, can scarcely be at present effected. Mr. M'Culloch states, that no documents exist from which a satisfactory estimate can be formed of the total agricultural produce of Ireland, but the eminent French statistician already quoted, M. De Jonnes, has endeavoured, by a discussion of all the available results to solve the question, and he concludes, that for each of the three kingdoms, in the years 1832 and 1834, the amount of produce was as follows. I have calculated the hectolitre, which he uses, as 2·8 bushels, in reducing his numbers to the British standard of measure.

COUNTRY.	WHEAT.	RYE.	BARLEY.	OATS, POTATOES, AND BEANS.
England,	75,000,000	2,800,000	53,000,000	39,000,000
Scotland,	4,312,000	17,640	10,500,003	61,740,000
Ireland,	29,680,000	7,840,000	44,100,000	107,520,000

In the case of Ireland at least, it is probable, that M. De Jonnes includes bere and bigg under the head of rye, for otherwise it is not easy to understand how the number for rye becomes so great.   It may afford some additional interest to mark the quantity of different kinds of corn exported to Great Britain.   Three decennial periods are taken for comparison. The quantities expressed are quarters.

YEARS.	WHEAT AND WHEAT-FLOUR.	BARLEY AND BERE.	OATS AND OATMEAL.	BEANS AND PEAS.
1820,	403,407	87,095	916,251	8,835
1830,	529,717	189,745	1,471,252	21,573
1840,	174,439	95,954	2,037,835	15,976

Among other interesting inquiries as to the social physics of Ireland, which are included in the census of 1841, is the estimate of the numbers and value of live stock.   The numbers are given in the following table, the values are not of interest here, but the total money value may be mentioned as somewhat above twenty millions sterling.

STOCK.	LEINSTER.	MUNSTER.	ULSTER.	CONNAUGHT.	TOTAL.
Horses and Mules,	168,753	160,378	155,425	68,013	552,569
Horned cattle,	488,858	530,273	525,854	295,840	1,840,825
Sheep,	657,118	695,622	212,671	525,788	2,091,199
Pigs,	366,772	522,895	292,512	170,922	1,353,101
Poultry,	2,236,941	2,834,752	1,895,678	5,397,056	12,334,427
Asses,	23,599	23,970	13,337	29,409	90,315

The horses kept for luxury are here included amongst those employed in agricultural and other labour.

In connecting with this notice of the actual circumstances and fertility of the soil, the important question of how its powers may be augmented, or at least protected from that deterioration to which the experience of ages has proved cultivated land to be exposed, it becomes necessary to advert to the kind of action which plants exercise upon the soil, by which, in fact, their growth is sustained, and the materials of food and other crops brought into existence. I shall touch upon the subject but succinctly; considered in its proper compass, it embraces at once the principal objects of agricultural chemistry, and of vegetable physiology, departments, upon the extensive and interesting domain of which I shall not enter, but glean from them such characteristic facts and principles, as may best illustrate the immediate objects of this chapter.

The vegetable kingdom is placed in nature intermediate between the mineral kingdom, which is submitted solely to the operation of physical laws, and actuated only by means of mechanical forces, and the animal kingdom, in which vital organization is most complex and most perfect, and where physical and chemical affinities are subordinate in energy to the refined influence of nervous power.   Every thing in nature is referrible to one or other of these three divisions, of which the first, the mineral, is distinguished by an absolute fixity of constitution, whilst the materials of which the animal is composed are in a constant state of change. If we consider a piece of marble, it contains carbon, oxygen, and calcium, and as long as it has been a piece of marble, the same proportions of these elements have formed it: but if we consider an animal, it is composed of numerous elements which have little permanence of arrangement. By the very act of its living force, the materials of which it consists die, and are thrown off from the remainder, and other new elements of the same kind must be taken in their place, or else the whole animal dies. The living being, therefore, requires food to supply this want of new materials; for this food it must look abroad in nature; it must prey. The more highly organized animals (carnivorous) prey on those of an inferior vital power (herbivorous): these again on the vegetable kingdom.   Thus ultimately the different kinds of plants must supply the means of sustenance to all animal bodies, for in no case is an animal able to assimilate to its organism, or use as nutritious food, a mineral material.

When, however, the term of existence of the animal has expired, and that vitality ceasing, the physical and chemical forces come into play, its constituents are restored to the mineral kingdom. The various elements which had formed its bones and muscles, its nerves and viscera, pass into simpler forms of combination, diffuse themselves in the atmosphere, or are carried off, dissolved in water; or else, entombed beneath the surface, may reappear after the lapse of many ages, in rock formations, and thus become the indices of animal existence, of which all other trace might long before have vanished from the earth. From this mineral form the elements of animal existence are rescued by the aid of plants. The vegetable, penetrating with its roots deep below the surface of the ground, stretching with its stem and branches into the atmosphere, and moistened by the showers, takes from these various sources the elements necessary for organic beings, elaborates them into the numerous products which are capable of being used as food, and on which animals are fed. The various departments of nature are thus correlative and mutually compensating. The same elements pass successively from the mineral to the vegetable, and from that to the animal existence, and by the dissolution of the latter, again back to the mineral kingdom, to be the foundation of another and similar series. When we see in Summer the country rich with luxuriant crops, gay with foliage and flowers, where in Winter all had appeared dead and desert-looking; when we find new generations of animals replacing those that die, and that the number of living beings does not diminish, it is important for us to recollect, that there is still no new element added to those already existing on the globe, that the condition of the materials of our earth is of unceasing change; assuming many forms, they pass from mineral to plant, from plant to animal, and hence the growth and sustenance of an animal depend on the nature of the plants on which it is fed, and the growth and development of a plant upon the nature of the soil and the atmosphere, by which the mineral elements may be supplied to it.

The number of elements which are found existing in animals and plants amount to sixteen, of these the atmosphere and water may be considered as capable of supplying four, carbon, hydrogen, nitrogen, and oxygen, and these are they which constitute by far the greatest proportion of every organic substance. The remaining elements, though usually present in much smaller quantity, are not less essential to the healthy existence of the plant, and must be obtained from the soil on which the plant is cultivated. The soil must, therefore, be highly complex in constitution, in order that it may yield those elements. If it do not naturally contain them, they must be artificially supplied in order that the plants may grow. Each crop removing from the soil quantities of those materials, diminishes its power of producing future crops, and hence to sustain the fertility of any soil, the exhausting tendency of its vegetation must be compensated for by suitable additions. In those few and simple propositions is contained the clue to the most refined and successful systems of agriculture, and the objects of the philosophical agriculturist, as well as the most effective means of practically advancing husbandry, consist in :

1st. Studying the composition of the soil.

2nd. Studying the action of plants upon it.

In neither point of view has the agriculture of this country been as yet considered, and hence I shall rather endeavour to indicate the route to be pursued in such inquiries, than be able to describe what has been accomplished.

The soil is formed by the decomposition of the minerals, of which the crust of the globe consists. The water which flows over the surface is absorbed into the pores and fissures of the rocks ; and in winter, on freezing, it expands with such irresistible force, as to crumble down even the materials of the densest and hardest stone. The pulverulent or gravelly material so afforded, is carried down by rains or floods to the lower grounds, and spreading over the more level country forms the cultivatable soil. Independent of the mechanical action of water, the constitution of numerous rocks is such as to cause their gradual decomposition by its chemical action, as in the case of felspar and other minerals ; and by the direct action of the atmosphere, all rocks which contain protoxide of iron very rapidly decompose and crumble down. Such being the origin

of the soil, its constitution will be easily understood to depend
on that of the rock from which it has been formed; and as on
this constitution its fertility, or its power of supplying plants
with the materials they require for their growth, mainly depends, it will be seen that the agricultural capabilities of a
country are immediately connected with, and dependent on,
its geological character. A district, of which the rock is simple in constitution, cannot furnish a fertile soil. A pure quartz
rock, or a pure limestone, could only furnish from its soil to
plants, lime or silica, and they should hence languish for want
of other equally important elements. The edges of a geological district, where various rocks are in contact, will, therefore, always be more fertile as to soil than its interior, and the
more numerous are the rocks in the neighbourhood, and the
greater the diversity in their mineral character, the more
complex will be the soil furnished by their decomposition, and
by its power of furnishing the elements of growth to different
kinds of plants, the greater will be the range and energy of
its fertility.

If these principles be applied to the actual condition of fertility of the soils of Ireland, they will be found borne out in a
remarkable degree. The districts known to agriculturists, as
being of the most remarkable fertility in Ireland, are in Ulster,
about the valley of the Lagan, and in Munster, the Golden
Vale, which stretches from the end of the coal formation at
Cashel to near Limerick. On looking to the geological map,
these districts are found to contain a greater number of different kinds of rocks, than any other locality in Ireland. The
Lagan flows on a bed of new red sandstone, on one side of
which rises the trap district of Antrim, with its underlying
chalk and gypseous marls, whilst the clay-slate of Down
bounds it on the south, until it is closed by the old red sandstone and mica-slate, the coal formation and tertiary clays,
which occur all at the southern extremity of Lough Neagh.
The Munster district lies between the sandstone and clay-slate
mountains of the Galtees and Slieve Phelim. The principal
rock of the low country is limestone, through which, however,
protrude in various parts. masses of sandstone, and of volcanic

trap, itself of complex constitution: the western boundary
being the shales and grits of the Munster coalfield.

In the case of a river flowing through a great extent of
country, and intersecting various geological formations, the
earthy matter which it carries down, and deposits, when by
the widening of the stream and the meeting of the tidal water,
the force of its current ceases, possesses a similar complexity
of composition and equal fertility. Thus the flat lands along
a river are, when reclaimed, found to be highly productive,
such are the caucasses of the Shannon, so have been formed
the low districts of Holland and Belgium, whose agriculture
is so worthy of imitation. So also by the overflowing of the
Nile, and the deposition of its mud, the debris of the numerous
rocks of the upper country, Egypt was rendered the garden of
the ancient world.

It is necessary to remark, however, that the source of the
soil may be, and perhaps more frequently is, far distant from
the rock which actually underlies it; the soil being formed by
the decomposition of the mountainous country, and being deposited on the plain. The constitution of the most usual soil
of the central portions of Ireland is a remarkable instance of
this. The great limestone plain is covered by a soil which
contains scarcely a trace of lime, although it may be actually
mixed with limestone gravel. I have examined soil which was
not many inches deep, and had a subsoil of limestone gravel,
resting on bare limestone rock, and yet the soil itself was almost barren for want of lime, which it was necessary to apply
to it as a manure. This circumstance is very well illustrated
in the remarks of Mr. Murphy, in an agricultural tour, published in the Irish Farmers' Journal: he says, speaking of the
limestone country between Dublin and Slane: "The surface
soil of the extensive level, of which this rock forms the substratum, does not appear to have been formed by the disintegration of the subjacent rock, as between it and the surface a
layer of gravel or rounded stones, intermixed with earth, occurs very generally; these round stones, being for the most
part a limestone of much purer character, and suited for burning: but rather seems to have been deposited by the waters of

an immense lake, which probably at some distant period occupied this extensive flat. It has not, so far as we are aware, been analysed, but evidently contains a large portion of alumina (clay); is stiff, retentive of moisture, and if worked or trodden when wet, becomes as hard as a road in dry weather, so that no harrowing or rolling can reduce the clods, but which fall just like roche lime on being wetted."

It is very difficult to trace, in any case, the origin of soils which are mostly due to such complex sources, and especially in Ireland, where analyses are almost absolutely absent, and where the attention of scientific men has been as yet scarcely at all fixed on agricultural problems; yet, it may not be uninteresting to follow up what has been said, by noticing at least a possible source of the heavy clayey soil of the limestone plain. The coal districts of Ireland, as described in a former chapter, are not shut in, as in most other countries, and contained in basins between more elevated formations of older rocks, but stand out insulated, and rising several hundred feet above the general level of the limestone plain on which they rest. Were they always of their present limited dimensions? Were not, for instance, the Leinster and Tipperary coal fields once connected? Were not the places where the lower limestone is now the surface rock, originally covered by an extension of the calp and upper limestone, the tearing off of which laid bare the lower and produced a portion of the present soil?

The great heaps of limestone gravel known as Eskers, which are found over the central plain, and which afford abundant proof of there having been at one time currents of vast force in operation over the surface, render it highly probable, and that certainly in some localities such has occurred is beyond doubt. In the Railway Report, Mr. Griffith, describing the coal strata of Lough Allen, says: "The millstone grit forms the surface, not only of Cuilcagh, but of many similar mountains of the neighbouring district. Had they been one hundred feet higher, they would have all contained the main coal of Brahlieve mountain, but unfortunately that valuable coal bed, which no doubt once existed there, has been washed away by the action of currents, proceeding from the north-west, and deposited in broken fragments, accompanied by sandstone and blue-clay, on the surface of the limestone valley which extends to the south-east, towards Belturbet, Killeshandra, and Mohill. In many instances large pieces of coal have been discovered by well-sinkers, in the diluvium, throughout the district above mentioned, and in some cases the quantity of coal was so considerable, as to induce the belief, that by sinking deeper, a bed of coal might be found." If we contemplate similar, only more extended actions than those just now described, we shall have easily accounted for the coating of clayey soil which covers the limestone country, and which certainly has been produced by the decomposition of slate-clay strata, such as exist abundantly in the coal formations and in the calp.

I have mentioned that we are almost totally destitute of analyses of the soils of Ireland. This is a deficiency which it is most important for our scientific chemists, with the assistance of enlightened agriculturists, and of such institutions as the Royal Dublin Society, to endeavour with all energy to supply. In preparing the Geological Memoir for the Ordnance Survey of Londonderry, Captain Portlock had analyses made of several soils from that county, of which the following table presents a summary sufficient for present objects. The soils are arranged according to the nature of the underlying rock, and the names of the townland of each are given.

SOILS ON MICA-SLATE.

	MOYARD.	BALLY-BANEDIN.	KILLU-NAUGHT.	MONEY-HANEGAN.
Water, ...	9·6	8·5	15·8	3·2
Organic matter, . .	11·8	20·8	24·0	6·0
Sand and gravel, .	104·2	131·7	101·2	112·0
Fine insoluble matter,	65·8	37·0	38·7	67·8
Oxide of iron, . . .	7·1	3·1	0·2	8·0
Alumina, ...	0·7	6·0	2·7	3·0
Carbonate of lime, .	0·2			
	199·4	207·1	182·6	200·0

SOILS ON TRAP ROCKS.

	BALLYMA-COMB.	DOWNING.	EDEN.	SLAGHT-NEILL.
Water, ...	24·3	19·6	6·6	25·2
Organic matter, . .	22·6	17·9	2·9	15·1
Sand and gravel, .	71·3	68·2	85·6	41·9
Fine insoluble matter,	54·6	70·8	77·4	88·6
Oxide of iron, . . .	16·4	10·3	11·7	17·6
Alumina, ...	5·5	6·0	5·3	5·9
Carbonate of lime, .		3·6	9·3	0·7
	194·7	196·4	198·8	195·0

SOILS ON SANDSTONE ROCKS.

	DOON	GORTNAS-KEY.	DERRY-CHRIER.	TULLY-VERY.
Water, ...	7·8	8·5	12·2	5·5
Organic matter, . .	11·2	8·2	21·6	7·3
Sand and gravel, .	124·5	105·4	123·8	142·9
Fine insoluble matter,	53·2	62·3	38·2	38·6
Oxide of iron, . .	4·5	5·0	3·9	6·2
Alumina, ...	0·7	2·4	2·1	,,
Carbonate of lime, .	0·2	0·2	0·2	,,
	202·1	192·0	202·0	200·5

It can be easily understood, that if we were in possession of
a series of analyses of the soils of the country, and could exhibit them in the form given above, they would furnish most
valuable data and assistance in agricultural operations, but I
must say, that really useful analyses should be very differently
executed from those above detailed. In none of these are the
alcalies, magnesia, the sulphates, nor phosphates, at all noticed as present or absent. Yet, these are highly important
elements of a soil, and indispensable to most plants. Moreover, there is a large amount of sand and gravel mentioned,
also fine insoluble matter, but no idea of the nature of the sand,
gravel, or fine matter; yet the nature of this being unknown,
what do we know of the soil? In fact the analysis of a soil

is an operation requiring the greatest precision. In order
that we may be satisfied of its correctness, we must have the
security of other and difficult problems in chemistry, successfully solved by the same analyst, whom, therefore, we can
trust, but in the case of the Ordnance Survey analyses, the
name of the operator is not even given, and hence we have no
other authority to rely on for their accuracy, even as far as
they go, than that of Captain Portlock, whose eminence in his
own departments of science is indeed worthy of praise.

In no case do the above analyses of soils enable us to judge
of the relation between the soil and subsoil or underlying rock.
The composition of mica has been noticed already (p. 172),
that of the trap or basaltic rocks which constitute the north-
east of Ireland, and which contain a great variety of minerals
in minute division throughout their mass, may be judged from
the following analyses. No. 1 is by Kennedy, No. 2 by Berthier, Nos. 3 and 4 by myself.

	No. 1.	No. 2.	No. 3.	No. 4.
Silica, ...	48	52·4	52·89	51·17
Alumina, ...	16	22·6	19·29	18·29
Lime, ...	9	5·8	5·39	6·12
Soda, ...	4	7·9	,,	,,
Magnesia, ...	,,	1·1	2·19	1·80
Oxide of iron, . . .	16	9·1	17·82	20·60
Water, ...	5	1·0	2·56	2·03
	98	99·9	100·04	100·01

From this complexity of constitution it might be expected,
that the soil formed by the decomposition of these basaltic
rocks should be well adapted for agriculture, but the manner
in which it decomposes has not been properly investigated.
The sides of the great trap dike, which near Croagh in Tyrone,
cuts through the chalk, are decomposed and soft, disintegrating rapidly on exposure, and a clayey substance, evidently the
result of its final change, rests against it in perpendicular beds,

separating it from the chalk   This substance was analysed by
Dr. Apjohn, and yielded:

Silica,	52·43
Alumina,	7·52
Magnesia,	7·13
Protoxide of iron,	3·70
Lime,	0·34
Water,	28·86
	99·97
Loss,	0·03
	100·00

Whether the "fine insoluble matter" of the soils of the trap
district, was similar to this decomposed trap, remains for future examination.   In the decomposition of the trap rocks, it
is certain that the oxide of iron is evolved in such a form, as
to be soluble in weak acids.   Hence the trap soils appear in
the Ordnance Survey analyses to contain so much oxide of
iron.   This metal is even dissolved out of the disintegrating
rock by the carbonic acid of the rain and spring water.   Almost every spring in that district is impregnated with iron;
of thirty specimens of water which I examined, twenty-three
contained iron, and some of them were strongly chalybeate.
It is hence probably, that the clayey substance formed by the
decomposing trap, and analyzed by Dr. Apjohn as above, contained so little iron.

When I come to speak of the flax agriculture, and of the
composition of the mineral manures, I shall have occasion to
notice some investigations which I have myself made, as to
the composition of soils, under the direction of two of our most
useful and enlightened associations, the Flax Improvement Society, and the Waste Land Improvement Society of Ireland.

Before passing from the consideration of the composition of
soils, it is necessary to add to this account of their constituents,
as derived from the rocks by which they are formed, some
notice of the peculiar organic matter which all fertile soils
contain, and to the functions of which I shall have to recur

after some time. After the death of a plant, its elements, yielding to the force of their chemical affinities, enter into new arrangements, and by a series of progressive alterations, are finally converted into a dark brown material, termed popularly vegetable mould, and by chemists, *humus* or *ulmine*. When perfectly pure, this subtance contains no nitrogen, and consists of, as prepared,

	FROM WOOD.	FROM SUGAR.
Carbon, ...	72·7	65·65
Hydrogen, ...	6·1	4·28
Oxygen, . . . , ...	21·2	30·07
	100·0	100·00

Such a material is totally destitute of power on vegetation, and the confounding of it with the substances which are produced in the natural rotting of the remains of plants in the soil, has been very prejudicial to the progress of agricultural chemistry.

It is in fact found, that when vegetable matter commences to decompose, it evolves carbonic acid, and absorbs oxygen from the air, but not merely does it unite with that element, but also the nitrogen of the air is absorbed in considerable quantity, and enters into the constitution of the new product, which actually acquires thus, almost the composition of an animal substance. Two equivalents of wood, $C_{72} H_{48} O_{48}$, take from the atmosphere five equivalents of nitrogen, and ten of oxygen, and evolving sixteen equivalents of carbonic acid, $C_{16} O_{32}$, are converted into a brown substance, which Hermann, whose results I am now quoting, terms nitrolin. The composition of this body, compared with that of animal flesh, is as follows :

	NITROLIN.	FLESH.
Carbon, . , ...	57·20	55·20
Hydrogen, ...	6·32	7·00
Nitrogen, ...	12·20	16·80
Oxygen, ...	24·28	21·80
	100·00	100·00

If this nitrolin remain in contact with air and moisture, it falls into decomposition, precisely as animal bodies do, evolves carbonic acid and ammonia, and produces different brown and black coloured substances, true humine, humic acid, &c., which are gradually less rich in nitrogen. It is by the gradual formation and decomposition of this body, that the organic matter of the soil becomes so powerful an agent in its fertilization. The roots and fibres of a crop, left in the soil, gradually rot, and become thereby the means of absorbing from the atmosphere a quantity of nitrogen, which is rendered available for the sustenance of the next generation of plants.

In estimating the fertility of a soil, therefore, it is most important to determine the quantity of these active organic matters, and particularly the amount of nitrogen which they contain. In the Ordnance Survey analyses, the quantity of organic matter is given, but its amount is such, often more than 20 per cent., as to shew that there are included all the unaltered roots and fragments of plants, which deprive the number of all absolute value. The mere presence of organic matter indicates nothing; thus a peaty soil may be absolutely barren, if the decomposition of its organic matter has been carried on under water, where the oxygen and nitrogen of the air have not access, and consequently only inert ulmine, destitute of the power of evolving carbonic acid and ammonia, be produced.

The office of the soil is not merely to afford such chemical elements as the constitution of the plant requires, but also, and what, in an agricultural point of view, is nearly of as great importance, to afford a mechanical support to the plant during its existence. This support must be consonant to the habits and structure of the plant, and hence is the special classification of soils, as adapted for the cultivation of various kinds of crops, quite independent so far of their chemical composition. Thus if we take a tenacious clay, which, when dry, becomes hard and solid, and when wet, forms an impervious paste, it is evident that plants which either required to extend delicate roots to a distance, or to generate a single root of considerable bulk, could not grow there in a healthy manner; whilst a light and very porous soil would be adapted naturally for such crops. On the other hand, a plant of which but little stretches under ground, the stem and other portions presenting a considerable mass and surface to the air, would find in a tenacious clay, a sure anchorage and support against the effects of the wind and rain. It is thus that wheat and turnip soils are almost synonymous with stiff and adhesive clays on the one hand, light and friable loams upon the other, and similar instances of the mechanical adaptation of soils to agricultural practices will have occurred in the experience of every practical farmer.

It is not merely, however, in this mechanical point of view, that the physical properties of the soil become important, but also, and indeed especially, as affecting the condition of drainage of the ground. The greater or less dryness of a soil influences powerfully the nature of the vegetation it tends to nourish. The plants of a marsh differ from those of a dry upland, not merely in greater or less abundance or luxuriance, but in nature and in organization. The plant which is naturally formed for dry ground will no more flourish in a wet situation, than an animal, inhabitant of the land or air, can seek its subsistence, and live habitually under water. It is, therefore, of vital importance to agriculture, that all superfluous water should be as rapidly as possible removed. Its presence not merely affects the character of the natural vegetation, and renders the soil unfit for the cultivation of plants which belong to a dry situation, but, what is even more practical in its consequences, it retards the progress of vegetation in a very material degree, by preventing the rays of the sun from warming the substance of the soil. A certain moderate heat is indispensable to vegetation; an increase of heat, provided it did not exceed certain bounds, augments its rapidity and force, in a remarkable degree, and the constitution of ordinary soil, by its dark colour and rugged dull aspect, is precisely such as to absorb the heat of the sun with most effect, so as to advance the vegetation on its surface; but if the soil be sensibly wet, no heating effect can take place, all the warmth will be absorbed in producing evaporation of water from the surface, and rather, as one may verify by holding a wet hand in the air,

even before the sun, an impression of greater cold will be produced. Long experience as to the result, has even fixed in
ordinary language the word *cold* as expressing the imperfection of such soils. The remedying of this evil, as of the former
one, consists in relieving the soil from the excess of water
which lies upon it, which is to be effected by attending to the
general drainage of the district, and by lessening the retentive quality of the individual soil, where such is economically
practicable.

The question of drainage becomes of very considerable importance in relation to the lands of the limestone plain, in which,
being situated at such moderate altitude, and with so gentle an
inclination of surface, the rivers and lakes, on any considerable fall of rain, are apt to overflow their banks, and flooding
considerable districts, destroy a serious amount of agricultural
produce. Thus the Shannon, above Lough Derg, was used
to flood, at ordinary rises, 32,000 acres of land along its banks,
which, on being relieved by the improvements in the channel
of the river, from such a source of loss, will be very materially
increased in value. The fall available for drainage in this
district may, in a general point of view, be calculated from the
fact, that the summit level of the Royal Canal is 322 feet at
Mullingar, that of the Grand Canal at the summit level 279 feet
above the level of the sea. The discharge of waters into the
Shannon occurs where the river is 120 feet, and to the east on
the edge of the limestone plain, a few miles from Dublin (about
Lucan), 150 feet above that level. The fall on the plain is,
therefore, but about 165 feet on each side of the summit, a
distance in average of forty miles, which gives little more than
four feet per mile. It is hence easily intelligible how, with the
obstacles of various kinds found in the course of every stream,
these flat portions of the country are liable to flooding in the
wet seasons. In many districts these accidents became almost
truly periodical, occurring once in three or four years to such
an extent as to destroy the crops ; the property lost in a single
year being so great, that it would, if judiciously expended, pay
the entire cost of remedying the evil. A great portion of such
lands is in wet seasons covered with water for three, six, or

even eight months in the year, and the injury extends also to those lands, which lying higher, are not actually flooded, but the corn and other crops of which are deteriorated by the damp fogs and vapours arising from the flooded lands, and the cold and early frost thereby produced.

These evils are often augmented by the position of mills or factories, which, from the injudicious construction of their dams or weirs, throw back the water on the land at one season, though they are left short of water for work at other times. In the majority of cases, the improvement of the waterpower of the mill and the effectual drainage of the lands are perfectly compatible. Such undertakings, however, cannot be carried out by any individual effort, except in very peculiar localities. This difficulty has, however, been recently removed, and power granted to the Board of Works to carry on drainage operations. From this the greatest benefit may be expected to result, principally to the agriculturist, but also to the manufacturer requiring water power. The land will be brought into a better state for cultivation, the supply of water to mills may be rendered steadier, and even increased, as the loss by evaporation from a great flooded surface will be obviated, and by the body of water being confined more strictly to the river channels, the navigation of these will be, in many cases, materially facilitated.

That the advantages derivable from effective drainage are fully appreciated by our agricultural proprietors, is shewn by the fact, that although the powers and regulations of the Board of Works are yet but little understood by the public, there had been applications made and surveys instituted between August, 1842, when the Act passed, and April, 1844, for the drainage of 48,293 acres of land liable to flood. The estimated cost of thoroughly draining these lands amounted to £129,811, or £2 18s. 6d. per acre. The expected increase in the annual setting value of the lands amounted to £16,489, or about 13 per cent. on the capital invested, and this capital is to be derived from the parties benefited by the improvement, to whom indeed the return is rendered somewhat larger by the fact, that

T

certain portions of the operations are carried on at the public cost.

Besides those cases in which surveys have been actually made, there have been applications for the examination of about 25,000 acres more, which makes 73,293 acres of land now about to be drained and improved, upon the voluntary application and assessment of the proprietors.

A feature in these drainage operations, which deserves notice, is the amount of employment which they afford. Of the £129,811 estimated above as the expense of the operations, it is calculated that £96,000 would be expended in labour alone. The works are of such a simple nature, cuttings and embankments, as may be performed by the least skilled labourers and with the simplest tools. Not being necessarily limited in time, the operations of each district could be executed by the labourers of that district when agricultural occupation was most deficient, and thus at once relieve for several years the localities from the pressure of an unemployed population, ameliorate the condition of the soil, so that it may furnish additional agricultural occupation, and train the labourers to habits of steady industry.

I have thus endeavoured to trace the general conditions under which the soil of Ireland is placed, as to the circumstances of composition and of drainage, which so powerfully affect its fertile quality. It is necessary to notice also the materials which are at hand for the restoration of its powers, when, by the ordinary course of agriculture, the land becomes more or less exhausted. These materials are manures of various kinds, some mineral some animal, or vegetable, all acting, however, in supplying to the soil the elements of which it had been originally deficient, or which had been removed from it by the crops previously grown upon the land. In order however, that the true action of manures and the necessity for them may be understood, it will be necessary to premise some brief observations.

The great object of agriculture is, to produce food for man. The agriculturist feeds various other animals, but only with the final object of rendering them also available as food. The plants must thus furnish to man the elements of which his body consists, and although there are certain exceptions arising from some kinds of food being more palatable than others, yet we may consider it as a principle, that the price of any kind of food is proportional to its nourishing quality. A stone of potatoes costs less than a stone of wheat, and this much less than fourteen pounds of beef; but to support the life of an individual it will require much more of potatoes than of wheat, much more of wheat than of beef, so that ultimately the same quantity of real nutritive material costs about the same money in all. In order that the plant may elaborate the various substances which serve the purposes of food, the plant itself must be sustained in health, and its parts properly formed, for which various substances are necessary, which are not required by the animal, and which, if the plant be eaten, are rejected. All these materials are derived from the inorganic sources described in page 261; from the air, or water, or from the soil, but it is chiefly from the latter. The atmosphere furnishes the carbon of plants, especially after they have passed the first stages of their growth, as has been shewn by Ingenhouz and many other philosophers, and so beautifully popularized by Liebig. From the atmosphere also many kinds of plants derive nitrogen, but it is from the decomposing organic matter of the soil the young plant finds a supply of carbon and of nitrogen: many of the most important plants depend on it alone for the nitrogen they contain, and in all cases the mineral elements of the vegetable are taken from the soil on which it grows. In order that the nature of these elements should be understood, I have drawn up the following tables, deduced from very accurate analyses by Boussingault, in the first of which the constitution of some of the most important plants used as food is shewn, and in the last the constitution of the inorganic portion, which in the first is marked as ashes.

100 parts of the following substances considered as dry, consist of:

	CARBON.	HYDROGEN.	OXYGEN.	NITROGEN.	ASHES.
Wheat, . . .	46·1	5·8	43·4	2·3	2·4
Wheat-straw, .	48·4	5·3	38·9	0·4	7·0
Oats, ...	50·7	6·4	36·7	2·2	4·0
Oat-straw, . .	50·1	5·4	39·0	0·4	5·1
Potatoes, . .	44·0	5·8	44·7	1·5	4·0
Turnips, . .	42·9	5·5	42·3	1·7	7·6
Red clover hay,	47·4	5·0	37·8	2·1	7·7

100 parts of these substances, in their ordinary state of moisture, contain usually :

	WHEAT.	WHEAT-STRAW.	OATS.	OAT-STRAW.	POTA-TOES.	TUR-NIPS.	CLOVER HAY.
Dry material,	85·5	74	79·2	71·3	24·1	7·5	79
Water, . .	14·5	26	20·8	28·7	75·9	92·5	21

100 parts of the ashes of the substances in these tables contain :

	WHEAT.	WHEAT-STRAW.	OATS.	OAT-STRAW.	POTA-TOES.	TUR-NIPS.	CLOVER HAY.
Phosphoric acid,	47·0	3·1	14·9	3·0	11·3	6·1	6·3
Sulphuric acid,	1·0	1·0		4·1	7·1	10·9	2·5
Carbonic acid,	,,	,,	1·7	3·2	13·4	14·0	25·0
Chlorine, .	traces.	0·6	0·5	4·7	2·7	2·9	2·6
Lime, . . .	2·9	8·5	3·7	8·3	1·8	10·9	24·6
Magnesia, . .	15·9	5·0	7·7	2·8	5·4	4·3	6·3
Potash, . .	29·5	9·2	12·9	24·5	51·5	33·7	26·6
Soda, . . .	traces.	0·3	0·0	4·4	traces.	4·1	0·5
Silica, . . .	1·3	67·6	53·3	40·0	5·6	6·4	5·3
Alumina, &c., .	,,	1·0	1·3	2·1	0·5	1·2	0·3
Moisture and loss, . . .	2·4	3·7	3·0	2·9	0·7	5·5	0·0

The investigations of Boussingault enable us also to calculate the actual quantities of these various elements which are taken from the soil by the growing crop. Thus, reducing his numbers to British standard weights and measures, he found the usual crop of wheat, from his farm in Alsace, per English acre, to weigh:

	AS STORED.	DRIED.	CONTAINING ASH.
Grain, ...	1500℔	1285℔	33℔
Straw, ...	3400	2550	178

The ash consisted of, per acre:

	GRAIN ASH.	STRAW ASH.
Phosphoric acid, ...	15·51℔	5·52℔
Sulphuric acid, ...	·33	1·78
Carbonic acid, ...	,,	,,
Chlorine, ...	traces.	1·07
Lime, ...	96	15·13
Magnesia, ...	5·25	8·90
Potash, ...	9·73	16·37
Soda, ...	traces.	·53
Silica, ...	·43	120·33
Alumina, &c., ...	,,	1·78
Moisture and loss, ...	·79	6·59
	33℔	178℔

The usual crop of oats:

	AS STORED.	DRIED.	CONTAINING. ASH.
Grain, ...	1210℔	975℔	40℔
Straw, ...	1700	1180	59

The ashes were found composed of:

	GRAIN ASH.	STRAW ASH.
Phosphoric acid, ...	5·96℔	1·77℔
Sulphuric acid, ...	·40	2·43
Carbonic acid, ...	·68	1·90
Chlorine, ...	·20	2·78
Lime, ...	1·48	4·91
Magnesia, ...	3·08	1·65
Potash, . . . , ...	5·18	14·60

Soda, ...   „   2·60
Silica, ... 21·30   23.85
Alumina, &c. . . . .   ·52   1·24
Moisture and loss, ... 1·20   1·27
                             ─────   ─────
                             40℔   59℔

The other crops, of which the composition per cent. has been given above, yield usually, per statute acre, as follows:

	AS STORED.	DRIED.	CONTAINING ASHES.
Clover hay, . . .	4620℔	3680℔	283℔
Potatoes, ...	14560	3509	142
Swedish turnips, .	44800	3360	255

These ashes consisted of:

	POTATO ASH.	TURNIP ASH.	CLOVER ASH.
Phosphoric acid, .	16·05℔	15·55℔	17·82℔
Sulphuric acid, .	10·08	27·79	7·08
Carbonic acid, .	19·03	35·70	70·85
Chlorine, . . .	3·82	7·39	7·35
Lime, ...	2·55	27·79	69·62
Magnesia, . . .	7·67	10·96	17·83
Potash, ...	73·15	85·97	75·18
Soda, ...	traces.	10·45	1·41
Silica, ...	7·95	16·32	15·00
Alumina, &c., . .	·71	3·06	0·85
Moisture and loss,	·99	14·02	„
	142℔	255℔	283℔

hese analytical results shew how numerous are the materials which the plants remove from the soil, and also the quantities which in each year are taken from a given area. Most of these, it will be observed, are bodies which exist in ordinary soils, but in comparatively small quantity. Thus it requires very accurate analysis to determine the presence of phosphoric acid, or of magnesia, or of potash, in a soil; and yet these bodies are found in the ashes of the growing crop in abundance. It is, therefore, easily intelligible, that plants removing thus such substances from the soil, should ultimately leave it so far destitute of them, as to be unable to afford material for the healthy growth of similar plants; the soil should become barren, and it would require long repose, indeed time sufficient for the formation of a new soil, before a similar cultivation could be renewed with success. This time cannot, however, be given without such interruption of agricultural labour as should ultimately produce serious loss, and hence the necessity of producing, by the application of manures, an artificial soil, such as may supply all the materials necessary to the plants, and render the farmer, to a great extent, independent of the slower process by which natural soil is generated. Of these manures, it falls only within the object of this work to notice such as exist naturally in Ireland.

To the different varieties of cold clayey soils, of which so large a part of the central surface of Ireland consists, there is no manure more suitable than lime. It is also the material most easily accessible, as but one county in Ireland is destitute of it, and in the central districts it forms in general the underlying rock. It is useful first as supplying a necessary constituent of plants, next, that when applied fresh slaked and caustic, it promotes the decomposition of the vegetable remains of former crops, and thus leads to the rapid formation of thos azotized organic matters which are so active in promoting the fertility of the soil, and finally, by intermixture with lime, the cohesion of the clays is so materially diminished, that they be-some much less strongly retentive of water, Perfectly pure lime, arising from the calcination of a pure marble, would often give only such advantages to the farmer as I have just described, but it is to be recollected, that no limestone is absolutely pure. That class of rocks are formed of the aggregated remains of animals, more or less analogous to the crustacean and molluscous animals of the existing seas, and hence contain traces of other ingredients derived from that origin. In fact if we consider the composition of existing shells, which has been found to be

	CRAB SHELL.	LOBSTER SHELL.	OYTER SHELL.
Animal membrane, . .	28·6	44·76	0·5
Carbonate of lime, . .	62·8	49·26	98·5
Phosphate of lime, . .	6·0	3·22	1·0
Salts of soda, . . .	1·6	1·50 ⎱	
Phosphate of magnesia,	1·0	1·26 ⎰	,,
	100·0	100·00	100·0

it will appear that limestone may be expected to contain similar materials, and such is absolutely the fact. The quantities are very minute, but become not unimportant in agricultural operations, from the very large amount of materials that is acted on. The different kinds of limestone also contain frequently silica and alumina, and thereby acquire often the property of setting under water and forming hydraulic limes or cements, although inferior limes for ordinary purposes. Most of the middle limestone or calp is of this quality.

Independent of the true magnesian limestone described already, page 246, the beds of ordinary limestone are, in various places impregnated with magnesia in small quantities, which might make them desirable for some purposes of agriculture, but injurious in other cases. The composition of such forms of limestone is exemplified in that of the stone of Murloch Bay, and of Donegal marble, the analysis of which by Dr. Apjohn is given in the following table, along with the composition of pure limestone, of that of Brown's Hill, Carlow, which belongs to the lower series, by Mr. Griffith, and of the calp of Dublin, analysed by Knox. The phosphoric acid is not counted in these analyses, as its quantity is too minute, seldom amounting to one-thousandth of the entire.

	PURE	BROWN'S HILL.	CALP.	MURLOUGH BAY AND DONEGAL MARBLE.
Lime, ...	56	53·0	38·1	54·40
Carbonic acid, .	44	42·0	29·9	43·49
Silica, ...	,,	4·5	18·0	·98
Alumina, . . .	,,	,,	7·5	,,
Organic matter,	,,	0·5	4·5	,,
Magnesia, . .	,,	,,	,,	1·13
Oxide of iron, .	,,	,,	2·0	,,

Marl, which under many circumstances is a most useful manure, is found to occur abundantly in Ireland. It supplies to the soil, lime, though but in a mild form; it serves to loosen the more densely aggregated soils, as it would also serve to bind those of too loose a texture. It is, in fact, a mixture of carbonate of lime and clay, and hence participates in the different properties of each. Almost all of the bogs rests on a marly bottom, intermixed with beds of clay, or of limestone gravel, in such manner that these wastes, where they become unnecessary for fuel, contain underneath the best materials for their own reclaiming. The general constitution of these marls and marly clays is shewn in the following analysis, given in the Bog Reports by Mr. Griffith and by Mr. Edgeworth.

STRATA BENEATH TIMAHOE BOG (GRIFFITH).

	MARL.	BLUE AND YELLOW CLAY.
Carbonate of lime, ...	64	6
Silica, ...	24	22
Alumina, ...	12	72

STRATA UNDER BOGS IN WESTMEATH (EDGEWORTH).

	BLUE LIME-CLAY.	WHITE MARL.	BLUE CLAY.
Carbonate of lime, . .	44·4	87·3	53·0
Carbonate of magnesia,	1·4	,,	,,
Alumina, ...	27·2	1·1	36·0
Silica, ...	27·0	·9	11·0
Bog stuff, ...	,,	10·7	,,
	100·0	100·0	100.0

Elsewhere I shall have occasion to notice the more direct application of these materials.

Some interesting deposits of marl have been laid open by the lowering of Lough Talt, on the Gleneask estate of the Land Improvement Society in Sligo, and they promise to be of considerable service in ameliorating the condition of the soils of that locality. The following analyses of those marls, and of the subsoils of the district, are extracted from a report which I drew up for the Society, and which was appended to a very interesting and valuable account of the condition of that estate, published by Mr. Beamish, one of their directors. These marls yielded on analysis:

	BLUE MARL.	WHITE MARL.
Siliceous sand,	2·35	20·72
Alumina,	0·36	0·74
Oxide of iron,	0·24	0·32
Phosphate of iron,	0·03	0·02
Carbonate of magnesia,	0·43	0·53
Carbonate of lime,	90·98	77·04
Organic matter,	2·42	trace.
Water,	2·52	1·03
	99·33	100·40

The subsoils from under bog, on this estate, gave for the composition of two specimens the following results:

	No. 1.	No. 2.
Siliceous sand,	88·07	87·40
Alumina,	2·83	4·18
Oxide of iron,	1·89	4·02
Carbonate of lime,	0·65	0·32
Carbonate of magnesia,	0·19	0·08
Water,	4·08	2·26
Organic matter,	2·04	1·98
	99·75	100·24

The sand contained intermixed minute particles of mica and grains of felspar, and was evidently formed by the disintegration of the underlying gneiss and mica-slate rocks of Slieve Gauff.

A manure, of which the practical value is undisputed, although difference of opinion exists as to the mode of its action, is gypsum or sulphate of lime. The localities in which this mineral exists in Ireland have been described. Its composition is:

Sulphuric acid, ...	46·5
Lime, ...	32·6
Water, ...	20·9
	100·0

Its peculiar value consists in supplying lime for the rapid growth of clover and other papilionaceous crops, which its moderate solubility in water enables it to effect, better than any other compound of that earth.

TURF AND ASHES AS MANURE.

The ashes of turf arise partly from the inorganic matter belonging to the plants of which the turf was formed, and partly from intermixture of the earthy matter of the subjacent soil. It is hence that the quantity of ashes varies so considerably, as shewn in page 36, and its composition will, of course be different as it is affected by its origin. The ashes of pure turf may be supposed nearly similar to those of other plants, except that as the material must be considerably acted upon by water, the more soluble ingredients will be found, for the most part, absent; thus the quantity of potash present in most ashes of plants is not found in turf ashes. The more compact varieties of turf are frequently intermixed with iron pyrites in considerable quantity, produced by reactions, not as yet thoroughly examined, and which in burning react so upon other ingredients of the plants, as to produce sulphate of soda and sulphate of lime, leaving oxide of iron free, by which the ash becomes coloured red. Hence the general rule, founded on popular experience, that red ashes are more fertilizing than white ashes, the latter being little more than clay mixed with some lime, whilst the former contains generally sulphuric acid and soda.

In a letter to the Commissioners of Irish Bogs, Sir Humphrey Davy states, that he has found a difference between the turf ashes of England and of Ireland to consist in the presence of sulphate of lime in the former, and its absence in the latter. It may be absent in certain localities, but it certainly is present in the majority of cases, as I have satisfied myself by experiment, although hitherto my opportunities have not enabled me to institute absolute analyses of the ashes of the different varieties of Irish turf, in which indeed we are as yet absolutely deficient, for Davy, though making the above remark, did not communicate any numerical results.

The following analyses of turf ashes from various localities, made by Continental chemists, will suffice to indicate their general composition.

	ICHAUX.	VOITSUMRA.	VASSY.	FRA- MONT.	HAGENAU.
Carbonic acid, ⎰ Lime, . . ⎱	63·0	⎰ 2·7 ⎱ 3·7	22·5 ⎱ 39·7	30	6·0
Clay, ...	7·5	,,	11·0		,,
Silica, . .	15·0	36·5	,,	40	65·6
Alumina, . .	7·0	17·3	,, ⎰		16·2
Oxide of iron, .	9·0	33·0	11·5 ⎱	30	3·7
Potash and soda,	·5	,,	,,	,,	2·3
Magnesia, . .	,,	3·5	,,	,,	0·6
Sulphuric acid,	,,	3·0	15·3	,,	5·4
Muriatic acid, .	,,	0·3	,,	,,	0·3
	100·0	100·0	100·0	100·0	100·0

It is hence seen that whilst certain ashes, as that of Framont, could only act as a form of calcined marl, and hence be but moderately useful to vegetation; others contain a great number of elements, as magnesia, potash, soda, sulphuric acid, &c., which may prove in the highest degree beneficial. Differences of this kind are probably the origin of the conflicting evidence as to the results of the application of such substances as manures, by which practical agriculturists are so much puzzled, and we thus see that before employing those materials a correct knowledge of their composition should be obtained.

In none of the ashes above analysed was there phosphoric acid found, and as its presence or absence affects very materially some of the most important actions of manure, Boussingault endeavoured to ascertain whether it was at all present. He never could detect it in turf ashes, yet Sprengel names it as a constant constituent of the turf ashes of Holland and Luneburg, in the proportion of from one to two per cent. I consider Boussingault the higher authority in such a case, which, however, is really one of the most difficult problems of chemical analysis, and, therefore, it is very desirable that special investigations should be directed to that point in the examination of the ashes of Irish turfs.

The phosphoric acid so abundantly deposited in those parts of plants employed as food, is destined to the formation of the osseous skeleton of the animal, and on its death returns to the soil, to be again absorbed into the composition of plants, and become the material of the bones of a new race of animals. Phosphate of lime and other compounds of phosphoric acid are thus most essential elements of plants, and, under the form of bones, ground or otherwise prepared, hence become one of the most usual manures. It is to be feared that before very long considerable loss will accrue to the corn and other food crops of this country, from the deprivation of the soil of this essential ingredient. The cattle exported from Ireland carry out in their bones a vast quantity of phosphoric acid derived from the soil. Of the cattle whose flesh is eaten in the country, the bones form a considerable article of export, as the attention of our agriculturists has not yet been awakened generally to the importance of restoring them to the soil. Let it be recollected, that in 1℔ of bone there is the phosphoric acid belonging to 28℔ of wheat, or of 250℔ of potatoes; that this phosphoric acid is indispensable to the healthy growth of the plants and of the animals by which they are consumed, and hence will appear the vital importance to agriculture of preserving, as far as possible, these valuable materials, and returning them to the soil.

The coast of Ireland furnishes vast quantities of valuable manure in the sand which is dredged from a greater or less depth in the various bays, and in the sea weed which is collected at low water. Of the sea sand there are two kinds, one containing intermixed abundance of small shells, univalve and bivalve, which in many cases contain their living tenants, so that this sand used as manure supplies a very appreciable quantity of animal matter. Its general composition may, therefore, be understood, although as the proportions of its elements continually fluctuate, a single analysis of it could have but little authority. The silicious sand usually amounts to from 30 to 60 per cent.; the shells to from 20 to 50, and, beside carbonate, yield some phosphate of lime and of magnesia; there is generally from 3 to 6 per cent. of animal matter, which yields nitrogen by its decomposition, and, finally, from 5 to 10 per cent. of water, which holds in solution common salt, and the other ingredients of sea water. This manure furnishes actually thus a great variety of substances to the soil, and although its principal action must be analogous to liming, yet the farmers are certainly right in preferring it to ordinary lime.

Another variety of sea sand used as manure is the coral sand, which is found but in certain localities, as Bantry Bay, and some of the inlets of Connemara. It consists of silicious sand, intermixed not merely with ordinary sea shells, but with fragments of a material usually termed coral, but which naturalists now consider to be of vegetable origin. This, however, does not affect its chemical composition, as the organic matter, whether animal or vegetable, is very rich in nitrogen, and exceedingly active as a manure. The usual proportions of sand and coral fragments are each about 40 per cent.; the remainder being organic matter and water. The coral contains some phosphate of lime, and this variety of sand is popularly esteemed as being much preferable to that more commonly found. Boussingault considers the quantity of azotized matter in it, as dredged on the French coast, where also it is much used for manure, such as to render it equal in utility to its own weight of farm-yard manure.

Roundstone Bay is the principal depository of this kind of coral upon the west coast; it there forms banks, and occurs of several species. As it has been separated under the name of

Nullipora from the true corallines, and its place in the scale of
nature a good deal disputed, I thought it important to make
an accurate analysis of the usual form of it (Nullipora poly-
morpha), which might, at the same time, illustrate its scientific position and its agricultural value.

I found it to consist of:

Carbonate of lime, ...	77·31
Carbonate of magnesia, ...	7·54
Phosphate of lime, ...	0·37
Organic matter, ...	10·50
Water, ...	4·28
	100·00

The organic matter was found to contain a very decided
quantity of nitrogen.

That I may give an idea of the extent to which the shell
banks on our coasts are available as sources of these manures, I shall extract briefly some estimates of the quantities
raised at Derry, and on the southern coast of Cork. The former is taken from Captain Portlock's Report on the Survey of
Derry and Tyrone, the latter from a most interesting communication by Mr. Francis Jennings.

" The shell banks of Lough Foyle form, when the tide is out,
extensive flats, which are firm enough to be walked on without
any inconvenience, and they are resorted to by numerous boats
for loads of shells, and though this system has been pursued
for more than a century, they exhibit no appearance of a failure in the supply. The shells hitherto examined are all of
recent species ; and it becomes a question whence they came.
There are engaged is raising the shells

285 men for 26 weeks, at 10s., ...	£3,205
50 boys . . . . at 6s., ...	390
The cost of the labour alone is thus, . . .	£3,595

There are annually employed about ninety-four boats, of
tonnage from below eight to sixty tons. The aggregate tonnage of forty-one of the largest boats is 1306 tons. The total

quantity of shells raised each summer is about 59,496 tons,
which on the shore immediately opposite the bank sell for 1s.
per ton; but at Derry and Strabane for 1s. 6d. to 2s. per ton.
Altogether Captain Portlock considers the shell banks of Lough
Foyle to be worth £5,000 per annum to the country. "They
are particularly useful in bringing bad lands into cultivation,
and in ameliorating stiff wet clays, deficient in calcareous matter, being applied at the rate of from thirty to sixty barrels
per acre. They are preferred to lime, as warming and brittle-
ing the land." In this the silicious sand is probably most useful by giving porosity to the clay.

Mr. Francis Jennings, to whose union of zeal and scientific
knowledge I am indebted for much information regarding the
industrial condition of the south of Ireland, has kindly drawn
up for me the following account of the use of sea sand as a manure, along the coast of Cork. I present it without alteration,
that its value and authenticity may not be lessened.

" The harbours and coasts of the south and west of Ireland
abound in a calcareous sand, which is employed by the agriculturists for manure in very considerable quantities; that
raised in Bantry Bay and the west, is termed coral sand, from
the similarity of its appearance to portions of coral, but is in
reality a semi-vegetable; that kind is, however, unknown in
the harbours of Kinsale, Youghal, and the intermediate districts of the coast, which, from a microscopical examination,
is composed of comminuted shells, pulverized rock, portions of
the shells of the crustacea, and in many cases no inconsiderable
number of minute spiral and bivalve shells, containing the fish,
either dead or alive.

" To the large proportion of phosphate of lime contained in
the crustaceous remains, and the nitrogenized matters of the
fish, much of its importance, doubtless, is due. Its colour
varies from a reddish brown to a blue and brownish black,
dependant not alone on the remains of the shells, but also on
the prevailing rock in the vicinity. The sand raised in the
harbours of Cork, Kinsale, Oyster Haven, and Ringabella, is
dredged from depths varying from about ten to thirty feet;
that taken in Youghal, and the bays and strands intermediate

between it and Kinsale, excepting those already mentioned, is
shovelled from the strand into carts and boats, generally at
low water, and then taken up the country to its various desti-
nations.

"In a few of those places already named, I have been able
to ascertain, with tolerable precision, the average amount
raised per annum, which from Youghal harbour and strand is
about 300,000 tons, 130,000 of which are taken by boats, of
various degree of tonnage, to the different landing places on
the Bride and Blackwater, as far as Cappoquin.

"In Oyster Haven, an inconsiderable creek west of Cork
harbour, there are thirty-two boats, of about twelve tons bur-
den each, employed in dredging sand, some of which make
about 150 boat loads each, in the year.   These principally belong to the farmers, and the men, when paid in money for their
work, earn 1s. 4d. per man for each cargo delivered, and a
boat-load or two at the end of the season, as a perquisite, there
being three men employed in filling and working each boat,
which takes about twenty full dredges to complete its cargo ;
in many cases the men are partly paid by the use of a portion
of land for a sufficient length of time to raise a crop of potatoes.
The sand can only be raised in calm weather, and the labour
is very severe.   The annual amount raised in this creek is
about 57,000 tons, and a boat-load, when sold, brings, according to the weather, from 6s. 6d. to 7s. 6d.   These data, in
connexion with the quantity raised in Cork, Kinsale, and
Ringabella, which is a very small creek off Cork harbour, are
by no means accurate ; the amount in those places taken together is, I am confident, considerably underrated at 1,000,000
tons.   Much of that raised in Cork harbour is, after a water
carriage of ten or twelve miles, taken into the country on one-
horse cars by working farmers, a distance of ten and twelve
miles on hilly roads, which affords strong evidence in favour
of its value as a manure; and it is placed on limestone ground
as well as on the soil resulting from the decomposition of the
old red sandstone and carboniferous slates. It is not, however,
to be supposed that the raising of sand on the coast is confined to those places already mentioned.   Every strand, nook,

and bay to which access can be had, by either a horse with panniers, or a cart, is taxed to supply its quota of sand; and in many places of small extent, I have seen over fifty carts taking it at low water; that which is raised then being considered the best, and only inferior to that which is dredged. When it is, therefore, considered the number of places from which sand is raised, an approximation can only be obtained by inquiries requiring no ordinary degree of care and attention.

" The amount of carbonate of lime contained in the sand varies considerably; some of a dark blue colour, from Oyster Haven, which I tried a few years ago, contained 65 per cent.

" It may be inquired, is the supply inexhaustible? The answer, as far as regards the dredged sand, might probably be given in the affirmative, but in many places the strands, formerly covered to the depth of many feet, at present yield none except after heavy gales, and the inhabitants must either give up its use, or resort to the dredge for a supply. The amount of sand to the acre varies according to its price. In those places where it is about 6d. per ton, 800 cwt., or 40 tons, is by no means an unusual quantity to be applied every season, for many years together.

" In considering its agricultural value, the quantity of salt water it contains must not be omitted, for the calculations are made not as to the amount of dry sand, but the state it is in after some hours' draining; moist to the touch, but not wet. From its daily increasing consumption, and great value when taken far inland, I believe it would form one of the most considerable branches of internal traffic, at least in the south of Ireland, if canals existed which would allow of its being forwarded at moderate charges."

From a note furnished by the Duke of Devonshire's agent to Mr. Jennings, it appears that there are engaged in the procuring of sand at Youghal

363 horses, with carts containing 14 cwt.

18 donkies, with carts containing 7 cwt.,

each drawing twelve loads per week.

35 lighters, of 35 tons average tonnage, which take two loads per week.

And the total quantity of sand raised annually is estimated at 293,503 tons, in the harbour of Youghal alone.

Along the coast, large quantities of seaweed are collected for the purpose of being applied as manure, especially for potatoes. It is found that the deeper the water where it is taken up the more powerfully it acts. This is probably owing to its greater luxuriance, and containing in its tissue a greater mass of sea water, which yields valuable saline materials to the soil. Exact analyses of the seaweeds used in Ireland have not yet been made. Boussingault found those used on the coast of France to be the fucus digitatus and the fucus saccharinus. These contain, when fresh, about 40 per cent. of water, and the dry material contained from 1·58 to 2·29 of nitrogen. He considers it, when fresh, equivalent to about its weight of farm-yard manure. Latterly this material has been transported to considerable distances into the interior, having been first dried by exposure to the sun. Its saline constituents are, of course, those of sea water, muriate and sulphate of soda, and of magnesia, with traces of lime and iodine.

Such are the manures which the existing physical structure of the country places at the disposal of the agriculturist. They are in origin and constitution principally mineral, and are usually poor in one important element necessary to the support of plants, nitrogen. I have already noticed that to certain plants the atmosphere is itself a source of nitrogen, but it is not so to all, not even to the most important; the giving of nitrogen to the soil is, therefore, a most essential office of manures. To effect this a variety of means have latterly been afforded to the farmer, as the nitrates of potash and of soda, the salts of ammonia, the decomposed excrements of sea birds, guano, and numerous other even more complex bodies, all of which serve the purpose, all of which promote the fertility of the soil and favour the growth of plants, when judiciously applied, but none of which possess any real utility over the manure available on the farm, suitable to every crop, and most ready in its action. To this manure it is, therefore, highly important for the economical farmer to direct attention, in order that correct ideas may be formed as to the care which it deserves, and the relation which it bears to the crops, and feeding operations of the farm.

If we consider the final application of farm produce, it will appear that comparatively little of it is absolutely removed from off the ground, and that by much the larger proportion is consumed within the limits of the farm, in the provisioning and stalling of the various animals. The corn which is sold, or the animals which are sent to market, remove from the farm certain quantities of inorganic materials and of nitrogen, which must be replaced, in order to sustain its fertility, and the cost of replacing which must be considered a necessary and fair deduction from their money price; but the straw of the corn crops, the tops of turnips and potatoes, contain a much larger quantity of those materials which need not be removed from off the farm, but, on the contrary, should be most carefully returned to the soil, to serve for the support of future crops of plants. It is similarly with the produce consumed by the animals as food. Each day's food serves but to replace in its organization the materials which are daily thrown off from its frame. The dejections and excretions of the animal must, therefore, represent the food which it consumes, and thus by returning to the soil all such materials, the sustenance of the animal is really deprived of any power of diminishing the fertility of the soil. I do not here consider the case of fattening animals, but only such as are sustained in an uniform condition and health; but the fattening does not affect the principle in any important degree.

Now these various materials, the straw of the corn crops, the tops of the potato and turnip crops, the excretions and dejections of the animals sustained upon the farm, all mixed and subjected to the reaction which soon sets in amongst their chemical ingredients, constitute farm-yard manure It is made up of the remains and products of every kind of crop: it contains, therefore, the elements of every kind of crop. Its state is continually changing, as it is more or less rotted, and hence no two specimens of it would probably agree exactly in constitution, but still, as illustrating in a general point of view the nature of its elements, I shall add the results of analyses made by Boussingault of that which, in a half rotted condition, he puts out on his experimental farm.

The manure, in its usual form, contains in average 79·3 per cent. of water, and 20·7 of perfectly dry material.

The dry material contained:

	RICHEST.	POOREST.	AVERAGE.
Carbon, ...	40·0	32·4	35·8
Hydrogen, ...	4·3	3·8	4·2
Nitrogen, ...	2·4	1·7	2·0
Oxygen, ...	27·6	25·8	25·8
Salts and earth, . . .	25·7	36·3	32·2
	100·0	100·0	100·0

The ashes of this manure contain in 100 parts:

Carbonic acid, ... 2·0

Phosphoric acid, ... 3·0

Sulphuric acid, ... 1·9

Chlorine, ... 0·6

Silica, sand, and clay, ... 66·4

Lime, ... 8·6

Magnesia, ... 3·6

Oxide of iron, and alumina, ... 6·1

Potash and soda, ... 7·8

On comparing this with the analyses of the ashes of various plants, given in page 276, it will be at once evident, that every constituent which they require is present in the farm-yard manure. It is, therefore, of the most vital importance to those whose livelihood depends upon the produce of their farms to economize as completely as possible this valuable material. A dung heap formed on the ordinary ground of the farm-yard, allows of the escape of the most valuable portions of the manure by drainage through the porous soil   By ex-

posure to the weather during wet seasons the most active of
its elements may be washed away.   These disadvantages may
be removed at very trifling cost by the adoption of such modes
of collecting and preserving the manure as are employed in
other countries.   The dung heap should be formed upon an
impervious floor of brick-clay or of cement, this to dip towards
the centre, so as to form a shallow tank, towards which the
floors of the various stables should have such inclination as
would enable the drainings to be conveyed by suitable channels to the central tank.   By such an arrangement nothing
goes to waste; the liability to loss by rain is obviated, and
even the smallest farmer will very soon find the cost and trouble well repaid by the improvement, as well in the quantity as
in the quality, of his stock of manure.

I am not disposed to underrate the importance of the various
artificial and foreign manures, the effects of which on the fertility of the soil have been in many cases wonderful, often by
their activity producing results to which the farm-yard manure would be incompetent, and by their portability presenting,
in many localities, a real advantage.   Nevertheless, in the existing state of education in this country, it is, as I conceive,
far more useful to point out to the struggling farmer how to
take advantage of the materials which now run to waste about
his stables, than to send to him to lay out ready money, of
which he generally has so little, for a fertilizer, of whose special properties and nature he is probably quite ignorant, and
which has seldom any great advantage over well prepared
farm-yard manure.

CHAPTER VIII.

AGRICULTURAL INDUSTRY CONTINUED OF ROTATIONS. RE-
LATION OF CORN CROPS AND GREEN CROPS. AMOUNT OF
FOOD PRODUCED BY VARIOUS SYSTEMS OF CULTURE. INFLU-
ENCE OF DIFFERENT CULTURES IN THE EXHAUSTION OR
AMELIORATION OF THE SOIL. SIZE OF FARMS IN IRELAND.
PRINCIPLE OF CONSOLIDATION, NOT AS APPLICABLE TO AGRI-
CULTURE AS TO MANUFACTURES. RELATION OF THE SIZE OF
FARMS TO THE POPULATION. RELATIVE PROFIT AND EM-
PLOYMENT AFFORDED BY LARGE AND SMALL FARMS. AVE-
RAGE AVAILABLE FARMS FOR EXISTING POPULATION.

SECONDARY USES OF FOOD CROPS. MANUFACTURE OF POTATO
STARCH, SUGAR, AND SPIRITS. COMPOSITION OF DIFFERENT
KINDS OF POTATOES. MANUFACTURE OF BEET ROOT SUGAR;
ITS ECONOMIC CIRCUMSTANCES. OF FIBRE CROPS. CULTI-
VATION OF FLAX AND HEMP. COMPOSITION OF LIGNEOUS
FIBRE. MODE OF CULTURE AND PREPARATION OF FLAX.
PRINCIPLES WHICH IT GIVES OFF IN STEEPING. AVERAGE
CROP OF FLAX; ITS VALUE. USES OF THE FLAX PRODUCTS AS
FOOD AND AS MANURE.

FLAX MANUFACTURE AND LINEN TRADE. TOTAL VALUE OF
FLAX GROWN IN IRELAND. EXERTIONS OF THE ROYAL DUB-
LIN SOCIETY AND FLAX IMPROVEMENT SOCIETY, AND THEIR
RESULTS. EMPLOYMENT GIVEN BY THE FLAX AND LINEN
TRADE. TABLES OF MILL POWER AND OF EXPORTATION OF
FLAX AND LINEN. LOCALIZATION OF THIS INDUSTRY. FA-
VOURABLE SITUATIONS FOR IT. CULTURE AND COMPOSITION
OF HEMP. CONCLUSION.

I HAVE so far considered the exhaustion of the soil by plants,
with a view to the restoration of the deficient ingredients
through the agency of manures.   There is, however, another
mode of restoring fertility which is of practical importance,
as it has led to the greatest of all improvements in husbandry,
the *rotation of crops*. A soil which has been exhausted becomes restored by lying at rest for a certain time, particularly
if it be well broken up and fresh surfaces be exposed to the
action of the atmosphere, in fact then by the decomposition of
the mineral masses which the soil contains, a fresh soil is produced.   The organic remains of the former crops become also
rotted, and assume a form suited for the nutrition of young

plants, and thus after a season's fallowing, still more after
lying out of cultivation for some years, the soil resumes a very
considerable degree of fertility. But it is evident that this
process entails considerable loss by the land being so long idle,
and it becomes of great importance to the farmer to make
some use of the land, whilst this process of regeneration is
going on. This is actually done by changing from one kind of
culture to another; whilst the land is recovering from the effects of one plant it is capable of sustaining a plant which does
not act upon it in the same way, and after this a third, differently exhausting from either of the others, will give a *course*
or rotation of three years, during any two of which the ground
is recovering from the exhausting action of the plant grown
during the third. I take this only as an example, for it is
found that three years is too short a term to be of much practical utility.

In selecting the plants adapted for such a rotation, we must
be guided by their chemical composition, and by their mode of
growth. The results of both, however, lead to the same conclusion. In addition to those elements which are common to
all plants used as food, certain plants are remarkable for the
great quantity of silica they take from the soil, such are the
grasses and corn plants; certain others for the potash they
take up, such are turnips, the beet, the potato; others again
for the quantity of lime, as the pea, vetch, clover, tobacco, &c.
Such are the kinds of plants that should succeed each other in
a rotation, and the proportionate action of each class may be
judged from the following table derived from Liebig's investigations. From a space of land of 2·47 acres, he found there
were taken up by

	ALKALINE SALTS.	SALTS OF LIME AND MAGNESIA.	SILICA.
A crop of wheat, .	120¼lb	78¼lb	260lb
A crop of peas, . .	198¼	371½	46
A crop of beet with-out the leaves, .	361	37¾	,,

The quantity of phosphates taken up by these crops are

PEAS.	WHEAT.	BEET.
117℔.	112℔.	37¾℔.

The reason of the beet taking so little phosphoric acid is, that it is not allowed to form its seed, and in all plants it is in the seed that the phosphates are principally deposited.

From these numbers it is evident, that on such a field, if by the gradual decomposition of its soil it could furnish but 200℔ of alkaline salts, and 200℔ of lime and magnesia salts each year, we could grow upon it but half the proper crop of beet, for a full crop would require 360℔ of alkaline salts, and also only a half crop of peas, for the full crops would require 371℔ of lime and magnesia salts. The continuous culture of either plant would, therefore, be most unprofitable and injurious, but if we cultivated beet one year and peas the other, the soil would have two years to prepare the materials which each crop would require to take up in one. There would be available 400℔ of each kind of salts, and thus so far from exhaustion, there should be a surplus steadily increasing the fertility and augmenting the produce of the soil.

As it is seen in the above table that the quantity of alkaline and earthy salts taken up by the corn crop (wheat) is so much less than that required for the other kinds of plants, and that the principal demand of the corn crop on the soil is for silica, of which we may consider it certain that no soil is in danger of being exhausted, it might appear natural to conclude that the corn crop should be that least detrimental to the ground, whilst it is well known to practical agriculturists, that white or corn crops are amongst the most exhausting. Their injurious action on the soil is, however, not so much due to the inorganic materials they take up as to the nitrogen, for which element they are altogether dependent on the soil, whilst other kinds of plants act upon the atmosphere, aborbing nitrogen, and actually serving rather to enrich the soil upon which they grow, than in any degree to impoverish it. This in in fact what constitutes the remarkable relation between the *white crops* and *green crops* as members of a rotation. The former exhausting the soil of nitrogen, the other fixing in the soil nitrogen derived from the air, and thus preparing for the nutrition of the corn crops that may succeed it.

The complete illustration of this principle is due to Boussingault, who has established it as well by experiments on individual plants in the laboratory as by the operations of an extensive farm. Thus on growing corn in artificial soil deprived of nitrogen, it was found that the plant, when arrived at its full maturity, contained only the nitrogen that had originally existed in the seed. On the other hand, on growing peas in the same way, the quantity of nitrogen in the mature plant was found to be much greater than had been in the seed, and for this there was no other source than the atmosphere. The following tables will shew how fully this result is borne out on the large scale.

In a three years' cultivation of two successive crops of wheat manured and then a year of fallow, the produce was 3318 kilogrammes of wheat, and 7500 kilos straw per hectare, from 20,000 kilos of manure. Now taking these dry, the following table shews their composition and the relation of their constituents.

	WEIGHT DRY.	CARBON.	HYDRO-GEN.	OXYGEN.	NITRO-GEN.	ASHES.
Wheat,	2836	1037·4	164·5	1230·8	65·2	68·1
Straw,	5550	2686·2	294·2	2159·0	22·2	388·5
Sum,	8386	3993·6	458·7	3389·8	87·4	456·6
Manure,	4140	1482·1	173·9	1068·1	82·8	1333·1
Difference, }	+4246	+2511·5	+284·8	+2321·7	+4·6	—876·5

It is here quite evident that the crop contained only the nitrogen of the manure, as the difference 4·6 is so slight as to be within the unavoidable errors of experiment in such cases. On the other hand the carbon of the crop is nearly treble that of the manure, verifying, in an admirable manner, the atmospheric origin of the carbon of plants, to which I have already alluded. Hydrogen and oxygen were also gained abundantly, and almost exactly in the proportions to form water.

In contra-distinction to this corn culture may be placed the results of the continued growth of lucern for five years, followed by a crop of wheat, all at the expense of 44,000 kilos of farm-yard manure per hectare, put out on the land at the commencement of the period. These results were published by M. Crud, an eminent agriculturist.

CULTURES.	PRODUCE PER HECTARE.	CONTENTS IN NITROGEN.
Lucern dry, 1st year,	3,360 kilos.	79 kilos.
,, 2nd ,,	10,080 ,,	237 ,,
,, 3rd ,,	12,500 ,,	294 ,,
,, 4th ,,	10,080 ,,	237 ,,
,, 5th ,,	8,000 ,,	188 ,,
Wheat, . 6th ,,	1,580 ,,	31 ,,
Straw, ...	3,976 ,,	12 ,,
Total nitrogen, ...		1078
Manure employed contained of nitrogen,		224 kilos.
Gain in nitrogen, ...		854

Or for the five years of lucern, 171 kilos per year, as the wheat of the last year did not take any from the atmosphere.

Now as the residues of these green crops which remain in the soil, contain a corresponding quantity of nitrogen, they are the means of transferring to it such portions of that element as serve, if not fully to sustain its fertility, at least prevent the exhausting action of the white crops from being so soon or so severely felt. This is still more fully carried into effect when these crops, or the last growth of them, in place of being consumed, are ploughed into the soil, where they act as the best form of manure, their fresh and juicy structure facilitating their decomposition, and their composition being such as to provide almost every element subsequently required.

The substitution of these plants as sources of food for the animals of the farm, for the common, or as they are called, the natural grasses, has been one of the most important improvements in husbandry. The following table, which is collected from the best authorities, exhibits the quantity of actual nutritious material which is usually derived from an acre of land.

CROP.	WEIGHT.	STARCH AND SUGAR.	GLUTEN.	OIL.	TOTAL.
Wheat,	1500℔	825℔	185	45	1055
Oats,	1700	850	230	95	1175
Peas,	1600	800	380	45	1225
Potatoes,	9 tons.	3427	604	45	4076
Turnips,	20 ,,	4500	540	,,	5040
Carrots,	25 ,,	5600	1120	200	6920
Meadow hay	1½	1360	240	120	1720
Clover hay,	2 ,,	1800	420	180	2400

It is here seen, that turnips and carrots yield from five to seven times the actual quantity of food that the corn crops give, also that potatoes and clover yield twice as much, and as it should be always the object of the farmer to do as much as possible in a given time, on a given space of ground, he should fix his attention on those systems of culture which thus produce the greatest quantity of food, and by the least exhaustion of the soil.

Practical experience bears out fully the principles I have here endeavoured to explain. The Board of Agriculture in England directed special inquiries as to this point, and the result led to the general conclusion, that one year of tares, rape, potatoes, turnips, or cabbage, gives thrice as much food as one year of medium pasture grass. In his very useful Lectures on Agricultural Chemistry, Professor Johnstone adopts the same general proposition, but he couples it with some money estimates which I consider it important to notice. He says:

" With the exception of rich pastures, it is said that land under clover or turnips will produce three times as much food for cattle as when under grass. If such a green crop then alternates with one of corn, the land should every two years produce as much food for stock as if it had been three years lying in grass, besides the crop of corn as food for man, and of straw for the production of manure." Professor Johnstone then proceeds to discuss the money value of the produce of similar pieces of ground under such crops, and concludes, that " although more food is raised by converting the land to arable purposes, and more people may be sustained by it, yet more money would be made by meadowing the land, where a ready market exists for the hay, where it is allowed to be sold off the farm, and where abundance of manure can be obtained for the purpose of topdressing the land every year." In order to arrive at this result he takes the prices of produce as follows:

Hay, £5 per ton.   Turnips, 10s. per ton.
Barley, 4s. per bushel.   Wheat, 7s. per bushel.

Such a price for the hay could certainly be obtained only in exceptional cases: the other circumstances he mentions could only be realized in some few localities, and there is no doubt, but that, as a general principle in agriculture, the cultivation of green crops and artificial grasses is not only that by which the largest quantity of food is raised, but also that by which the greatest money return is afforded to the farmer.

The natural moisture of the climate of Ireland, coupled with the general fertility of the soil, and especially that of the central district, where the subsoil is limestone gravel, produces a tendency to rapid growth of a sweet and luxuriant grass, in consequence of which the lands of these localities are almost exclusively devoted to grazing. It is certain that on the western coast the humidity of the atmosphere is such, as on an average of years may present a serious obstacle to the ripening of corn crops and the safe completion of the harvest, but it is

also certain that the tendency to adopt grazing in preference
to tillage-agriculture, as a pursuit, is much more connected
with the habits of the agricultural classes than with the nature
of the soil, or the character of the climate. Mere industry
has been in Ireland, for many generations, connected with the
idea of a vulgar and depressed caste. The possession of the
land with perfect idleness constituted in itself the criterion
of respectability. The working of a tillage farm, even if
more profitable, was thus fatal to the social position of the
occupier; whilst if he kept only a herd to mind some cattle,
and spent his time and money in hunting and in drinking,
trusting to protection for high prices, and to Providence to pay
his debts, he mixed with the notables of the land and looked
down with scorn ineffable on all that savoured of occupations
vile, of industry or intelligence.

Those ideas have been already very considerably disturbed.
Prior to the introduction of turnip husbandry, and to the cultivation of the artificial grasses, it might be a question between
the relative profits of grazing and of a very imperfect tillage,
which gradually reduced the land to a condition of almost perfect barrenness; especially where the advantage of capital was
altogether in favour of the former : but grazing is in reality but
the production of food as well as tillage. An animal makes
no food, it only assimilates that which is produced by the plants
on which it feeds. A crop which produces three times as much
food will, therefore, feed three times as many cattle, and it is
hence unavoidable that as agriculture progresses the ordinary
grass crops will be replaced by the more nutritious carrots,
turnips, clover, &c. ; the animals, in place of roving over extensive grounds which recal the idea of the prairie existence of a
half civilized hunting population, shall be suitably confined, that
their food may not be wasted in muscular efforts inconsistent
with their ultimate perfection as food for man. The rearing of
cattle will thus, in itself, become a branch, as it is really one
most important, of tillage husbandry, and the manure thus rendered available will serve most efficiently to the production of
corn and other exhausting crops. It is in such form that agri-

culture should finally be carried on in Ireland, and as it actually is in other countries, where industrial intelligence has been more active. There are, however, many difficulties to overcome and prejudices to remove before that point can be arrived at, but in the mean time, every even trivial effort will lessen the obtacles on the way.

The greater amount of food produced by the system of turnip and potato husbandry, is noticed by M. De Jonnes, in relation to its influence on the social circumstances of the people of this 'country, in words which are worthy of quotation.

" On seeing what immense riches are obtained in England by the cultivation of the various species of green food, as supplementary to corn crops, and which are obtained, like them, by plough husbandry on a great scale, we are astonished at how recently this agricultural improvement, which has nearly doubled the means of subsistence, has been carried into effect. It was only in the middle of the seventeenth century, that turnips have been cultivated in England, and that the use of clover had been introduced. Scotland, more backward in every respect, obtained the potato culture only in 1739, and these precious vegetables were first cultivated in the Highlands in 1743. But it is particularly in Ireland, where the soil is fresh and fertile, that these new kinds of crops have prospered. In that island the potato gives an annual produce of 42,000 to 52,000℔, per hectare. (2·47 acres S.) On dividing that number by four to reduce it to the standard of nourishment which wheat affords, the hectare thus cultivated affords 10 to 13,000℔ weight of subsistence. Newenham even considers three pounds of potatoes as equivalent to one pound of wheat, and if so the 10,000℔ of nutriment given by the hectare, as a minimum, when it is cultivated with potatoes, represent 45 hectolitres of wheat and the 13,000℔, are equal to 58. This is the double and treble of the best crops of wheat. This vast productiveness has multiplied potatoes in Ireland, so that they form the basis of the subsistence of the entire country. That is an evil, for a social condition where each family, or nearly each individual, has his

field, which furnishes his immediate nutriment, without any necessity for marketing, without the assistance of the miller or
the baker, without occasion to demand assistance from his
neighbours, that society is deficient in the elements most necessary to the progress of its civilization, From the great produce of its corn crops it would be easy to establish a mixed
system of nutriment in Ireland."

There are few questions regarding agriculture which have
been more keenly discussed, and there is certainly none more
vitally important to this country, than the circumstances, as regards the magnitude of farms, and the mode of applying labour,
under which the greatest amount of produce can be obtained
from the land and the greatest quantity of employment given
to the people.   It is well known that in Ireland the subdivision
of farms has been carried on to an extent which has been productive of most serious evils, moral and industrial.   It is not
within the objects of this work to discuss either the causes or
the effects of the existing state of things, but first exhibiting
the mere statistical facts of the number and size of farms, and
some connected circumstances that will hereafter require comment, I shall proceed to consider the general principle of how
the greatest quantity of produce can be obtained from the
soil.

By the returns of the census of 1841, the number of farms in
Ireland, and their magnitude, was

PROVINCES.	FARMS FROM 1 TO 3 ACRES.	FARMS. FROM 5 TO 15 ACRES.	FARMS FROM 15 TO 30 ACRES.	ABOVE 30 ACRES.	TOTAL.
Leinster,	49,152	45,595	20,584	17,889	133,220
Munster,	57,028	61,320	27,481	16,557	162,386
Ulster,	100,817	98,992	25,099	9,591	234,499
Connaught	99,918	45,221	5,790	4,275	155,204
Total,	306,915	251,128	78,954	48,312	685,309

The following table exhibits the number and the average
size of farms, compared with the total area and area of arable
land of each province.

PROVINCE.	NUMBER OF FARMS.	TOTAL AREA IN ACRES.	AREA OF ARA-BLE LAND.	AVERAGE SIZE OF FARMS.
Leinster,	133,220	4,860,642	3,961,188	29·7 acres.
Munster,	162,386	6,049,886	3,874,613	23·8 ,,
Ulster,	234,499	5,466,648	3,407,539	14·5 ,,
Connaught	155,204	4,388,166	2,220,960	14·3 ,,

It is thus seen that in every province the great majority of the farms are under fifteen acres, and the average magnitude of the farms in the north and west, appears to be but one-half that of the southern and eastern provinces. This geographical association is very much at variance with other social circumstances, and it will form just now an interesting object of inquiry.

The wonderful revolution effected in the mechanical arts by the invention of spinning and weaving machinery, and the application of steam power, by means of which these operations were concentrated within the walls of factories, and carried out on an immense scale by the application of enormous capital, had fixed the attention of agriculturists, especially in Scotland, where the very generally sound education of the people had rendered them active in the utilization of new ideas. It hence became the leading principle with agriculturists, that in the cultivation of the land the same methods were to be followed as had been so successful in the cotton manufacture; that small and individual holdings should be concentrated into one vast agricultural establishment; that human labour should be dispensed with as much as possible, and replaced by mechanical power: and the activity of head and hand which accompanied the introduction of this system had certainly the effect of so efficiently improving the modes of cultivation, and increasing the amount of produce, as to have gained almost universal approbation for the principles upon which the proceedings of its advocates were based.

Yet it is not difficult to trace between the conditions of manufacturing and agricultural industry, differences so essential and so great as to render very doubtful whether any methods can be really common and successful with both   The raw material of a manufacture is subjected to a series of processes which are carried on under the same roof, or at least within a small space, and which occupy but little time. Every thing in the mechanism is constructed for rapidity of work, its superiority to human labour consisting not in greater excellence, but in greater velocity of action. The materials are brought to the seat of power, which is fixed, and all its parts being made solid, are little liable to injury, and the cost of the exertion of power is reduced to a minimum. If we compare with this the condition of a farm, we shall find almost entire discrepancy. The operations are not confined to a house, but are spread over, perhaps, several hundred acres. The processes require for their completion many months, from seed time unto harvest, and do not admit of any important interference. The power necessary must be exerted at different times, in different places, and, therefore, cannot be fixed; it must be locomotive, and as such, the power of animals is cheaper, under the circumstances, than the power of steam. Thus the fundamental conditions of a farm are quite different from those of a factory, and the question of the relative advantages of small or of large farms must be considered on other grounds.

This comparison is, however, independent of certain subsidiary operations of agriculture, which are really mechanical in their nature, and which are more economically accomplished by machinery, such as threshing and winnowing, certain modes of preparing food, &c.; these are, however, no more agricultural than the grinding of corn to meal and flour. They need not be accomplished on the farm. If we suppose a farm of 1000 acres, which requires the aid of threshing machines and other instruments for the preparation of its produce, it is evidently the same as if there were a 100 farms of 10 acres, from which the produce was sent to a central point, where a mill and machinery were erected, for the use of which they paid as much as should reasonably remunerate the proprietor. The question, as to whether the large farm or the many small farms should give the greatest amount of benefit in produce and employment, is evidently not thereby affected.

The question is, in fact, one almost incapable of perfect solution, from the very different aspects which it presents in different localities, and under different conditions of proprietorship. But I certainly consider that if there be a final advantage in favour of farming on a great scale, and by all mechanical advantages, it cannot be of any considerable amount. If the question be put to a farmer of Scotland, or of the north of England, he will answer, decidedly and at once; invest great capital, throw aside manual labour, and introduce machinery; cultivate several hundred acres: but has this method led to great results in the hands of these very men? In the mechanical arts we know that the corresponding system has organized a new social power, that colossal fortunes have been on every side created, that large cities have sprung into existence, and employment has been given to the majority of the inhabitants of Great Britain. The wholesale system of agriculture has nothing whatever of such results to shew; on the contrary, every day new demands are made for amelioration in its condition. The assistance of science is on the one hand invoked, the protection of the legislature is on the other hand demanded; the agricultural labourer is thrown for existence on the workhouse, or for employment on the manufacturing town, where, even under existing circumstances, he obtains a rate of wages which the agricultural capitalist cannot afford to pay.

Although the general question is thus so difficult to decide, yet if we proceed to the application of it to the actual state of Ireland, it becomes essentially simplified. Large farm cultivation is possible only in countries possessing a thin and scattered population, or else in countries where the existence of extensive manufacturing employment removes the inhabitants of the agricultural districts to other places. Thus certain Scotch counties had actually a smaller population in 1841 than in 1831, owing to the migration of the labourers to the manufacturing districts. In such counties the tendency must be to increase the size of farms, and to introduce, as far as possible, mechanical substitutes for human labour. Also in the north of England, where there is a constant drain of population from the country districts to Newcastle, to Leeds, to Manchester, and Liverpool, it is evident that the tendency being to take the agricultural labourers from their farming occupations, the farmer must endeavour, as best he can, to make himself independent of them. In Ireland, however, the circumstances are widely different; a large population is totally dependant on the land for its subsistence. As shewn in page 250, two-thirds of the inhabitants are exclusively devoted to agriculture, and if the agricultural operations of the country, that is to say, the production of food from the soil, and its exportation to feed the inhabitants of another country, be carried on with a system of cultivation which does not afford employment, the great majority of the people of Ireland must either die of starvation, or be supported in idleness, by a money tax on the earnings of the industrious classes, or finally, be removed from the country, at an expense which, if judiciously applied at home, would enable them to support themselves and families in positive comfort and independence.

Voluntary emigration carries off in fact just the class of persons whom it is most important to keep at home; persons of both foresight and enterprize, and possessed of some small capital. The expatriation of the very poorest classes, whether at the public expense or at the cost of individuals desirous of removing them, has been found, from the expense, impossible, in any degree sufficient to affect the rate of increase of the population. The other alternatives are not likely to meet with approval, either upon moral or on prudential grounds, and hence as the great fact, the existence of the people, still remains, the question of what can be done with them must one time or another be fairly met. The only answer is, enable them to support themselves. Give them employment, and as, especially in this country, any manufacturing system, to be healthy, must be slow in growth, the employment must be agricultural, and I am convinced that such employment may be given, without any injury to the interests of the land-owner or farmer, nay with a positive amelioration of their condition, provided the proper means be taken to ascertain the true conditions of the problem.

Destitute of personal agricultural experience as I have no hesitation to own myself, and consequently feeling competent

to interpose my own opinion only in such physical and chemical
portions of these subjects as stand in immediate connexion
with my special professional pursuits, I should not have entered
upon this subject, but that I have found the evidence of the
most eminent and intelligent persons connected with Irish
agriculture to agree completely with the views I have expressed. Thus, as to the comparative profit of small and large
farms, Mr. Blacker, by whose exertions so much benefit has
accrued to Armagh, in his Essay on the Management of
landed Property in Ireland, which was honoured with a gold
medal by the Royal Dublin Society, says: "Supposing, then,
an extensive estate to have recently fallen out of lease (under
which circumstances alone such a consolidation as I have recommended would be at all practicable), and that such a division had been actually made, by which it may very generally
happen that two-thirds of the farms will be found not to exceed five to eight acres, it may be asked, how can these tenants
live upon such small portions, and still more, how can they
pay rent? I answer without hesitation, they can live comfortably, and pay as high a rent as any large farmer whatever,
if the plan is pursued with them which I have recommended,
and have characterized as one in which was involved the happiness and comfort of thousands." And again, he remarks in
a note: "I am firmly persuaded, that the small farmer who
holds his own plough or digs his own ground, *if he follows a
proper rotation of crops and feeds his cattle in the house*, can
undersell the large farmer, or in other words, can pay a rent
which the other cannot afford; and in this I am confirmed by
the opinion of many practical men who have well considered
the subject, and I think it will not appear extraordinary, that
such should be the case, to any one who reflects that the
English farmer of 700 to 800 acres, is a kind of man approach-
ing to what is known by the name of a gentleman farmer in
this country. He must have his horse to ride, and his gig,
and perhaps an overseer to attend to his labourers; he certainly cannot superintend himself the labour going on in a farm
of 800 acres. Add to this, he must appear himself, and have
his family also to appear in a superior rank, and his farm must

not only enable him to pay his rent, and yield him the support
he requires, but it must also be chargeable with the interest of
the large capital which is necessary to its cultivation; besides all
these drawbacks, which the small farmer knows little about,
there is the great expense of carting out the manure from the
homestead to such a great distance, and again carting home
the crop. A single horse will consume the produce of more
land than would feed a small farmer and his wife, and two
children; and what is more than all, the large farmer says
to his labourers *go* to your work, but when the small farmer
has occasion to hire them, he says *come;* the intelligent reader
will, I dare say, understand the difference perfectly. Now if
it is really the case that the *small* farmer has the advantage
over the *larger*, it will be easy accounting for what Mr. Paulet
Scroupe observes in his letter to the agriculturists of the west
of England, of the Irish farmers being able to undersell the
English in their own markets, because the Irish farmers are,
generally speaking, *small* farmers, and the English are *large*
farmers."

I am indebted for some numerical statements regarding this
question to a gentleman, upon whose judgment I would place
the fullest reliance, from his being at once practically acquainted with the system of large farms of North Britain, and
minutely conversant with the relations of science to agriculture,
Mr. Butler of Ballyconra. In answer to some queries which I
sent to him upon this head, he says:

" In the first place, what number of persons might be taken
as deriving steady employment from the labour of such farms
through the year, and in each case, besides men, what employment may be afforded to women and children? In reply, I shall
take two farms, one of 200 acres, the other 20 acres, in preference to 100 and 10.

" FARM OF 200 ACRES.

16 men constantly.
1 boy   ,,
12 women about one-half the year.
20 men, 3 weeks in Spring.

40 men, 3 weeks in Harvest.

20 women   ,,   ,,

20 men   ,,   potato digging.

20 women ,,   ,,   ,,

Reduced to cash value, ...	£300	0	
7 horses constantly, ...	185	0	0
Occasional horses, ...	15	0	0
	£500	0	0

" FARM OF 20 ACRES.

In constant employment one average family, say a man and wife and six children, varying from 1 to 16 years, and one servant maid. This, I think, should not be estimated at less than . . .	£50	0	0
Extra labourers, chiefly men, at intervals, to the amount of about . . .	10	0	0
Horse work, ...	17	0	0
	£77	0	0

" Second. Supposing in each case rent regularly paid, and that in the larger farm the produce be charged with all interest of capital invested, and wear of machinery and horses, and that the sum allocated to the support of the farmer's family, be such as should be derived from any other kind of industry by a man of the same capital and intelligence, should there be any difference in the amount of rent per acre which the large and small farm could pay, and what would you consider that difference to be, and on what side?

" According to a comparative calculation I have made, it appears to me, that a farm of 20 acres would bear as high a rent as a farm of 200 acres, and such has been my experience as an agent in this country; at the same time it is stoutly asserted in some of the best cultivated districts in England and Scotland, the larger the farm the higher the rent it is able to bear, and they have experience on their side. But I do not think that the small farm system ever got a fair trial there. I dare say that where the landlord builds and keeps up the tenants' houses it might be cheaper to him to build and keep up one house and steading suitable to a 200 acre farm, than to build and keep up ten cottages, &c., on ten farms of 20 acres each, and it would certainly save him trouble. So perhaps in proportion to the outlay, he might get a higher rent for 200 acres, than he would get from 20 acres.

"THOMAS BUTLER."

Without proceeding to further quotation on a subject which has already far exceeded the limits originally designed, I shall only remark, that the fact of small farms being able to pay at least as high a rent as large farms appears well-established, and the greater amount of employment that is given is beyond any question. This latter circumstance it will be useful to consider a little further, in connexion with the population and the quantity of cultivatable land in Ireland.

In his valuable work on agriculture, Professor Low gives some estimates, from which it results that he considers a 500 acre farm to give an amount of occupation equivalent to the employment of twenty persons throughout the entire year. Now it has been already shewn that the area of land available for cultivation is about 18,000,000 of acres, made up of :

> Land actually cultivated, ... 13,464,300
> Land capable of cultivation, ... 4,600,000

Now if this be divided into 36,000 farms, of 500 acres, there will be given by their cultivation employment for 720,000 individuals, but as the actual agricultural population amounts to 5,406,743, the difference, or four millions and a half of human beings will be thrown on the world without any means of subsistence. They may be considered as forming 850,000 families, and as it is found that the emigration of a family costs at least £50, the removal of these multitudes, whether paid for by themselves or by the State, should cost the enormous sum of forty-two millions and a half of money.

On the other hand, as the total number of existing agricultural families is 974,188, it results that from the available land there could be allocated to each a farm of seventeen statute acres. That this quantity is sufficient to support a family, paying full rent, is a matter of which there is no doubt, and it is thus evident that the finding means of employment for the population is not so difficult, nor requiring such hidden resources as is often thought. It does require, however, one condition, at present unfortunately scarcely obtainable, and on which attention is not yet sufficiently fixed, an amount of general industrial and agricultural education, that may enable the landlord to set an example to his tenantry in the disposition to improve the agriculture of his district, and may enable the tenantry to follow that example, and to apply his precepts each to his individual case. The landlord should be, in fact, not merely the proprietor of his peasantry : he should be their preceptor and their friend.

That the greater or less magnitude of farms is not in any way necessarily connected with the condition of agriculture, or with any other elements of social comfort of the population, becomes fully evident on reference to the table of the sizes of farms given in page 305. It is there seen that in Connaught the average size of farms is almost exactly the same as in Ulster, and yet these two provinces are the extremes of ignorance and of intelligence, of activity and of industrial indolence, which this island presents. The difference has certainly nothing to do with the smallness of the farms, and that such farms are sufficient, when properly managed, for the support of even more than the average number of individuals in a family, is shewn by Mr. Blacker, in a passage which disposes so perfectly of the redundant population question, that I shall not again allude to it. In his valuable Essay, Mr. Blacker says :

"I cannot conclude without endeavouring to answer one objection, which may be made to the opinions I have supported in the foregoing ; I allude to my objecting to the expulsion of small holders for the purpose of consolidating farms, in regard to which it may be asked, if this is not done, the population is increasing so rapidly, that as families grow up, subdivision must go on, until at length the whole community will become *paupers ?* I might fairly ask in return, how the plan of turning out these families will prevent *pauperism ?* It seems to me that the latter plan is by much the surest way to produce such a result. But the most satisfactory answer to the question will perhaps be arrived at, by endeavouring to ascertain how far the apprehensions of a superabundant population, at present so generally entertained, may or may not be justified by facts ; for if it should appear there was land enough in the kingdom for all its inhabitants, now existing, and for as many more as could be anticipated in any reasonable time, and that nothing more was wanting but proper regulations to make it available for their wants, then the objection may be fairly considered to be set aside. In a late publication entitled ' Ireland as it was, is, and ought to be, a table is given of the acreable contents and population of each county in Ireland, which may be supposed, at least, so far *relatively* accurate, as to afford data for the following calculations. From this table t appears that the county of Armagh contains 212,755 acres, and a population of 220,653 souls, and that the entire kingdom contains 17,190,726 acres, and 7,839,469 souls; now, in the county of Armagh, by a recent survey, more than one-seventh of the surface is taken up by lakes and unprofitable land, and the remainder is, for the greater part, but indifferently cultivated, and yet the peasantry are better clothed, lodged, and fed than they are in most other counties in Ireland. I cannot, therefore be accused of taking away from the comforts of the rest of the kingdom, by taking the county of Armagh as a standard, and its proportion of unprofitable surface is not very remote, I believe, from the average of the others ; if, then, 212,755, the number of acres in Armagh, give a population of 220,653 souls, 17,190,726 acres, the entire contents of the kingdom, ought to give a population of 17,828,888, in place of 7,839,469, the population at present. It, therefore, appears, that supposing the other parts of Ireland to be as well cultivated as Armagh, it would support about two and a half times the number of its present inhabitants, and be able to export provisions largely besides; for Armagh, notwithstanding its population, exports pork, butter, and grain in great quantities. But before deciding finally upon the population which the kingdom could support, it ought to be examined how far the county of Armagh (the standard taken) has arrived at its full complement; and in regard to this I would say, from a pretty general knowledge of it, that under an improved system of agriculture, and a regular rotation of crops, the produce would be *treble* of what it yields at present, and I think this may be considered as practically proved, if I can shew farmers possessing land of average quality, who being induced to change their manner of cultivation in the way already described, are now receiving fully treble produce from the identical same farm to what it formerly yielded; but supposing it only to yield *double* as much, it would follow, that the population of Armagh, if that beneficial change became general, might be *doubled* also, without in any degree lessening the comforts of the inhabitants; which increase being taken as the basis of the calculation, and applying it to the whole of Ireland, would make it adequate to the support of better than thirty-five millions of souls. When, therefore, it is considered what unexhausted, I might say unexplored, resources remain for the maintenance of any increase of inhabitants that can be expected in any definite period, it must, I think, be evident to every reflecting person, that all fears as to a *surplus population* are perfectly ideal, and that it is its unequal distribution, and not its aggregate amount, which is to be deplored."

The primary object of agriculture, as hitherto discussed, is the production of food, which process necessarily requires the numerous elements essential for animal subsistence, and causes the exhausting action upon the soil which has given occasion to the great diversity of crops, of manures, and of rotations, of which I have endeavoured to explain the principles. There are, however, certain kinds of crops, and those of great practical value, which, when their culture is considered in a proper point of view, become almost free from exhausting action, and as some of these are actually of the highest importance to industry in Ireland, I shall pass to the description of their leading features.

I have mentioned as being well established by experience, that after the first stage of growth of a plant, the assimilation of its carbon is carried on by the decomposition of the atmosphere, as may be exemplified in the case of the corn crop and fallow, of which the numerical conditions are given in page 298. The mere woody portion of the stem is thus formed almost exclusively from the air and water, as the ligneous fibre, independent of some minutiæ of its structure not affecting the present question, is composed of carbon united to oxygen and hydrogen in the proportions which form water; its formula being $C_{18} H_{12} O_{12}$. This composition of woody fibre, as affecting the cultivation of fibre crops, leads to important agricultural results, which will require full examination. Ligneous fibre is, however, but one of a class of bodies having the same character. The different varieties of starch and sugar are of precisely similar constitution, all being composed of carbon and of the elements of water; thus in chemical formulæ they are expressed by

Starch, ...	$C_{12} H_{10} O_{10}$
Crystallizable sugar, ...	$C_{12} H_{11} O_{11}$
Grape sugar, ...	$C_{12} H_{12} O_{12}$

None of these bodies contain nitrogen, or, when pure, any inorganic matter. The plants which contain these bodies require for their healthy growth, nitrogen and mineral elements, and consequently exhaust the soil; but when we take out of a potato its starch, or when we extract from the sugar-cane or beet-root its sugar, the residual portions of the plant contain all the materials that had rendered the plant exhausting, and are capable, if restored to the soil, of acting as a most valuable manure, and in fact enabling the land to produce successive crops of starch or sugar without any sensible diminution of its fertility.

Of all the starch-bearing plants the potato is that which affords the greatest quantity of produce from a given surface of land. The different varieties of potato differ, however, very much, and the following table will indicate exactly the circumstances of the most important kinds. The plants were grown all on the same quality of land, and the analyses are by Payen, the eminent French agricultural chemist.

VARIETIES.	1 CWT. SEED PRODUCED	1 STATUTE ACRE PRODUCED	100 PARTS CONTAINED		
			WATER.	STARCH.	GLUTEN AND FIBRE.
Rohan,	58 cwt.	14½ tons.	75·2	16·6	8·2
Large yellow,	37 ,,	9¾ ,,	68·7	23·3	8·0
Scotch,	32 ,,	8 ,,	69·8	22·0	8·2
Slow Island,	56 ,,	14 ,,	79·4	12·3	8·3
Legonzac,	32 ,,	8 ,,	71·2	20·5	8·3
Siberian,	40 ,,	10 ,,	77·8	14·0	8·2
Duvillers,	40. ,,	10 ,,	78·3	13·6	8·1

These results shew that the quantity of starch is not largest necessarily in those varieties which yield the greatest weight of tubers. Thus an acre of large yellow potatoes, which gives but 9¼ tons of tubers, produces two tons three cwt. of starch, whilst the acre of Slow Island potatoes, which produce fourteen tons of tubers, give only one ton fifteen cwt. of starch. In cultivating the plant for the purpose of extracting this material, it is, therefore, of the greatest importance to attend to the existence of these varieties.

The preparation of starch from the potato is an operation of very simple kind, and well adapted for the industry of the smaller towns, where potatoes would be usually cheap. It requires only the most ordinary skill, and involves little machinery, the greatest nicety in it being perfect cleanliness, and care that the washings be well finished and with pure water. The operations of the manufacture are

1st. Washing the tubers.
2nd. Rasping them to a pulp.
3rd. Pressing the pulp.
4th. Washing the rough starch.
5th. Draining and drying the produce.
6th. Bolting and storing.

Of these operations it is only necessary to notice one or two in detail.

The breaking up of the tubers into a pulp is accomplished by means of cutting cylinders, to which the potatoes are supplied from a hopper, nearly as grain is to a mill. The more rapidly the cutters move the finer is the pulp produced, and the more perfect the subsequent extraction of the starch, and hence they generally make 600 to 900 turns in the minute, and as these cylinders are usually about twenty inches in diameter, their periphery moves with a velocity of from 1000 to 1500 yards in a minute. A single cylinder of the above dimensions, and of sixteen inches long, making 800 revolutions in a minute, will reduce to pulp about fifty bushels of potatoes per hour. This for the twelve working hours is about ten tons.

The object of pressing or sifting the pulp is to separate the fecula from all foreign substances, especially from the cellular tissue, which, being coarser, rests on the sieve through which the fine starch passes. A great variety of mechanical arrangements have been constructed for this purpose, which fulfil their object, but there remains always with the residual pulp 2 or 3 per cent. of the fecula, which it is impossible to obtain.

The starch, diffused in the current of water by which it has been washed out from the pulp, is run into vats, where it is poured off, and fresh water put on: finally the starch is taken out and dried on floors. As it consolidates into very firm masses, it requires finally to be broken down by a kind of bolting machine, before being put up for sale.

It is necessary to add some valuation of the money circumstances of this manufacture. An acre of potatoes, very well manured, and on good land, may be considered to produce nine tons of potatoes, which may be taken as worth £15. From such potatoes it may be expected, that, with proper care, 15 per cent. of pure starch may be extracted, and hence, from the 9 tons, 27 cwt. The market price of the potato starch is variable; it has been 30s. per cwt., but it only on rare occasions falls below 20s. Taking it at 20s. the value of the produce of the acre becomes £27, leaving for cost of manufacture and profit £12, and of this certainly a large proportion should be profit. I do not think I value the potatoes too low, as, of course, the manufacturer, if not himself the grower, would purchase for store at proper seasons, and avail himself of the lowest terms.

But this calculation of advantage supposes the starch to be the only valuable matter extracted from the potato, which is far from being the case. The residual pulp, which, when perfectly dry, amounts to about 5 per cent. of the entire weight of the tubers, has been found a most nourishing food; in fact, it contains most of the nutritious part of the root, the mere starch which was removed being comparatively much less important in nutrition. This pulp, if moist, putrefies rapidly, it is rich in nitrogen, and in fact analogous to animal substances in composition, and consequently, if not required for food, would form, by being made with lime and clay into a compost, a manure of great value, and especially suitable for restoring to the potato ground the substances which the crop in growing had removed. The waters, with which the pulp is first washed, dissolve a quantity of the soluble constituents of the potato. They rapidly putrefy, and exhale an odour so rotten as to have rendered the starch factories near Paris a nuisance to the neighbourhood, until it was suggested to employ this water as a manure, which has been perfectly successful, and at once removed an important drawback to this branch of industry, and materially increased the fertility of the surrounding farms.

If these residues be properly economized, it is evident that the cost of growing the potatoes may be materially diminished. The atmosphere, in itself, furnishes in fact the carbonic acid and water from which the starch is formed, and if the matters taken from the soil in each crop, be returned to it in the residues of the manufacture, the cost of manure, so heavy for this particular plant, may be almost entirely obviated.

In this country, where the extensive use and culture of the potato have become almost a national characteristic; where labour not requiring considerable skill is to be had so cheap; where potatoes are at their minimum price; it is not merely to be regretted but absolutely disgraceful to ourselves, that we import from Scotland and from France, large quantities of the potato starch to be consumed in Ireland.

The starch is not the only material extracted from potatoes, and extensively available in the arts. The potato itself, re-

duced to flour, is at present extensively employed upon the
Continent in the preparation of a very wholesome quality of
bread, and the starch itself is consumed in making confec-
tionary, jellies, sago, tapioca, in thickening paper, and in a
variety of uses, by which such quantities of it are employed as
to render its manufacture a really important and extensive department of industry. The most remarkable of all the applications of potato starch is, however, one to which the excise
laws of this country would probably present invincible impediments. It is the preparation of sugar and of spirits. Under
the influence of certain chemical agents, simple, yet peculiar
in their action, and to which it would not be my province here
to refer in detail, starch is converted into sugar, and this
sugar, by fermentation, yields spirits. On the Continent the
manufacture of spirit from corn is almost abandoned. Potato
spirit is almost universally used; and in flavour it so resembles
brandy that it is well known that a large quantity of the
French brandy brought into London, is potato spirit from Ham-
burgh coloured with burned sugar.

A branch of industry which has acquired considerable development upon the Continent of Europe, is that of preparing
sugar from the root of the red and yellow beet. The circumstances of this country do not appear to favour its introduction, but as it is immediately connected with the starch manufacture already noticed, and that very exaggerated ideas regarding it are often conceived, I shall briefly notice the general
conditions of its preparation. For this purpose the documents
recently published, during the inquiry instituted by the French
Government, afford satisfactory data. In order to render
the results more immediately intelligible, I shall reduce the
weights, values, and measures, from the French to the English
standard.

The crop of beet roots which is usually obtained in France,
varies from ten to sixteen tons per statute acre. The mean
produce may be taken at twelve tons. For the cultivation of
the acre, it appears that the labour required is, forty-six days
of a man's work, and fourteen days of a horse's. The total

cost of the crop to the farmer appears to be, in average, £7 11s. 6d., made up of

Rent and taxes,	£2	0	0
Manure,	2	3	6
Labour,	1	13	0
Seeds, &c.,	1 -	2	0
Pulling and carriage,	0	13	0
	£7	11	6

The average crop, of twelve tons per acre, stands the farmer, therefore, in 12s. 6d. per ton.

A disadvantage of the crop is usually considered to be, that it occupies the ground so long, as often to interfere with the wheat-sowing in autumn. The seed of the beet is placed in the ground as early as it can be considered at all safe from frost, and it continues growing very decidedly to September, and hence the pulling of it is retarded to the latest moment. Now it is, at that season, peculiarly liable to injury from frost, or from wet. A fact discovered by Peligot will, however, if borne out by practical experience, remarkably simplify the cultivation. He found that the juice of the young beet root is so much richer in sugar than that of the mature plant, that the total quantity of sugar in the plant may be considered to be the same at all ages, and hence, if the roots be pulled up in summer, although the weight of the crop is much less, yet, as the quantity of sugar is not smaller, the market value of the crop is the same. Thus the ground becomes available much earlier, for other agricultural operations, and the plants being pulled in a drier and steadier season, are much less liable to injury from exposure to the weather.

The mode of treatment of the roots, in order to prepare the sugar, is not complex. The roots are broken up, by suitable machines, into a soft pulp, and this is submitted to excessive pressure, between folds of cloth, in hydrostatic presses. The juice which flows out is clarified by lime, and evaporated down, first in ordinary boilers, but subsequently in pans heated by steam, sometimes by evaporation in vacuo, precisely as is adopted for the clarifying and refining of ordinary cane sugar, with which the product, when obtained pure, is identical in properties and composition.

The following estimate of the cost of production of the beet-root sugar, in a factory working up thirty-six tons of roots daily, is taken from the summary of the official results given by M. Dumas. The numbers are reduced to the British standards, and the price of coal in Ireland substituted for the French value. The daily expenses of the factory are

36 tons of beet-root, at 16s. 8d. . . .	£30 0 0
5½ tons of coals, at 12s.	3 6 0
Bone-black, ...	3 6 0
Lime, ...	0 8 0
Labour, 52 persons, ...	5 19 0
Cloths, for pressing, ...	0 16 0
Repairs, lighting, insurance, rent, taxes, and sundries, ...	6 13 0
Interest on the capital invested, which is shewn to be, by other estimates, £12,500, ...	4 3 0
Total daily expense,	£54 11 0

The quantity of sugar actually contained in the beet-root varies from 7 to 10 per cent. in its weight, and, from good materials, and the employment of the best methods, 7 per cent. is available as pure product, after all waste of manufacture; but the ordinary produce to be calculated on is 5 per cent., which, from the thirty-six tons of beet-root, amounts to thirty-six cwt. of refined sugar, delivered daily from such a factory, which, on the above outlay, would cost the manufacturer 30s. 4d. per cwt.; but there are some important deductions to be made from this.

It will be recollected, that the sugar is a material which, like starch, contains no nitrogen, and, when pure, no inorganic matters. It hence is formed, during the growth of the plants, by the mere concurrence of air and water, and the other materials of the beet-root, which remain behind after the sugar is extracted, contain the nitrogen and salts which render the beet useful as food, or available as manure if returned to the soil.

Hence the waste pulp of the sugar works is greedily purchased up by the farmers, and also the skimmings of the boilers, which are found to be a powerful manure, and are sold at a certain price. As it is impossible to obtain all the sugar crystalline, a certain quantity is converted into molasses, or treacle, and this is sold to the distillers for the manufacture of spirits. The expenses must, therefore, be credited by the values of these products, which are daily as follows :

18 cwt. of pulp, at 6s. 3d.	£5 12	6
12 cwt. of treacle, at 1s. 8d.	1 0	0
6 cwt. of skimmings, at 1s.	0 6	0
	£6 18	6

The nett expenditure is, therefore, for each day, £47 12s. 6d. and at 5 per cent. of produce, the sugar costs per cwt. 26s. 6d. or, $2\frac{7}{8}d$. per ℔. As by suitable culture and manipulation the produce may be increased to 7 per cent. without any notable increase of outlay, I may add,

At 6 per cent. the sugar costs 22s. 2d. per cwt., or $2\frac{1}{2}d$ per ℔.
At 7 per cent. the sugar costs 19s. per cwt., or 2d. per ℔.

It, however, is not to be supposed that the Government would allow of a manufacture, which, although giving extensive employment to the population of this country, and opening out a new field for agricultural enterprize, might seriously diminish the revenue now derived from duties on sugar imported from abroad. Beet-root sugar, if manufactured here, should be, of course, submitted to the same duties as are levied on sugar of colonial origin, and as this amounts to 27s. per cwt., or 3d. per ℔, the final cost to the manufacturer, of sugar made in this way, should be therefore so far increased. This may not allow, at present prices, a profit sufficiently large to tempt capital and enterprize into so novel a track.

It will be remarked, that the factory estimate supposes the beet-root bought at 16s. 8d. per ton. It cost the farmer, as shewn above, 12s. 6d. ; he has, therefore, 4s. 2d. per ton nett profit, or, for the twelve tons, £2 10s. per statute acre. In estimates which I have seen of the beet-root sugar manufacture, the produce per acre is often taken at twenty or forty tons, as may really be obtained; but in such case there is little or no sugar; it has been used in forming the woody matter of the roots, and hence the light crop described above is that finally most productive.

In relation to the actual agricultural and manufacturing industry of Ireland, it is still more important to describe the circumstances of those crops which have for their ultimate and valuable product, the vegetable fibre. Of these fibre crops, those of most interest are flax and hemp, especially the former, on which so large a proportion of the population of the north of Ireland may be considered to depend for subsistence.

The flax plant, to which I shall first direct attention, may be cultivated on any soil of moderate fertility, but, of course, will grow in greatest luxuriance, and yield its largest produce, where the land is most fertile. It is, however, indispensable, that the soil be rendered thoroughly open, and perfectly clean. The order of rotation with other crops varies in different countries, but on the Continent, as in Belgium, where its cultivation is best understood, the ordinary custom is, to bring it in after a corn crop, and not to introduce it into the course more frequently than once in seven years. The flax is a very exhausting crop, and hence requires abundance of manure, which is supplied to it in Belgium, in the most effective form, as liquid manure. It will be shewn, immediately, that the flax contains but little lime, the presence of which, in a caustic form, in the soil, appears to be injurious to the plant, hence it is proper, where lime has been necessary to the soil, to intermit the culture of flax for a certain season.

The composition of the soil on which the cultivation of flax may best be carried on, being a problem of the highest practical interest to this country, the Flax Improvement Society of Ireland, in pursuance of their laudable objects in promoting this branch of industry, commissioned me to make analyses of some soils which had produced remarkably good crops of flax. The soils were all light clay loams, and afforded the following results, which I extract from the Report of the Society.

	No. 1.	No. 2.	No. 3.
Silica and silicious sand, . .	73·72	69·41	64·93
Oxide of iron, ...	5·51	5·29	5·64
Alumina, ...	6·65	5·70	8·97
Phosphate of iron, ...	·06	·25	·31
Carbonate of lime, ...	1·09	·53	1·67
Magnesia and alkalies, with traces of sulphuric and muriatic acids, ...	·32	·25	·45
Organic matters, ...	4·86	6·67	9·41
Water, ...	7·57	11·48	8·73
	99·78	99·58	100·11

The organic matter in these soils was rich in nitrogen; their fertility is, therefore, from the analyses, easily understood.

A point which may be noticed in relation to the growth of flax is, that its quality is essentially improved by thick sowing. This arises, not from there being more flax grown, but from the closeness of the plants forcing them to grow upwards with a single stem to gain access to the air, and thus to prevent their branching, by which the fibre is shortened, and rendered irregular. Every thing in the cultivation of this plant is subservient to the formation of a long and delicate woody fibre, and it is owing to this fact in the practical history of the flax, that certain sources of economy in its agriculture, which I shall point out, become practicable.

The ligneous or woody fibre, which finally is converted into the linen thread, is composed of the same elements as starch and sugar, and in nearly the same proportions. Omitting certain minute differences between the true fibre and the matter which occupies its cells, its composition may be expressed by the formula $C_{18}H_{12}O_{12}$ and, when pure, it contains no inorganic matter. Its elements are, in 100 parts:

Carbon, ... 50·00
Hydrogen, ... 5·55
Oxygen, ... 44·45

Hence this fibre, which constitutes the entire money value
of the flax crop, is produced during the life of the plant, by
the elements of the atmosphere, and the materials taken from
the manure and from the soil are, in reality, employed by the
plant in organizing substances which do not make any return
to the farmer, but which are, on the contrary, under certain
circumstances, considered to be positively a disadvantage. It
is, therefore, of importance, that it should be understood, that
by a proper system, the growth of flax and similar fibre crops
should be destitute of all exhausting influence. That the materials drawn from the soil by such a crop should be found in
the waste products of its manufacture, and should be available
by being returned to the soil, to restore it to its original condition of fertility. In order to render this principle fully intelligible, I shall enter into some detail regarding the processes
to which the flax is subjected, and the nature of the products
obtained from it.

The flax, when it has grown to suitable maturity, according
as the design is to allow it to ripen its seed or not, is pulled,
and either immediately, or in the next spare season, according
to the circumstances of the locality, it is subjected to the
process termed rotting or watering. In the stem of the flax
there may be recognized three structures, the outer skin or
epidermis, covering a close network of fibres which encloses the
plant as in a sheath, and in the centre a stem of dense pithy
material. The fibrous network is connected together by a
glutinous matter, which must be decomposed before the fibres
can be separated from the stem, and it is to soften and rot this
substance that the plant is steeped. If the steeping be continued too long, the fibre itself may rot, and be weakened and
injured in quality; if the steeping be not continued long enough,
the fibres are not thoroughly separated from each other, and
the quality of the flax is coarser than it might be. The general tendency is not to rot the flax enough, but it is a process
requiring very careful management and attention, to conduct
it with the greatest advantage.

In order to ascertain what occurs during the steeping of the
flax I instituted chemical examinations of the substances and

process. I have already given the composition of the pure
ligneous fibre, and in the following tables are shewn the results
of my analyses of the composition of the flax stem as it grows,
and of the ashes which it yields, These are in fact its organic
and its inorganic elements. The composition of the ash varies
very sensibly with that of the soil upon which the plant is
grown, but it is not necessary to introduce that consideration
for the present object.

FLAX PLANT.

Carbon, ...	38·72
Hydrogen, ...	7·33
Nitrogen, ...	·56
Oxygen, ...	48·39
Ashes, ...	5·00
	100·00

ASHES OF FLAX PLANT.

Potash, ...	9·78
Soda, ...	9·82
Lime, ...	12·33
Magnesia, ...	7·79
Oxide of iron and alumina, ...	6·08
Silica, ...	21·35
Sulphuric acid, ...	2·65
Chlorine, ...	2·41
Carbonic acid, ...	16·95
Phosphoric acid, ...	10·84
	100·00

When the flax is steeped, the water acquires a darker
colour, a disagreeable odour, and, it is well known, becomes
poisonous to fish. This arises from the solution of the glutinous material which had cemented together the pure fibres.
To examine this material, I employed it as it is produced
when the steeping water is dried down, and the following
tables shew its organic composition, and the composition of the
ashes which it yields. I term this substance, for brevity sake,
flax-steep extract.

	FLAX-STEEP EXTRACT.	FLAX-STEEP EXTRACT WITHOUT ASHES.
Carbon, ...	30·69	52·93
Hydrogen, ...	4·24	7·31
Nitrogen, ...	2·24	3·86
Oxygen, ...	20·82	35·90
Ashes, ...	42·01	,,
	100·00	100·00

It is thus seen, that the steep-water dissolves out a great quantity of nitrogen, and of the inorganic materials of the stem; in fact, that it removes from the plant almost every thing that the plant removes from the soil. This is confirmed by looking to the composition of its ashes, which are shewn by the following analytical results. There are found 42 parts of ashes, in every 100 parts of flax-steep extract, consisting of

Chloride of potassium, ...	3·8
Sulphate of potash, ...	4·4
Carbonate of potash	3·8
Carbonate of soda, ...	13·2
Silica, ...	5·5
Phosphate of iron and alumina, ...	3·2
Phosphate of lime	2·1
Carbonate of lime, ...	4·0
Carbonate of magnesia, ...	2·0
Total quantity, ...	42 per cent.

The steep-water thus dissolves, especially, the alcaline ingredients, and the phosphates of the plant, and hence leaves the rotted stems in a condition of almost pure ligneous matter.

The stems of the plant, after having been thus steeped, undergo a rough bleaching and drying, by being *grassed* for some days. They are then broken by the hackle, and finally, the fibre separated from the residual woody pith or chaff, by the operation of scutching. These operations may be carried on either by hand or by machinery, and the relative value of the systems may hereafter require attention. The fibre, after these processes, is sent to market; it passes into the hands of the linen manufacturers, and becomes the element of mechanical industry, such as has been treated of in the earlier chapters of this work.

Now the agriculturist should steadily bear in mind, that the fibre which he sells to the flax spinner has taken nothing from the soil: all that the crop took out of the soil he has still in the steep-water, and in the chaff of the scutched flax, and if, after suitable decomposition, these be returned to the land, the fertility of the latter will be restored, and thus materials, at present utterly neglected, and even a source of inconvenience, may be converted into most valuable manure.

That the water in which flax has been steeped possesses powerful influence as a manure, has been observed by various persons; thus round the edges of bog holes used for steeping, a luxuriant and tender herbage often arises in vivid contrast to the surrounding barren peat. Various agricultural authorities have noticed its beneficial effects when experimentally used, but I shall only quote, in order to shew the attention it deserves, the following notice by Mr. Wakefield: " The water in which flax has been immersed is, in Ireland, entirely neglected, but Mr. Billingsby mentions it as an excellent manure, and no country in the world, perhaps, affords better opportunities of employing it than Ireland. I made frequent inquiries about it, but could never hear of a single instance of its being used. The author of the Survey of Somersetshire (Mr. Billingsby) says: ' it is observable, that land on which rotted flax is spread to prepare it for heckling, is greatly improved thereby, and if it be spread on a coarse sour pasture, the herbage will be totally changed, and the best sorts of grasses will make their appearance. Having myself cultivated flax on a large scale, and observing the almost instantaneous effect produced by the water in which the flax was immersed, I was induced, some years ago, to apply it to some pasture land, by means of watering carts similar to those used near London for watering the roads. The effect was astonishing, and advanced the land in value ten shillings per acre.' "

The chaff remaining after the scutching might also be formed into manure, and has actually been found of as much value as its composition would indicate. Thus, in fact, the farmer sending to market only the fibre of the flax, which derives nothing from the soil, has the opportunity of economizing in other and highly remunerating modes all the residual materials.

This chaff was found to consist of

Carbon,	50·34
Hydrogen,	6·33
Nitrogen,	·24
Oxygen,	41·52
Ashes,	1·57
	100·00

Its nutritive quality cannot be material, but mixed with the water of the flax-steep, it should complete the restoration to the soil of the constituents of the growing flax.

The average produce of scutched flax, as given by Wakefield, reduced to the statute acre, is 543℔ from nineteen gallons of seed. This is thirty-four stones of sixteen pounds. The usual produce of Scotland is stated by Low, to be forty stones, and at present by the Reports of the Flax Improvement Society, the produce in the north of Ireland may be taken as averaging forty-two stones. The weight of the flax-straw, when quite dry, may be taken as approximating to about two tons.

Mr. Crosthwaite, whose intimate acquaintance with all branches of this industry renders his authority highly valuable, considers that there are about 100,000 acres under flax in Ireland, and that the produce is about 30,000 tons, of an average value of £50 per ton. This is 6s. 3d. per stone, and should give about £12 10s. for the usual produce of the statute acre. The quantity of flax grown appears to be on the increase, and its quality also to be improving, as by the Report of the Flax Society it appears, that the amount of the crop in 1841 was 25,000 tons, averaging £45 per ton, whilst in 1843 it was 36,465 tons, and the average value was considered to be at least £55. This increase of value being, if not wholly, certainly in great part, attributable to the exertions of that very useful Society.

The value of the flax crop depends in a very material degree, indeed it might be said entirely, on the care taken in the preparation of the fibre. The value which it may assume under careful management, and the final amount of employment which it gives, is shewn by the following fact:

"Mr. William Blakely, a tenant of the Dean of Dromore, on the townland of Corcelany, near Waringstown, grew, last season, three statute acres (about 1A. 3R. 16P., Irish measure) of flax, which he managed strictly according to the directions of the ' *Society for the Promotion and Improvement of the Growth of Flax in Ireland.*' The produce of this field has been recently purchased for 15s. per stone, by Messrs. M Murray, and Hening, of Waringstown, the eminent cambric manufacturers, who say, *it is equal, if not superior, to any flax they ever saw before,* and that they have given 36s. per stone for foreign flax, of an inferior quality.

" A large portion of this flax has been delivered to Messrs. M'Murray and Co.; but some still remains to be dressed by the celebrated machinery of Mr. Henry, of Keady. Should this part be as productive as that already furnished, the entire produce of the three acres will be 120 stones; which, at 15s., will give to the farmer £90; but he has a *certainty* of 100 stones, which will realize him £75.

" This flax is now in process of conversion into cambric pocket-handkerchiefs; it is capable of being spun to thirty hanks to the pound, and is to be spun by hand. Mark, now, the employment this will give.

"It will give constant employment, for twelve months, to 158 women to spin it; eighteen weavers will be occupied a like period in weaving; and it will employ forty women for a year to hemstitch (or vein) the handkerchiefs, thus giving constant employment, for twelve months, to 210 persons.

" It is curious to trace the result of the process which this flax is now undergoing:—It will produce 210 webs of cambric, each web containing five dozen handkerchiefs; each dozen

will be worth 50s., and the entire, when finished, will be worth
£2,600."

" If arguments in favour of the Flax Improvement Society
were needed, the case specified in the above letter would furnish them. The farmer alluded to was induced to try what
he could do in the way of growing flax, by reading a small
tract issued by this Society, which accidentally fell into his
hands. The land on which he sowed the seed was the most
barren part of his farm."

Where so much depends on the mechanical and chemical
treatment of the plant after the crop has been pulled, it is
easily conceivable that under the ordinary circumstances of
the Irish farmers, it is difficult to carry out the preparation of
the fibre, so as to give it the best quality, and in fact in Belgium and Holland, where the flax cultivation and manufacture
are in their most advanced state, the growth of the plant and
the fabrication of the fibre are totally distinct occupations.
The crop is purchased by a factor, who takes the dressing into
his own hands, and, being devoted to that one department, is
acquainted with all mechanical arrangements and details necessary to success, and it frequently happens that the farmer
actually obtains for the crop, as grown, more money than he
should have obtained for the imperfectly dressed produce of it,
and is spared the loss of time, of labour, and interference with
other business, which, retaining the mechanical treatment of
the flax in his own hands should necessarily entail upon him.
In the present state of industry, I conceive the general adoption
of the system of factors as indispensable to progress. Without improvement in quality of product, the manufacture cannot extend, and without the preparation of the fibre being
taken up, and cultivated as a distinct profession, no important
amelioration in it can be expected.

From the importance of the flax culture, as well to the farmer as to the manufacturer, it might be supposed that it
should be at least cultivated to such an extent, as to supply
our own industrial wants. Such, however, is far from being
the case ; every year a large quantity of flax is imported into
Great Britain and into Ireland from the Baltic ports, and from

Belgium; the total quantities for three late years are shewn in the following table:

FROM WHENCE IMPORTED.	1840. TONS.	1841. TONS.	1842. TONS.
Russia, ...	43,520	48,472	40,720
Prussia, ...	6,779	5,533	5,624
Germany, . . , . .	405	519	815
Holland, . . : . .	5,650	6,024	4,828
Belgium, ...	4,032	4,865	2,475
France, ...	2,164	1,477	866
Other countries, . . .	99	478	385
Total tons, . . .	62,649	67,368	55,713

It is worth observing, that the diminished importation of 12,000 tons of 1842, is almost exactly the quantity by which, owing to the exertions of the Flax Improvement Society, the home crop had been increased at the same period.

The agricultural employment which the flax crop gives, may be estimated from a statement by Mr. Blacker, whose ability as a judge is so well known; he says: "After the most minute calculation by practical men engaged in the growth of flax, the labour necessary for every acre of flax is computed to be seven days of a man, fifty-four days of a woman, and four and a quarter days of a horse. Now 55,610 tons weight [which was the import in 1833, when Mr. Blacker wrote], supposing each statute acre to produce four cwt., which is a full average crop, would be the produce of 278,050 acres, which, according to the above estimate, would require in labour equal to the employment of 6,488 men for 300 days in the year, 50,015 women for the same number of days, and 3,939 horses for ditto."

It appears thus, that there is twice as much flax imported into Great Britain from foreign ports, as there is grown in this country, and yet there is no actual impediment to its cultivation, for it appears to be uniformly a remunerating crop, where attended to with ordinary care, and may, by the proper application of scientific principles to its culture, be rendered one of the least expensive or exhausting crops that the agriculturist can have to do with.

There is finally to be noticed, in relation to the secondary advantages of the flax crop, the utilization of the seed, either as food or for sowing. It appears now well established, that the fibre is not injured by allowing the plant to form the seed, and that the seed may be saved in good condition under the ordinary circumstances of our climate. This is a very important addition to the value of the crop : the seed being employed for preparing oil : the residual linseed cake being a very valuable food for cattle, or for manure ; or the unripened seed in the capsules, or bowes, as they are termed, may be at once given to cattle. The husks of the seedvessels have been used as food for cattle in the north of Ireland, and by the testimony of Mr. Nevin, and of Mr. Charley, with remarkable advantage. In fact, it would appear that there is no part of this very remarkable plant that is not directly or indirectly capable of being applied to useful purposes.

The great value of it to this country is, however, that its cultivation supplies not merely a source of agricultural, but also of manufacturing employment. In this respect, it is far more beneficial than a food crop of the same money value, or occupying the same ground. The flax, as it leaves the hand of the farmer, gives a livelihood to the dresser, from him it passes to the spinner, to the weaver, the bleacher, and perhaps to the embroiderer, according to its destination. Mr. Andrews illustrates the actual profit and employment given by the crop described page 33, in a calculation which, after correction of a few typographical errors, stands thus:

" 100 stones at 15s.— £75 ; each stone calculated to produce 5½℔. of *dressed* flax—in all 550℔.—spun to 30 hanks to the ℔, will produce 16,500 hanks. About 158 females will be employed twelve months in spinning, at the rate of two hanks per week (six working days) ; wages for spinning each hank, about 1s. 8d., or nearly 7d. per diem for each spinner. This quantity of yarn would make 210 webs of cambric pocket-handkerchiefs, each web containing five dozen. About 18 weavers would be twelve months weaving this quantity, allowing each

man a month for each web (17½ weavers exactly); wages per
web, £2: or from 9s. 6d. to 10s. per man per week.   About
40 females would be employed twelve months in needlework
(hemstitch or veining) ; each could do *one* handkerchief on
each working day; wages, 8s. per dozen, or 8d. per day.
The goods, when finished, would be worth £2 10s. per dozen.

" 158 spinners 12 months, or 52 weeks, at about 3s. 4d. per week, . . .	£1,369 6	8
18 weavers 12 months, at £24 per annum, ...	432 0	0
40 needlewomen 52 weeks, at 4s. each per week, ...	416 0	0
216 persons employed.		
Amount of wages, ...	£2,217 6	8
Cost of flax, ...	75 0	0
	£2,292 6	8
Value of 1,050 dozen handkerchiefs, at £2 10s. per dozen, ...	£2,625 0	0
Profit,	332 13	4"

The realizing of this great amount of value depends on the
delicacy given to the fibre, and it is hence that so much is due
to the leading members of the Flax Society, for their exertions by example and by publications, for the introduction
of the most approved Belgian methods.   While thus recog-
nizing the benefits which are likely to accrue to Irish industry from this modern institution, it is important not to forget
how much we owe to others.   The Royal Dublin Society, almost
immediately on its foundation, applied itself anxiously to promote the culture of flax, and to improve the methods of its
preparation.   They obtained the assistance of persons well
experienced in the Belgian processes, and so early as 1739
published a volume of papers, principally occupied with directions for the growth and treatment of flax, and which contained,
intelligibly laid down, almost every detail of the processes
now being introduced as the newest and most advantageous.
Owing to the disastrous social condition of the country, which

has so kept it back in every branch of peaceful enterprize, the beneficent intentions of the Royal Dublin Society were not carried out, but now that with renewed energy, it labours to awaken Irish industry, that it possesses in numerous junior societies, so many active co-operators, and that the people, by education and steadiness of habits, are become more fitted for the pursuits of peaceful industry, it is to be hoped that the seed shall no longer be scattered upon an unfruitful soil, but spring forth with a sound and vigorous vegetation, which may bring peace, abundance, and contentment to the land.

It only remains to indicate, in a general manner, the extent to which the mechanical manufacture of flax is prosecuted in this country. In the work on Ireland, published by Mr. and Mrs. Hall, some statistical results are given, which they obtained by personal inquiry in Belfast, and which, though probably above the truth, are not more exaggerated than is usual with such general estimates. They consider that there are in Belfast, now at work, 155,000 spindles, consuming 210 tons of flax per week, and that there are employed in the manufacture of flax, 170,000 hands. They estimate the total number of persons supported by the linen trade as not less than half a million: that the annual value of the linen cloth manufactured in Ulster is not less than £4,000,000 : the capital involved in its production not less than £5,000,000, and that the annual amount of wages paid to those engaged in the manufacture amounts to £1,200,000. This sum, for the 170,000 above mentioned, would make the average wages to be only 2s. 9d. per week.

The extent of this manufacture stands in such relief from the usual absence of all manufacturing industry in Ireland, that we frequently attach to it a degree of importance and an idea of absolute magnitude that it does not really possess. Thus we often hear the linen manufacture spoken of as being the staple of this country, whilst wool and cotton are in return the natural manufactures of the sister kingdom. In reality, however, Ireland is almost as much behind in this as in every other branch of industry. The town of Dundee alone is considered to manufacture as much linen as all Ireland, and the relation which the manufacture of flax bears in the three kingdoms, is exactly shewn in the following table, which is extracted from the Report of the Factory Inspectors for 1839, since which period no sensible alteration has taken place.

In England there were 169 mills, worked by 4,260 horse power, and employing 16,573 persons.

In Scotland 183 mills, worked by 4,845 horse power, and employing 17,897 persons.

In Ireland forty mills, worked by 1,980 horse power, and employing 9,017 persons.

It is difficult to reconcile this official return with the estimate of Mr. Hall, just before quoted; as the proportion of home-spun and woven linen goods can scarcely be so considerable as to account for the discrepancy.

Finally, the following extracts from official tables will shew, as far as documents allow, the actual, or, at least, recent, extent of the export trade in linen products.

EXPORT OF WOVEN LINEN GOODS, IN YARDS.

YEARS.	TO GREAT BRITAIN.	TO FOREIGN PARTS.	TOTAL.
1810	32,584,545	4,313,725	36,898,270
1815	37,986,359	5,496,206	43,482,565
1820	40,318,270	3,294,948	43,613,218
1825	52,559,678	2,553,587	55,113,265

RE-EXPORT OF IRISH LINEN AND SAIL-CLOTH, FROM GREAT BRITAIN TO FOREIGN PARTS, IN YARDS.

YEAR.	IRISH LINEN.	IRISH SAIL-CLOTH.
1824	17,933,195	1,593,291
1827	14,022,496	2,211,529
1830	13,244,269	1,922,211
1833	9,561,277	2,229,777

Latterly an extensive trade with the Continent has sprung up, in the exportation of linen yarns, replacing, to a certain extent, the export of woven linens. The money values exported were

YEAR.	LINEN.	YARN.
1837	£77,272	£3,164
1840	63,847	172,602
1842	31,404	169,449

Such are the general conditions of this important branch of manufacture. It is needless for me to point out how strenuously our efforts should be directed to the extension of a branch of industry, which, in its various departments, affords, from a given surface of land, employment to a greater number, and a greater variety of individuals, than any other branch of human occupation. The agriculturist, the mechanist, and the chemist, are all equally occupied with its preparation; and, certainly, the natural circumstances of the country are such as to adapt it, in a singularly perfect manner, for the development of the flax and linen manufacture, to an indefinite extent.

The linen manufacture has been, hitherto, almost exclusively confined to the north of Ireland. This does not arise from any physical circumstances of soil or climate, or from the greater facilities of access to mechanical power; on the contrary, the soil of Ulster, if we except the valley of the Lagan, and some scattered districts, is not, by any means, equal to the soils of the south and centre. The growth of this department of industry in Ulster, is owing rather to moral causes. Its population was, essentially, of a class devoted to industrial pursuits, and eager after the independence and power which pecuniary success confers, and which was within their reach; whilst in the south, the wretched remnants of feudal barbarism paralysed all tendency to improve. The lord was above industry; the slave was below it; and hence, although the circumstances of a fertile soil, easy access to markets, and abundance of motive power, were, in themselves, favourable, the blessings which nature presented were left unutilized, by the ignorance and inertness of the people.

In fact, if we consider the situation of those countries in which the manufacture of linen and other flax products has become the characteristic fact of their industrial history, we shall find the soil and geographical condition quite different from those of the north of Ireland. In Egypt, whose dignitaries were clothed in purple and fine linen, and from which the culture of flax has spread over the civilized world, the soil was formed by the mud carried down in the overflowings of the Nile, and spread over the surface of the lower country along its banks. The soils of Belgium and Holland, the countries now most remarkable for the excellence and abundance of their flax industry, have been produced by the accumulated mud deposited by the vast rivers, which, draining the greater part of Europe, discharge their waters into the German Ocean, by numerous channels. The rivers which flow into the Baltic afford, also, on the low grounds along their banks, the seats of the flax agriculture of Russia, and Northern Prussia; and, guided by these analogies, may we not ask, where are the similar soils, or districts, in our own country? They are abundant, and available along the line of the principal river. The lands hitherto liable to flood, by the irregular risings of the Shannon, but, by the improvement of its channel, about to be permanently rendered available to agriculture, amount to not less than 32,500 acres above Limerick, whilst below that city, the caucasses, or marshy grounds, of the extraordinary fertility mentioned by Wakefield, are to be found. Such soils afford the most complete parallel to those districts of Egypt and of Belgium, which have been for ages the seats of the growth of flax. The water power at Killaloe, fully described at page 83, places at the hands of the manufacturer, the means of every mechanical preparation of the crop. The river furnishes for 200 miles the most convenient access to domestic markets, and the port places him under equally favourable circumstances for the foreign trade. So remarkable a combination of facilities for industrial success is rarely to be met with.

The flax had formerly been actually cultivated to some extent in certain parts of the south and centre of Ireland, and the quantity of produce obtained was found decidedly greater than the average of the crops given in the north of Ireland. I am informed by experienced persons, also, that the quality of the fibre was of a delicacy but seldom met with in the ordinary flax of Ulster. Neither the cultivation nor the manufacture was adopted by the people with the energy and patience which alone can lead to success. The encouragement to industry was unhappily associated with other objects, which deprived it of all power of really bettering the condition of the people; which interposed between those who might have served as efficient teachers, and those who were to derive instruction, a barrier which, it is to be hoped, the experience of centuries has at last shewn cannot be removed by measures of cruelty or menace.

Connected with the cultivation of flax, as a department of agriculture, and of subsequent mechanical industry, is that of hemp, which, in all its states, indeed, bears an almost perfect analogy to the growth and preparation of flax. During the war, when access to the Baltic, from whence the great supply of hemp is drawn, was difficult, this plant was cultivated in this country with some success. The crop appears to require a good soil, and in its preparation a degree of care, which the general run of farmers were not capable of applying to it, and hence, since that period, the attention of agriculturists having been exclusively fixed on corn and other food crops, its cultivation has been totally abandoned.

The constitution of the hemp plant is almost exactly like that of flax. It is pulled, with suitable care, in regard to the ripening of the seed, which its diœcious structure requires. The plants are steeped, until the gummy material which connects the fibres is softened, and rotted off, and then, after drying, and a certain amount of bleaching on green land, the fibrous skin is peeled from the stems, and the fibre obtained clean by scutching with appropriate instruments. The hemp fibre, like the flax fibre, consists of purely woody matter, having the chemical composition of $C_{18} H_{12} O_{12}$, and contains neither nitrogen nor saline matters. It is hence formed in the plant by the agency of the atmosphere alone, and the materials which the plant extracts from the soil, or from the manure used in its cultivation, are found, not in the fibre, but in the waste of the processes of its preparation. The water in which it had been steeped, the chaff which remains when the fibre is cleaned off, contain various substances, which, when properly returned to the soil, give it back all that the plant in growing had removed from it, and hence would restore its original condition of fertility. In this way the hemp may, like flax, be rendered one of the least exhausting crops, and the profit on its cultivation increased, of course, in the same proportion.

In order to establish these principles by chemical analyses, I instituted an examination of the hemp plant and its products, analogous to that which has been already noticed regarding flax. The following were the results. The hemp plant consists of:

	THE STEM.	THE LEAVES.
Carbon,	39·94	40·50
Hydrogen,	5·06	5·98
Oxygen,	48·72	29·70
Nitrogen,	1·74	1·82
Ashes,	4·54	22·00
	100·00	100·00

The ashes of the plant (stem and leaves), consisted of

Potash,	7·48
Soda,	·72
Lime,	42·05
Magnesia,	4·88
Alumina and oxide of iron,	·37
Silica,	6·75
Phosphoric acid,	3·22
Sulphuric acid,	1·10
Chlorine,	1·53
Carbonic acid,	31·90
	100·00

When the hemp is steeped, the water acquires very strongly narcotic properties and a disagreeable odour. On drying it down a brown extract is obtained, which was composed of

Carbon,	. . . .	28.28	or	55·66
Hydrogen,	. . . . . .	4·16	,,	8·21
Nitrogen,	. . . .	3·28	,,	6·45
Oxygen,	. . . .	15·08	,,	29·68
Ashes,	. . . .	49·20	Without the ashes.
		100·00		100·00

This material contains so large a quantity of nitrogen, as well as of saline matters, as to shew that when it had decomposed it should become a most valuable fertilizer.

The steeped hemp stem, as it remains after pulling off the loose fibrous coat, is little more than ordinary wood. It contained

Carbon,	. . . .	56·80
Hydrogen,	. . . .	6·48
Nitrogen,	. . . .	0·43
Oxygen,	. . . .	34·52
Ashes,	. . . .	1·77
		100·00

The cultivation of the hemp is not likely to be in future as important as hitherto it has been. The substitution of iron for hemp in the standing rigging of ships, and the introduction of coarse Egyptian flax in the manufacture of various fabrics where previously hemp had been used, will probably limit very much its consumption. It is only from its close analogy to the flax, and the identity of principle by which so much economy may, as I believe, be introduced into the cultivation of both, that I have here noticed it, even thus briefly.

I have endeavoured, in the foregoing observations, to notice briefly the questions regarding Irish agriculture, which appeared to me most intimately connected with its position as an important branch of industry. It has been shewn that the amelioration of the processes of cultivation requires a very extended knowledge of chemical and mechanical science. That husbandry as an art, so far from presenting the monotonous and almost passive routine in which rustic existence has been dreamed away, requires to be placed parallel with the other great departments of human occupation, in the amount of intelligence which its successful practice calls into play.

Until, by suitable education, the minds of the agricultural population of all classes are awakened to a knowledge of what their art really depends upon, all secondary exertions for its improvement must be completely futile.

There exist in Ireland millions of acres of land perfectly well adapted for cultivation, but which have never yet supplied a morsel of food for man.

It is well established that on the lands actually cultivated there might be raised three times the amount of food that is now produced, were a suitably improved system of agriculture brought into general use.

And yet there exists in Ireland a population, starving and unemployed, wearing out a miserable existence on the charity of those only a degree less wretched than themselves, or supported by a tax levied on the industry of the more energetic and more instructed classes.

Were the true conditions of agricultural success generally understood such could not be the case. The cultivation of these wastes, which, as evidence of the most decisive and practical character has shewn, can be easily and economically reclaimed, would give remunerative occupation to hordes of those who now are among the weightiest burthens of the land. The productiveness of the soil being augmented by proper drainage and deep working, and the pastoral system replaced by the turnip and green crop husbandry, by which so much more food is raised and so much more employment given, it would be found that, so far from the existing numbers of the people being too great to be supported by the soil, the new conditions of agricultural activity would provide means of profitable occupation for a much greater number than that proportion of our population, which can, even now, be considered as dependent on it for the means of life.

CHAPTER IX.

IMPORTANCE OF MEANS OF INTERNAL COMMUNICATION TO THE
INDUSTRY AND MORALITY OF A PEOPLE. INFLUENCE OF THE
CONSTRUCTION OF ROADS ON THE SOCIAL CONDITION OF THE
INHABITANTS. THE EXPENSE REPAID MANIFOLD BY THE
INCREASE OF REVENUE. UTILITY OF PUBLIC GRANTS TO
ASSIST IN THE EXECUTION OF WORKS OF LOCAL IMPROVE-
MENT.

OF INLAND NAVIGATION. FAVOURABLE NATURAL CONDITION
OF IRELAND. NAVIGATION OF THE SHANNON. EXPENDITURE
ON ITS WORKS. AMOUNT OF EMPLOYMENT GIVEN. TRAFFIC
ON THE SEVERAL PARTS OF THE SHANNON BY STEAM AND
OTHERWISE. OTHER NAVIGABLE RIVERS OF IRELAND. THE
BARROW NAVIGATION. EXTENT AND DIRECTION OF THE
CANALS OF IRELAND. GRAND AND ROYAL CANALS. AMOUNT
OF TRAFFIC AND TOLLS. THEIR BRANCHES. LAGAN NAVI-
GATION. NEWRY AND ULSTER CANALS. TYRONE AND BOYNE
NAVIGATIONS. PROPOSED CANAL TO PLACE IN CONNEXION
LOUGH NEAGH, LOUGH ERNE, AND THE SHANNON.

OF THE IRISH LAKES IN RELATION TO THE MEANS OF INTER-
COURSE. LOUGHS NEAGH AND ERNE. LOUGH GILL. THE
CONNAUGHT LAKES. IMPORTANCE OF DEVELOPING THEIR
NAVIGATION. PROBABLE BENEFITS TO THE INHABITANTS OF
THAT PROVINCE, AND TO THE COUNTRY AT LARGE.

OF RAILWAYS AS REGARDS IRELAND. EXISTING LINES. DUB-
LIN AND KINGSTOWN. ULSTER RAILWAY. DROGHEDA LINE.
REPORT OF RAILWAY COMMISSIONERS. LINES RECOMMENDED
THEREIN. NOTICE OF THE GENERAL CONDITIONS OF THE
VARIOUS LINES OF RAILWAY NOW PROPOSED TO BE FORMED.
COST OF LOCOMOTIVE POWER. OF THE ATMOSPHERIC RAIL-
WAY. ITS PECULIAR RELATIONS TO THIS COUNTRY. ITS
MECHANICAL AND ECONOMICAL ADVANTAGES.

IMPORTANCE OF THE RAILWAY SYSTEM AS A MEANS OF INTER-
COURSE TO THE PEOPLE. NOTICE OF THE QUESTION OF GO-
VERNMENTAL CONTROL IN THE CONSTRUCTION AND MANAGE-
MENT OF RAILWAYS.

It is not enough that a country may possess, in the fertility
of its soil, or the richness of its mines, the materials for the
creation of industrial wealth, but also there must be the means
of bringing these resources into play by land and water communication. By their aid the different substances necessary

to manufactures are brought to the localities where the processes to which they are to be subjected can be carried on with most advantage, and the produce be conveyed to the situations where its sale may be effected with most profit to the owners. Direct and safe modes of communication are, therefore, indispensable to the development of industrial pursuits, as well for the procuring access to raw materials, as to secure markets for the manufactured goods. It is, however, not wonderful that, industry having received so little extension until a few years back, the means of communication should still remain in Ireland comparatively undeveloped.

The internal communications of a country demand attention, however, on grounds of far higher order than their merely facilitating mercantile transactions; they are connected with the highest moral aims of the legislator, by their influence on the habits and the conduct of the people. The isolation in which man is condemned to live, in a district destitute of roads, or where transport is difficult and expensive, is fatal to his progress in civilization and humanity. He grows up in ignorance of his fellow-men; his mind, limited to the circle of a few ideas elsewhere obsolete, looks upon all deviation from them as fraught with injury and ruin. The results of new methods in the management of land or labour, which within a few miles are actually producing the greatest benefits, remain utterly unknown to him. The stimulus of contact with persons above him, and yet not too far removed from his own sphere to prevent the ambition arising within him of exerting himself to attain the comfort and consideration which they enjoy, does not present itself to his mind. His isolation and his ignorance remove him equally from the instructor, and the instructor from him, and he resists with violence, by which, in the absence of reasoning, he can alone shew his will, the intrusion of all novelties calculated to break through the miserable monotony in which his forefathers and himself have vegetated. An enlightened French minister, in speaking of the cost of the manufacture of iron in France, as affecting railroads, said: "The question of the price of iron,—it is the question of roads, the question of communications, of intercourse between man and man, of the obliteration of prejudices, of the production of mutual amity, of morality, and civilization."

These considerations are borne out in a very remarkable manner by the results of the construction of roads in certain parts of Ireland, that had been previously destitute of the means of transport. The consequence of not having roads is illustrated by the evidence of Mr. Fetherstone, who, describing some of his important bog improvements to a Committee of the House of Commons, says: "The oats these lands grow is so very fine, and of such a rich gold colour, that if we can possibly get it down to the lowlands, we sell it freely for seed oats, but the roads being so bad, we put it to the purpose of illicit distillation. It is a great deal cheaper to distil it than to bring it to market, for we could only bring a sack at a time, and we distil it on the spot at once, and on that account very little of it finds its way to the market." . . . "There are no roads at all. I was obliged to take my carts to pieces and carry them on horses' backs, and then I made the roads through my part of the mountain. The mountain is alluvial land, and produces anything. The oats are beautiful, and an enormous crop; but what is the good of it? you cannot send it to market. There are no gentlemen residing in that mountain country, and the people are in a lawless state.' The combination of facts is here important. A fertile soil, its produce available only by outraging the laws, demoralizing the people, and rendering them fit for the perpetration of those insane outrages, which we too often have to record. For this the remedy is not Draconic legislation, but making roads; not blindly punishing the people for being savage, but opening to them the means of civilization and honest industry.

When this is done, it is remarkable how instantly the very poorest of the people hasten to avail themselves of its benefits. When Mr. Nimmo was engaged in the construction of the Connamara roads, his workmen were actually inconvenienced by the country cars conveying produce and objects of traffic, even up to the spot which the engineers were at the moment commencing to render passable. Similar instances occurred elsewhere. In the district called Pobble O'Keefe's country, on the limits of the counties of Cork, Limerick, and Kerry, which had been a place of refuge for malefactors and desperadoes of all kinds, and had remained totally uncultivated, a set of roads were made under the direction of Mr. Griffith. As the roads advanced, cottages and farm houses sprang into existence along their sides; cultivation extended itself from their edges into the waste. The bad characters that had inhabited it disappeared, and a single policeman has marched a prisoner through the entire district, without any other than the most friendly greetings along his way. The whole organization of the locality has been changed, and at the same time with a pecuniary benefit to the public funds, which I shall hereafter notice.

The effects of opening out with roads some very desolate parts of Clare, are thus described by a gentleman of intelligence and station, in a communication to the Board of Works, the accuracy of which the Commissioners guarantee.

"Communications have been effected between large towns through mountain districts, whereby the distance will be in each case shortened, and in which districts, previous to the construction of these roads, no wheel carriages of any kind could be used.

"The immediate effect has been to excite the minds of the people to the pursuits of honest industry; they can now bring lime into the mountains, and they can carry produce out of them.

"Illicit distillation has been checked, first by a market being opened for the sale of grain, and secondly, by the facilities afforded to the revenue officers in their search after private stills: the consequent benefit in a moral point of view is immense.

"The soil of the mountain districts having been hitherto unworked, has been found, by burning and liming, to produce potatoes in such abundance, and of such excellent quality, that very large quantities have been taken from the neighbourhood of Lough Grana (the parts most known to the writer) to the county Limerick, the excellence of the roads making the transport easy; thus the deficiency of food in some parts of the

country has been made good by the superabundant crops in
these mountains.

" Gentlemen who before could never reach their properties
in these districts, are now led to visit and reside on them, and
form plans for their improvement.

" In the execution of these roads the resources of the country have been developed; quarries of stone fit for building, of
slate, and of limestone, have been discovered, which will be of
incalculable advantage in the improvement of the country, and
in thus stimulating the industry of the inhabitants.

" In a few years the lands will contribute to the county rates,
and thus repay fully the sums assessed for their formation,
while the Government will be amply indemnified by the improved habits of the people, and the growing consumption of
exciseable articles."

Such being the results of the opening out of communications
through the country, it may well be supposed that it should
form one of the dearest objects of a Government anxious for
the improvement of the people, and that the sums necessary
for such purposes should be most heartily afforded. It is to
be regretted that such is not found always to be the case.
The benefits derivable are often so remote, and are spread
over so great a space of country and of time, that they do not
present, to ordinary statesmen, a sufficiently definite aspect to
justify the actual advance of sterling money; it may, therefore,
be not without interest to point out that such advance is
really an investment of capital on the part of the Government,
and one generally yielding profits of a high, even usurious
return.

The town of Clifden in Connamara, and the surrounding
country, were, in 1815, in such a state of seclusion that it contributed no revenue whatsoever to the State, and up to 1822,
its agriculture was so imperfect that scarcely a stone of oats
could be got. In 1836, Clifden had become an export town,
having sent out 800 tons of oats, and it produced to the revenue annually £7,000. From the expenditure in Connaught
in eleven years of £160,000 in public works, the increase of

annual revenue derivable from the province has become equal to the entire amount.

In Cork, where Mr. Griffith expended £60,000 in seven years, there has been stated to be an annual increase of customs and excise of £50,000 immediately derivable from the territories benefited by those works.

Those should not be called grants of money, but investments of capital, with realization of enormous profit. An individual would most happily advance the money if he were allowed to appropriate a fourth of the returns. Such sums, therefore, when advanced by the State, should not be looked upon as boons or favours, as they too frequently are, but as a part of the ordinary duties of a Government.

Three quarters of a century ago, when Scotland, poor, barbarous, and ignorant, lay at the feet of England, withering under the results of two unsuccessful rebellions, the central Government saw the necessity of creating at once such a system of internal communications, as whilst it enabled the instruments of Government to penetrate to every portion of the country, should also place at the disposition of the inhabitants the means of pacific intercourse and trade. Hence between canals and roads a million and a half of money was given to Scotland. Of this there was to be no repayment. Other large sums, as a quarter of a million to Leith Harbour, were lent at very moderate interest, and an arrangement was made, that for all roads required in Scotland, the State pays one-half of the expense, and the locality is burthened only with the other moiety. It is not with any idea of objecting to those grants that I here mention them. On the contrary, they were perfectly proper, and the Government did its duty to Scotland nobly, although some of the plans, such as the Caledonian canal, were failures as to the particular result: but what has been the consequence to Scotland? How much of the intelligence and business habits, the general morality, and amenability to law, by which the people of that country are distinguished, is due to the abundant means of intercourse with each other, and with their richer and more cultivated neighbours?

Certainly a great deal. Scotland furnishes to the State more revenue, in proportion to her population, than Ireland does, but she certainly does not return a larger proportion of profit on the sums which the State has expended in the sound improvement of her people.

A great deal has been latterly done towards improving the roads of the more remote districts, as also in erecting fishery piers and forming harbours, as shall be hereafter noticed, by the Board of Works, who were enabled to grant loans of small sums of money, for such objects, on other sums being contributed by individuals. Although the restrictions placed upon the Board by its constitution limited its powers very much, forcing it to require a high rate of interest and an unusual amount of security, yet these loans were in many cases of exceeding use. The grant from the Board of Works formed a nucleus, round which the subscriptions of the local gentry generally accumulated, so that objects for which otherwise no means could be obtained, were thus carried rapidly into effect. Such local works were also of the peculiar use that they could be carried on in general at times when other employment was slack, and they required principally the rough labour furnished by the inhabitants of the district. Thus, not long ago, a part of Kerry, near Kenmare river, was suffering under the miseries of almost famine. By the aid of the Board of Works the construction of some roads was started, and the population was set to work. Being paid their weekly wages, they were enabled to purchase abundant food. Their cottages have ceased to be the abode of disease and misery. A way being opened for the produce of their fields, their agriculture has become more active. A school has been erected on the road side, and industry and education having been now introduced among that so lately wretched people, there is every hope of a steady progress in social comfort.

The total sum granted by the Board of Works since its establishment, about twelve years, appears to have been about £104,000. The fund so productive of good consequences was, therefore, about £9,000 per annum. This grant either has been or is immediately to be abolished.

The expense of land carriage is so considerable, even on the best roads, as to present material obstacles to the extension of commercial intercourse. It may be estimated for general goods throughout the country at 6d. per ton per mile, and even under the conditions of steady traffic with returns, as in the case of the carriage of coals from the colliery districts, I have been obliged to estimate its minimum amount at 3d. per ton per mile. The cost of manufactured goods as well as of produce is thus heightened considerably by the cost of carriage; their use is limited to a smaller circle of the people, and, therefore, every means that can be devised for lowering the cost of transport should be energetically made available.

The most important reduction in the cost of transport is made by the substitution of water for land carriage. For this Ireland is peculiarly fitted, the extent of her principal rivers, and the number and magnitude of her lakes presenting natural means of communication, such as are seldom equalled, and the structure of the central country affording facilities for the construction of canals not easily surpassed. In fact Ireland is a country peculiarly fitted for inland navigation and for traffic, there being no point on the surface of the island more than twenty-five miles distant from the sea, or from a navigable lake or river. Without entering into lengthened detail I shall proceed to notice each of the principal lines of navigation.

In every point of view, the Shannon, which has already obtained so much of our notice in relation to the coal fields and iron mines, the agricultural districts, the slate quarries and sulphur ores upon its banks, deserves to rank as the main channel of water communication throughout Ireland. Its navigable length is divided into several portions, on which the vessels differ in build and magnitude according to the circumstances of the river. Below Limerick the estuary is navigated by steamers of considerable size, which ply daily to Kilrush and Tarbert. From Limerick to Killaloe the navigation, partly canal and partly in the narrow portion of the river, is effected by passage boats drawn by horses. The expanse of

Lough Derg and the river to Athlone admits again of steamers ;
some of considerable size, which ply upon the lake, others
smaller for the river channel.   Beyond Athlone regular steam
traffic has not yet penetrated, but Lough Ree, Loughs Boda-
rig and Boffin, and Lough Allen, will admit of being navigated
by vessels of the first class, and after a little time the river
channel will be throughout so much improved as to allow of
the large steamers passing from Killaloe to its most northern
termination, and thus dispense altogether with the use of
smaller vessels in the narrow waters, and the cost and trouble
of trans-shipment.

It is singularly illustrative of how little reflection was devoted to Irish subjects—of how slightly the true and only
means of consolidating a people by giving them common habits
of industry, of sociality, and of traffic, was thought about in relation to this country, that the Shannon was for so many generations looked upon as an useful barrier and defence against the
uncivilized tribes, who dwelt beyond its boundary.   The cost
of maintaining in good repair, the various fortifications at what
were called the passes of the Shannon, was defrayed with pleasure, but the idea of rendering fortifications useless, of erecting the bulwarks of the State in the hearts of the inhabitants
by fostering their industry, by encouraging their commerce
and agriculture, and promoting their education, did not occur
to the statesmen of that epoch.   Let us hope that a better era
has arrived.

It is not within my object to enter into any account of the
successive steps taken towards the improvement of the Shannon.   Large sums have been expended on it, and these form
very frequently a subject of public complaint, from those who
either do not or will not understand the vast results to Ireland, which must flow from the completion of the navigation.
A few miles of a canal in Canada, has cost more than treble
the entire money laid out upon the Shannon, with this difference, that every improvement of the latter river leads to an
increase of revenue which repays the money expended, whilst
in the case of the Canadian canal, the money was an absolute
and final grant.   The alterations now being carried on under

the care of the Board of Commissioners, are defrayed partly
by public funds and partly by a rate levied on the counties
along the river. This principle is very equitable, and there is
no doubt but that the final result will be so advantageous to
those districts as fully to atone for the necessity of advancing
money, which certainly is inconsistent with the usual financial
habits of the western province.

Works such as those in process of execution on that river,
are, in fact, lessons in industry to the population of the neighbourhood. The people are not only employed so as to earn a
subsistence, but being brought into contact with workmen of
a higher class, and of steadier habits, they become themselves
gradually improved in character. "Such public works," in
the words of Mr. Spring Rice (Lord Monteagle), "produce, as
their ordinary effect, extended cultivation, improved habits of
industry, a better administration of justice. the re-establish-
ment of peace and tranquillity in the disturbed districts, a domestic colonization of a population in excess in certain districts, a diminution of illicit distillation, and a very considerable increase of revenue."

The total sum expended by the Commissioners for the improvement of the Shannon, up to the 4th March, 1844, is
£316,346 11s. 3d. The amount of employment given in the
construction of locks, &c., along its course, may be judged
from the following return of the average number of persons
employed daily:

	1841.	1842.	1843.
Lower Shannon, . . .	233	394	138
Middle Shannon, . . .	538	1412	1310
Upper Shannon, . . .	106	705	978
Total,	877	2511	2426

This number of hands is, however, not constantly at work,
and I have, therefore, calculated the total number of men

2 A

whose occupation throughout the entire year is represented by the preceding totals. They are in

1841.   1842.   1843.

727 men. . . . 1884 men. . . . 2064 men.

It is now time to close this notice by recording the actual amount of traffic, according to the latest returns that have been published.

The actual length of navigation on the lower Shannon, from Limerick to Kilrush, is forty-four miles. The number of passengers by steamers in 1836 was 23,851. The quantity of goods carried at the same time is not given in the returns to the Railway Commissioners.

The navigation by track-boat between Limerick and Killaloe, which is partly river and partly canal, extends for fourteen miles, in a circuitous course. In 1836 there were taken by packet boats 14,600 passengers, and the traffic was:

In 1831, 28,212 tons, paying £1092 14s. 0d. tolls.
In 1836, 36,018 ,,   ,,   £1514 2s. 0d. ,,

On the Middle Shannon the navigation is lake, river, and partly canal. There are on it five steamers of a total tonnage of 710 tons. One of 100 horse power; the others of from 20 to 30. In 1836 the number of passengers was 4083. The quantity of traffic at two distant periods is shewn by the following numbers. The smallness of the tolls is owing to the relations of the Companies of Inland Navigation, and of the Grand Canal.

YEARS.	NO. OF BOATS.	TONNAGE.	AMOUNT OF TOLLS.
1829	430	10771	£279 18 2
1835	597	19475	184 10 0

The Upper Shannon, consisting of a series of lakes, connected by the river and a canal with six locks, extends from Athlone to Lough Allen. The boats upon it are of from 30 to

50 tons. The freight is usually one penny per ton per mile, including tolls. The traffic was in

> 1834, 8,672 tons, producing £93 9s. 8d. tolls.
> 1835, 9,770 ,, ,, £100 2s. 9d. ,,

There are no passenger boats, nor, as yet, steamers.

From the Fifth Report of the Shannon Commissioners, it appears that the traffic on the river, under their control, that is above Limerick, was :

YEARS.	TONNAGE LANDED.	TONNAGE LOADED.	TOTAL.
1840	40,882	31,180	72,062
1841	33,405	37,335	80,740
1842	46,435	39,880	86,315

The number of passengers conveyed on that part of the river by the City of Dublin Steam Company's boats, was in the year 1843, 15,583 persons.

Of the other rivers which penetrate to such considerable distances into the interior of the country, there are few available for navigation beyond the points where the estuaries terminate. The Blackwater, which, at least to Fermoy, a distance of thirty-five miles, might be so easily adapted to navigation, is as yet available only to Cappoquin. On the Suir, the trade boats ascend to Clonmel; on the Nore to Innistiogue. The Barrow, however, affords an example of our river navigation fully developed, as by means of it, and of a branch of the Grand Canal, a water communication is established between Dublin and New Ross. The total length of the navigation opened out from Dublin to the sea below Waterford, is upwards of 120 miles. The boats are from 30 to 50 tons. The traffic was in

> 1800, 19,828 tons, producing £1,405 tolls.
> 1820, 41,262 ,, ,, £3,827 ,,
> 1835, 66,084 ,, ,, £4,966 ,,

Some other rivers, as the Foyle, the Slaney, are navigated

to a certain distance with the assistance of the tide, but they are not at all navigable in the proper sense, as applied to their ordinary river channels.

The natural difficulties which rivers often present to navigation, as well as their not being found in the precise localities where other conditions render means of communication important, render it often more economical to create a perfectly new route by a canal, than to alter or improve the circumstances of a river.

The canals of Ireland are referrible to two systems; one destined to connect the Shannon with the Irish Sea at Dublin, the other to connect the great inland sea, Lough Neagh, with the British Channel at Newry and Belfast.

The Royal Canal from Dublin to the River Camlin, by which it enters the Shannon, at Tarmonbarry, has a total length of ninety-two miles. Its summit level is at Mullingar, where, at fifty-three miles from Dublin, it is 322 feet above the level of the sea. Its supply of water is derived from Lough Owel.

The income from goods and passengers, and expenditure, were, in the

YEARS.	PASSENGER RECEIPTS.	TOTAL RECEIPTS.	TOTAL EXPENDITURE.
1834	£6,299 11 10	£24,000 0 11	£11,376 10 0
1836	7,468 8 3½	25,148 19 7	11,912 2 10
1843	8,259 4 5	24,122 10 0	11,389 9 9

The average toll levied upon this canal appears to be from 1d. to 1½d. per ton, per mile. The total number of passengers who travelled by this canal, in the year 1837, was 46,450.

The *Grand Canal*, leaving Dublin by the southern extremity, passes nearly parallel, and at a very few miles distance, from the Royal Canal, for a certain portion of its length. It joins the Shannon at Shannon Harbour, and, on the other side of the river, is continued to Ballinasloe. Its total direct length is ninety-nine miles. Its branches are numerous; to Kilbeggan, and to Edenderry; to Athy, where it communicates with the

River Barrow, to Portarlington, to Mountmellick, and to Naas. In addition, there are two branches into the great boggy district of the central countries, the drainage of which partly supplies the canal with water. These branches serve also as reservoirs, there not being any natural lakes along this line. The total length of these extensions of this navigation, is sixty-five miles, making, in all, 164 miles of canal. The summit level is about Robertstown, at a distance of twenty-six miles from Dublin, and 279 feet above the level of the sea.

The number of passengers travelling by the packet boats on the Grand Canal, was, in 1833, 54,812; in 1835, it rose to 72,748, and, in 1837, was 100,695. Since which time the number has increased but little.

The total amount of tonnage carried, and the tolls levied, together with the nett income from passage boats, were, in the

YEAR.	TONNAGE.	TOLLS.
1827	179,173	£33,587 4 9½
1832	216,418	34,552 16 6
1837	215,910	37,557 7 1
1842	191,958	35,774 18 5

Of the canals in connexion with Lough Neagh, the Lagan navigation is the most important. It commences at Belfast, its entire length from which is twenty-eight and a-half miles. Its course is partly tidal, partly river, and partly canal. The usual tonnage of the boats is fifty tons. In 1836, there passed 894 boats, carrying 44,700 tons of goods, and paying £2,060 10s. 8d. tolls. The toll is 9½d. per ton for the entire length, and the freight, from 5s. to 6s.

The Newry Canal, communicating with the sea, about two miles below the town, passes northwards, for sixteen and a-half miles (Irish), to Whitecoat, where it joins the Bann, and by it passes into Lough Neagh. There are no passenger boats on this canal. In 1837, the traffic was, 102,332 tons, producing, in tolls, the sum of £3,505 11s. 5d.

The coal field of Tyrone, so fully described in the first chapter, had been originally supposed to be of much greater extent than subsequent examination has proved, and a canal was constructed, at the public expense, for conveying its produce to a distance. This canal, of about eleven miles, extends from Coal Island to the River Blackwater, a short distance from its confluence with Lough Neagh. The mining operations of that district being now so limited, the trade on this canal is proportionally small. In 1836, its total traffic was 7,291 tons of coals.

Within the last few years, an important line of canal communication has been opened, the *Ulster Canal*, which, commencing from the River Blackwater at Charlemont, near its junction with Lough Neagh, passes to the south-west, by Monaghan and Clones, and joins, after a course of forty-eight miles, the Upper Lough Erne. The eastern and western seas are thus nearly connected, by a line of water communication, which only requires some improvements at Enniskillen, and in the lower lake, to be perfectly continuous from Ballyshannon to Belfast, a distance of about 150 miles. This line has been in operation too short a time, to test its efficiency by the amount of traffic hitherto called into play, yet it is gratifying to observe, that, already, the *facilities of transport* have produced a considerable increase of industrial activity along its course. Thus, in the years ending April 1st, the traffic was

    1843, tons, 13,371, producing £1,261 toll,
    1844, ,,   17,585,   ,,   £1,976 ,,

The increase being, one-third of tonnage, and one-half of tolls, shewing the increase of traffic in the more valuable commodities.

Through the valley of the Boyne from Drogheda, by Slane, to Navan, a distance of nineteen miles, and below Drogheda for two and a-half miles to the sea, a navigation is carried on, partly by the river channel and partly by canal. There are no passage boats. In 1836. the total traffic was 10,194 tons, producing about £640 in tolls.

Such being the circumstances of the canal and river navigations, it remains to notice the numerous lakes available for the purposes of communication. Some of these have been already mentioned, as, in fact, expansions of the Shannon, and need no further reference.

In many places, lines of canals have been proposed, and some surveys executed, which, however, have not led to further results. A very useful project of this kind, was the improvement of the navigation of the Nore, above Innistiogue. Perhaps, however, the most important line of inland navigation proposed, in addition to those already existing in Ireland, is that for which surveys were executed by Mr. Mulvany, and which would connect the Ulster Canal and Lough Erne with the Shannon, at Leitrim. The length of canal on this line would be twenty-eight and a-half miles, and twenty-one miles of steam navigation on Lough Oughter, to Killeshandra. The estimated total cost was £170,000. The importance of this connexion may be estimated by a glance at the map, when it will be seen, that the network of inland navigation of the north-east of Ireland, is separated from the water communications of the south and centre, by the tract which this canal would intersect, and that, consequently, the two systems of traffic, now isolated, would by it be placed in connexion. Limerick would thus come into direct communication with Enniskillen and Ballyshannon, on the western, and with Belfast on the eastern, coast of Ulster, and a total line of 716 miles of inland navigation be opened out. The want of water carriage, in that part of the country, is shewn by the fact, that the heaviest articles of traffic, even timber, are brought from Newry, to Ballina, within a few miles of the Shannon, more by land, at an expense of 6d. per ton per mile, whilst water carriage, including all expenses of freight, tolls, &c., never exceeds $2\frac{1}{4}d$.

Inquiries lately made with reference to the drainage of the districts along this proposed canal, have shewn the feasibility of an important modification of it, in which the line passing from Leitrim by a series of small lakes and river courses, at present navigable but not connected, should reach Lough Erne direct, and the artificial water cuts, in place of being twenty-eight and a-half miles, should be but eight. The cost of completing this important navigation in this form should be but £80,000 beyond the expenses of drainage for agricultural purposes.

Ireland possesses not only the largest river in the British Islands, but also the largest inland sea, Lough Neagh, the coasts of which are formed by the Counties of Derry, Antrim, Tyrone, Armagh, and Down. Its area is estimated at about 100,000 acres. Its height above the sea is forty-six feet. It drains a considerable extent of the east of Ulster, the rivers Blackwater, Upper Bann, and Ballinderry flowing into it, and its superfluous water being removed by the Lower Bann. The shores possessing but little elevation, it is destitute of the picturesque character which heightens the interest of so many of our lakes, but as it presents above 100 miles of coast in a country swarming with an intelligent and industrious population, and by the Coal Island, Newry, Ulster, and Lagan Canals it is placed in communication with a large extent of the north of Ireland, it promises to be the future centre of extensive internal traffic. Already a commencement has been made. Steam vessels have been placed upon the lake, which collecting at various ports on the northern and western shores, the goods and passengers, convey them to the south and east. Portadown, which unites the advantages of being placed on the Bann, near the junction of the Newry Canal, and of being the present terminus of the Ulster Railway, is the principal emporium of the traffic on Lough Neagh. This precise amount of the steam traffic, I am not able to state in exact numbers, though it is certainly considerable.

The upper and lower Lough Erne, extending altogether a distance of about thirty miles, have been rendered in great part available for internal communication to Enniskillen, by the completion of the Ulster Canal. In fact, the multiplicity of islands in the upper lake renders its navigation similar to that of a canal. The lower lake, however, presents an important field for the introduction of steam traffic upon its ample surface. Its area is 27,645 acres. It is situated in average 150 feet above the level of the sea, and the channel contracting above Belleek to the river form, its waters are precipitated over a ledge of rocks, forming a magnificent cascade. Again at Ballyshannon a similar cataract occurs, by which the waters of this great basin are finally passed into the sea. The power of these falls of water has not been accurately calculated. It is certainly equivalent to many thousand horse in constant operation, and, if utilized with the facilities which those lakes and the canal would give for distribution of produce, the result should be most beneficial to the population of the surrounding districts. After the Shannon at Killaloe and Doonas, there is nothing in Ireland comparable as a source of mechanical power to the Erne at Belleek and Ballyshannon.

The picturesque solitudes of Lough Gill have been invaded by the power of steam for communicating between Sligo and Dromohaire. When the Shannon improvements are completed, the steamers on Lough Allen will be separated from those of Sligo by only a few miles of hilly country, presenting no insuperable obstacle to intercourse.

The province of Connaught is, however, that which deserves most attentive notice in relation to its navigable lakes. Its soil is not inferior to that of the rest of Ireland; some of the sweetest pastures, and most productive lands, are found within its limits. Its coasts abound with fish; its mountains are rich in ores; its people are willing to work, and travel hundreds of miles seeking for work, even at a rate which only allows them to sustain existence. Yet that province is the reproach of Ireland and the bye-word of Great Britain. Its population is relieved by charitable subscription from recurrent famines. Little more than one-half of its area has been made available for cultivation, and it is but a few years since its interior was first rendered accessible to industry by the formation of proper roads.

There exist in Connaught, independent of the Shannon Loughs which form its boundary, two groups of lakes, peculiarly fitted for navigation. The most important of these, consisting of Loughs Mask and Corrib, communicate with the sea at Galway by a river about three miles long, with a fall of fourteen feet, of which the water-power is described in page 86.

The area of Lough Corrib is 50,700 statute acres. Its length from Galway to Maam by Cong is about twenty-five miles, its breadth very variable, at greatest about fourteen miles. Its depth of water is fully sufficient for navigation. Its islands contain more than 1000 acres of fertile land. The waters of Lough Mask are poured into Corrib, but by subterraneous channels, the lakes being separated by a ridge of land of three miles broad. The area of Lough Mask and of Carra, which is an offset from it, is 26,265 acres. Its height eighty feet above the sea level.

To bring these three lakes into navigable communication with each other and with the sea, there would only be required about three miles of canal. The direct length of navigation opened would be about forty miles, and a coast of nearly 200 miles would have a cheap and ready outlet for its agricultural produce.

The second group of lakes in Connaught stands in connexion with that fine river, the Moy, which draining 1033 square miles of country, falls into the sea at Ballina. These are Loughs Conn and Cullin. Their area is about 14,000 acres. They present a direct navigation of eleven miles and fifty-three miles of coast. The height and power of the fall from these lakes is given in page 86.

Surveys of this district, with a view of opening this extensive lake navigation to the coast, and thus enabling the inhabitants to send out for export the produce of their fields at a low cost, were made by Mr. Bald. He shewed that the carriage by water would be in those localities not more than one-sixth that by land. That by an arrangement of canals, including but seventeen locks, a navigation of fifty-three miles direct could be secured, available to a district containing 800,000 inhabitants, who now possess none but the rudest and most expensive means of intercourse.

It is to be hoped that such criminal neglect as has hitherto impeded the progress of all such plans for ameliorating the condition of the people, may not continue. When a famine occurs in Connaught, money is raised in London to buy them bread as charity. It is much fitter that suitable means should

be adopted for enabling the people to earn it by honest labour.

When the navigation of the Connaught lakes is proceeded
with, it will become an important problem to determine on the
mode of communication with the Shannon. For this, various
plans have been proposed, but it would be premature for me
to enter upon the discussion of any of them.

A mode of transport which at the present day occupies public
attention much more than the common roads, or water-ways
which I have so far noticed, is the railway. Though totally
modern, not yet a generation old, this new agent in intercourse has assumed an importance, which entitles it to be considered as a power in promoting the development, not merely
of industry, but of civilization.   I shall of course not enter
into any general description of the theoretical circumstances
of railways, or of steam power as used upon them, but having
first noticed the condition of the existing and proposed railroads in Ireland, I shall apply myself to the brief discussion
of two questions which I consider important to this country,
that is, in whose hands the general control of railways should
be placed, and by what kind of power motion should be produced upon them.

We possess in actual operation but four railways in Ireland.   The Kingstown Railway, extending from Dublin to the
pier at Kingstown Harbour, six miles, lies along the southern
shore of the bay, and may be considered as altogether a passenger line for that extensive suburban villa district.

In the years ending March,

YEAR.	PASSENGERS.	TOTAL INCOME.
1842	1,632,085	£40,208 2 4
1843	1,758,878	42,401 3 1
1844	1,962,051	45,255 8 2

The financial and mechanical conditions of the line are illustrated by the following numbers:

For the year ending 27th March, 1844.

Total number of trains dispatched,	29,564
Miles travelled, ...	177,384
Average number of coaches per train, ...	7½
Passengers per train (average), .	66⅓
Consumption of coke per train per mile, ...	24¼lb
Average sum paid per passenger per mile, ...	0·968 penny.
Cost of locomotive power per train per mile, ...	11 pence.
Total weight moved *one mile*, . .	7,095,360 tons.

The Ulster Railway, which is completed, and has been for some time in actual work. From Belfast, it passes by Lisburn, Moira, and Lurgan, to Portadown, twenty-five miles. The traffic upon it appears steadily increasing.

For the years ending 1st March, there were,

YEAR.	PASSENGERS.	RECEIPTS.
1842–3	425,864	£21,148 15 10
1843–4	436,317	25,145 2 1

There is some traffic in goods on this line, and it appears to increase more rapidly than the passenger traffic; thus the receipts for carriage of goods, included in the above, was in 1842–3 £5123 10s. 9d., and in 1843–4 it became £8269 6s. 11d. The reports of the company do not state the weight of merchandize carried.

The railway from Dublin to Drogheda passes circuitously along the coast by Malahide and Balbriggan. Its length is thirty-one and three quarter miles. It has been open for public traffic, from May, 1844. In the period from 24th May to 31st December, the total number of passengers carried was 402,414, and the total receipts £19,625 18s. 9d.

None of the lines here mentioned, require any special notice as to the nature of the ground passed over, and details as to their cost and financial condition would be out of place.

The importance of railways as a means of developing the industrial resources of a country, especially in the absence of those other aids, by which, in many countries, their necessity is rendered less urgent, had long been felt by all seriously interested in the prosperity of Ireland, and led to the formation of the Railway Commission in 1838, which, under the principal guidance of the late Mr. Drummond and Sir J. Burgoyne, published a Report, which, although some details of its propositions may be combated or deviated from, remains a masterpiece of physical and statistical investigation, and will connect the names of its eminent authors permanently with the records of Irish progress. The strictness of official caution led to an estimate of the final return of profit, probably less than the circumstances justified, certainly much less than projectors were disposed to promise in the share market, and hence the effect of the Report was to damp the enthusiasm of railway speculations.

The principal of governmental control which was strongly advocated in the Report, and to which I shall by-and-by return, was also adverse to the feelings of those disposed to invest money in such undertakings, and was opposed to the existing English practice. Owing to these and other still more unreasonable influences, the provisions of the Report have not been in any one instance carried into effect, and the improvement of the condition of the people, which its authors had so fondly anticipated, remains as distant as six years ago, when the Report was written.

The Commissioners proposed the formation of two great lines of railway, one to the south-west, and the other to the north-west, from Dublin, starting from Barrackbridge: the south-western line was to have passed by Palmerstown and Lucan to Sallins, Rathangan, Monasterevan, Portarlington, and Maryborough. Near the latter, at the summit of the limestone country, between the valleys of the Nore and Barrow, it was proposed to form a branch to Kilkenny by Abbeyleix and Ballyragget.

" The distance between Dublin and the commencement of this branch is 52½ miles, and thence to Kilkenny is 26½ miles, making a total length, from Dublin to Kilkenny, of 79 miles.

"From the Maryborough summit, the line has been continued though the limestone country to the road from Borris-in-Ossory to Rathdowney, which it crosses at the distance of 66 miles from Dublin, and three miles from Borris-in Ossory, on the Limerick road; and this point, which will serve as a station for passengers and merchandize from the towns of Roscrea, Borris-in-Ossory, Castletown, Mountrath, and the districts surrounding them, must eventually become a point of very general resort.

"From the road to Borris-in-Ossory, the line pursues its south-western direction, passing near to the towns of Rathdowney, Templemore, and Thurles, to Holycross, in the county of Tipperary, where it is proposed that the line to Limerick should diverge.

" This line has been laid out with great care, skirting as close as levels would permit to the south-eastern base of the range of the Keeper Mountains, and thence, without encountering any difficulty, proceeding in a direct line to the city of Limerick.

" The distance by the proposed line of railway between Dublin and Holycross is 89¾ miles, and between Holycross and Limerick 35¾ miles, making a total distance between Dublin and Limerick of 125½ miles. This distance is only six miles longer than the direct post-road between those points, a circumstance we deem very satisfactory, when it is considered that the proposed railway communication between Limerick and Dublin will be effected by a divergence from the Cork line of only 35¾ miles in length.

" From Holycross the main Cork line proceeds in a southern direction to Cashel, and thence to Marhill, near New Inn, in the county of Tipperary, at which point it is intended that the line to Clonmel and Waterford should commence; but, to complete a direct railway communication between Limerick and Waterford, it is also proposed that this branch-line should be continued in a western direction, from Marhill towards

Limerick, and, crossing the River Suir at Golden, join the line from Holycross to Limerick at Donaghill.

" The distance from Marhill, by Golden, to Donaghill, is 13 miles; and by adopting this arrangement there will be a saving of distance between Limerick and Waterford of 14½ miles; without it, all the traffic from Limerick to Waterford must necessarily pass from Donaghill, round by Holycross to Marhill, in order to reach the commencement of the Waterford line.

" Continuing in a southern direction from Marhill, the Cork line follows the valley of the River Suir to Cahir, situated at the eastern extremity of the Galtees Mountains, at which point, owing to the physical structure of the country, it has been necessary to adopt a south-western course, passing through the narrow valley interposed between the Galtees and Kilworth Mountains, whence it continues by Michelstown to Kildorrery, and thence to the town of Mallow, situated on the River Blackwater.

" From Mallow the main line takes a direct southern course to Cork, and necessarily crosses a ridge of slate country, which intervenes between the limestone valleys of the River Blackwater, at Mallow, and the River Lee, on which Cork is situated.

" Here experience fully confirms the remarkable circumstance to which allusion has been made, in treating of the geology of the country, that throughout the whole of the lines which have been described, no engineering difficulties worthy of notice occur, as long as we continued in the limestone country; but the moment we attempt to cross the slate district, situated between Cork and Mallow, we encounter an elevation of 222 feet in 7 miles 3 furlongs, which must be overcome by adopting steeper gradients than those required for any other part of the lines we have described, and which never leave the great limestone district of the interior of the country. Owing to this favourable nature of the ground, we have not found it necessary to cross any of those high table lands, which can only be traversed by tunnelling; but by allowing the lines to undulate to a certain degree with the surface of the country, according to the revised system of gradients, all deep cuttings have been avoided. Hence the several railways which we recommend for the south of Ireland can be formed at the comparatively moderate expense stated in the estimate contained in Mr. Vignoles' Report."

For the northern line it was proposed to form a trunk to Navan, and from thence two main branches, one west to Enniskillen, and one north to Armagh, which, communicating with the Ulster Railway, would thus reach Belfast. The surveys for this line were executed by Mr. Macneill. The Report proceeds:

"By reference to the map it will be seen that the first 28 miles, namely, from Dublin to Navan, are common to both the Armagh and Enniskillen lines; at Navan they diverge, that to Belfast taking a north course, passing near to Carrickmacross, and through Castleblaney to Armagh; the distance between Navan and Armagh being 57½ miles, and the total distance from Dublin to Armagh 85½ miles.

"Between Dublin and Navan, where the line crosses the limestone country, the gradients are better, and the average cost per mile will be £4,200 less than where it passes through the slate country already described, which extends nearly for the whole distance from Navan to Armagh.

"The north-west or Enniskillen line, on diverging from the Armagh line at Navan, has been laid out in the valley of the River Blackwater, passing through Kells and Virginia. As far as Kells the country is unusually favourable, but between that point and Cavan, and from thence to Newtown-Butler, in the County of Fermanagh, the cost of forming will be considerable, owing to the hilly character of the slate district. Beyond Newtown-Butler the line passes through the flat country skirting the north-eastern margin of Upper Lough Erne. In such a locality the gradients, as might be expected, are excellent, and the cost is proportionally reduced.

"The town of Enniskillen, situated between Upper and Lower Lough Erne, may be considered as a central station, towards which both passengers and commercial traffic may be expected to converge for a considerable circuit, including the important towns of Londonderry, Letterkenny, Strabane, Omagh, Donegal, Ballyshannon, and Sligo, and hence, for the present, it is considered to be the most suitable for the termination of the north-western railway.

" In forming a comparison of the advantage which the lines to the north and north-west of Ireland, recommended by us, possess over the others to which we have alluded, there is only one which traverses the interior of the country, to which we think it necessary to refer, namely, that from Dublin to Armagh, passing through Ardee and Castleblaney, already mentioned.

" For general purposes this line would not be favourable to the views adopted by us; it is not sufficiently near the coast to be used for connecting the important commercial towns of Newry and Dundalk with Dublin; and, on the other hand, it does not strike far enough into the interior to render any portion of it suitable for a main line to the north-west.

" In an engineering point of view it is likewise inferior, inasmuch as it is proposed to cross the River Boyne, by an embankment, about 460 yards in length, the greater portion of which, as shewn by the section, would exceed 100 feet in height; while the line which we propose crosses the river above Navan, by an embankment of 260 yards in length, and at an average height of but 33 feet; and likewise between Castleblaney and Armagh the line is not so advantageous, either in length or gradients, as that laid out under our direction.

" In respect to the coast line, which has been surveyed from Drogheda by Dundalk to Newry, we have to observe, that it may be considered altogether in the light of a speculation which has no reference to the internal commercial traffic of the country, but as one which will afford a desirable facility for passenger intercourse between the important commercial towns which it is intended to connect."

Such were the propositions of the Railway Commissioners in 1838. There were also various lines proposed by private companies, of which the following are the most important.

A line to Kilkenny, which leaving Dublin at Kilmainham, passed parallel to the line adopted by the Commissioners, but at a higher level, and crossed the Grand Canal at Sallins: it then passed across the Curragh of Kildare to Athy, and followed the left bank of the Barrow by Carlow to Leighlin Bridge, from whence, along the foot of the Colliery Hills, it passed to Kilkenny. This line, considered solely as regarding Kilkenny, was perfect, but it was not adapted for such continuations and branches as could render it a part of a general southern system.

A railway from Limerick to Waterford was one of the first proposed in Ireland, and surveys were executed by Nimmo, whose favourable opinion of the locality has been confirmed by all succeeding engineers. Regarding it the Report says:

" By reference to our passenger and traffic maps it will be seen, that between Limerick and Clonmel the present intercourse is comparatively trifling; but the known resources of the country are so considerable, that rational expectations might be entertained of a favourable result from a railway which would open a direct communication from the counties of Clare, Kerry, Limerick, and Tipperary, to the markets of Bristol, the south of England generally, and to London.

" Still we cannot admit that, if abandoned to its own local resources, this railway would yield profits sufficient to remunerate a company for its construction. But blended, as we propose that it should be, with the general lines of intercommunication between Dublin, Cork, Limerick, and Waterford, we conceive that the expense of the connecting branch, thirteen miles in length, between Donaghill and Marhill, already alluded to, will be considered as a minor consideration when compared with the advantage which the country must derive from the completion of a direct railway communication between Limerick and Waterford."

A company is now formed for constructing this line, and there is little doubt but that it will be one eminently useful and remunerative.

From the period of the Railway Commissioners' Report until some few months back, the establishment of extended railway intercourse through Ireland had been almost totally lost sight of. The formation of the Dublin and Cashel Railway Company has been, however, the herald to a period of activity and enterprize which, although possessing many of the characters of a speculative paroxysm, cannot pass over without conferring vast benefit upon the country, by creating a network of the most efficient means of communication, and leading indirectly to a rapid advance of industrial ideas and operations. The number of railway projects now under consideration is so great, and many of them competing and conflicting lines, that they cannot be expected or desired all to be carried into effect, and it will, therefore, suffice for the majority to mention, in very few words, their general direction.

The Dublin and Cashel Railway, the works for which have been just commenced, and which will probably be the main stem of all the lines branching to the south and west, passes by Sallins and Kildare, to Monasterevan, and thence by Portarlington, Maryborough, and Thurles, to Cashel. This route differs but little from that recommended by the Commissioners. The country through which it passes is highly favourable. It is thrown rather more into connexion with the intervening towns, and thereby, probably, the facilities for traffic augmented. Cashel is but a small change of terminus from Holycross, which the Commissioners recommended, and which will be in practice, most probably, the point of derivation of the secondary lines.

There are proposed, in connexion with the main Cashel stem, an extension to Cork, which, passing from Holycross by Tipperary to the north of the Galtee mountains, should proceed by Kilmallock, Buttevant, and Mallow, into Cork. In competition with this, other parties propose to carry out the Commissioners' line, which, proceeding south of the Galtees, passes by Mitchelstown to Mallow, from whence the course of both lines nearly coincide to Cork. Beyond Cork a line will probably be extended to Bandon.

From Tipperary a branch is proposed to proceed westward to Limerick, and to be continued on the north bank of the Shannon and Fergus to Ennis.

Very important branches of the Cashel line, are those proposed to Wexford and Kilkenny, the former starting from the trunk at Kildare, enters the valley of the Barrow, and passes by Athy to Carlow. From thence it crosses through the gorge in the granite ridge, and entering the valley of the Slaney, descends by Newtownbarry and Enniscorthy, to Wexford. The Kilkenny branch is proposed to skirt the western edge of the Leinster coal field, passing by Ballyragget and Abbeyleix, and joining the main stem at Maryborough.

Short lines connecting Kilkenny and Wexford with Waterford are proposed. The Kilkenny connexion is proposed to be laid down, as an experiment, with wood, impregnated with plaster of Paris, after trying which the company will probably adopt some more rational method of proceeding.

To bring the western coast at Galway into direct communication, by railway, with the metropolis, is the object of several plans, one of which is to form a branch of the southern line at Portarlington, which, proceeding by Tullamore to Athlone, should then pass by Ballinasloe to Galway. A very simple and economical line might be formed on the bank of the Grand Canal, joining the Cashel trunk at Sallins. and extending to Ballinasloe. Another proposal is to form a line on the banks of the Royal Canal to Mullingar, from whence branches should extend to Longford and Athlone, but it is said that this Company objects to going beyond the Shannon. This is quite fair, as regards the speculators, who naturally wish to have to do only with the most profitable portion, but the Government should look to the benefit of the country at large. The line to the Shannon should not be granted to any company which would not go beyond the Shannon to the western coast.

To connect Dublin with Belfast, a line is now proposed, in continuation of the Drogheda line, to Portadown, where it will communicate with the Ulster Railway. The distance of this junction line will be fifty-six miles; with the exception of the vicinity of Newry the route does not present any important difficulties, and Sir John Macneill's estimate for its construction is £12,000 per mile. The general direction is the same as the coach road. From Drogheda there is also contemplated a railway to Navan and Kells, a distance of twenty-three miles; this line, being principally in the valley of the

Boyne, along the junction of the limestone and slate districts, is peculiarly favourable, and is estimated to be completed for £10,000 per mile. By an extension of this branch a communication may be formed with the Shannon by Longford, and thence to Sligo, which would give the north of Connaught a very direct means of access to the eastern coast for the exportation of agricultural produce, and also probably bring into more active play, the field for enterprize which the vicinity of Lough Allen presents.

The Ulster Railway Company are about extending their line by Armagh to Monaghan, and thus opening out the central counties to Belfast. The line to be pursued beyond that point is not determined on.

The inland line abutting on Enniskellan, proposed by the Commissioners, has been already noticed. This being abandoned now, it is proposed to connect that important town with the Dublin and Belfast coast line, by a railway which should proceed either by Monaghan and Armagh to Newry, or by Castleblaney to Dundalk. The latter line certainly appears the more favourable in its general character. From Enniskillen a line is projected by Omagh and Strabane to Londonderry, and from Omagh also a line has been proposed by Dungannon to Coleraine.

From Belfast a line is projected to pass by Carrickfergus to Ballymena.

Such are the principal plans now under consideration for forming railways in Ireland. It is to be hoped that the decisions of those, to whose lot judgment will ultimately fall, may be guided by an enlightened desire for the sound prosperity of the country.

In all of the lines of railway so far noticed, whether in actual work or only proposed, the source of power in use or contemplated is the ordinary locomotive engine. There has, however, been recently brought into play a means of locomotion on railways which bids fair to replace, at least in many localities, that hitherto in use; it is by atmospheric propulsion, of which, in fact, this country has become the most remarkable example, by the specimen of it which is in action for a mile and three-quarters from Kingstown to the village of Dalkey.

On an ordinary line of railway, as, for example, the Kingstown line, the weight of the train and engine is usually about forty-five tons, of which the engine weighs fifteen tons, and the carriages and passengers about thirty. It hence follows that of the total power required to move the train, one-third is actually absorbed in the motion of the engine without any return. The cost of fuel necessary to produce steam is thus half as much again as should suffice if there were only the useful load to move, and the importance of this difference will be at once felt, on considering that the cost of power is by far the largest item in the expense of working a railway, and in the cost of power the fuel is again the predominant item. Thus, in the years ending respectively March 6th and 27th, 1844, the expenses on the existing railways were:

	ULSTER.	KINGSTOWN.
Cost of power, ...	£3729 12 8	£8128 18 8
Of which the cost of coke was, ...	1850 9 10	2264 17 11
Whilst the cost of maintenance of way was but	1048 10 7	2253 11 8
And the total gross expenditure, ...	14539 0 0	20599 12 6

The annual cost of the fuel expended in giving motion to the engines, without reference to the carriages, goods, or passengers, and on which no profit accrues, is, consequently, on the Ulster line, about £600, and on the Kingstown line, about £750 per annum, besides a proportion of the general expenses which cannot be well separated.

The great massiveness and weight of the locomotive engine render necessary also a degree of strength in the rails, bridges, and embankments of the line, which otherwise might well be dispensed with. Thus we may consider a passenger carriage to weigh, as is usual, three tons, and to contain twenty-eight passengers, which, at fourteen to a ton, gives two tons, making the whole weight five tons, or we may allow it to be even six tons, which, if the carriage be provided with but four wheels, gives a pressure upon each wheel of a ton and a half. The construction of all the bearing parts of the railway must be in accordance with this amount of pressure. If, however, the locomotive engine be taken into account, its weight being considered, as is usual, as fifteen tons, and that it be supported on six wheels, the pressure on each wheel is two tons and a half, and the strength of every portion of the line must be augmented beyond what would suffice for the paying part of the train, in the proportion of 5 to 3. Now to make the railway stronger, in the ratio of 5 to 3, involves far more than an increased expense in the proportion of 5 to 3, and it may be safely asserted that so far as all the parts which are common to both systems of locomotion on railways are concerned, the existence of the locomotive engine considerable increases the necessary expense of construction.

On the principle of atmospheric propulsion, which is now in action upon the short railway from Kingstown to Dalkey, the power is applied at a fixed point to work an air pump, by which the air is continually removed from an iron pipe, which is laid down along the centre of the line. The carriages are connected with this pipe by a piston, upon which, when the internal air is exhausted, the external air presses, and as it is found practicable, on the line of a mile and three-quarters, to obtain a vacuum of twenty-four inches in the barometer, there is generated an effective pressure of twelve pounds per square inch of piston area, or for the pipe of fifteen inches diameter, a force of 2129lb. The valve mechanism which regulates the passage of the air, and opens and closes the apertures in the tube as the train passes, is found in practice to be so far perfect as to leave, after all leakage, a force equivalent to that of the most powerful locomotive engines, generated in the most economical manner, and possessing in its application peculiar advantages for railway intercourse.

In the cost of power it has been shewn, that one of the largest items is the cost of coke. On the Ulster Railway, the coke cost 34s. per ton, until they began to manufacture for themselves, and even then it cost 26s. The Dublin and Kingstown Company pay for coke at the Gas Works 23s. 4d. per ton. Now in the locomotive boiler the coke does not evaporate more than eight times its weight of water : but if the fuel be burned under a fixed engine, and that in place of coke, coal be used, which can be had for 12s. per ton, the ton will evaporate, with Cornish boilers, at least twelve tons of water, and the steam power, to produce which should cost £1000 for coke in a locomotive engine, may be generated with the fixed engine for £333 worth of coal. Not merely may coke be burned to work the air pump of an atmospheric line, but in localities where coal might be expensive, turf may be used, and thus the system becomes at once applicable to the centre and west of Ireland, where gas coke should be unattainable except at a great expense. The advantages of fixed power do not even stop here. The power need not be that of steam. At every change of level along a line of railway in this country, water power may be made available, and in such case the economy in substituting it for the most expensive form of steam power may be estimated from what has been so fully discussed in the third chapter.

A further important economy in the principle of fixed power communicated by the flexible medium of the atmosphere, is that its effect does not alter with the inclination of the road. On an incline the locomotive engine has to draw up itself as well as the train. Let us suppose an incline where the total drag on the engine is doubled ; now unless the velocity of the transport is sacrificed, or an additional engine employed as help, the size of the train must be reduced, and this reduction must be made altogether at the expense of the paying part of the train, so that finally at certain inclines the engine could only draw itself up, and be incapable of bringing any load. It is this peculiarity of the locomotive engine that has hitherto rendered it the object of engineers to avoid inclines, and to retain the lines as nearly horizontal as possible, even at a vast sacrifice of cost in the construction. If, however, the power be fixed at a distance, and be brought into action on the train by the flexible medium of the atmosphere, the mechanical force will always move a proportional amount of carriages or goods, while the heavy locomotive being absent, all tend to remunerate the line for the loss of transport. Hence, inclines are available on the atmospheric plan, which would be absolutely impracticable on a line worked by locomotives, and by this, as well as the other considerations previously noticed, the general engineering conditions of the railway become exceedingly simplified.

The more intimate connexion with the line by the pipe and piston which gives steadiness to the atmospheric train, and enables it to traverse curves too sharp for the safe passage of an ordinary train, is another advantage : besides that the absence of the locomotive, from which, in most cases of accidents, the injury is sustained, presents an additional source of safety.

The only source of expenditure on an atmospheric line, which does not exist to as great an extent on the locomotive line, is that of the iron exhaustion pipe. This, however, cannot be equivalent to the sources of economy I have described, and hence I do not hesitate to conclude, that in regard to facility of execution, of economy in working and construction, and in safety and rapidity of transit, the principle of fixed power working by atmospheric pressure deserves the most attentive consideration on the part of those engaged in railway enterprizes, especially in this country, where the substitution of cheap coal, or turf, or still cheaper water power, for expensive coke, may, in many districts, make the difference between a profitable line, or a losing speculation.

Such being the general conditions of the application of atmospheric power to locomotion, it remains to notice the general construction of the trial line now in operation between Kingstown and Dalkey. It is erected on a line of tramway formerly used for conveying stone to Kingstown Harbour. The total length is a mile and three-quarters. Its average inclination is 1 in 115, but in some parts it is 1 in 57: a slope on which a locomotive engine could move little besides itself. It presents several curves sharper than any constructed on ordinary lines of railway, one of less than an eighth of a mile radius, so that on this short line there are actually so many obstacles, that its success may be considered as decisive, so far as the application of the power is concerned. The engine at Dalkey is of 100 horse power; this is, for ulterior objects, much greater than that required. The usual average velocity of the trains ascending the line is thirty miles, but a velocity of sixty miles per hour is easily attainable. The trains descend the line from Dalkey by the force of gravity. They occupy usually about three minutes and a half in the ascent, and about four minutes in the descent of the mile and three-quarters. The pipe used on this line is fifteen inches diameter. It is in ten feet lengths, which weigh each twelve cwt. There should be, therefore, per mile 528 lengths, weighing 317 tons, and the iron in the screws and valves might amount to about sixteen tons, making a total of 333 tons of iron per mile of single way, which is the only point in which this mode is more expensive than the ordinary railway.

The Dalkey atmospheric line will probably be extended to Wicklow, or even farther south along the coast, and thereby satisfactorily bring into play the full powers of this remarkable mechanism of locomotion.

The influence of the railway system on the industrial and social circumstances of the country, is so great, as to demand, upon the part of the Government, the most careful supervision. This has not been as yet accorded to it. When railways were first proposed, their results were not foreseen, nor their vast power understood, even by their advocates, still less by the Government, and hence, being looked upon as individual speculations, into which every capitalist should be at liberty to enter, when and where he liked, and to realize as much profit as he could, there was only required a parliamentary procedure, similar to that necessary for obtaining permission to open a new line or branch of common road. The railway, when once opened, took possession necessarily of the entire intercourse between its terminations. It instantly abolished the usual and previous modes of travelling, and this once effected, all fear of competition was removed, and the cost of the transport was rendered such as the managers thought would be most remunerative. The velocities were also kept far below what the system is capable of producing, for the expense increases very rapidly with the velocity, and hence to obtain the greatest amount of profit the speed must be kept low.

When a proposition for a new railway is brought before Parliament it is inevitably opposed, either by those who, desirous of forming a line in a different direction, advance their claims to a monopoly of their own; or by such as, having property along the line, are desirous of obtaining the greatest possible amount of compensation, and seek to enhance their importance by strong representations of the injury they sustain. By such opposition the expense of obtaining the necessary bill is enormously increased; landed proprietors of influence in either house, through whose localities the line may pass, require to be conciliated ; the energies of the law agents and others employed for the adverse parties, are exerted to the uttermost, as, no matter how the railway eventuates, whether the proprietors ever realize a fraction on their investment, or the public derive any increase of means of intercourse, the law and engineering expenses must be paid, no matter how enormous they may have become. Those expenses have actually amounted in many cases to £2000 per mile on the entire line, and in average are not less than £1000 per mile, wherever there is opposition, no matter whether well founded or not. All this must ultimately be defrayed by the public. The companies regard it of course only as a part of their investment, on which profit is to be made equally with that for the construction of the railway, or for the expenses of the power. These preliminary operations furnish, however, a rich harvest to solicitors and engineers, and hence have arisen throughout England a vast number of railway enterprizes, which, undertaken without suitable investigation as to their final results, have brought ruin upon those persons who were induced to embark their property in them. There are altogether in operation in the British Islands 1732 miles of railway. Of these 1014 miles pay an interest of £6 6s. 7d. per £100 on their capital, which amounts to £4 19s. 4d. per cent. on their market price. There are 571 miles of railway on which the return in no case ex-

ceeds £4 per cent. on the paid up capital : in a few it amounts
to £2 10s., and in some but to 10s. per £100.   The remaining
147 miles consist of branch lines, subordinate to the first class,
and producing about from 3½ to 4 per cent.   It is thus evident
that nearly one-third of the entire extent of railway in England
has been an absolutely unfortunate speculation, and yet on
these bad lines a total capital of £18,500,000 has been expended, the present value of which is now not more than
£13,000,000.

On the other hand the companies which are in possession of
the great lines of intercourse realize enormous profits.   The
London and Birmingham having cost £5,923,000, pay £11 2s.
per cent.   The Liverpool and Manchester, and Grand Junction, having cost respectively £1,515,000 and £2,319,000, pay
each £10 per cent., the maximum allowed by law.   The lines
of intercourse being thus absolutely private speculation, one
set of capitalists are ruined, another set are enriched, but the
public, so vitally interested in the main question of facility of
intercourse, is left totally out of consideration.

With those examples of profit on one side and of loss upon
another, it is easily understood that no difficulty would be
found in obtaining capitalists ready to construct those leading
lines which are certain of being the great means of intercourse
with the capital of the country.   But capitalists will not be
forthcoming to extend those lines into the variety of districts
where the means of intercourse are most required ; where the
railroad would be a source of social stimulus towards improvement, and by connecting together the most remote parts of the
island, and the extremes of our civilization, diffuse the activity
of industry and good example over all its parts.   That would
not pay.   The great trunks near Dublin will certainly pay ;
and hence the capitalists will obligingly take possession of
them.   And similarly, if all the provisions which come up for
the supply of Dublin, were conducted to the same market, and
that the power was given to an individual to levy what toll he
liked before the inhabitants could get any food, there is no
doubt but that we would find capitalists ready to build the

market. Such a case is just the parallel to the main trunk railways.

Let us conceive this country destitute of roads, and that an individual undertook to make a road, on condition that no person should be allowed to travel or hold communication with his neighbour except by his road ; that no person should, when on the road, travel at a greater or less speed than the owner of the road approved of; that no person should travel at any other hours than those which the owner ordered ; and that the owner should have the power of charging any sum he chose for the use of his road; and finally, that this power should be eternal; that no matter what advances the district made in industry, intelligence, activity, it should still remain bound to the conditions of this road proprietor. Would not this be an intolerable grievance ? And yet every item in that catalogue is realized in the actual circumstances under which railways are placed. For the idea of competing lines, which shall keep the existing companies on their good behaviour, is perfectly chimerical; the practical fact being, that the railway, once formed, is a monopoly of the strictest kind.

Similar considerations have presented themselves to almost every person who has had occasion to study the general relations of railways. The following passage from the concluding section of the Irish Commissioners' Report, is illustrative of the general argument, and valuable in addition, as shewing the deliberate opinion of some of the most eminent men by whom questions of the kind have been considered.

" It is a favourite opinion with many that all undertakings of this description are best left to the free and unfettered exercise of private enterprise, and that the less the State interferes, either in prescribing their execution, or controlling their subsequent operation and management, the better.

" We are fully sensible of the great advantages to be obtained by allowing full scope to the vigour, energy, and intelligence of individuals associated for such important purposes ; and that it would be equally inconsistent with the interests and with the rights of society were such exertions crippled or restrained by unnecessary or impolitic regulations. But we ap-

prehend that the essential difference between railways and any
other description of public works has been overlooked, and
that power and privileges have been conceded to private companies, which should be exercised only under the direct authority of the State, or under regulations enforced by effective
superintendence and control.

" So great are the powers, so vast the capabilities of a railroad, that it must, wherever established, at once supersede the
common road; and not only will all the public conveyances now
in use disappear, but even the means of posting will, in all pro-
bability, rapidly decline, and eventually, perhaps, cease to be
found along its line.   These effects may be expected as the
necessary consequences of opening a railway.   Its superiority
is too manifest and decided to admit of rivalry; it possesses
almost unlimited means of accommodation; no amount of traffic exists on any road, or is likely to exist, which a single railway is not capable of conveying; no concourse of passengers
which it cannot promptly dispose of; the velocity of the locomotive, when impelled even at a very considerable reduction
of its full power, surpasses the greatest speed which the best
appointed coach on the best made road can maintain : in short,
where the capabilities of the system are brought fully into operation, they present such an accumulation of advantages, as
to render it an instrument of unequalled power in advancing
the prosperity of a country.

" It therefore deeply concerns the public, whose welfare is
inseparably connected with all that tends to improve the internal resources, or to maintain the commercial and manufacturing superiority of these countries, that such works should
be promoted; and consequently, every encouragement, consis-
tent with the regard due to other interests, should be given to
capitalists who may be willing to undertake them.   Their propositions should be submitted to a competent and duly constituted tribunal; and if approved, should be adopted and stamped
as national enterprizes.   As such they should be protected from
all unnecessary expense—from extravagant demands for compensation—from vexatious opposition, and from the ruinous

competition of other companies. To that extent they have a strong claim on the protection of the State.

"But, on the other hand, the public interest would require that they should be bound by such conditions, and held subject to such well-considered regulations and effective control, as shall secure to the country at large the full benefit and accommodation of this admirable system.

"The practice hitherto followed in England has been almost the very reverse of that which we here recommend. No preliminary steps are taken on behalf of the public, to ascertain whether the proposed railroad be well adapted to its specific object, or calculated to form a part of a more general system. The best and the worst devised schemes are entertained alike, being equally exposed to opposition, and left equally unprotected against the difficulties which interested parties may raise up against them. Nay, a railway bill may be passed, or it may be rejected; but the fate of the project merely proves the number and influence of its respective supporters or opponents. Its failure or success is no test whatever of its merits, as a measure of general utility; for that consideration forms a very small part of the inquiry before Parliament."

It appears from all these considerations that the great channels of public intercourse should not be rendered private property; that, in the language of an enlightened Belgian minister, to whose reports on other subjects I shall have occasion elsewhere to refer: "the object desired in the construction of a railway should be not the gain of an individual, but the extension of the traffic and communications of the country to the utmost limits of the public capability, at the lowest rate of charge, at which the original outlay can be reimbursed." . . . "The project undertaken by Government is an establishment which should neither be a burthen nor a source of revenue, and requiring merely that it should cover its own expenses, consisting of the charge of maintenance and repairs, with a further sum for the interest and gradual redemption of the invested capital." The systems upon which the railways of England and of Belgium have been constructed are thus completely

opposite, and the way in which each works, is such as might
have been expected from this opposition of principles.   As the
able author of the pamphlet entitled Railway Reform says :
" The object of the one is to tax the public the maximum of
the most profitable rate, that of the other the minimum of the
most economical expenditure ; the one to produce the greatest
profit to private individuals, and the other to confer the greatest
benefit on the whole community.   What are the relative charges
by each ?   On one of our railways, from London to Birmingham for instance, the distance is 112 miles, and the fare by the
mail is £1 12s. 6d.   For the same distance in Belgium, in a
similar class carriage, the fare would be fourteen francs, or
just one-third of what it is in England."

I have endeavoured thus to explain the reasons which have
induced me to conclude, that it is, at the present time, a vital
question with this country, on what plan the organization of a
network of railways should be constructed.   I have left out
of question the argument which has often been advanced with
much force, that private companies proceed to the execution
of such works with a carelessness of expenditure which could
be avoided if the entire were under strict central superintendence.   It is true that many lines of railway in England have
cost sums so enormous, as to manifest the most wasteful ex-
travagance, or the most discreditable carelessness, but I consider that a great part of this high expenditure arose from
the ignorance and timidity of engineers, who, the system being
in its infancy, considered themselves limited to a horizontality
of line, which enormously increased the outlay.   The future
lines, whether private or governmental, will be much more
economically executed than such undertakings have hitherto
been.   This, however, does not alter the general conclusion
that the great highways of the country should belong to the
country, and that the means of intercourse of the population
should be under the regulation of the State.

It is of course not within my duties nor my powers to propose
such measures as would give the public a proper control over
the times, charges, and velocities of the means of intercourse.
Such plans have been brought forward, and by those whose

knowledge and position rendered them peculiarly competent
to the task. Thus let capitalists make the railway, but let
their investment be not a speculation but a stock, on which they
should get a secure but limited interest, and at $4\frac{1}{2}$ per cent.
abundance of capital could be obtained; let the districts
within a certain distance of the line secure that interest; if
the railway realize a higher interest, let the difference go to
alleviate the other burthens on the land of the vicinity. Now
it must be recollected that no prudent capitalists will make a
railway for themselves, unless with a moral certainty of its paying more than $4\frac{1}{2}$ per cent., so that the difference of result is,
that should the line be made by the capitalists for the country,
if it paid 6 per cent. the country would have $1\frac{1}{2}$ profit to apply
to other local objects, and could control velocities, arrange
hours, and reduce fares as they thought fit, whilst if the capitalist make the railway on his own account, he pockets the
entire 6 per cent. of profit, and the public has no control, but
must submit to any regulations he likes to make.

The landed proprietors in many of our counties were, however, terribly frightened at the idea of the localities being
made liable for the interest, and the most exaggerated statements were circulated as to the amount for which the districts
would thus be responsible. I believe that if the subject was
generally understood, this alarm, which was so fatal to the important principle of keeping in their own hands the control of
their own highways, would be dissipated. The probable lia-
bilities have been in fact accurately calculated, and are as follows:

If we suppose, as was at one time contemplated, three trunk
lines issuing from Dublin, and passing northwards to Armagh,
westwards to Mullingar, and southwards to Cashel, their cost,
according to the highest estimate which had been made, should
be,

To Cashel, 100 miles, ...	£1,300,060
To Mullingar, 49 miles, ...	459,600
To Armagh, 92 miles, ...	1,185,100
Total, 241 miles, ...	£2,944,700

2 c

And to secure the repayment of 4½ per cent. interest, the districts through which the lines passed should be liable to assessment, in proportion to their vicinity to the railway, and the probable benefit derived from it. If the line realized 4½ per cent., of course the districts had nothing to pay. If it realized more than 4½, of course the districts had the overplus as absolute gain. But if there were a deficiency of receipts of 1 per cent., then the localities should be assessed in the amount of from nine-tenths of a penny, to one and two-tenths penny per statute acre of arable land per annum, for the lands judged most benefited, and in from one-sixth to one-tenth of a penny for those least benefited. Supposing no return whatsoever on the railway, and that the entire interest had to be made up, the tax should be per acre of arable land, from 4d. to 5¼d. for the districts most, and 1d. to 1¾d. for the districts least benefited.

It may appear that I have unne ssarily dwelt on these topics, now that the question appears definitely settled, and that not merely in England, where the system was already in operation, but also in this country, where, the field being practically new, a different mode might have been tried, the property, control, and construction of railways are to be left to private capitalists. I am satisfied, however, that the defects of the existing system are so rapidly augmenting in importance and notoriety, that before long, the question must be discussed anew, and as it is important that sound ideas should be placed before the public for consideration, prior to the period of actual judgment, I have so far entered upon their discussion.

From the geological and topographical details regarding the surface of the country, which have occupied so much of the preceding chapters, it will be easily understood, that Ireland is most favourably circumstanced for the construction of railways. The great limestone plain, which occupies an area in the interior of the country of not less than 10,000 square miles, presents facilities for railway engineering scarcely to be equalled. In the north and south the mountain ranges afford some obstacles, which, however, are not beyond the usual run of engineering difficulties, that are every day overcome in such undertakings, and there is hence no physical reason why this country should not rapidly acquire an efficient system of railway intercourse. In nothing is the difference between Ireland and England more marked than in the extent of navigable rivers, of canals, and railroads, possessed by the two countries.

Independent of common roads, of which I do not know any estimate, there are in

		ENGLAND.	IRELAND.
Canals,	(statute miles), ...	2478	362
Navigable rivers,	,, ...	1820	380
Railroads,	,, ...	1742	64

What renders this contrast the more remarkable is, that the great majority of these facilities of internal intercourse are spread over a surface not greater than that of Ireland. In fact, the inhabitants of almost every district of the sister kingdom have placed at their very doors the means of the most perfect access to markets for their produce and the materials of their manufactures. They are thus enabled to prosecute their various departments of industry under the most economical conditions. Time is money: labour is money: the canal, the river, or the railroad, which places its facilities at the disposal of the manufacturer or farmer in England, is an increase of money price for what he brings to market, which enables him to undersell and ruin the Irish artizan, whose country is left in a condition of comparative barbarism, and the energy which might clear out the course of rivers, might cut canals, and construct railroads, is spent in fighting about theories which few of either party are in a condition to understand.

It only remains for the present subject, to notice the circumstances of Ireland as to her capabilities and position for foreign trade. In this respect there is no country in the world her superior. She is placed, as it were, by nature, the key of the two hemispheres, the point by which America first communicates with Europe, and the last on which the traveller to the west can pause. Her westerly situation enables vessels from her ports to escape the perils of channel navigation, and at once to obtain an offing, which enables them to bear out for any port of either continent. The evidence collected by parliamentary inquiries as to the advantages of harbours on the western coast is quite decisive. The voyage from America to the west of Ireland and back again, could frequently be made in the time that vessels take in clearing the channel from Liverpool, from London, or from Glasgow.

Lord Sheffield, whose acute judgment will be admitted, and who certainly was not biassed by Irish prejudices, notices this position in a passage which is amusingly candid. He says, when speaking of the impolicy of repealing the navigation laws between England and Ireland, which was then clamourously demanded by this country: "Her object is to become the mart of Europe for the trade of America, for which she is so well suited, by her western situation immediately open to the ocean, and accessible almost with every wind; her vessels often crossing the Atlantic in a shorter time than the shipping of London require to clear the channel. In addition, her ships can be victualled infinitely cheaper, and every necessary of life being low, as well as public taxes, the general charge of conducting trade will be proportionately less." Now this object, which Lord Sheffield so much feared, is precisely what should be the ambition of this country. Her position fits her for it, and it is only by the absence of the general means of improvement in industrial pursuits, that its success has been so long prevented.

It is sometimes supposed that the introduction of steam upon the Atlantic has neutralized the westerly position of this country, and removed the disadvantages of the channel navigation. This is not the case. The freight of goods in steam-vessels on long voyages, is far too high to allow of their being generally used. Passengers and letters are conveyed by them, but now, as formerly, the merchandize is sent by sailing vessels. Hence for goods, the relative positions of the harbours of this country and of the sister kingdom, remain as when Lord Sheffield wrote. But were the access to the western coast as direct and easy as it might and should be made, the passengers also

would naturally prefer to start from the extremest point of
land. Railroads from Dublin to Valentia or Beerhaven, or to
Tarbert on the Shannon, would render Ireland the leading
highway between the hemispheres.

It is not my province to enter into a guide book description
of the individual harbours which are found along our coast.
The evidence of nautical men of the soundest judgment has
characterized them as being competent to any, even the most
extensive, commercial or other wants, and I shall, therefore,
conclude this chapter by noticing what appears to me a feature in our industrial circumstances, which deserves consideration.

At present, whatever industrial activity exists in Ireland is
distributed along the eastern coast, and is, in fact, sustained
by the exportation of raw agricultural produce, which is paid
for by the importation of manufactures from the more developed industry and higher civilization of the sister kingdom.
Any trade or manufacture which we find in the western districts, is there in spite of their situation, and not as a consequence of it. If, however, with the growth of education, of
steady habits, and of business tastes, our domestic industry
should, as I fondly trust it may, revive, our farmers would
meet a safer and a better market for their produce, amongst
their neighbours, and consume the cloth, the linen, cotton, and
other products manufactured within our own bounds. In such
case the differences which are now so marked between the
north and south, the east and west of Ireland, would disappear,
and each locality would manifest a power of industry, commensurate with its natural structure, and the energy and intelligence of its people. In such case there is no doubt, but that
the greatest development of activity and wealth should be
towards the west, and especially along the districts of the
Shannon. Let us conceive that river, forming at its source,
250 miles from the sea, an extensive lake, surrounded with
coal and turf, and the richest ironstone, then cutting through
a district containing some of the most fertile land in Ireland,
capable of producing the largest returns of flax, of corn, and
cattle; presenting an alternation of lake and river, fitted for

steam navigation from end to end, and in one locality, within the distance of four miles, affording water power for mechanical manufactures on the greatest scale. In the hills, a few miles only from this seat of mechanical power, are mines of lead, of copper, and of sulphur, of slate, and marbles. Again, this great line of navigation is placed in immediate access to the eastern coast by two canals, and may be brought into contact with the north by a canal to Loughs Erne and Neagh. Finally, it possesses a capacious port, and estuary superior to that of the Thames, and roadsteads capable of giving certain accommodation to the most extensive navy.

Those natural facilities, of which no such combination exists in any other part of the country, promise to render, at some future time, the Shannon the line of industrial activity in Ireland. Of that line, Limerick, if not dethroned by some more active competitor, may be the key. It is a future upon which every Irishman must look with deepfelt interest, and with the hope that the people may, by morality, by steadiness, and intelligence, shew themselves worthy of the benefits that have been placed thus within their grasp, and may be found competent to apply them in the proper manner.

CHAPTER X.

CIRCUMSTANCES OF IRELAND REGARDING CERTAIN STAPLE AR-
TICLES OF INDUSTRY. COTTON, WOOL, SALT. OF THE COST
OF LABOUR IN IRELAND. SKILLED AND UNSKILLED LABOUR.
CHEAP LABOUR AND LOW WAGES NOT IDENTICAL. LABOUR-
ING FORCE OF MEN ESTIMATED. SKILLED LABOUR RARE AND
DEAR IN IRELAND. FREEDOM OF LABOUR NECESSARY TO ALL
INDUSTRIAL PROGRESS. COMBINATIONS IN IRELAND MORE
INJURIOUS THAN IN GREAT BRITAIN. HOW TO BE COUNTER-
ACTED. EVIDENCES OF IMPROVEMENT IN THE HABITS OF
THE WORKING CLASSES.
SUPPOSED WANT OF CAPITAL IN IRELAND. REAL EXTENT OF
ITS INFLUENCE. ENGLISH CAPITAL NOT AVAILABLE FOR
ACTIVE INDUSTRY. USEFUL FOR THE SECONDARY OPERA-
TIONS OF PASSIVE INDUSTRY, AND THUS LEAVING NATIVE
CAPITAL FREE FOR THE MORE ACTIVE PURSUITS.
NECESSITY FOR INDUSTRIAL KNOWLEDGE IN IRELAND. POS-
SESSED BY ENGLAND IN AN EMINENT DEGREE. OBSERVA-
TIONS OF M. BRIAVIONNE. FALSE IDEAS OF EDUCATION.
UNION OF SCIENCE AND PRACTICE NECESSARY FOR INDUSTRY.
INDUSTRIAL KNOWLEDGE MORE EXTENSIVE AND MORE DIF-
FICULT TO ACQUIRE THAN PROFESSIONAL KNOWLEDGE.
MANNER OF CONDUCTING IT. EXERTIONS OF THE ROYAL
DUBLIN SOCIETY FOR PROMOTING INDUSTRIAL EDUCATION.
SPECIAL EDUCATION IN AGRICULTURE BY THE ROYAL DUB-
LIN SOCIETY, THE ROYAL AGRICULTURAL SOCIETY, AND
PRIVATE AGRICULTURAL SCHOOLS. OF THE SYSTEMS OF NA-
TIONAL EDUCATION, IN REGARD TO AGRICULTURE. RELA-
TIONS OF INDUSTRY TO MORALITY, TEMPERANCE, AND IN-
TELLIGENCE. CONCLUSION.

IN the preceding chapter I have endeavoured to point out the circumstances of this country, as to the most important material elements of mechanical and agricultural industry. The extent and quality of our supplies of fuel; the distribution and amount of our sources of water power; the localities of our mines of iron, of copper, and other useful metals, have engaged attention, as well as the condition of the soil, the amount of its produce, and the general principles upon which its cultivation should be based, as regards equally the profitable investment of capital, and the comfort of the people. With such elements of material prosperity lying at our hands, it becomes a problem of high importance, to resolve why they have not been made available, and why this country has been left behind in the path of physical improvement by other nations, whose natural circumstances are in few instances superior, but in many points, certainly less advantageous. The examination of this general question is, however, foreign to my object, and would involve considerations far apart from those on which alone the man of science desires to dwell, or, probably, is competent to judge. Although thus waiving its discussion, I shall endeavour to fix attention on certain circumstances, of which some have been described as peculiarly facilitating the development of industry in this country, whilst others are usually looked upon, as the most characteristic disadvantages under which it labours. The inquiries I have made, and the consideration I have been enabled to give the subject, have led me to believe, that the popular impression is in both cases wrong, and as the establishing of a more correct idea becomes important, as affecting future progress, I shall notice those topics in detail. Before entering upon their discussion, however, it is necessary to advert briefly to the conditions of this country, with regard to some staple articles of manufacturing industry, that have not hitherto been described. Some of these are strictly of foreign origin, but the others are at least of possible home production, although their circumstances did not allow them to be noticed earlier.

Cotton wool, which now forms so large an article in British industry, is not imported directly into Ireland, because this country has no articles of manufacture to send in place of it. For the use of such factories as exist upon our eastern coast, it is purchased in Liverpool, and transhipped for Ireland. This is an additional expense, but although it would be of course desirable to get rid of it, it is not so heavy as might be supposed, when reduced to the per centage proportion of the general cost of the manufacture. In the case described, page 68, where the precise proportions of a factory are given, the total expenses of transport to Ireland are 1·4 per cent. of the result. This is probably not exceeded, if it be equalled, upon any other part of the eastern coast. In the case, however, of the development of manufacturing enterprize upon the western coast, and along the Shannon, the cost of transport of cotton from Liverpool would be much heavier. If paid for by manufactured goods, the cotton of the Southern States, or of Surat, would be delivered in Limerick or Galway, freed from the delays and danger of a channel voyage. It will be, indeed, an epoch in the history of Ireland, when a bale of cotton direct from New Orleans is spun and woven at Killaloe, and in part returned as printed calicos or muslins from Limerick to the States. The man who first accomplishes that, or any equivalent result, will have effected a revolution.

The woollen manufacture has been at all periods considered as of high importance in this country, so that at certain times it was deemed necessary to take measures to moderate its prosperity. Where ill-judged efforts for its encouragement alternated with violent attempts at its suppression, the object of the latter was of course finally accomplishod, and at present the woollen trade does not form an exception to the general stagnation of industry, which is so unfortunately characteristic of this country. In considering how far the natural condition of Ireland leads us to expect the development of this industry to any important degree, it is necessary to consider the growth of wool which we possess, not merely in relation to its quantity, but also to its quality and structure.

A very large quantity of wool is grown in Ireland. The grazing counties of the limestone plain afford an herbage peculiarly agreeable to sheep. The total number of sheep in Ireland is given in page 258, as somewhat above two millions. In Ulster, where industry and agriculture are most advanced, the pastoral habits are weakest. In Connaught the reverse conditions exist. To 100 acres of arable land, there are in Ulster but six sheep, whilst there are in Connaught twenty-four. It would be useless to attempt to calculate from this, the quantity of wool, as in fact each fleece yields numerous kinds of wool, which form quite distinct objects of manufacture. There is no doubt, however, but that were the wool grown

in Ireland manufactured in it, there should be called into play
so great an amount of mechanical industry, as would afford
employment to a large portion of the people. At present great
quantities of wool are exported from this country, particularly
to France, and several French houses have established agencies
in the centre and west of Ireland for the more direct purchase
of the wool. This wool is in France manufactured into the
mousselines de laine, so deservedly popular amongst our coun-
trywomen, by whom, I trust, they would not be less esteemed,
had they been spun, and woven, and printed without leaving
Ireland, and thus have given comfortable means of living to
thousands of our countrymen.

There are two kinds of woollen goods, which are formed by
different modes of manufacture, and these, again, are founded
on essential differences in the structure of the wool. Worsted
goods are formed of wool, the fibres of which are long, and
have little twist. In such goods the web is formed only as the
web of cotton or linen goods, by the opposition of the fibres,
alternately crossing and parallel. But, in what are properly
woollen goods, as in broad cloths, after the web has been so
formed, it is subjected to a violent beating, in the tucking or
fulling mill, during which the cloth shrinks very much in length
and breadth, but thickens, and the individual threads of the
web so mix in with each other that they cannot be distinguished,
until it is much worn, and becomes thread-bare. Now, for
such goods, a different kind of wool must be taken than for
worsted goods. The fibre must be short, and more twisted.
These varieties of wool are known as short and long stapled.
The cause of this difference is, that each fibre of wool consists
of a series of joints, and at each joint there are a set of pro-
jections, like the barbs of a fish hook. In long stapled wool
these barbs are few, and very weak; in short stapled wool they
are numerous, and strong. If a handful of the latter be worked
in the hands, the fibres will gradually interlace, and, by these
barbs catching in each other, will lock into a kind of web, quite
independent of spinning and weaving: they will felt. It is in
this way that the bodies of hats are made, as all furs possess
the same property. Hence, the making of cloth requires the

spinning and weaving of the web, in the first instance, and the subsequent partial felting of the fibres, in the tucking mill.

I notice these particulars, as the climate and vegetation of a country exercise remarkable influence on the staple and structure of the wool which the sheep produce, and thus, finally, on the description of manufactured goods. In moist cold climates, such as that of the British Islands, the natural wool of the adult sheep is universally long stapled, and unfit for felting: whilst in dry climates, with hot summers, the wool is short stapled, and felts strongly. The wool produced not merely in Ireland, but in England also, is thus exclusively adapted for the worsted trade; and that of Ireland being of an excellent quality of fibre, is much sought after for the finer kinds of worsted, such as those already noticed of French manufacture. For woollen cloths, and similar goods, the wool is imported from the Continent. The great plains of the east of Europe support vast flocks of sheep, from whence we derive our Silesian and Saxon wool. The dry plains of South Australia are also favourable to that growth of fibre, and hence has been created, within a few years a branch of trade most important to that colony. It has been often an object with English wool-growers, and landed proprietors, to produce this felting wool in England, and thus get rid of the necessity of purchasing abroad; but it has been found impossible, after the most expensive experiments in importing sheep of particular flocks. It has been found that in two or three generations, even of the pure breed, the influence of the climate and food totally changed the character of the wool, and brought it to the same quality as that of the native animals.

It is thus evident that the manufacture of the native wools of Ireland can lead but to one department of that important branch of industry, that is, the worsted trade. With regard to woollens, this country, like England, must import wool, and hence will be under the same conditions of access to raw materials as the sister kingdom. In no degree are we less favourably placed. The Messrs. Willans, so extensively and so favourably known in Dublin, and who have also large factories at Leeds, have often and in public declared, that they carry on trade as

favourably in Ireland as in England: the low price of coals in
Yorkshire being fully counterbalanced by the cheapness of
water-power, and a certain advantage in wages here.

A substance which is the basis of more chemical manufactures than any other, is common salt. It yields chlorine, and
is thus the original material of all the beautiful arts which involve bleaching processes. It yields soda, and this is an ingredient in soap, in glass, and numerous other substances not so
universally known. In curing provisions, and as a manure, it
is of extensive use, and as a condiment, it becomes a part of
our daily food. There is, probably, no one material, the ab-
straction of which would occasion so many deficiencies in the
habits of a civilized people. Of this important substance, there
is no natural deposit in Ireland. Salt is found usually in the
new red sandstone, aud the gypseous marls which lie above the
coal strata; and thus about Chesshire are situated the great
salt mines and pits of England. These formations exist in
Ireland only in the north-eastern district, about Belfast, as
described page 179, and they have not been found to contain
any indications of salt mines. We are, therefore, dependant
on England for our supply of this valuable material. Its price
is so low, that the cost of transport increases its cost in a very
important degree, and hence the various chemical manufactures, which require large quantities of salt, labour under a
much greater proportional disadvantage in this country than
the mechanical manufactures do, in regard to fuel, to produce
steam. Salt, however, could be obtained, although not so
economically, by the evaporation of sea-water. It is thus
formed on the coast of Southern Europe; the strong heat of
the sun drying down the water, which is run into shallow reservoirs. With us, the sun is not strong enough, and rain is
too frequent to allow of such methods being adopted; but by
employing the plans that are actually adopted in Germany, to
concentrate the waters of the weak brine springs in those localities, where there are no mines of rock salt, the sea-water
of our coasts might be concentrated partially, perhaps to a half,
and then the evaporation should be finished by means of coal

or turf. It would occupy too long, and would, indeed, be superfluous, to describe those plans of evaporation. I shall only
notice that the cost of the fuel that would be at least required
to obtain a ton of salt, should be about 18s., and the other expenses would probably make the salt from sea-water cost, on
the coast of Ireland, not less than 25s. per ton. The ordinary
English salt seldom costs more in Liverpool than 10s. or 12s.
per ton.

Such are the conditions of these three important materials
of industry, cotton, wool, and salt, as regards Ireland. We
arrive now at the consideration of a most influential element
in manufacturing calculations—the cost of labour, the lowness
of which has been popularly considered as the most eminent
inducement this country can present to the capitalist to embark in industrial undertakings.

That human labour can be obtained in this country on lower
terms than almost any other in Europe, is too well known to
require example. A population, for which the existing modes
of cultivation do not supply occupation on the land, and which
is not, as in the sister kingdom, drafted off to manufacturing
employments in the towns, must, in order to live, accept of
any terms of remuneration which they can get in exchange for
labour. It is thus that 8d. or 10d. per day is found to be the
usual rate of wages, at a distance from large towns, and that,
even on such terms, thousands of men remain unemployed
during the greater portion of the year: this nominal cheapness is, however, by no means necessarily economy in final
cost. A wretched man who can earn, by his exertion, but
4s. or 5s. a week, on which to support his family and pay the
rent of a sort of habitation, must be so ill fed, and depressed
in mind, that to work, as a man should work, is beyond his
power. Hence there are often seen about employments in this
country a number of hands, double what would be required to
do the same work, in the same time, with British labourers.
The latter would probably be paid at least twice as much
money per day, but in the end the work would not cost the
employer more; although the wages, therefore, in the former

398   INDUSTRIAL RESOURCES

example were lower, labour was not cheaper, on the contrary,
somewhat higher, as the trouble of overseeing twice the number of men is a source of additional expense.

When I say that the men thus employed, at low wages, do
so much less real work, I do not mean that they intentionally
idle, or that they reflect that as they receive so little they
should give little value; on the contrary, they do their best
honestly to earn their wages, but supplied only with the lowest
descriptions of food, and perhaps, in insufficient quantity, they
have not the physical ability for labour, and being without
any direct prospect of advancement, they are not excited by
that laudable ambition to any display of superior energy.   If
the same men are placed in circumstances, where a field for
increased exertion is opened to them, and they are made to
understand, what at first they are rather incredulous about,
that they will receive the full value of any increased labour
they perform, they become new beings : the work they execute
rises to the highest standard, and they earn as much money as
the labourers of any other country; wages are no longer low,
but labour is not, on that account, anything dearer than it
had been before.   An occurrence at a certain public work will
exemplify this principle.   Many hundreds of men were employed at 10*d.* per day.   They worked slowly, and ineffectually;
the work was not progressing, and as time was an object, a
parcel of English labourers were introduced, who were paid
18*d.* per day, which they fully earned.   None of the Irish labourers were dismissed, but they struck work, and demanded
that all should have 18*d.* per day.   The Englishmen feared
for their lives.   The police and military were called out, and
the affair might have eventuated in a scene of blood, adding
another to the tales of horror so industriously circulated about
the savageness of the native Irish.   At this moment one of the
principal engineers, an Irishman, respected by the people for
his abilities, and esteemed by them as a countryman, came
amongst them, and penetrating into the mass of excited labourers, arrested and gave into custody all the ringleaders.
The crowd of labourers would not do him an injury.   He
then, in place of the common practice of saying they were

brutes, and none but English labourers were fit for any useful purpose, quietly explained to them that the Englishmen did much more work and deserved to be paid higher, but that he would be very willing to secure 18d. per day to every man, who would do as much work as the Englishmen, and more, if they could do more. He shewed them that from their rude way of managing their tools they wasted their strength, and that by simple improvements a great deal of time could be saved in their operations. The people knew and trusted him; the police and military were withdrawn; the whole body of labourers went to work, and after the first Saturday night they found, that without combination or violence, they could earn more money by laying themselves down steadily to do more work. After some weeks there were very few of the men earning less than 18d., and many of them were earning at the rate of 2s. 6d. per day.

In this case wages ceased to be low, precisely as the efficiency of work increased. The cheapness of labour is thus shewn to be quite different from the nominal rate of wages. This difference is not peculiar to this country, it exists as forcibly in regard to certain countries of the Continent. Thus the iron manufacture in France is actually more retarded by this cause than by the greater proportional cost of fuel, which is popularly considered the most important.

The manufacture of iron, including the extraction of the fuel, and of the iron ore and flux, as well as the actual smelting and refining of the metal, occupies as many hands in France as it does in England, although the quantity of produce is not one-third so great. In fact, an iron work in Great Britain producing 10,000 tons of iron per annum, would employ 145 men, or a man for every sixty-nine tons of iron. In France it would require two furnaces for the same quantity of metal, and they would employ 445 men, or a man for every twenty-three tons. Hence, there are three times as many hands for the same work, and although provisions are so much cheaper and wages lower in France, more money must be paid to workmen there than in England to produce the same quantity of

iron. In fact, in trades requiring considerable mechanical
skill, wages are actually lower in England than in any other
country, in consequence of there being so much more competition amongst persons so qualified.

In every industrial occupation there are actually involved two
totally distinct offices, which are paid for in very different degrees. These are the animal force, and the mental exertion
which directs it. The question of relative cheapness or dearness of labour altogether depends on the relative proportions
we want of those, and the proportions in which they are possessed by the man we hire. Now, owing to the general absence
of industrial activity in this country, the mental power is not
at all so universal as in Britain. It is hence dearer in Ireland,
whilst animal force, destitute of industrial skill, being less
abundant in Great Britain, is dearer there than it is with us.
A bricklayer in London gets 22s. per week, and his labourer
14s.; a bricklayer in Dublin gets 25s. per week, and his labourer but 9s. These proportions are often said to be caused
by combination and threats against employers. It is not so;
the fact being that men who know how to set bricks are proportionally more abundant in London, and men who do not
know how to do it are more abundant with us. This diversity
produces both the power of combining, and the difference of
wages.

Considering man merely as a source of animal power, it is
gratifying to have it proved, that when at all well fed, there
is no race more perfectly developed, as to physical conformation, than the inhabitants of this island. Professor Forbes instituted an extensive series of observations of the size and
strength of the students attending the University of Edinburgh, who may be considered as fairly representing the middle classes of their respective countries; and I have subjoined
the similar results of Professor Quetelet, regarding the students of the University of Bruxelles. The strength indicated
is that shown by pulling out the stem of a spring dynamome-
ter.

	AVERAGE HEIGHT IN INCHES.	AVERAGE WEIGHT IN POUNDS.	AVERAGE STRENGTH IN POUNDS.
English,	68½	151	403
Scotch,	69	152½	423
Irish,	70	155	432
Belgians,	68	150	339

The Irish are thus the tallest, strongest, and heaviest of the four races.

Mr. Field, the eminent mechanical engineer of London, had occasion to examine the relative powers of British and Irish labourers, to raise weights by means of a crane. He communicated his results to the Institute of Civil Engineers in London. He found that the utmost effort of a man lifting at the rate of one foot per minute ranged:

> Englishmen, from 11,505℔ to 24,255℔.
> Irishmen,   ,,   17,325   ,,   27,562

The utmost effort of a Welshman was 15,112.

In all operations, therefore, where brute force is required, there is no question but that we possess in Ireland, in the actual population, a vast amount of power; but the progress of art and of intelligence must lead us to consider such employment as unsuited to a being endowed with the noble capacity for improvement that belongs to man. It should be his prerogative to subdue the greater strength of other animals, and to adapt the wondrous forces of external nature to his ends, by virtue of the intelligence with which he is provided, and the labouring force of man must be considered as lying truly dormant, so far as its true uses are concerned, until it be quickened by the energetic fire of industrial education. It is in this regard that Ireland is actually weakest, and that most difficulty may be expected in any future development of our industry. No matter to what side we turn, or what problem of manufacturing or agricultural improvement we proceed to, we find the difficulty of procuring skilled workmen or superintendents, and hence all such positions are occupied by natives of the

sister island, to the exclusion, as it would appear unfair, of
the natives of this country. Such an idea is, however, quite
unjust. Irishmen are not appointed to those situations because
they are not educated for them. Scotchmen and Englishmen
obtain them because they learn what is necessary for such
duties. The remedy for this is not to declaim against intrud-
ing foreigners, but to learn those trades so well as to make it
the direct interest of the employer to give his countrymen the
preference. Every intelligent Englishman or Scotchman who
comes to Ireland should not be looked upon as an intruder, but
as a schoolmaster. If there did not exist a blank in our industrial system which it suits him to fill up, he would not
come. He is a-head of us in practical skill and habits, and it
should be our object to imitate him, learn from him, and, if
possible, excel him, and when he finds that we know as much
as he does, he will not come. He then would be better off at
home.

Skilled labour is thus shewn to be certainly dearer in this
country than in Great Britain, whilst unskilled labour is much
cheaper. The final question of whether, for manufacturing
industry in general, labour is cheaper here, is therefore not
capable of receiving a decided answer. It must depend altogether on the proportions which the skilled and unskilled labour bear to each other. The total cost may actually be
greater than in England. I am disposed, however, to conclude, from tolerably numerous inquiries, that in most of the
departments of manufacture, the balance is in favour of this
country, and that the total cost of labour is so much less as to
counteract many of the smaller advantages, as in fuel and
freights, which the manufacturer of the sister kingdom should
otherwise possess. That, however, no such real difference in
cost of effective labour here and in England exists, as is popularly thought, may, I trust, be considered as established by the
foregoing evidence.

A condition absolutely essential to industrial progress is
freedom of labour. This freedom must be complete ; it must
exist as regards master, as well as regards man. A workman must have the most perfect liberty to place what value he

likes upon his labour. If he does not wish to work for certain wages, it is his affair; and it were intolerable tyranny to control his will; but with that limit the right of the workman ceases. As he should not be controlled himself, he has no right to control others, and all interference of men to prevent their fellow-operatives from working below a certain rate, must be denounced as not merely contrary to existing law, but to the plainest principles of common sense, and utterly destructive of the best interests of industry, not merely the interests of the employer, but, in an equal degree, of the men themselves. It would lead me too far from my proper object, were I to enter upon this question, so important to be truly understood by the working classes. I shall, therefore, pass from considerations which should be but general in their applications, and notice only one point in which the topic concerns this country.

It is often asserted that an important obstacle to the introduction of manufactures into this country, is from the combinations which exist among the several branches of trade, and which subject the employer to laws and to restrictions so intolerable, as to prevent him from venturing amongst us. He, therefore, remains in England or in Scotland, where he is free to use his capital and machinery, to employ or not employ, as he thinks fit, and is not disturbed by clamour of combinators. To judge how far this cause can influence this country we must probe deeper than the surface.

No person really conversant with the progress of industry in the two countries would assert that there is more combination here than in Great Britain. The history of industry in England for the last century presents a series of the most violent outbreaks, riots, and combinations, murders of the most amiable employers, destruction of machinery and mills; in fact, such an array of illegal interference with the just rights of property and labour, as would, if judiciously worked up by an active editor, supply materials for a history of Great Britain that has not yet been written. But these events are lost sight of by the public in the vast extent of British industry. The ringleaders are punished; the general mass return

to their work; in no case has the object of the strike been at
all successful, for the unfortunate artisans seeking to enforce
from particular localities or employers what the general progress of industrial discovery opposes, must yield before the
movement of the age, and by warring against, in place of
moulding themselves to it, suffer too often under its evils,
without being able to participate in its good.

In this country, however, cases of combination derive an ex-
trinsic importance from causes quite independent of their true
nature. Our industry is so limited in amount, that a disagree-
ment, which in England would never be heard of, except by
those immediately concerned, becomes a topic of universal
comment, and, unfortunately, the organs of public opinion are
too often hurried by the eagerness of political feeling into speaking of a quarrel between an employer and a few men, as if it
were a general outbreak of the working against the employing
classes. Thus some time ago a sugar bakery was erected in
Cork, and the proprietor very prop rly brought over from
England bricklayers conversant with the modes of setting the
pans and other apparatus. For the rough work, to which only
they were really competent, Irish bricklayers were employed,
but these, finding that the Englishmen worked for lower wages
than the Cork standard, refused to work with them. In this
they were perfectly justified. The Irish bricklayers had a
clear right to leave work and stay idle, if they preferred it to
earning money. But they went further, and demanded that the
English bricklayers should be dismissed, and that none but the
workmen at high rates of wages should be employed. Here
they were totally in the wrong, and the proprietor very properly refused to comply. The idle workmen stood about the
gates for a few days; their wives favoured the proprietor with
a course of Munster billingsgate; but the intervention of a few
policemen restored order, and the matter was really so unimportant that in a week it was forgotten in Cork.

But it was not forgotten elsewhere. The journals took it
up, and concealing that the whole affair was a dispute about
working for wages under the ordinary rate, they seized on the
question of English and Irish, and poured out on the poor

ignorant Cork workmen and their unhappy country, column after column of vulgar abuse and contumely. We were savages, brutal rioters; the whole was but one indication of the hatred we bear to Englishmen; of the stupid obstinacy with which our barbarism repels the introduction of intelligence and civilization from the sister kingdom: and not only were such absurdities printed by the most eminent daily press, but the articles were reprinted in works pretending to be purely statistical, and it was inferred, that Ireland is in a state of social barbarism; that if mills were erected they would be burned; if masters gave employment their throats would be cut; that the means of earning wholsome food and healthful habitations, of dressing comfortably, and educating their children to useful trades, are looked upon in Ireland as objects sedulously to be avoided; that the native Irish have an indomitable and natural taste for rags and dirt, for sloth and hunger, for violence and murder. We can afford to laugh at such tirades now. After all the schoolmaster is abroad.

Besides the fact of the importance of such strikes being magnified by the unwholesome appetite for political excitement which pervades this country, there is another, perhaps still more influential in its operation upon trade. Employers are in Ireland much less able to stand out against strikes than in the sister kingdom. They possess less capital; its rapid circulation is a matter of more pressing necessity, and hence any temporary interruption is more felt. But still more important is the circumstance, that in Ireland, employers are more dependent on their men, than those of the same class in England. They do not in general know their own trade as well. If an English workman refuse to do a piece of work, the master can, if he chooses, do it himself, and this gives the employer a moral superiority and power, which the Irish manufacturer, in too many cases, does not possess. To this there are, I am aware, many and brilliant exceptions, and these exceptions are the more important, as their success, well merited by their energy and industrial knowledge, becomes a beacon to others on the same track. In every case that I have known of, in this country, where the master shewed himself possessed of the really high qualities, which the direction of extensive industry requires, combination has been unknown, or, if attempted, has eventuated in the establishment of the employer, and of his trade, in a better condition than before.

There is but one remedy for combination; education. Not merely intellectual education; not merely to brighten up the faculties of a man, as you polish and smooth the parts of a machine, that it may do more work, and with less friction: but that education which developes equally the moral and intellectual mind. And this education is as much required for the employer, as for the employed. If knowledge alone be given, it will confer power; whoever knows most must ultimately command, be he master or man, and if his morality be low, he will oppress; he will insist upon rights, and neglect his duties. Educate, therefore, the moral faculties of all classes. There may thus be generated what is more than all else wanted to give happiness, tranquillity, and wealth to Ireland, a sympathy between the higher and lower classes, a sense of their mutual dependence, and mutual duties, a pleasure in the recognition of each other's joys, and reciprocal condolence in those sorrows which fall to the lot of every rank. Manufacturers, otherwise well informed, have said, " what have I to do with my workmen, but to receive their labour and pay them for it? I have no connexion with them once they leave the factory?" That is not right. Is it nothing to the employer whether his workmen spend their evenings happily with their families, or in drunkenness, in gambling, or perhaps theft? Which would be most likely to make honest servants, and steady workmen? Which would be most likely to prevent an attempt to destroy his property, or perhaps his life? There can be but one answer. Independent of moral grounds, the kindness, sympathy, and attention of an employer to his workmen, is the safest and most profitable money speculation in which he can engage.

So far from the habits of the working classes of this country being adverse to the introduction of industrial occupations, they have made, within the last few years, unparalleled strides in the habits which best conduce to industrial success. I do not hesitate to assert, that the existing generation in this country is half a century in advance of that which is dying off, and that the generation now at school will be a century in advance of us. We were reckless, ignorant, improvident, drunken, and idle. We were idle, for we had nothing to do; we were reckless, for we had no hope; we were ignorant, for learning was denied us; we were improvident, for we had no future; we were drunken, for we sought to forget our misery. That time has passed away for ever.

In Ovoca, on pay days, where 2000 men are employed, 500 gallons of whiskey used to be bought by the miners, and drunk upon the works. The men spent the night in fighting, whilst their wives and children begged in vain that some of their wages should go for provisions and for clothing.

There is now upon pay days no whiskey whatsoever sold. The wives of the workmen receive their wages for them, and quarrelling is unknown.

Some years ago, the village of Bonmahon presented, on pay days, a scene of strife and drunkenness. which always required the intervention of the police, and often rendered the position of the superintendants dangerous. At present nothing of the kind is known, a temperance hall for social quiet meetings, and extensive school rooms for the education of the children, are now built, and the same number of individuals are able to earn £300 per month more than they formerly received, by the greater steadiness and attention to their work, which accompany their improved domestic habits.

I might adduce a great number of such examples, but it is not required. The children are at school; the parents are sober and steady. The revenue collected on ardent spirits has been diminished to one-half; notwithstanding that the export trade has augmented. The sums in the Savings Banks are not materially augmented yet, and it is better not; the mere desire to amass money is, after all, not what we want most. Greater desire to live comfortably, to eat of better food, to live in better houses, to wear superior clothing, to buy good books, these are passions far more useful to the people, and more important to encourage, than the mere accumulation of money, which there is no danger will come, if it be not already present, and will lead to its usual results.

Labour, as it exists in Ireland, if it be unskilled, is thus now in the best possible condition for receiving the impulse of skilled direction. It becomes, hence, vitally important to provide for the proper direction of the nascent energies of the people. We have passed the line which separates progress from inactivity. May our future course be guided by intelligence and morality.

There is another circumstance, so popularly counted on as a most material obstacle to the development of industry in Ireland, that I cannot leave the subject without briefly adverting to it, that is the want of capital. This has been the bugbear of Irish enterprize for many years. England has capital, Ireland has not; therefore England is rich and industrious, and Ireland is poor and idle. But where was the capital when England began to grow rich? It was the industry that made the capital, not the capital the industry. An idle or ignorant man will lose his capital where an active and intelligent man will create a capital. We leave our fields in barrenness, our mines unsought, our powers of motion unapplied, waiting for English capital. Labour is capital; intelligence is capital; combine them and you more than double your amount of capital. With such capital England commenced, as Ireland must commence, and once that we have begun and are in earnest, there will be no lack of money capital at our disposal.

The subject must, however, be more numerically stated. So far from being unable to extend our industry for want of capital, we do not employ the capital we have in active industry. When money is made in England it is re-invested in the same or in a similar branch, concerns are increased, and transactions multiplied, until the amount of capital attains the vast dimensions which we now see. If some money be made in trade in Ireland, it is not so treated, it is withdrawn from trade, and stock is bought, or land is bought, yielding only a small return, but one with the advantage of not requiring intense exertion or intelligence, and free from serious risk. Capital cannot, therefore, increase with a rapidity at all commensurate with English progress; but that capital of great amount does truly exist in Ireland available for industrial uses, if the owners had a taste therefor, is certain. More than two millions of Irish capital is transferred every year to England in purchase of English Government stock. Many of the English railways have a numerous Irish proprietary. The property in steam vessels belonging to Dublin is only exceeded in amount by that of London, and is actually greater than the united steam property of Bristol, Hull, and Liverpool. With such facts, it is useless to say we have no capital; we do not want the capital so much as we do the knowledge and disposition to employ it.

Let it not be supposed I object to English capital; on the contrary, money is too good a thing to refuse, and especially from our dear sister, who has got abundance of our money on much better terms than she is likely ever to give any of her's. But I do not think that English capital will be employed in the direct advancement of our manufactures or agriculture, although it certainly will, indirectly, and thus be of immense service to us. But suppose an Englishman possessed of £50,000, and wishing to invest it in spinning cotton: he has his choice to go to Manchester or Killaloe. In the former place, he has coals cheap, workmen of every class at hand, machinery made at his door, market established, and if he wants to sell in Ireland he has canal and railway to Liverpool, thence steam to Dublin, and canals then to the Shannon. If he comes to Killaloe, he has to bring his machinery, and all his higher workmen, to bring cotton, and to settle amongst a people concerning whom his ears have been stuffed with newspaper stories, some unfortunately true, but mostly false. His sympathies are at his home, and unless profits were considerably higher, he should remain at home, and such would certainly be his course. Now profits cannot be sensibly higher in Ireland than in England. There is, therefore, no inducement for him to come. Take woollens, or any other branch, in place of cotton, and, by a similar chain of facts, we shall be led to the same conclusion.

But some English capitalists have settled amongst us, it

may be said, and hence the above reasoning cannot be absolute.   There are some, as the Willans, who have cloth mills
here and in Leeds, but they settled here at a time, when, by a
system of differential duties, trade between England and this
country was impeded, and to which it would be a most barbarous retrocession in industrial economy to think of returning.
They have not dismantled their factory, because cloth can be
made as cheap with us, but they have not materially extended,
because cloth is as easily brought from Leeds.   English capitalists will establish factories in France, Austria, and Belgium,
because the tariffs of these countries secure them higher returns than English competition allows.   They are paid higher
as schoolmasters for the natives.   This country does not afford
such advantages, and hence we cannot expect them to come.
To this there may be individual exceptions, arising from peculiar instances of enterprize, but this does not affect the question as regards the country generally.   For active industry,
English capital cannot be expected, and if it do revive, it
must be by Irishmen and Irish capital.

English capital may, and, I have no doubt, will, be highly
useful in the operations of what I may term passive industry ;
in the creation of the various collateral aids to commercial
business.   If an English capitalist have a few thousand pounds
to invest in shares, he will as soon put it into an Irish railway
or a canal as into an English one, if it promise the same returns.   Hence the vast accumulation of money of the sister
kingdom may be most usefully employed in rendering our
rivers navigable, in completing our water intercourse by canals,
in constructing our lines of railway, and thus, whilst it brings
to the owner at least as must profit as it should do if laid out
in England, it will prevent such works from absorbing the capital of Irishmen; who, on the spot, and familiar with the
people, if they were properly acquainted with the structure and
capabilities of the country, and thoroughly educated in their
trades, might apply their individual capitals to the creation of
active industry.   By means of English capital also, agricultural
industry may be, and is in progress of important amelioration.
The owners of land were very generally loaded with monetary

obligations incurred at a high rate of interest, which are now being rapidly removed by means of loans from England, at moderate charges; the estates thus freed will enable their proprietors to devote more money, and, it is to be hoped, intelligence, to their improvement, and therewith the improvement of the people. The large amount of Irish capital thus liberated from the land, will become available for active industry, and must, indeed, be very energetically employed to produce the equivalent of what had been received.

Acting in this way the sister kingdom may be most useful and most powerful in advancing the industrial condition of this country; it will be profitable, and, therefore, she will finally do it. The investment of English capital and of Irish enterprize must, however, go hand in hand. The railway is of no use unless there be a suitable increase of traffic. The means of transport are not wanted f there be not products of industry to convey. English capital, therefore, even where it might be most useful, may totally fail in its object, and its investments give no profit, unless the morals of the people, their taste for industrial pursuits, and their education, be promoted with the utmost zeal.

Numerous companies have been, from time to time, formed in England, for the purpose of developing some branches of the industrial resources of Ireland, especially our mines. They have been almost universally failures, and Ireland, as a field of enterprize, has been hence at a discount in the English market. It is not difficult to see why they failed; the causes were ignorance of the country, and want of economy. Thus, to work a coal mine in Ireland, an overseer and miners are employed, who know perfectly how coals are worked at Newcastle, and who bring over steam engines and gins, on a scale proportionate to the English beds, but totally unfitted for the localities of our coal fields; the natural disadvantages are heightened by the want of adaptation on the part of the system pursued; the overseer is not himself vitally interested, his employers are at a distance, and under such circumstances it need not be a matter of wonder that the concern does not pay.

It is thus shewn, that many of those conditions as dearness of fuel and want of capital, to which is popularly attributed the absence of extended industry in this country, are, in reality, by no means so powerful, and in fact do not present obstacles to our progress greater than what are every year surmounted in other places; on the other hand, we find, in the abundance and economy of water power, in the extent of our mines, and the fertility of our soil, in the capabilities of our rivers and harbours for water transport, and of the general surface of the country for land carriage, so many circumstances in an unusual degree favourable, and leading to the most sanguine expectations of the results of industrial enterprize. To what then is it due that we have made so little way? Why is it that our people are unemployed, or are driven to seek the means of living by periodical emigrations to fulfil the lowest offices in another land? Why is it that our harbours are bare of ships, our rivers undisturbed by the bustle of industry and intercourse, our fields producing but a third of what they might supply? that where activity exists, or that progress is now being made, it is to be traced, with but few exceptions, to the introduction of the natives of the sister kingdom, into whose possession there thus pass the most valuable domains of enterprize which this country offers, whilst the Irish population rests in the lowest grade, and but rarely manifest the qualities which the time requires.

The fault is not in the country, but in ourselves; the absence of successful enterprize is owing to the fact, that we do not know how to succeed; we do not want activity, we are not deficient in mental power, but we want special industrial knowledge. England, which in absolute education and in general morality is below us, notwithstanding our criminal violence, is far above us in industrial knowledge. The man who knows not how to read or write, who has never been at church, who never taught his child to reverence the name of his Creator, will be a perfect master of his trade. The machines he constructs, or the products he elaborates, will be most perfect in their parts, most suited to their purpose, and most economical in their cost; from the task which he undertakes nothing will turn him aside; he knows that time as well as labour is required for an industrial result; he invests his time as he invests his money, as regularly and as extensively; his steadiness and perseverance in his pursuits are thus part of his industrial knowledge; his acquaintance with the probabilities of his trade prepares him for difficulties, and hence enables him to surmount them. Such things, he knows, must be in ordinary course, and thus he works constantly on, through alternations of success and failure, to his final triumph.

In this industrial knowledge we are deficient. An Irishman takes up a branch of trade; after a time he finds it requires more capital than he expected, and he becomes involved. He finds that the profits are less than he had hoped, or he discovers that for a long time he can make no profit, and he is discouraged. Circumstances arise which he is not prepared to meet; the conditions of the branch of industry may have changed since he first entered into it, and finally he loses, perhaps, all that he had embarked in trade, simply because he did not know his trade well enough. An eminent Belgian minister, M. Briavionne, having occasion to describe the importance of attending to the education of the working and commercial classes in that country, drew his examples of the consequences of neglect, and of attention to it, from the existing position of the British Islands. He asks: " What has produced the difference between the rich and flourishing condition of England, and the poverty and weakness of Ireland? Industrial knowledge." He strenuously urges on the Belgian legislature the necessity of attending to industrial education, lest Belgium should become like Ireland.

The education necessary for industrial pursuits is very generally underrated in this country, and from this cause alone springs a great deal of our want of industrial knowledge. Our ignorance is so great, that we are even incapable of estimating its extent. If a boy is to be sent to a profession, great care is taken with his education. Literature and science present themselves to him hand in hand. A reputation, the best passport to professional success, may, it is said, be founded on school and college character, and his ambition is excited by

the social and political eminences which professional men may
attain. But if he is going to trade, education, it is thought,
would be thrown away on him. If he can read and write and
cypher, it is supposed to be enough.   Should an ambitious
parent desire to give his son a good education, although he is
to be in trade, he puts him through college.   He devotes the
best years of his youth to reading Grecian poetry, and Latin
plays; to learning by rote the dialectics of the middle ages, and
principles of abstract metaphysics, and awakens, after the so-
lemnity of getting his degree, to find that he is to obtain his
living by principles and pursuits to which his education has
had no reference whatsoever.   He finds that the safety of his
property may depend on the navigation of a sea, of which he
never heard whilst labouring for months to understand the geo-
graphy of the Odyssey; that the mode of growth, or the chemical composition of a plant, of whose existence neither Greek
nor Roman knew, may be the means of gaining or of losing
fortune, and of it he has been left in ignorance ; that his daily
commercial intercourse is with men and nations, of whose languages and whose customs he is totally ignorant, whilst he has
spent his youth in learning how he should have spoken had he
lived three thousand years ago.

It is very well for those, who, independent in fortune, and
devoted rather to ease than enterprize, wish to dream through
an existence which offers to them but roses they did not plant,
to seek in the literature of past ages, an elegant and innocent
occupation. Indeed, to all classes the literature of present and
of former times, of our own and of foreign countries, presents a
relief from the weary continuity of action, which industrial progress requires.   To the man of business, there can be no en-
joyment greater than to transport himself from the anxieties
of the desk or factory, to communion with the best lessons,
which human intelligence has handed down, or to obtain, within
a few volumes, the records of the greatest deeds, the noblest
struggles, and the holiest thoughts which have been allowed to
man. But this is not his business. This knowledge is not
that by which he is to live, and the first object of one dependent on his own exertions must be to learn to employ them, to

educate his faculties specially with regard to their future use
in the development and the improvement of every part of whatsoever line of business he embarks in.

The idea of there being no direct connexion between trade
and education, has derived support, with many persons, from
the examples of individuals, highly educated, failing entirely
when they engaged in trade, whilst other men, of no education
whatsoever, have been brilliantly successful in industry. This
argument is, however, when analysed, strong on the other
side. What is called education by those persons, is not so, it
is, on the contrary, worse than no education whatsoever. If a
man knows Greek and Latin, if he can expound all the niceties
of metaphysics, what does it avail him when he proceeds to
spinning cotton, or to smelting iron; quite the reverse. His
habits and modes of thought are at every moment shocked by
the rough clashing of the realities on which his fate depends.
His mind, accustomed to discussions, which, whether right
or wrong, leave life as it has been before, becomes appalled
at the stern calculations of a problem, in which his liberty,
his home, his fortune is involved. The man is not able for
his position, and he fails; but he fails not because he was
an educated man, but because he was not educated for his
trade.

On the other hand, who are those uneducated men that succeed in trade? A young man, wanting to sell spectacles in
London, petitions the Corporation to allow him to open a little
shop without paying the heavy fees of freedom. He is refused.
He goes to Glasgow, and the Corporation refuse him there.
He makes acquaintance with some members of the University,
who find him very intelligent, and permit him to open his shop
within their walls. He does not sell spectacles and magic
lanterns enough to occupy his time; he occupies himself at
intervals in taking asunder and remaking all the machines he
can come at. He finds there are books on mechanics written in
foreign languages; he borrows a dictionary, and learns those
languages to read those books. The University people wonder
at him, and are fond of dropping into his little room, in the
evenings, to tell him what they are doing, and to look at the

queer instruments he constructs. A machine in the University collection wants repairing, and he is employed. He makes it a new machine. The steam engine is constructed, and the giant mind of Watt stands out before the world, the author of the industrial supremacy of his country, the herald of a new force of civilization. But was Watt educated? Where was he educated? At his own work-shop, and in the best manner. Watt learned Latin, when he wanted it for his business. He learned French and German; but these things were tools, not ends. He used them to promote his engineering plans, as he used lathes and levers.

Arkwright began his career a barber; he had a taste for mechanical combinations, and spent all he could save by cutting hair, in putting together wheels and levers, making little machines, which sometimes answered his purpose, and sometimes not. At last, he put them together after a manner which has led to momentous· consequences. He invented, or at least he rendered practicable, the spinning by rollers, and created the basis of the cotton trade in England. Was he not educated? Did he not educate himself, whilst carrying his wigs and barber's apparatus from house to house, thinking about his models of machines, and so wrapt up in them, that his wife, in a passion, burned them all, for which he removed from her, and stipulated that she should let him invent in quiet. He was not as great a man as Watt. His education did not go so far, but it was his real industrial education which made him the founder of a vast manufacturing art, and enabled him to become one of the wealthiest subjects of Great Britain.

Tracing the history of men successful in a less prominent degree than Watt and Arkwright, we are led to the same result. Their success is proportional to the conjoint action of their mental power and knowledge. That knowledge is often difficult to acquire. So far from industrial pursuits not requiring education, they do require it in much greater degree than any of the so-called professions. Industrial knowledge is much more difficult to acquire, and much more extensive in its range, than professional knowledge; and yet, in Ireland, its acquisition has not been attended to in any efficient degree, nor have the general principles, upon which its communication should be founded, been at all generally understood.

Every department of agricultural and of manufacturing industry has its origin in scientific principles, practically applied. The weaving of a woollen cloth, the rolling of an iron rail, or of a brass ornament, the construction of a clock, the preparation of soap, or of oil of vitriol, all require the discovery of a certain principle, which, working by a certain process on certain materials, elaborates the product. Sometimes a process, with particular materials, is hit upon long before the principle of its action becomes known, and the art exists, but cannot extend itself, for with any other materials, the process cannot answer, whilst with any other process, the materials are not suited; and hence, although the art may arrive in that limited form to great perfection, it is impossible to transplant it to other places or into other hands. On the other side, a scientific principle may be discovered, and yet remain long barren of practical results. Science and art, which should distribute, by progressing hand in hand, the highest blessings of industry and civilization, are thus often separated, and the more so, that the persons by whom each is cultivated are kept asunder by the false ideas as to what really constitutes education. The man of science, occupying himself with the interesting paths of abstract discovery, thinks not of community of objects, or of feeling, with the dark, coarse-handed operatives, who, in the furnace or the forge, work up the really practicable solution of his problems; whilst the worker, equally ignorant of the importance of bringing together their respective modes of experiment and inquiry, considers science, like the dead languages, as characterizing the position of the upper classes, from whom, intellectually as well as socially, he keeps apart.

The real fact is, that only of late years has science attained a position of such accuracy and power as that it could efficiently come to the assistance of the arts in devising new methods, or in suggesting the use of new materials. The phenomena of a manufacturing process are so complex, are so affected by little details of working, by temperature, by moisture, by presence or absence of air, by mechanical conditions,

2 E

and by molecular forces, that the problems were really too complex and difficult for science, in its existing state, to grapple with; and, in most cases, a process was brought to practical perfection, not by the direct advice of a man of science, but by the continued working of a number of practical men, who, at great expense, intense labour, and numerous trials, brought it to succeed. The man of science may then be able to tell him why it succeeds; but the artizan is often tempted to say, that he is not particular as to why, provided it does succeed, and he is disposed to consider as unnecessary, and practically inapplicable, that scientific knowledge which alone ordinary scientific men can supply.

The artizan is, however, as much in error in neglecting abstract theory as the philosopher in regarding practical results distinct from science. When theory teaches us what is really essential in a process, it enables us often to simplify that process and to render its working more economic; or it may enable us to modify it so, as to carry it on in other places, where the materials originally necessary could not be had. It is thus, that even where the practice of the art has preceded theory, the latter facilitates the extension and improvement of the art. But such cases are much less numerous than is really thought. He who devises a process has almost universally a theory, and the only difference is, that if the theory be wrong, he stumbles in the dark, until, by long continued practice, he works rightly in spite of his theory, whereas, if he had known the true theory, he would have lighted upon the proper practice in the beginning. In every great improvement that has been effected in the arts, a distinct idea of the object and of the means of effecting it, that is, a scientific theory, has been first conceived. Watt had the idea of the steam engine distinct in his mind before he ever made an engine. Under these circumstances, it is evidently of the greatest consequence to render the theoretical ideas of the practical worker and inventor, as distinct and exact as possible, that is, to superadd upon his already practical education, so much acquaintance with science, as may enable him fully to understand the properties of the substances upon which he operates, and the laws of action to which they are subjected.

To give an industrial education, therefore, it is necessary to unite the two elements—science and practice. Science should be taught especially with a view to the application of its principles. Practice should be followed with constant reference to the principles upon which it rests. In this way, the elements of the highest industrial progress should be obtained. The economy of any process, the effective duty of any machine, the real value of any material, would be tested by the application of direct calculation to the results produced. The manufacturer never could be taken by surprise, for the different operations of his works would all be conducted under a system of numerical control, which should render it impossible that anything important could escape his observation.

The practice of the arts is that which is most difficult to be learned, and that in which we labour under the greatest disadvantage. In England, every manufacturing town is a great school of practical education, where each branch of mechanical and chemical industry is carried on, on a vast scale, and by a variety of processes. Her workmen, thus educated, though otherwise illiterate, pass into other countries, and are thus serving, most efficiently, to develope throughout Europe the different branches of native industry. Amongst us, such schools of industrial education, are, as yet, scarcely existant. For the acquisition of this practical knowledge, we must look therefore to Manchester, Leeds, and Birmingham. These are the universities, in which the persons desirous of developing the industrial resources of Ireland must graduate. The English workmen, although perfect in thus carrying out the processes to which long experience has conducted them, are destitute, owing to the low state of general education in that country, of the power of applying the aids of science to their modification, or further improvement. The processes adapted to the nature of materials in certain districts of England, are inapplicable in others, and still more in other countries, and it is on this account that so many schemes for utilizing our sources of industry have failed totally in the hands of the English workmen imported to carry them out; because they found themselves under new circumstances, and with materials which differed from what they had been used to, and did not know the principles of their trade at all sufficiently to enable them to introduce proper modifications.

A person about to be educated for industrial purposes should, therefore, be first thoroughly grounded in the general principles of the natural and physical sciences, and in elementary mathematics. All this can be done with far less expenditure of time, of trouble, and of money, than is usually incurred with the Greek and Latin, for which, in industrial pursuits, there is seldom the slightest use. Thus grounded in general education, he should pass to his special branch, according as he is to be a chemist, a maker of machines, a worker in metals, or of other trade. Of all the objects used in his peculiar occupation he should acquire the most minute knowledge; their properties and composition; their adulterations; where they are found; how they are obtained; what can be substituted for them; how they can be made. All these are things on which may depend, at each step of his future progress, whether he follows a losing trade, or whether he be eminently successful.

To this general education should be added the experience of the workshop. The simplest operation in the arts requires a degree of manipulative skill that no books, no words can give. The most perfect theoretical acquaintance with the construction of machines and the nature of various materials used would not enable a man to do good work. But if the man has obtained the manual skill by working practice, there is no doubt but that the knowledge of the tools he is using and of the materials he works upon, will enable him to do it better than he otherwise could. The practical education of the artizan in the place of actual working is, therefore, of all the most important, and requires most time. The ultimate object of the previous discipline in science is to enable him fully to avail himself of the opportunities of improvement in his art which the workshop continually affords.

This subject of industrial education is, as it appears to me, specially important to this country, as without it any available development of our industrial resources must be almost impossible. In every branch of manufacture England is already in possession of the field, and if we only learn from her, and are competent merely to follow her routine processes, we must remain always behind in the march of industrial improvement. There is no physical disadvantage in this country to render it necessary that we should always remain destitute of manufactures as we are at present. But we certainly do not possess any advantage over England. On the contrary, her character is already made; her mechanism is already in operation. To keep a market does not require at all as much exertion as to obtain one; and hence it is only by the most strenuous exertion, and by the most perfect knowledge of his trade, that an Irish manufacturer can have any chance of success. To succeed against his English competitor, he must know more than him. It is evident that we have much to change, yet it is not impossible.

The practical part of education for industry must be effected in the factory. But all that part which consists in general and special scientific discipline might be most efficiently carried on by means of institutions of a collegiate character. The central School of Arts and Manufactures in Paris, founded under the direction of Professor Dumas, deserves, in this point of view, to be considered as affording an excellent example. In Prussia and Austria similar institutions have been organized under the care of the government; and in England and Scotland also the necessity of adding scientific knowledge to practical education has been acknowledged by the foundation of departments for that purpose in connexion with various local institutions.

A century ago, long before the necessity of connecting scientific knowledge with the arts was felt elsewhere, an association was founded in this country expressly for that purpose. The Dublin Society, whose exertions in the advancement of husbandry and the other useful arts were so eloquently described by Arthur Young, and admitted by him to be the origin of all the similar societies in England, has, from that period to the present, undeviatingly promoted the objects for which it was founded. The liberality of the government of that time placed at its disposal great sums of money, which were applied to the prosecution of various plans conceived to be advantageous to the country. That it effected vast good is undeniable. But at that period it was too much in advance of the general population for its beneficial power to come fully into play. The country was not ready for an extensive industrial movement. Since that time its funds have been progressively diminished; its departments necessarily curtailed; its scientific and industrial organization limited in extent and still more in powers. But there appears some hope that the darkness which overhung those days is about to dissipate, and that the Royal Dublin Society may be enabled again to become the centre of industrial education for this country.

Its means of effecting good, were it supported by anything like the sum to which this country is entitled for such objects, are very great :—its fine Botanic Garden, in which all experiments regarding agriculture might be so efficiently put in action; its Museums of Agriculture, and for Natural History, as well as for all industrial products and materials; the resources of its extensive Laboratory, in which investigations calculated to smooth down the many difficulties which beset the path of enterprize in Ireland might be so well conducted; its almost continuous courses of lectures on every branch of applied science, and the means recently placed at its disposal of having similar courses of lectures delivered in provincial towns; the triennial exhibitions of manufactures, the annual cattle shows, in which the progress of our artizans and agriculturists may be registered, and rewards stimulating them to honourable ambition may be distributed; and, finally, the Schools of Art, which, although not exclusively connected with industrial objects, are yet most powerful adjuncts thereto, by enabling the manufacturer to bring to bear upon the improvement of certain branches of trade, a force of fancy and cultivated taste that not only may be, but has been found most conducive to success. With such facilities for communicating all that general scientific education which I have described as the basis of sound industrial knowledge, the Royal Dublin Society may be the source of important advantages to Ireland. It is not now, as half a century ago, when its members were so far before their age, and were so separated from the general population, that their plans of improvement, their premiums, and their bounties, falling upon a soil unprepared by previous workings for the reception of the seed of energy and science, yielded not a commensurate return. The people now are competent to work out the precepts of the Society. The Society has before it the noble task of giving to the people such precepts and example as may draw forth the slumbering energies of Ireland, and create employment, with its constant attendants, comfort and tranquillity.

To the middle classes of Ireland, to whom specially the industrial fortunes of the country must be committed, the Royal Dublin Society should become the source of scientific education. It belongs to the middle classes: not to any section or subdivision of the people, but to Ireland. Its objects are truly Irish. Its office is not to perpetuate the middle age absurdity of an exclusive university, but to explain to all the modes by which we may become more learned in our respective trades; more skilled in all the processes by which we have to support our families; how we may become more intelligent and more wealthy, and hence inevitably more powerful and more respected. It deserves fully the sympathy and co-operation of every Irishman.

In discussing the general question of the relations of scientific knowledge to the pursuits of industry, I have spoken of industry more as regards manufactures than agriculture, because it simplified, in a corresponding degree, the conditions of the question, and enabled me to treat of it more briefly. Every argument proving the necessity of knowledge to the manufacturer, applies however, equally to the agriculturist; and, as in the existing circumstances of Ireland, manufacturing industry can only come into play by slow degrees, it is by improvements in agriculture, for which education is absolutely necessary, that the most rapid and most extensive amelioration in the condition of the people must be effected. Agricultural education is, therefore, the object on which immediate attention should be concentrated in

this country. It should, like other industrial education, consist of the general scientific discipline which has been already
described, and be perfected by the practical education of a well
conducted farm. For the commencement of this education,
the arrangements of the Royal Dublin Society are eminently
adapted, and the co-operation of the Royal Agricultural Society,
which embodies almost every landed interest in Ireland, will be
a most powerful stimulus to those who have to live by agriculture, to avail themselves of such means of increased knowledge.
The practical education of the farmer or land-steward can be
completed in those schools, of which so many are now in operation, or about being formed, as at Templemoyle and Lough-
Ashe. That contemplated on a larger scale, at Leopardstown,
cannot fail, if carried out upon a proper plan, to be of great
utility. We will hear no more of the superiority of Scotch
farming, or of the exclusive employment of Scotch stewards,
if Irishmen set themselves about learning their trade as well,
and fit themselves, by steadiness and practical knowledge, for
such situations.

That these views are in no material degree unsound, is fully
shewn by the fact, that the Commissioners of Education have,
in organizing the plan of instruction for the poorer classes,
always considered industrial education as a necessary element
of their system. What can be of higher beneficence to a population, than the instruction of the child in the general principles of the trades, by one or other of which the man will have
to support a family. This object, however, could not be fully
carried out by the means hitherto available; and hence the
Commissioners have, for reasons such as are described above,
concentrated their efforts upon agricultural education. Even
in this, their plans cannot be yet fully brought into play. The
schoolmasters have to learn the principles of agriculture, before they can teach them; and this education of the educators,
is the step now in process of working out. The scientific lectures, by eminently qualified teachers; the practical workings
on the model farm, under the directions of a highly skilful
agriculturist, will, after a little, enable the Commissioners of
Education to settle in each parish a schoolmaster, who will be

also a minister of industrial progress, and by whose precepts and example, the seed of practical intelligence shall be cultivated, and return hundred fold. With such a system of education, and with the habits of temperance, of moral conduct, and fixity of purpose, which, it is acknowledged, are growing rapidly upon the Irish character, there is no fear for the working classes. It is the middle classes that have most difficulties to overcome, most bad habits to break from. I have endeavoured to indicate to them at once the sources of material prosperity, which the country possesses, and the means by which alone, as I conceive, they can acquire the power of properly utilizing them.

I have been asked, whilst engaged in the consideration of this subject, " Would you seek to introduce into Ireland that manufacturing system, which, whilst creating vast wealth for a fortunate few, throws the majority of the population into a state of moral and physical wretchedness and destitution, to which there is, absolutely, no parallel in this country ?" The Reports of the Employment Commissioners have revealed a depth of moral and social ignorance, of degrading barbarism, in the midst of the very pinnacles of civilization and of wealth, which it were guilt even to contemplate being disseminated amongst our population. No, if it were necessary, in developing our industrial resources, to become as parts of England are, I would not desire the change. But the condition of the working classes in England does not belong to the fact of their being industrious. Isolated districts in that country, numerous localities in America, and on the Continent, shew the perfect feasibility of the union of the most steady industry with education, with morality, and with cleanliness. If a large proportion of the working classes in England are ignorant, are immoral, are drunken, and are unhealthy, it is because no efficient system of moral and intellectual education has ever been in operation with them; that their habitations are crowded into filthy and unwholesome lanes, and that, when released from the toils of their working rooms, they rush to the ale-house to seek a destructive stimulus to their exhausted frames. Is it wonderful that such a condition of society should produce unwholesome fruit? Individual associations in England have endeavoured to remedy this deplorable condition. Their active benevolence and their wealth have founded schools for temporal and spiritual instruction, have opened mechanics' institutes and reading-rooms, and thus have given to thousands the opportunities of elevating themselves from the darkness in which their fellows are still immersed. But these local and individual efforts cannot remedy the system.

The causes which have led to the bad results of the manufacturing system in the sister kingdom, do not exist with us. Ireland can never become a great manufacturing country, such as England is. Her physical constitution does not supply materials. The proportion of the people employed in factories can, therefore, never be so great. Her sources of power, whether it be coal or turf, or water, lie distributed so uniformly through the land, that the concentration of manufactures, on a few localities, as in England, cannot occur. Hence the evils of vast, unhealthy, manufacturing cities need not be feared. Above all, with temperate habits, and with the education which the National system will give to every individual of the growing race, there is no danger but that industry may be accompanied by intelligence, intelligence by morality, and all by the steadiness of purpose, and tranquillity of habits, on which the happiness of the family and the peace of the community depend. This is the result which it should be the object of all to gain. This would render us independent of the wretched political differences on which we waste our strength.

Vast in its consequences, it is yet simple in its means of attainment. It only requires that each man intending to live by the land, should learn what the land is, and what can be done with it. That, having so learned, he should apply himself steadfastly to the practical working of his occupation. So he is certain of success. Success will render him independent; independence will render him respected, and respect will bring him power. Thus knowledge is power. Practical knowledge; for power is essentially practical.

Such are the circumstances influencing industry in Ireland, which, falling within the range of subjects connected with my professional duties, I have thought it not unimportant, at the present time, to offer for public consideration. I have not entered into every source of employment which this country could afford. Thus I have touched but lightly on the details of the cultivation of waste lands, and not at all alluded to the subject, so important in itself, of fisheries. These topics I did not introduce, because their importance and their practicability are universally recognized. My object was to point out that the constitution of the rocks and soil of Ireland, its contents in ores and fuel, its supply of water, its extent of lakes and rivers, its harbours, all fitted it for industry in agriculture, in manufactures, and in commerce, in a degree, which, although not entitling it, like England, to grasp at the commercial and manufacturing sceptre of the world, would certainly enable it to be the source of employment and comfort to its own people. For the attainment of this end, it was necessary to remove some errors regarding the true foundations of industrial success, to describe, with a certain detail, how far the materials for industry exist naturally in Ireland, and to point out, how indispensable to the employment of even the richest gifts of nature is practical education in industrial knowledge. If even a few are induced, by the facts and arguments I have brought forward, to reflect upon these topics, to discuss them, and, if satisfied, to act steadily upon them, I shall consider my object as being gained.

INDEX.

———◆———

A.

AGRICULTURE, relation of, to manufactures, 251.
———— connexions of, with geology, 261.
———— principles of, 259.
———— importance of, 249.
———— of flax, 324.
———— of hemp, 340.
———— of beet-root, 320.
———— with small and large farms, 304.
Agricultural education, 423.
———— success, requisites for, 343.
———— produce of Ireland, 255.
Alum, manufacture of, 227.
———— district of Munster, 229.
Allihies copper mine, 194.
Alternation of crops, 295.
Ammonia, source of, to plants, 269.
Analyses of soils, 265, 282, 325.
———— of iron ores, 126, 128.
———— of clay ironstones, 132, 135.
———— of plants, 276.
———— farm-yard manure, 293.
———— limestones, 281.
———— of flax and its products, 327.
———— of ashes of plants, 276.
———— of hemp and its products, 341.
———— of marls and clays, 233, 281.
———— of turf ashes, 284.

Analyses of bituminous coals, 23.
———— of anthracites, 28.
———— of corallines, 287.
———— of turf, 37.
———— of lignite, 32.
———— of potatoes, 317.
Antimony, ores of, 222.
Anthracite, composition of, 28.
———— use and economy of, 29.
———— smelting iron with, 151.
———— districts of, 8-12.
Antrim, coal field of, 14, 26.
Ardmore lead mine, 209.
Arigna Iron Company, 17.
———— iron ores of, 133.
———— production of iron at, 145.
———— refining of iron at, 157.
Ardtully copper and lead mine, 196.
Arsenic, ores of, 223.
Arseniuret of cobalt, 197.
Assay of Wicklow gold, 220.
Ashes of turf as manure, 283.
Athlone, water power at, 84.
Atmospheric railway, 375.
Audley mines, 192.
Aughabehy coal, 23.

B.

Ballycastle coal, 26.
Ballymurtagh copper mine, 185, 188.
Ballygahan copper mines, 186.
Ballydehob copper mine, 192.
Ballycorus lead mine and works, 207.
———— native silver at, 221.

Ballyhickey lead mine, 213.
Ballybunion, alum rocks of, 229.
Bann, water power of the, 85.
—— reservoirs, 99.
Barrow navigation, 355.
Basaltic rocks of Antrim, 180.
Basalts, value of, in building, 240.
—— composition of, 267.
Barytes, minerals of, 245.
Berehaven copper mine, 194.
Beet-root sugar, 320.
Blende, localities of, 223.
Bog, mode of formation of, 33.
—— extent and nature of, 35.
—— distribution of, 39.
—— as sources of fuel, 37.
—— marls found under, 281.
—— subsoils under, 282.
Bog iron ore, analysis of, 128.
Bonmahon copper mine, 189.
Bones, composition of, 282.
Board of Works, results of the, 350.
Breast wheel, 88.
Brosna, power of the, 105.
Brick clay, localities of, 236.
Building materials, 239.

C.

Caime lead mine, 208.
Calp limestone, position of, 7.
—— analysis of, 281.
Callows of the Shannon, 253, 339.
Canals, Grand and Royal, 356.
——— of the north of Ireland, 357.
——— proposed connecting, 359.
Capital, supposed want of, in Ireland, 408.
——— uses of English, 410.
Carboniferous slate, 178.
Carbonization of turf, 41.
Catchment basins of rivers, 78.
Caucasses of the Shannon, 253.
Charcoal made from turf, 43.
——— manufacture of iron by, 158.
Chalk of Antrim, 180.

Chalk, as a building stone, 240.
China clay, localities of, 230.
Civilizing effects of roads, 344.
Clare lead mines, 211.
Clay ironstones, analyses of, 132, 135.
—— slate, localities of, 173.
—— composition of, 233.
—— preparation of, 237.
—— localities of pure kinds, 231, 236.
—— marls under bogs, 281.
—— slate, for roofing, quarries of, 242.
—— for building, 240.
Clover, composition of, 276, 278.
Coal, origin and constitution of, 6.
—— formations, structure of, 5, 13, 178.
—— varieties of, 8.
—— fields of Ireland, 7, 15.
—— analyses of, 23, 28.
—— fields, iron ores of the, 130.
——— clays of the, 232.
—— seat, nature of, 13, 234.
Cobalt ore, localities of, 223.
Coking of coal, 141, 150.
——— of turf, 41.
Coke from Arigna coals, 150.
Connaught coal districts, 16.
——— lakes, water power of, 86.
——————— navigation of, 361.
Combinations in Ireland, 403.
Connoree copper mine, 184.
Construction of railways, 363.
Consumption of coal in England, 49.
Copperas, manufacture of, 227. 230.
Copper mines of Wicklow, 184.
——— South Cork, 192.
——— north of Dublin, 200.
——— general nature of, 183.
——— Kerry and Tipperary. 197.
——— Waterford, 194.
——— ores, analyses of, 182.
——— smelting of, 201.

Copper mines, total produce of, 204.

Coral sand as manure, 286.

Cork, clay deposits in, 236.

———— copper mines of, 192.

———— lead mines of, 209.

Cornwall, produce of copper from, 204.

Cosheen copper mine, 194.

Cost of steam power, 49, 53.

———— of water power, 106.

———— of iron smelting, 142, 155.

Cotton manufacture, cost of power in, 64.

———— manufacture of, in Ireland, 68, 392.

———— trade, statistics of, 63, 67.

Course of cultivation, 295.

Crops, nature and amount of, 275.

———— rotation of, 295.

———— production of food by, 300.

———— without exhaustion, 315.

———— action of, on the soil, 259.

———— white and green, nature of, 296.

Cronebane copper mines, 185.

Croghan Kinshela gold mines, 219.

Cupellation of lead, 216.

Culture, alternation of, 296.

D.

Derrynoos, lead mine, 209.

Deer's meadow reservoir, 99.

Dodder, water power of, 105.

Dolomite, localities of, 246.

Drainage basins of rivers, 78.

———— importance of, to agriculture, 272.

———————— to navigation, 273.

———————— beneficial results from, 274.

Duhallow, collieries of, 11.

Dungannon, coal district of, 12.

———— copper mine, 200.

E.

Economy of water power, 107.

———— of hot blast in making iron, 148.

———— of fuel in smelting iron, 163.

———————— in reducing copper, 203.

———— of manures, 292.

Education, industrial, 412.

———— false ideas on, 414.

———— practical, necessity for, 417.

———— means of, in Ireland, 421.

Educated labour dear, 400.

Elba iron ore, 126.

Elements taken up by plants, 260.

———— of various crops, 276.

Elevation of surface, 76.

Employment of the people, 250.

Employment given by farms, 310.

———————— by flax trade, 334.

———————— by public works, 350.

———————— on the Shannon, 353.

English capital, uses of, 409.

Evaporation, rate of, 74.

Evaporative powers of fuels, 43, 47, 50.

Exhaustion of soils, 274, 295.

Expansive action of steam, 50.

Experiments on building stones, 239.

F.

Fallows with wheat crops, 298.

———— principles of, 278.

Farm-yard manure, 292.

Farms, size of, in Ireland, 304.

———— small, productiveness of, 313.

———— employment given by, 310.

———— in Connaught and Ulster, 313.

Fertility of the soil, 253.
Flax trade, cost of power in the, 65.
—— rotting, nature of, 326.
—— water-steep as a manure, 329.
—— importation of, 333.
—— extent of manufacture, 337.
—— localities of the trade, 339.
—— mode of growth of, 324.
—— analyses of plants and ashes, 327.
—— nature of soils, 325.
—— residues as manure, 329.
Feldspar, nature of, 171.
Flags of Valentia, Clare, and Carlow, 242.
Flesh, composition of, 269.
Flints of Antrim, 237.
Food, manufacture of, 251.
—— given by various crops, 300.
Forests, ancient, in Ireland, 3.
Fuel, localities of, in Ireland, 8.
—— importance of, in industry, 1.
—— economy of, in Cornwall, 51.
—— consumed in smelting iron, 142.
—————— copper, 203.
—————— lead, 216.
—————— in making glass, 239.
—— economy of, in iron works, 163.

G.

Gas, of high furnaces, use of, 163.
—— generated by steam, 165.
Geology of Ireland, 168.
—————— connected with agriculture, 261.
Glasgow ironstone, 137.
Glendore manganese mines, 222.
Glass manufacture in Ireland, 238.
Glendalough lead mine, 205.
Glenmalur lead mine, 207.
Gold mines of Wicklow, 219.

Granite, localities of, 170.
Granite, mines in, 183, 205, 221.
—————— as building stone, 240.
Green crops, rotations of, 298.
Greenock water reservoirs, 102.
Gypsum, localities of, 180.
—————— use of, as manure, 283.

H.

Height of Ireland above the sea, 76.
Hematite, analyses of, 127.
Hemp, analysis of, 340.
—————— steep water of, 342.
Hibernian Mining Company, 14.
High iron furnaces, 139.
Hot blast for iron smelting, 149.
Horse power, meaning of, 46.
Howth, manganese mine of, 222.
—————— clay, deposits of, 236.
Humus, nature and origin of, 269.

I.

Importance of iron in the arts, 118.
Importation of flax, 333.
Industrial education, necessity for, 412.
Industry connected with science, 417.
Inland navigation, 351.
Intercourse aids civilization, 344.
—————— moral effects of, 348.
Ireland, scarcity of wood in, 2.
—————— cost of fuel in, 53.
—————— geology of, 168.
—————— copper mines of, 181.
—————— lead mines of, 204.
—————— gold mines of, 219.
—————— population of, 250.
—————— coal districts of, 8.
—————— bogs of, 33.
—————— elevation of surface, 76.
—————— water power of, 71, 80.
—————— produce of copper in, 204.

Ireland, agricultural produce of, 257.
———— live stock of, 258.
———— size of farms in, 304.
———— fertility of soils in, 253.
———— available land in, 312.
———— distribution of surface of, 257.
———— linen trade of, 336.
———— flax grown in, 330.
———— means of intercourse in, 344.
———— inland navigation of, 351.
———— geographical position of, 387.
———— railways in, 363.
———— cheapness of labour in, 397.
———— external trade of, 387.
———— combinations in, 403.
Ireland, want of capital in, 408.
Irishmen, physical excellence of, 401.
Iron, ancient manufacture of, 118.
——— ores, localities of, 120.
——— analyses of, 127, 132, 135.
——— smelting, process of, 139.
——————— charges of, 142.
——————— by hot blast, 148.
——————— by anthracite, 152.
——— refining in Wales and Ireland, 155.
——— manufacture by turf, 158.
——— pyrites of Wicklow, 224.
——— of the coal fields, 26, 227.

K.

Kaolin, nature and localities of, 230.
Kenmare copper and lead mines, 196, 209.
Kilbricken lead mines, 212.
——————— antimony ore, 222.
Kilkenny coal district, 8.
——————— clay, deposits of, 234.
——————— ironstone of, 131.

Kilkenny, manufacture of iron at, 152.
Killaloe, water power at, 82.
——————— slate quarries of, 242.
Killarney, mines at, 197.
Knockmahon copper mines, 198.

L.

Labour, cheapness of, 397.
——————— skilled and unskilled, 402.
Labouring force of man, 400.
Lackamore copper mine, 199.
Lansdown steamer, turf used in, 57.
Land available for farms, 312.
Large farm system, 305.
Lead ores, analysis of, 204.
——— mines of Clare, 211.
——— of Wicklow, 205.
——— of Cork, 209.
——— elsewhere, 206.
——— ores, smelting of, 214.
——— separation from silver, 217.
Lee, water power of the, 84.
Leinster coal field, 8.
Ligneous fibre, growth of, 324.
Lignite or wood coal, 31.
Lime as a manure, 279.
Limestone strata of Ireland, 6, 178.
——————— lead mines in, 210.
——————— for building, 240.
——————— magnesian, localities of, 246.
——————— plain, drainage of the, 272.
——————— composition of, 281.
Linen trade, extent of the, 336.
——— goods, export of, 337.
——— manufacture of, 331.
Live stock, amount of, 258.
Lough Allen, structure of, 16.
——— coal field, 18.
——— Neagh, lignites of, 31.
——— Derg, capacity of, 82.
——— Allen, water power of, 84.
——— Ennell, water power of, 105.

Lough Shinney copper mine, 200.
—— Neagh, clays of, 31.
—— Allen, clays of, 233.
—— Neagh and Erne, naviga-
tion of, 360.
—— in Connaught, power of, 86.
—— navigation of, 361.
Lucerne, crops of, 299.
Luganure lead mines, 206.

M.

Magnesian limestone, 179.
Magnesia, minerals of, 246.
Malleable iron, making of, 155.
Manufacture of food, 251.
Manures, native in Ireland, 279.
—— sea sand as, 286.
—— sea weed as, 291.
—— turf ashes as, 283.
—— farm yard, 292.
—— of green crops, 299.
—— flax steep as, 329.
—— hemp steep as, 341.
—— potato residues as, 319.
—— beet residues as, 322.
Marls, localities and natures of
281, 283.
Manganese ores, localities of,
222.
Marbles, localities of, 239.
—— coloured varieties of,
244.
Meelick, water power of, 84.
Meenashama, coal of, 23.
Mica slate, localities of, 172.
—— soils formed of, 265.
Millstone grit formation, 7,
178.
Mill power of England, 69.
—— by reaction of water, 93.
Miltown lead mine, 211.
Millstones, quarries of, 245.
Mines of iron in Ireland, 120.
—— of copper, 181.
—— of lead, 204.
—— of gold, 219.
Moisture of climate, 72.
Monaghan coal field, 15.
Mucruss copper mine, 197.

Munster coal field, 11.
Murlough bay, coal beds of, 14.

N.

Navigation of the Shannon, 352.
—— Barrow, 355.
—— Grand and Royal Canals,
356.
—— northern canals, 357.
—— Ulster lakes, 360.
—— Connaught lakes, 361.
New red sandstone rock, 179.
Newtownards lead mine, 209.
Nitrogen fixed by green crops,
299.
—— source of, in plants, 269,
298.
—— of manures, 275, 293.
Nitrolin, nature of, 269.

O.

Oats, composition of, 276.
—— materials in crop of, 277.
Old red sandstone, localities of,
176.
Ores of iron, 120.
—— analyses of, 127, 132,
135.
—— smelting of, 140.
—— of copper, analyses of, 182.
—— smelting of, 201.
—— of lead, analyses of, 204.
—— smelting of, 214.
—— produce of, 216.
—— of sulphur, 224.
—— of antimony and arse-
nic, 222.
—— cobalt and chrome,
197, 223.
Ores, metallic, distribution of,
183.
Organized beings, composition of,
259.
Organic matter of the soil, 268.
Origin of soils, 261.
Overshot water wheel, 87.
Ovoca valley, copper mines of
the, 184.

P.

Pasture and tillage, 300.
People, occupations of the, 250.
Pipeclay, localities of, 231.
Plants, composition of, 260.
—— ashes of, 276.
—— mode of growth of, 259.
Pollough coal, 27.
Power, cost of steam, 54.
—— value of the unit of, 46.
—— evaporative of fuels, 47, 50.
—— water of Ireland, 71.
—— of the Shannon, 83.
—— of the Bann, 85.
—— cost of, 108.
—— cost of, on railways, 374.
Poncelet's wheel, 89.
Porcelain clay, localities of, 230.
—— nature of, 171.
Pottery, clays adapted for, 232.
Potatoes, composition of, 276. 317.
—— nutriment in, 303.
Potato husbandry in Ireland, 302.
—— starch, making of, 316.
—— residues, economy of, 319.
Population, not excessive, 312.
Prices of fuel, 53.
Pressure, water engines by, 90.
Practical education, importance of, 401, 412.
Produce of Ireland, 255.
Puddling of iron, 155.
Public works, employment by, 346.
—— grants, profit on, 349.
Pyrites of the coal fields, 26.
—— of copper, 182.
—— iron, of Wicklow and Tipperary, 224, 227.
—— oxidizable, 228.

Q.

Quartz rock, localities of, 175.
—— sand of Donegal, 238.

R.

Rain, annual quantity of, 72.
Railways in Ireland, 363.
—— actual traffic on, 364.
—— proposed, 371.
—— report of Commissioners on, 365.
—— atmospheric, nature of the, 373.
—— management of, 381.
—— necessity of control for, 378.
—— cost of power on, 374.
Railway, atmospheric, to Dalkey, 373.
Reaction water mill, 93.
Reservoirs of water power, 96.
—— on the Upper Bann, 98.
—— at Greenock, 102.
—— for tide mills, 112.
Relations of agriculture to manufactures, 250.
Reclaiming of bogs, 281.
Report of Railway Commissioners, 365.
Ringabella lead mine, 209.
Rivers, navigable, 351.
—— catchment basins of, 78.
Roads, making of, beneficial, 345.
—— profitable outlay on, 348.
—— Connaught, effects of, 346.
—— Highland, effects of, 349.
Rover coal, 24.
Rooskey, water power at, 84.
Ross, copper mine, 198.
Roscommon, clays of, 232.
Rotation of crops, 295.
Rushes coal, 27.

S.

Salt, manufacture of, 396.
Sand for industrial uses, 238.
—— shelly and coral as manure, 286.
Sandstone of the coal fields, 9.

Sandstone rocks, localities of, 176, 179.
——— for building, 239.
——— soils, formed of, 266.
Santnavena coal, 23.
Science and industry connected, 417.
Scotch iron ores, 137.
Scotland, hot blast used in, 148.
Seaweed as manure, 291.
Sea sand dredged in Ulster, 285.
——— Cork, 288.
Shannon, use of turf on the, 57.
——— water power of the, 83.
——— drainage of the, 272.
——— navigation of the, 351.
——— traffic on the, 354.
——— industrial position of the, 389.
——— floods on the, 98.
Shaw's water reservoirs, 102.
Shells applied as manure, 286.
Sheep, number of, in Ireland, 258.
Silica for industrial uses, 238.
Silurian slate, localities of, 174.
Silver mines, copper and lead district, 199, 209.
Silver produce from lead ores, 217.
——— native in Ireland, 221.
Skilled labour, dearness of, 397, 400.
Skull, copper mine, 194.
Slate of the coal fields, 9.
——— roofing quarries of, 242.
Smelting of copper ores, 201.
——— lead ores, 214.
——— iron at Arigna, 145.
——— with anthracite, 152.
——— with turf, 158.
Soils of Ireland, fertility of the, 253.
——— composition of, 282, 325.
——— geological relations of, 261.
——— average produce of, 253, 275.
——— connected with plants, 259.

Soils of Ireland, origin of, 261.
——— mechanical uses of, 270.
——— materials taken from, 274.
——— exhaustion of, 295.
——— drainage of, 271.
——— sources of fertility in, 260, 296.
St. Etienne, coal district of, 15.
Staffordshire, iron ores, 137.
Starch, composition of, 316.
——— manufactured from potatoes, 317.
——— uses of, 319.
Steadiness of water power, 109.
Steam engine, construction of, 46.
——— of Cornwall, 50.
——— vessels, use of turf in, 57.
——— power, cost of, 60.
——— combined with water, 111.
——— expansive action of, 51.
Stock, live, amount of, 258.
Strength of building materials, 239.
——— of labouring men, 401.
Sugar, composition of, 316.
——— manufacture of, 320.
——— probable cost of, 323.
——— beet, culture of, 321.
Sulphate of iron, manufacture of, 227.
——— of zinc, manufacture of, 223.
——— of alumina and potash, 228.
Sulphur ores of Wicklow, 224.
——— of Tipperary, 227.
——— of coal fields, ib.
Surface of Ireland, distribution of, 257.
——— elevation of, 76.
Sweetvein coal, 27.

                      T.

Tarmonbarry, water power at, 84.

Tertiary formations of Ireland, 30, 180.

Tide mills, nature of, 112.

Tigrony copper mine, 185.

Tillage and pasture, parallel of, 300.

——— production of food by, 302.

Timber in bogs, origin of, 3.

Tinstone of Wicklow, 222.

Tipperary coal field, 11.

——— clay deposits of, 231.

Trade, education required for, 413.

Traffic on the Shannon, 354.

——— on the Irish canals, 356.

——— ——— railways, 363.

——— ——— River Barrow, 355.

Trap rocks of Antrim, 180.

——— soils of the, 266.

——— analyses of decomposed, 268.

Tribute paid to Normandy, 221.

Turbine, nature and power of the, 93.

——— as a tide mill, 115.

Turf, mode of formation of, 33.

——— used in Shannon steamers, 57.

——— coke and charcoal, 37, 43.

——— localities of, 35, 54.

——— in manufacture of iron, 158.

——— composition of, 38.

——— composition of ashes of, 283.

——— practical value of, 38.

——— evaporative power of, 55.

——— modes of preparing, 39.

Turnips, composition of, 276.

Tyrone coal, districts of, 12.

——— clay, deposits of, 232.

U.

Ulmine, nature and source of, 269.

Undershot water wheel, 88.

V.

Valentia, slates and flags of, 243.

Vegetables, composition of, 276.

Vegetation, laws of, 259.

W.

Wages, in Ireland and England, 400.

——— and fuel, how related, 65.

——— low, not cheap, 397.

——— in England and France, 399.

Water power of Ireland, 71, 77.

——— of the Shannon, 83.

——— Lee and Bann, 85.

——— of Connaught lakes, 86.

——— cost of, 107.

——— advantages of, 108.

——— comparative use of, 110.

——— improved by drainage, 272.

——— wheels, 87.

——— pressure engines, 90.

——— mill by reaction, 93.

——— carriage, economy of, 351.

Waterford copper mines, 188.

Welch iron ores, 137.

West Cork mines, 192.

Wheat, composition of, 276.

——— materials in crop, 300.

White limestone of Antrim, 180.

——— crops, nature of, 296.

Wicklow copper mines, 184.

——— lead mines, 205.

——— gold mines, 219.

Woods, cutting down of, 120.

Wood, production of, 316.

Woody fibre, nature and source of, 324.

Wool, nature of Irish, 395.

Woollen trade, cost of power in, 64.
—————— in Ireland, 393.

Y.

Yellow sandstone rocks, 176.
Youghal clay, deposits of, 236.

Youghal sea sand as manure, 288.

Z.

Zinc ores, localities of, 211.
—— sulphate, manufacture of, 211.

THE END.

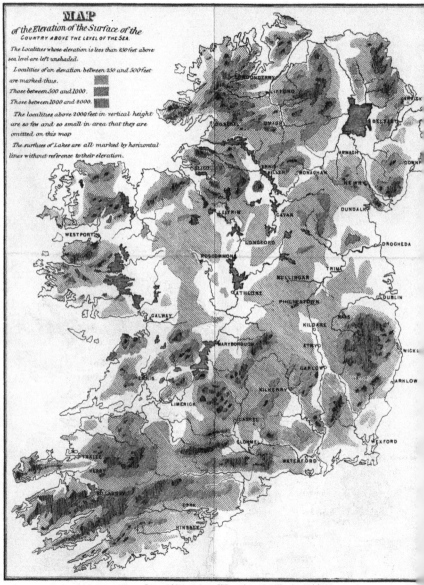

MAP

of the Elevation of the Surface of the
COUNTRY ABOVE THE LEVEL OF THE SEA.

The Localities whose elevation is less than 250 feet above
sea level are left unshaded.

Localities of an elevation between 250 and 500 feet
are marked thus.

Those between 500 and 1000.

Those between 1000 and 2000.

The localities above 2000 feet in vertical height
are so few and so small in area that they are
omitted on this map

The surfaces of Lakes are all marked by horizontal
lines without reference to their elevation.

LONDONDERRY
LIFFORD
CARRICK
DONEGAL
OMAGH
BELFAST
ARMAGH
DOWN
SLIGO
ENNIS
KILLEN
MONAGHAN
NEWRY
DUNDALK
LEITRIM
CAVAN
WESTPORT
LONGFORD
DROGHEDA
ROSCOMMON
TRIM
MULLINGAR
ATHLONE
PHILIPSTOWN
DUBLIN
GALWAY
KILDARE
NAAS
ATHY
MARYBOROUGH
WICKLOW
ENNIS
CARLOW
ARKLOW
LIMERICK
KILKENNY
CASHEL
CLONMEL
WEXFORD
TRALEE
WATERFORD
KILLARNEY
CORK
KINSALE

Engraved & Printed for Messrs. Houses & Smiths by J.O'Shaughnessy Trinity Place.

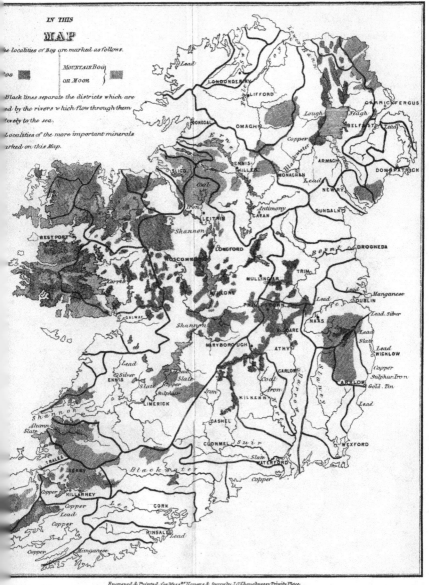

Lead

LONDONDERRY

LIFFORD

CARRICKFERGUS

DONEGAL

OMAGH

Lough Neagh

BELFAST Lead

Copper

Erne

ENNIS-
KILLEN

MONAGHAN

Blackwater

ARMAGH

DOWNPATRICK

SLIGO

Coal

Lead

NEWRY

Iron

LEITRIM

Antimony

CAVAN

DUNDALK

Shannon

LONGFORD

Boyne

DROGHEDA

ROSCOMMON

MULLINGAR

TRIM

Corrib

ATHLONE

Lead

Manganese

WEST PORT

Shannon

PHILLIPSTOWN

Lead

DUBLIN

GALWAY

Shannon

KILDARE

NAAS

Lead. Silver

MARYBOROUGH

ATHY

Lead
Slate

Lead
Slate

WICKLOW

Lead
Silver

CARLOW

Coal

Barrow

Copper

ENNIS

Slate

Coal

Iron

Sulphur.Iron

Slate

Copper

Slate

Iron

Nore

KILKENNY

ARKLOW

Gold.Tin

Sulphur

LIMERICK

CASHEL

Lead

Shannon

Altamin
Slate

CLONMEL

Suir

Slaney

TRALEE

KERRY

Blackwater

Slate

WATERFORD

WEXFORD

Copper

KILLARNEY

Copper

CORK

Copper
Lead

Lea

Copper

KINSALE

Lead

Copper

Manganese

Engraved & Printed for Mess.rs Houlston & Stoneman by J.O'Shaughnessy Trinity Place.

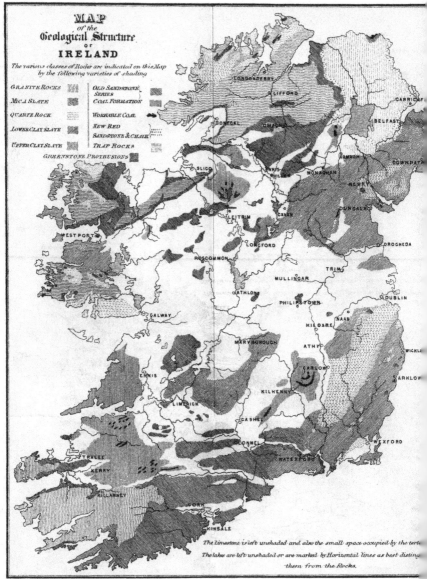

MAP
of the
Geological Structure
OF
IRELAND

The various classes of Rocks are indicated on this Map
by the following varieties of shading

GRANITE ROCKS

MICA SLATE

QUARTZ ROCK

LOWER CLAY SLATE

UPPER CLAY SLATE

OLD SANDSTONE
SERIES

COAL FORMATION

WORKABLE COAL

NEW RED
SANDSTONE & CHALK

TRAP ROCKS

GREENSTONE PROTRUSIONS

The Limestone is left unshaded and also the small space occupied by the terte

The lakes are left unshaded or are marked by Horizontal lines as best disting
them from the Rocks.

Engraved & Printed for Mess.rs Hodsons & Swans by J.O'Shaughnessy Trinity Place.

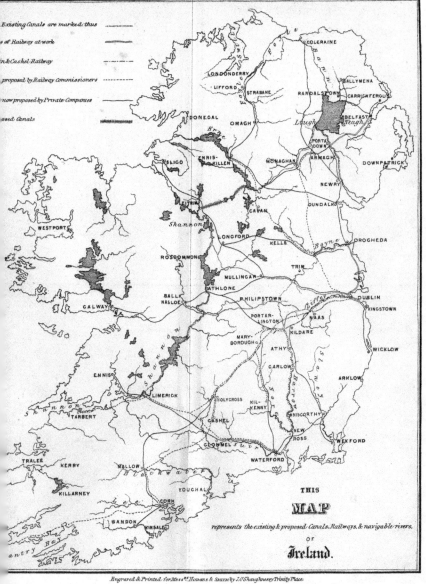

COLERAINE

LONDONDERRY
LIFFORD
STRABANE
BALLYMENA
RANDALSTOWN
CARRICKFERGUS

DONEGAL
OMAGH
Lough
Neagh
BELFAST
PORTA
DOWN

ENNIS-
KILLEN
SLIGO
MONAGHAN
ARMAGH
DOWNPATRICK

NEWRY

WESTPORT
Shannon
LEITRIM
CAVAN
DUNDALK

LONGFORD
KELLS
Boyne
DROGHEDA

ROSCOMMON
TRIM

MULLINGAR
ATHLONE
BALLI
NASLOE
P.PHILIPSTOWN
DUBLIN
GALWAY
PORTAR-
LINGTON
NAAS
KINGSTOWN

MARY-
BOROUGH
KILDARE
WICKLOW

ATHY
ENNIS
Shannon
CARLOW
ARKLOW

LIMERICK
HOLYCROSS
KIL-
KENNY

TARBERT
CASHEL
ENNISCORTHY

Shannon
NEW
ROSS
WEXFORD

CLONMEL
WATERFORD

TRALEE
KERRY
MALLOW
Blackwater

KILLARNEY
YOUGHAL

CORK

BANDON
KINSALE

antry Bay

THIS

MAP

represents the existing & proposed Canals, Railways, & navigable rivers,

OF

Ireland.

Engraved & Printed for Messrs. Howens & Sours by J.O'Shaughnessy Trinity Place.